Autism in Children and Adults

Etiology, Assessment, and Intervention

Autism in Children and Adults

Etiology, Assessment, and Intervention

Edited by
Johnny L. Matson
LOUISIANA STATE UNIVERSITY

Brooks/Cole Publishing Company
Pacific Grove, California

The trademark ITP is used under license.

Brooks/Cole Publishing Company
A Division of Wadsworth, Inc.

Printed in the United States of America
10 9 8 7 6 5 4 3 2 1

Library of Congress Cataloging-in-Publication Data
Autism in children and adults : etiology, assessment, and
 intervention / edited by Johnny L. Matson.
    p. cm.
  Includes bibliographical references and index.
  ISBN 0-534-23826-2
  1. Autism. 2. Autism in children. I. Matson, Johnny L.
  [DNLM: 1. Autism—diagnosis. 2. Autism—etiology. 3. Autism–
  –therapy.   WM 203.5 A93755 1993]
  RC553.A88A85 1994
  616.89′82—dc20   93-2902
                                                        CIP

Sponsoring Editor: *Vicki Knight*
Editorial Associate: *Lauri Banks Ataide*
Production Coordinator: *Fiorella Ljunggren*
Production: *Lifland et al., Bookmakers*
Manuscript Editors: *Jane Hoover, Jeanne Yost*
Permissions Editor: *Lillian Campobasso*
Interior Design: *Vernon T. Boes*
Cover Design: *Susan Haberkorn*
Art Coordinator: *Lifland et al., Bookmakers*
Typesetting: *Joan Mueller Cochrane*
Cover Printing: *Color Dot Graphics, Inc.*
Printing and Binding: *Arcata Graphics/Fairfield*

CONTRIBUTORS

Joseph A. Banken
Texas Tech University Health Sciences Center

Jill Belchic
Rutgers, The State University of New Jersey

Phillip J. Belfiore
Purdue University School of Education

Lisa Blum
Rutgers, The State University of New Jersey

Stephen M. Camarata
Vanderbilt University

David Celiberti
Rutgers, The State University of New Jersey

Marjorie H. Charlop
Claremont McKenna College

Michael Eberlin
Developmental Disabilities Institute, Smithtown, New York

Cynthia R. Ellis
Medical College of Virginia

Debra Farrar-Schneider
Louisiana State University

Sandra L. Harris
Rutgers, The State University of New Jersey

Linda K. Haymes
Claremont Graduate School

John W. Jacobson
New York State Office of Mental Retardation
and Developmental Disabilities

Lynn Kern Koegel
University of California at Santa Barbara

Robert L. Koegel
University of California at Santa Barbara

Bill J. Locke
Texas Tech University

Stephanie B. Lockshin
State University of New York at Binghamton

F. Charles Mace
University of Pennsylvania School of Medicine

Charles H. Mahone
Texas Tech University

Johnny L. Matson
Louisiana State University

Gary B. Mesibov
University of North Carolina at Chapel Hill

James A. Mulick
The Ohio State University

Carryl Navalta
State University of New York at Binghamton

Donald P. Oswald
Medical College of Virginia

Bernard Rimland
Autism Research Institute, San Diego, California

Raymond G. Romanczyk
State University of New York at Binghamton

Allen A. Schwartz
New York State Office of Mental Retardation
and Developmental Disabilities

Jay A. Sevin
The Kennedy Krieger Institute, Johns Hopkins University

Nirbhay N. Singh
Medical College of Virginia

Yadhu N. Singh
College of Pharmacology, South Dakota State University

Peter Sturmey
Abilene State School

Naomi Swiezy
The Kennedy Krieger Institute, Johns Hopkins University

Joseph Szempruch
Rome (New York) Developmental Disabilities Services Office

Douglas L. Wheeler
O. D. Heck/Eleanor Roosevelt Developmental Services Autism Program

v

CONTENTS

Chapter 13   241
Social Skills Training with Autistic Children
Johnny L. Matson, Naomi Swiezy

PREFACE

Autism is one of the most fascinating of the problems studied by mental health professionals. This fact is substantiated by the relatively large amount of research on the topic as compared to other psychological conditions. Given the extensive research literature and the fast-paced changes in this field, a book like this one seems warranted.

The purpose of this book is to provide a broad-based review of the field of autism—including background, general issues, and specific topics. Whenever one sets out to provide such an overview, others will suggest areas that should be included. Although many of those suggestions might be legitimate, what is included here represents my best assessment of the major areas of autism research. Because of the complexity and scope of the field of autism, I am convinced that the multidiscipline and multiauthor approach taken here is the best way to achieve the breadth and depth necessary to a wide-ranging overview.

The book begins with a first-hand account of the history of the field of autism by Bernie Rimland, who has been directly involved in most of its major developments. The next two chapters provide extensive background from Peter Sturmey and Jay Sevin on the definition and assessment of autism and a detailed description of the etiology of the condition by Bill Locke and his colleagues. Although discussion of training strategies has generally been integrated into chapters on topics such as aggression and self-help skills, an exception was made for facilitated communication. Because this strategy is currently receiving a great deal of attention from some professionals and many parents, a review such as that provided by John Jacobson and colleagues in Chapter 4 is essential. Chapter 5 addresses program design through a description of the TEACCH model written by Gary Mesibov, who has worked with Eric Schopler at North Carolina's Division TEACCH, arguably the best statewide system for service delivery to autistic persons. Two critical topics—differential diagnosis and behavioral assessment—have been reviewed in

Chapters 6 and 7 by Raymond Romanczyk and Sandra Harris and their colleagues. In Chapter 8, Donald Oswald and his colleagues thoroughly discuss self-injurious behavior, whose prevalence among autistic persons is not matched by extensive literature on the topic. Two chapters on the treatment of aggression are included to reflect the sizable empirical research on that topic: Chapter 9, by Robert Koegel and his colleagues, focuses on remediation through naturalistic language training, a relatively new but increasingly popular approach. In Chapter 10, Debra Farrar-Schneider describes behavior modification methods of remediation, which have been in use for a longer period of time. Given the trend toward deinstitutionalization of persons with developmental disabilities, the life skills curriculum described in Chapter 11 by Phillip Belfiore and Charles Mace has both topicality and importance. Marjorie Charlop and Linda Haymes review the speech and language characteristics of autistic persons in Chapter 11 and describe behavioral approaches to intervention in this functional area. Since another area in which many autistic persons show deficits is social and interpersonal functioning, Chapter 13 presents a review of social skills training of children with autism, by myself and Naomi Swiezy.

Many of the leading researchers in this field agreed to contribute to this volume, and the knowledge and experience they brought to the task have been invaluable. I thank all of them for their contributions. I am also grateful to Robert O'Neill of the University of Oregon and Richard Simpson of the University of Kansas Medical Center, who reviewed the manuscript and offered helpful suggestions. I hope that this book will be useful as a source for scholarly research on autism. Although it does not, and should not, present the only interpretation of what is important to the field, I believe it provides a succinct and solid overview of the rapidly growing research literature.

Johnny L. Matson

CHAPTER 1

The Modern History of Autism: A Personal Perspective

Bernard Rimland
AUTISM RESEARCH INSTITUTE

The editor of this volume has invited me to contribute a chapter on the history of autism from the vantage point of one who has participated in some of the important developments of the past several decades.

Since this is to be a personal view, let me start with some relevant background. I decided upon psychology as a career in my junior year of college. My intention was, and it has never wavered, to be a *research* psychologist. My interest was in the challenge posed by the *methodology* of behavioral science—how one determines what is true, or probably true—more than in the substantive content of the various fields of psychology. I was especially interested in individual differences and their measurement. To prepare myself for a career as a research psychologist, I took courses in experimental psychology, research design, statistics, and measurement.

As luck would have it, the Navy established its Personnel and Training Research Laboratory in my hometown of San Diego just before I completed my Ph.D. in psychology at Penn State (1953). I returned to San Diego and quickly found my niche as a research psychologist for the Navy. I soon became Director of the Personnel Measurement Research Department. A dream come true!

The dream continued: my wife, Gloria, and I were delighted when Mark, our first baby, arrived, after a picture-perfect pregnancy, on March 28, 1956. A beautiful healthy bright-eyed baby boy! End of dream—beginning of nightmare: Mark almost never stopped screaming. He screamed so violently he could hardly be nursed.

Infant Mark did not want to be held. He needed to be rocked to go to sleep, but he violently resisted being held. We found that by placing him in his baby carriage and rocking it back and forth we could get him to sleep for a few hours a night. I also discovered that by taping a yardstick to the floor and running the wheels of the baby carriage over the yardstick, we could impart a slight bouncing motion that helped relax him and let him sleep. (Now, with the benefit of hindsight and several decades of research on autism, we can understand that Mark craved vestibular stimulation but could not tolerate tactile stimulation. It is at least possible that the screaming was due to hyperacute hearing—more on that later.)

As Mark grew older, he manifested all the symptoms we now know to be characteristics of autism, including severe ritualistic behavior, rocking and headbanging, insistence on the preservation of sameness, eating oddities of various kinds, "autistic" staring into space, bizarre fears, failure to develop relationships with his parents, grandparents, or other humans, and fascination with mechanical objects, especially vacuum cleaners.

Our pediatrician, a venerable and respected physician with 40 years of experience, had never seen or heard of a screaming, ritualistic, alienated child such as Mark.

Mark started to say words at 8 months of age. His first words were "spoon," "bear," "all done," and "come on, let's play ball," all spoken with perfect articulation. The words were uttered in somewhat appropriate contexts, but Mark did not seem to be aware of what he was saying—like a living tape recorder.

One day when Mark was about 2 years old, walking aimlessly around the house repeating nursery rhymes and radio commercials in a hollow, parrotlike monotonic voice, Gloria remembered reading something in one of her college textbooks about a child with similar behaviors. We went to the garage, located the box of old college texts, and there found a point-by-point description of our little boy, accompanied by the strange-looking words "infantile autism."

I was now 5 years beyond my Ph.D. in psychology and was seeing the word "autism" for the first time. Today the term is familiar to almost every high school student because of films such as *Rain Man* and other media coverage.

Gloria's textbook listed several references to the literature. I jotted those down and went to the university library to see what more I could learn about this strange and puzzling disorder. I did not know it then, but I was hooked. Hooked on autism. I have stayed hooked on autism for almost three and a half decades now. Scarcely a moment passes when I do not think of autism.

These days my interest in autism can be described as strong and compelling. When I first started my quest, autism was no less than an obsession. I quickly read everything I could find on the subject and hungered for more. In the late 1950s and early 1960s, San Diego had no medical school, and medical library facilities were limited. When the Navy sent me to a conference in New Orleans, I spent my days at the conference and my nights at the Tulane University Medical Library, avidly reading papers not available in San Diego. While my fellow conferees savored the delights of Bourbon Street, I plowed through volume after volume of medical textbooks. I managed to persuade a kindly guard, who no doubt had grave misgivings about my sanity, to let me continue my studies while he locked up the library for the night.

More often, however, the Navy sent me to meetings in Washington, DC, where I could spend evenings devouring the miraculous holdings of the National Library of Medicine.

I was intent on reading virtually every word that had ever been published on autism, and I think I came close to succeeding. Articles in French, German, Dutch, Czech, and Portuguese were translated by friends or acquaintances competent in these languages. Today it would be impossible, but in the late fifties and early sixties it was possible—barely—to be conversant with the world literature on autism. As a student, I seldom took notes, depending instead on a near-photographic memory. But this was different. This was war. I envisioned autism as a powerful monster that had seized my child. I could afford no errors. I took meticulous notes.

Photocopy machines were becoming more accessible in those days, so it became feasible to request photocopies of articles. This approach, of course, was much easier than visiting the libraries where the books were held or requesting through interlibrary loan entire volumes of medical journals and textbooks, which the libraries were not eager to send.

My research led from autism to the bordering areas of genetics, biochemistry, and neurophysiology. I avidly read in these and other fields as my knowledge expanded. As a result, I began to develop a theory of autism as a cognitive disorder and a theory of how the normal brain functions. I filled many notebooks, and many thousands of 4 x 6 cards, with references, findings, and ideas. Although I had begun my work to satisfy my strong personal interest, after several years of study I decided to write a paper to stimulate research and to inform other parents and professionals about my findings. I wrote the paper, then revised and enlarged it, again and again. After 5 years of intensive work, Gloria commented one day that my "paper" on autism had grown so that it had really become a book. "Yes," I agreed, it had, much to my surprise.

At about this time the Appleton-Century-Crofts Publishing Company announced a new annual award competition for "A Distinguished Contribution to Psychology." I submitted my manuscript. A few months later I was notified that the judges had "unanimously and enthusiastically" selected my manuscript as the first winner of the Century Psychology Award. My book was titled *Infantile Autism: The Syndrome and Its Implications for a Neural Theory of Behavior.* From the moment its impending publication was announced, I began to receive letters and phone calls from parents of autistic children, who, like myself, were looking for answers. Those letters and phone calls continue to this day.

Publication of my book immediately made a huge difference in my life, and in the lives of many people, both parents and professionals. Within a short time I was invited to spend a year as a fellow at the Center for Advanced Study in the Behavioral Sciences on the campus of Stanford University. I was also invited as a guest speaker, lecturer, or visiting professor at scores of universities and medical schools.

After these lectures I was approached, on many occasions, by psychologists, psychiatrists, and other professionals who told me that reading my book had revolutionized their thinking. What I had written was so at variance with what they had been trained to believe, and so compelling, that they could not in good conscience continue the work for which they were trained. A woman who had just received her Ph.D. as a child psychotherapist switched careers and became a neuropsychologist. (One of the nicest compliments I received on my book was from a college librarian who told me that my book was the one most frequently stolen from the college library.)

The Cause of Autism

What did I say in *Infantile Autism* that had this effect? Most important, *Infantile Autism* attacked, and pretty well destroyed, the then-dominant belief that autism was an emotional disorder, brought on by the mother's mishandling of the child in some subtle, but devastating, psychological way. The theory that autism was psychogenic in origin had been presented not as a theory, but as a demonstrated, uncontestable, proven fact. Alternate hypotheses were not even considered. The experts, the authorities, the textbook writers, the professors, had proclaimed, as though they were blessed with some divine insight, that mothers caused autism in their children. In *Infantile Autism* I explicitly challenged this highly destructive belief, seeking out and very carefully examining any evidence or arguments that had been or that might be employed to support the thesis of psychogenic origin. I did the same with the arguments for biogenic causation.

Bruno Bettelheim, a prolific and persuasive writer in the field of child behavior, had published a number of books (e.g., *Truants from Life; Love Is Not Enough*) in which mothers were viciously condemned for their attitudes toward their children, which had caused, he claimed, their children to withdraw into autism. Bettelheim's books were very popular, and any mother of a newly diagnosed autistic child who went to a library looking for information on autism would be sure to be guided toward one of his books. To her grief would be added a heavy measure of shame and guilt. *She* had caused her child to become autistic. Her denial merely proved her guilt.

Most parents had no inkling that the professionals who blamed them for having caused autism were doing so out of blind faith and, in fact, could cite no evidence to support what was merely a weak hypothesis. *Infantile Autism* showed the psychogenic theory to be baseless and replaced it with a neural theory.

In 1979, 15 years after *Infantile Autism* was published, a national magazine commissioned one of its editorial writers to do a major article on autism. After traveling throughout the country and talking to a large number of parents and professionals, the editor wrote that "90% of the people in the field believe that Rimland blew Bettelheim's theories to hell." Bettelheim tried to fight back against *Infantile Autism* with his 1967 book *The Empty Fortress*, but to no avail. His time was past.

It was important to destroy the belief that mothers caused autism in their children. Not only did this belief cause the parents great harm in terms of guilt, grief, and loss of confidence, but, just as important, it discouraged the kinds of biological research I knew would be vital if the true cause of autism were ever to be found. A good deal of *Infantile Autism* is therefore devoted to hypotheses about the biological nature of autism. Autism is explained as being primarily a cognitive, rather than an affective, disorder.

Specifically, the hypothesis that the neurological underpinnings of autism lie in subcortical structures is developed in some detail. I argued that the brainstem reticular formation (BSRF) might well have functions different from those attributed to it in the neurophysiological literature and might, in fact, be the site of the brain malfunction that leads to autism. I suggested that the BSRF is the prime site where incoming sensory stimuli are transduced into the code that elicits, or makes it possible to elicit, the relevant memories that give meaning to sensory input—that convert sensation to perception.

Within the field of autism my neural theory has had relatively little impact, although neuroscientist Eric Courchesne, who has conducted landmark studies using brain magnetic resonance imaging (MRI) and cortical-evoked potentials with autistic subjects (e.g., Courchesne, 1987), credits his reading of *Infantile Autism* with arousing his interest in the study of brain function in autism and directing his attention to subcortical structures. Recently I

received an exciting paper from Japan in which the researchers report finding, through MRI, significantly smaller brainstems in autistic children than in matched control subjects (Hashimoto et al., 1992).

The neural theory of behavior as presented in *Infantile Autism* has had some influence in fields that may seem far removed from autism, such as aesthetics, philosophy, political science, and artificial intelligence. For example, Morse Peckham (1965) devoted an appendix of his book on aesthetics, *Man's Rage for Chaos,* to this theory. Artist Elizabeth Willmott cited the neural theory extensively in her essay "Creative Relationships" (1977). Political scientist R. I. Wolfe credited the neural theory with giving him the idea for his paper "War as a Surrogate" (1973). Biocyberneticist Harry Klopf presents in his book *The Hedonistic Neuron* (1982) an independently derived brain model strikingly similar to mine, including stimulus-seeking neurons and a brainstem reticular formation that serves functions crucial to intelligence and consciousness. Strange outcomes for a story that started with a screaming infant!

The Specificity of Autism

While I was successful in convincing the autism world of the vacuousness of, and the need to abandon, the psychogenic hypothesis, I was, alas, unsuccessful in achieving another goal of the book— bringing about recognition of the uniqueness of autism.

When Leo Kanner wrote his classic and frequently cited 1943 paper describing the first 11 cases of autism he had seen, there was already an extensive literature—a multitude of papers—relating to children who were diagnosed as "childhood schizophrenics," "childhood psychotics," "children with symbiotic psychosis," and "children with atypical development." Kanner had seen numerous children so diagnosed during his long tenure as director of the Child Psychiatry Clinic at Johns Hopkins University and had written about them in his chapter on childhood schizophrenia in his classic *Textbook of Child Psychiatry.* In a long series of papers, starting with his 1943 paper, Kanner tried to point out that within the larger population of children described as psychotic, schizophrenic, and so forth, there existed a small subgroup who shared a number of symptoms—that is, a subtype. It was only this small subgroup of children, *not* the total population of children with very severe behavioral disorders, that Kanner wished to label as having autism, or early infantile autism.

Despite Kanner's repeated protestations, others chose to ignore the very specific criteria for autism he had set forth, proceeding instead to attach the diagnosis of autism to the vast majority of children they saw who formerly would have been labeled "childhood schizophrenic." "Childhood schizophrenia" was not an attractive term—"autism" sounded much better.

Kanner asserted repeatedly that the two primary symptoms that differentiated the children he termed autistic from the much larger population of children generally referred to as childhood schizophrenic were (a) extreme self-isolation, present from the first years of life, and (b) excessive insistence on the preservation of sameness. Kanner presented many other less definitive criteria, particularly in the sphere of language, which helped to differentiate his autistic subgroup from the much larger population of children then called childhood schizophrenics. These speech symptoms (observed only in the non-mute children) included the failure to use the words "I" or "yes," extreme literalness, metaphorical language, and a number of other oddities described in detail in his papers as well as in *Infantile Autism*.

Despite Kanner's protests, the field seized eagerly upon the term "autism" and began applying it indiscriminately to children who did not meet Kanner's criteria. In 1958, Kanner observed that, in the 19 years since he had first identified infantile autism as a syndrome, many children had been brought to his clinic from all over the world for diagnosis. However, he had seen fewer than 150 children in those years—fewer than 8 patients per year—who were cases of true infantile autism.

When I first met Kanner, in 1962, he told me that fewer than 1 child in 10 diagnosed by others as autistic and brought to him for confirmation had really fit his criteria of early infantile autism. A decade later, after I had collected data on close to 2,000 "autistic" children, using my diagnostic checklist, Form E2, I found that Kanner was very accurate in his 1-in-10 estimate. That is, 9.8% of the children whose diagnostic checklists I scored achieved a score of +20 or higher, thereby indicating that they fit Kanner's criteria for early infantile autism (Rimland, 1971).

I had believed, rather naively, that if I presented the information clearly and compellingly, with solid documentation, the world would realize that Kanner was correct in insisting that he had sectioned off a small segment of the population of children with psychotic behavior, and that the small subgroup he had identified and labeled as having early infantile autism should remain differentiated, rather than be diluted and lost by having the entire population of psychotic children labeled autistic.

If you study the titles of articles written about the childhood psychoses (child schizophrenia, etc.) in the 1920s, 1930s, and 1940s, you will see that with the exception of the few articles written by Kanner in 1943 and after, none pertained to autistic children. If you go to the literature published in the 1970s, 1980s, and 1990s, you will find that virtually *all* of the articles published during these decades refer to autistic rather than schizophrenic children. If all of the children now being described in the professional literature are autistic, what happened to the schizophrenic children who were discussed and described in the decades before Kanner? Since it is not reasonable to believe that the population of children has changed much during these decades, it is obvious that what has changed is that the label "autistic" is now universally applied, whereas previously the vast majority of these same children would have been described as schizophrenic.

Unfortunately, the same poor scholarship that characterized the field when mothers were being blamed for having caused autism, without empirical evidence, is still rampant. People blithely continue to use Kanner's term "autism" to characterize a much larger and indiscriminate population than the small subgroup to which Kanner had insisted that the diagnostic of autism really belongs. It is interesting that the paper in which Kanner spoke out most clearly on this topic, "Specificity of Early Infantile Autism" (1958), does not appear in the volume of his collected writings on autism (1973). Also of interest, the journal Kanner edited from its inception in 1971 was titled *Journal of Autism and Childhood Schizophrenia*. After his retirement in 1974 it became *Journal of Autism and Developmental Disabilities*.

My diagnostic checklist, Form E2, which appears as an appendix to *Infantile Autism*, was intended to help differentiate children with true autism, as described by Kanner, from children who were autistic only in the loose sense of the word, whose disorder in previous decades would have been characterized as childhood schizophrenia or childhood psychosis.

One of the most interesting and striking findings reported by Kanner for his population of children with true infantile autism was that the parents remarkably often were professional people: psychiatrists, engineers, lawyers, physicians, and so on. This finding was met with a good deal of skepticism from Kanner's colleagues, especially those who did not trouble themselves to understand that he was speaking only of the parents of that small subgroup of children who truly met the criteria for early infantile autism. In Chapter 2 of *Infantile Autism* I examined all aspects of the issue of parental uniqueness presented by Kanner. The conclusion I reached then, and by which I stand today, is that Kanner's finding is irrefutable if, but only if, one uses the very strict and limited definition of autism insisted upon by him. That is, the parents of such children are remarkably often of high intelligence and are professionally trained.

A number of authors have claimed to have disproven Kanner's assertion about these parents (e.g., Callias, Lennox, & Rutter, 1977; Ritvo et al., 1971), but in every case they have ignored the distinction Kanner made between children with infantile autism and children who were autistic-like but not afflicted with infantile autism. When the distinction between truly autistic and autistic-like children is observed, however, Kanner's findings are supported (e.g., Lotter, 1967; Treffert, 1970). Kanner's report of the relationship between autism and parental intelligence has important theoretical implications for the genetics of attention and cognition, which are discussed in *Infantile Autism*. Recently, Robin Clarke independently came to similar conclusions (Clarke, 1993).

As Kanner pointed out, identifying subgroups within a large category of disorders is important if proper treatment is to be discovered. For centuries, physicians argued about something called "the fevers." Not until specific subtypes were found, such as malaria, typhoid, and diphtheria, did prevention and proper treatment become possible. The failure to recognize that "autism" is not a catchall term has led to serious problems in biomedical research (e.g., see Rimland, 1976).

Behavior Modification

Soon after *Infantile Autism* was published, I began hearing about the remarkable effectiveness of a new technique called "behavior modification" as a means of improving the behavior of autistic children. In October 1964, I visited the autism clinic run by Ivar Lovaas at the University of California, Los Angeles, and was impressed with his success in improving the condition of the autistic children with whom he worked. I had previously received letters from parents of autistic children in the Los Angeles area who had read my book and had made plans to meet with some of them for dinner. I invited Ivar along. He was quite reluctant. The newspaper articles I had read about him and his work showed that he accepted the then-universal view that autism was merely a psychological disorder brought on by maternal neglect, and he did not show great interest in meeting the parents. However, I managed to persuade him to join us for dinner.

After Ivar met these parents in a social setting, he could immediately see that they were very pleasant, normal people. He had arrived at an incorrect conclusion because of his training and because the parents he had met in his clinic setting were tense and guilt-ridden, keenly aware that they were regarded as the chief culprits in causing their child's autism. Several of the mothers at the dinner meeting asked Ivar if he would teach them how to use behavior modification so that they could help their own children. He agreed to do so, and later told me that it was one of the most important meetings of his life. He realized that parents could be strong allies for the children and for himself and should be supported, encouraged, and trained—rather than reviled and ignored—as had been the near-universal practice of professionals in the past.

Parents as Advocates

By this time I had received hundreds of letters from parents of autistic children throughout the country, and from many foreign countries as well. I decided that it was time for these people to learn about behavior modification as a means of helping their children, since the only other approaches then available were the use of drugs and of psychotherapy, both of which were likely to do much more harm than good.

In November 1965, the Navy sent me to a conference in Washington, DC. Checking my correspondence files, I could see they represented sizable numbers of parents both in the New York City area and in Washington, DC. I wrote to these parents, offering to meet with them and to speak to them about a new type of treatment that I thought would be helpful to their children. The first meeting was held in the home of parents in a suburb of New York City. About 60 people attended, some traveling from as far away as Albany. I told them about behavior modification and the significant improvements it could bring about in their children's behavior. I told them that Ivar Lovaas would be willing to send one of his graduate students to teach them and prospective teachers how to use this new technique. I proposed that we parents start a national organization, with chapters in various cities, to

be known as the National Society for Autistic Children. The response was enthusiastic, and the society (now the Autism Society of America) was formed.

The second meeting was held two evenings later, in the main auditorium of the National Institutes of Health in Bethesda, Maryland, with the assistance of dedicated parents in the Washington area. The parents were excited about the new approach to teaching their children I described ("very similar to the rewards-and-punishments method used to teach Helen Keller"). At last there was something constructive they could do to help their children.

As agreed, Ivar sent a graduate student—in most instances, David Ryback—to give weeklong seminars on behavior modification. The first seven or so chapters of the Autism Society of America were formed in this way, using the mailing list of parent correspondents I had collected. As of this writing, the Autism Society of America, headquartered in the Washington, DC area, has close to 200 chapters throughout the country and holds regional and national conventions yearly. These meetings are a great source of information and encouragement for parents and professionals alike.

The Autism Society has done monumentally important work in bringing about the public education of autistic children. While the psychogenic theory of autism reigned, autism was held to be an emotional disorder that fell within the purview of the psychiatric establishment, rather than a problem requiring educational intervention. In my home state of California, for example, the law required that autistic children be *excluded* from the public schools. Lifting the burden of shame, guilt, and blame from the parents of autistic children unleashed an enormous burst of productivity and creativity on behalf of the children. The parents insisted that autism be included in landmark federal legislation of the mid-1970s, which provided that *all* children had the right to public education.

Autism Research Institute

Meanwhile, I continued to receive mountains of mail from parents and professionals around the world who had read *Infantile Autism* and who wanted to share information. I had thought that my job would be done once my book was published, but that was not to be.

It was obvious that some of the information and ideas in the letters I was receiving could be important in terms of finding the cause, and eventually the cure, for autism. As a researcher, I felt it was important to systematically collect and analyze these data. By 1967, the cost of secretarial help, postage, office supplies, and the like began to become burdensome to our family, so with the help of friends I established a small nonprofit research organization, then called the Institute for Child Behavior Research and more recently renamed the Autism Research Institute (ARI). The Autism Research Institute serves as a world clearinghouse for information on autism and related conditions. We publish a quarterly newsletter, *Autism Research Review International*, which we send to over 6,000 subscribers in more than 50 countries.

One of the major activities of the ARI is to develop better methods of diagnosing autism. Our diagnostic checklist, Form E2, mentioned earlier, is possibly the most frequently used diagnostic tool in the world for identifying autism. We have in our files over 16,000 case histories, completed by parents worldwide. Form E2 is available in English, Spanish, German, French, Hebrew, Turkish, Polish, Japanese, Arabic, Serbo-Croatian, and several Indian dialects. When parents or professionals send us a completed E2 form, we score it by computer and send back a report. We do not charge for this service but use it as a means of helping parents and professionals and of collecting data. We are subjecting our database to sophisticated methods of factor analysis and cluster analysis in order to find, if possible, some of the subgroups of autism ("autism" in its loosely defined, generic usage) that have not yet been identified. In addition to providing research-based information and advice to parents and professionals worldwide, the Autism Research Institute conducts research on a variety of problems, including, especially, the evaluation of promising new treatment approaches.

Megavitamin Therapy

In the late 1960s I began getting letters from parents who had tried large doses of certain vitamins with their autistic children, often reporting good results. At first I was skeptical, but after many such cases had accumulated, I decided that the matter warranted systematic investigation. After an intense review of the literature, which assured me that the vitamins were safe, even at very high intakes, I conducted a large-scale study on over 200 autistic children, using high doses of four vitamins. Vitamin B6 proved to be the best of these, with close to 50% of the children on whom the high-dose vitamin had been used showing significant and worthwhile improvement. Because we could not assume that our population was homogeneous in its response to any treatment, the study used a unique computer-clustering experimental design, which precluded the possibility of arriving at an erroneous positive conclusion about the value of the vitamins (Rimland, 1973). Since we did not use the traditional, but overrated, double-blind crossover procedure, some critics with an inadequate understanding of statistical methodology have wrongly claimed that our study was merely anecdotal (e.g., Holm & Varley, 1989; Raiten & Massaro, 1987).

Our second study, conducted in collaboration with several researchers from University of California medical schools, followed the more traditional double-blind placebo crossover design, since we were able to use as subjects children found to respond to vitamin B6 in the first study. The second study confirmed the results of the first: vitamin B6 was helpful for a significant proportion of autistic children (Rimland, Callaway, & Dreyfus, 1978).

Shortly after our second megavitamin study, Gilbert Lelord and his research group at the Tours University Medical School in France became interested in our research on the use of B6 and magnesium in the treatment of autism. (I had learned in my first study that it was essential to give magnesium along with the B6.) The Lelord group has since published many studies on the use of high-dosage vitamin B6 (and usually magnesium) in autistic children and adults, all with positive results (see Rimland, 1987). As of 1992, 16 studies in the world literature, completed in five countries (the U.S., England, France, Germany, and Italy), confirm that approximately one-half of all autistic children and adults improve in many ways when given high doses of vitamin B6 and magnesium, and that none are harmed.

The record of safety and efficacy is far better for high-dosage vitamin B6 and magnesium than for any of the drugs used in the treatment of autism. The B6-magnesium combination not only improves the speech and behavior of approximately 50% of the population of autistic individuals, it also improves these individuals' electrophysiological functioning, as measured by cortical-evoked potential studies, and their metabolism, as measured by studies on the excretion of abnormal metabolites in the urine. Despite the remarkably consistent evidence for the efficacy and safety of the high-dosage vitamin B6 and magnesium treatment, most physicians attempt to convince parents that this form of treatment is not scientifically proven and/or is not safe.

Although a great deal of effort has been expended by myself and others on exploring the use of high-dosage vitamin B6 and magnesium in the treatment of autism during the past 25 years, it appears that a number of other nutrients may also be helpful. It is important to understand that the brain is a biochemical computer. To function properly it requires the right substances present in the right amounts. The "right substances" include vitamins, minerals, amino acids, and other factors typically used by the brain. The brain does not normally use such toxic substances as Ritalin, Haldol, Fenfluramine, Prozac, and the like.

I and many other researchers are convinced that when an appropriate biological treatment is found for autism (and most other disorders), it will be found among the natural substances ordinarily required by the brain to conduct its day-to-day affairs, rather than as any synthetic product of a high-tech chemistry laboratory. Of course, the synthetic products of high-tech chemistry laboratories can be patented by pharmaceutical companies, and

nutrients cannot be patented. For that reason—profit potential—far more funds are invested in looking for drugs than in searching for helpful natural substances.

With the assistance of parents of autistic children, many of whom are also scientists and physicians, the Autism Research Institute continues to explore natural substances capable of correcting at least some of the errors in brain chemistry that underlie autism. The use of substances found in foods, such as vitamin B6, vitamin C, folic acid, coenzyme Q10, certain essential fatty acids, and certain amino acids, represents a safe and rational approach to improving the quality of life for autistic children and their families.

In addition to our work in nutrition, we continue to explore other approaches to treating autism. Currently, my colleague Stephen Edelson and I are evaluating auditory integration training (AIT), which may be especially helpful to the large segment of autistic children whose hearing is hypersensitive to the point of being painful (Berard, 1982; Rimland & Edelson, 1991, in press; Stehli, 1991).

Looking back over the third of a century during which I have been involved in research on the diagnosis, cause, and treatment of autism, I am impressed not only with how much has been accomplished but, even more, with how much remains to be done. Having retired in 1984 from my job as a research psychologist for the Navy, I am now able to devote myself full time to autism research. Interesting new developments continue to occur, some of which may turn out to be important. As I finish writing this chapter in the pre-dawn hours, when I can write with few interruptions, I wonder if *this* will be the day when I hear of the discovery of a new and critical piece of the strange puzzle we call autism.

Afterword

Since this story started with my autistic son Mark, let me conclude with a brief update.

Mark had been so difficult and unresponsive that when he was 5, we were told, "He is hopeless—

institutionalize him!" We didn't. Instead, Mark was given every promising treatment I could learn about. Behavior modification and vitamins made the biggest difference. He said his first meaningful words, and asked his first question, at age 8.

Today Mark, at 36, is a polite, pleasant, helpful, very handsome fellow who lives at home and takes public transportation to an excellent day program for mentally handicapped adults. He enjoys life, listening to music, participating in Special Olympics, and taking care of his two pet cats. When Mark was in his twenties, it was discovered that he has remarkable artistic ability. His paintings have won many awards. We continue to investigate new approaches to helping him, and he continues to astonish and delight us by striding past milestones we had never dared hope he would achieve.

It would take a book to document what we have tried, and what Mark has accomplished. Watch for it.

References

BERARD, G. (1982). *Audition egalé comportment.* Sainte-Ruffine: Maisonneuve.

CLARKE, R. P. (1993). A theory of general impairment of gene-expression manifesting as autism. *Journal of Personality and Individual Differences, 14,* 465–482.

COURCHESNE, E. (1987). A neurophysiological view of autism. In E. Schopler & G. B. Mesibov (Eds.), *Neurobiological issues in autism* (pp. 285–324). New York: Plenum.

HASHIMOTO, T., TAYAMA, M., MIYAZAKI, M., SAKURAMA, N., YOSHIMOTO, T., MURAKAWA, K., & KURODA, Y. (1992). Reduced brainstem size in children with autism. *Brain and Development, 14,* 94–97.

HOLM, V. A., & VARLEY, C. K. (1989). Pharmacological treatment of autistic children. In G. Dawson (Ed.), *Autism: Nature, Diagnosis and Treatment* (pp. 386–404). New York: Guilford.

KANNER, L. (1958). Specificity of early infantile autism. *Zeitschrift for Kinder Psychiatry, 25,* 108–113.

KANNER, L. (1973). *Childhood psychosis: Initial studies and new insights.* New York: Wiley.

KLOPF, A. H. (1982). *The hedonistic neuron: A theory of memory learning and intelligence.* Washington, DC: Hemisphere.

LENNOX, C., CALLIAS, M., & RUTTER, M. (1977). Cognitive characteristics of parents of autistic children. *Journal of Autism and Childhood Schizophrenia, 7,* 243–261.

LOTTER, V. (1967). Epidemiology of autistic conditions in young children. II. Some characteristics of the parents and children. *Social Psychiatry, 1,* 163–173.

PECKHAM, M. (1965). *Man's rage for chaos: Biology, behavior and the arts.* Philadelphia: Chilton.

RAITEN, D. J., & MASSARO, T. F. (1987). Nutrition and developmental disabilities: An examination of the orthomolecular hypothesis. In D. J. Cohen & A. M. Donnellan (Eds.), *Handbook of autism and pervasive developmental disorders* (pp. 566–583). New York: Wiley.

RIMLAND, B. (1964). *Infantile autism: The syndrome and its implications for a neural theory of behavior.* New York: Appleton-Century-Crofts.

RIMLAND, B. (1971). The differentiation of childhood psychoses: An analysis of checklists for 2,218 psychotic children. *Journal of Autism and Childhood Schizophrenia, 1,* 161–174.

RIMLAND, B. (1973). High dosage levels of certain vitamins in the treatment of children with severe mental disorders. In D. R. Hawkins & L. Pauling (Eds.), *Orthomolecular psychiatry* (pp. 513–539). New York: W. H. Freeman.

RIMLAND, B. (1976). Platelet uptake and efflux of serotonin in subtypes of psychotic children. *Journal of Autism and Childhood Schizophrenia, 6,* 379–382.

RIMLAND, B. (1982). The use of megavitamin B6 and magnesium in the treatment of autistic children and adults. In E. Schopler & G. Mesibov (Eds.), *Neurobiological issues in autism* (pp. 389–405). New York: Plenum.

RIMLAND, B. (1987). The use of high-dosage vitamin B6 and magnesium in the treatment of autistic children and adults. In E. Schopler & G. B. Mesibov (Eds.), *Neurobiological issues in autism* (pp. 389–405). New York: Plenum.

RIMLAND, B., CALLAWAY, E., & DREYFUS, P. (1978). The effect of high doses of vitamin B6 on autistic children: A double-blind crossover study. *American Journal of Psychiatry, 135,* 472–475.

RIMLAND, B., & EDELSON, S. M. (1991). *Improving the auditory functioning of autistic persons: A comparison of the Berard auditory training approach with Tomatis audio-psycho-phonology approach.* San Diego: Autism Research Institute.

RIMLAND, B., & EDELSON, S. M. (in press). Auditory integration training in autism: A pilot study. *Journal of Autism and Developmental Disorders.*

RITVO, E. R., CANTWELL, D., JOHNSON, E., CLEMENTS, M., BENBROOK, F., SLAGLE, S., KELLY, P., & RITZ, M. (1971). Social class factors in autism. *Journal of Autism and Childhood Schizophrenia, 1,* 297–310.

STEHLI, A. (1991). *The sound of a miracle: A child's triumph over autism.* New York: Doubleday.

TREFFERT, D. A. (1970). Epidemiology of infantile autism. *Archives of General Psychiatry, 22,* 431–438.

WILLMOTT, E. (1977). Creative relationships. *The Structuralist, 7,* 23–34.

WOLFE, R. I. (1973, February). *War as a surrogate and surrogates for war: An application of the general theory of surrogates.* Paper presented at the annual meeting of the Peace Research Society, State University of San Francisco.

CHAPTER 2

Defining and Assessing Autism

Peter Sturmey
ABILENE STATE SCHOOL

Jay A. Sevin
THE KENNEDY KRIEGER INSTITUTE

The definition and assessment of autism has, over the years, been a controversial and heated topic. Implicitly and explicitly, this controversy reflects the importance of these issues. Several reviews (Parks, 1983; Rutter & Schopler, 1988) and books (e.g., Schopler & Mesibov, 1988a) have been devoted exclusively to this very aspect of autism. Why is this so?

Werry (1988) outlined seven functions that diagnosis of autism should fulfill. First, it should inform treatment, not just of isolated symptoms, but also of the whole person. Second, it should lead to accurate predictions about the future course of the disorder. Third, it should give information about the cause(s) of the disorder. Fourth, it should provide information about associated features of the disorder. Fifth, it should identify individuals who are, in some important way, homogeneous. Thus, it should facilitate communication among clinicians, researchers, and the public and should aid in replicating research findings. Sixth, it should provide information about strategies for preventing the disorder. Finally, labeling resulting from diagnosis should have a net benefit to the client and

family. It should provide a helpful explanation and summary of the client's behavior and facilitate access to resources and treatment.

The diagnosis of autism is not uncontroversial in clinical practice. Social stigma and other adverse consequences are frequently associated with receiving a psychiatric diagnosis (Seltzer & Seltzer, 1983; Turnbull & Wheat, 1983). Thus, the potential for abuse of the diagnostic process warrants caution. Schopler and Mesibov (1988b) noted that, in assigning a label to a person, psychiatric diagnosis may appear to oversimplify the person's complexities and individuality. Similarly, labels that may facilitate treatment for a particular disorder may limit access to services for other problems (Alford & Locke, 1984; Reiss, Levitan, & Szyszko, 1982). Further compounding the problem, diagnostic systems frequently serve functions other than those for which they were designed (Schopler & Mesibov, 1988b). Most notably, the *Diagnostic and Statistical Manual of Mental Disorders* (DSM-III-R) (American Psychiatric Association, 1987), originally designed for collecting data to be used for monitoring the clinical activities of psychiatrists, has since taken on a life all its own.

In spite of these problems, diagnosis offers advantages, both material and emotional, to individuals and their families. For example, Quine and Pahl (1986) found that parents of children with developmental disabilities showed greatest satisfaction with the disclosure process when diagnosis was made early, using a familiar label and expressed in a straightforward and sympathetic manner. Parents who received diagnoses late, with an unfamiliar label, showed the highest rates of dissatisfaction. Such findings have been used to form the basis for developing model procedures for disclosure. Autism is typically diagnosed some time after initial problems have been detected. For example, examining the diagnostic history of 10 individuals diagnosed with autism, Culbertson (1977) found that between 6 and 15 professional contacts were made before the first diagnosis. Thus, the disclosure of the diagnosis of autism may be especially difficult to manage well (Quine & Pahl, 1986).

Others have pointed to the political purpose behind developing diagnostic criteria to make a disorder a recognized part of current health politics. Rutter and Schopler (1988) noted that, although informed by scientific opinion, the definition of autism of the National Society for Autistic Children (NSAC) was primarily formulated to generate a favorable social policy toward the individuals and families for whom NSAC advocates.

Defining and assessing autism has been an evolutionary process, useful in refining conceptions of autism and related disorders. The remainder of this chapter deals with five topics. First, we review the major current conceptualizations of autism and their historical background. Second, we discuss problems in diagnosis related to the heterogeneous clinical presentation of autism. Third, we review the characteristics of good assessment instruments and develop criteria for evaluating current assessments of autism. Fourth, we critically review the four most frequently used autism scales. In the final section, we make recommendations for the future development and refinement of definitional systems and assessment procedures.

Definitions of Autism

Childhood psychoses received scant attention in the nineteenth century. Even as late as DSM-II, specific childhood disorders were not included in standard psychiatric nosologies (APA, 1952). In the first half of the twentieth century, greater interest was shown in this field with work on dementia precossisima (De Sanctis, 1906) and childhood schizophrenia (see Turner, 1989). At this time, childhood disorders were generally conceived of as adult-type psychoses with very early onsets (Rutter & Schopler, 1988). Kanner (1943) broke with this approach, developing a set of criteria that was not merely a modification of adult criteria. By implication, he also questioned the assumed link between childhood and adult psychoses.

Kanner's Definition

Kanner (1943) first proposed the diagnosis of infantile autism, reporting what he believed to be a previously unrecognized syndrome. As a basis for this diagnosis, he observed in 11 children a unique constellation of behaviors, including an inability to develop relationships with people, a delay in speech acquisition, noncommunicative use of speech after it had developed, delayed echolalia, pronomial reversal, repetitive and stereotyped play activities, insistence on sameness, lack of imagination, good rote memory, and normal physical appearance. These symptoms all had an early onset.

Kanner's definition of autism has had lasting impact in the field. Indeed, most of the criteria from his original list, with some revisions, are still included in current definitions of autism.

Creak's Definition

Almost immediately after Kanner's definition was proposed, controversy arose as to whether his syndrome constituted a distinct diagnostic condition. Like researchers of the early twentieth century, many believed that the behaviors associated with autism were very early signs of schizophrenia (Fish, 1976). This view, referred to as the "unitary" theory of child psychosis, was initially influenced by Creak (1961) and the British Working Party, who compiled a list of criteria to be used for identifying "early childhood psychosis." Characteristics included (a) gross and sustained impairment of emotional relationships with people; (b) apparent unawareness of personal identity to a degree inappropriate for age; (c) pathological preoccupation with particular objects or certain characteristics of them, without regard to function; (d) sustained resistance to change in the environment and persistent efforts to maintain or restore sameness; (e) abnormal perceptual experience; (f) frequent acute, excessive, and seemingly illogical anxiety; (g) speech either lost, never acquired, or failing to develop; (h) distortion in motility pattern; and (i) background of serious retardation in which islets of normal or exceptional intellectual function or skill may appear.

Interestingly, most of these criteria are similar to those reported by Kanner (1943), indicating that Creak and Kanner were describing similar conditions. However, Creak (1961) added items (e), (f), and (h) above and noted that most subjects in her sample were also mentally retarded. This was in contrast to Kanner, who believed, because of their good rote memory and normal physical appearance, that the children in his sample were of average intelligence.

The Working Party's criteria were not strictly a definition of autism. Nine criteria came from observations of 100 patients loosely classified as "psychotic." It is unlikely, therefore, that all 100 patients would be defined as autistic by current definitions. Nevertheless, Creak's nine points were frequently used as a definition of autism in following years, even by those who did not hold a unitary view (e.g., Rutter, 1965). For example, the Working Party's criteria were employed in the most frequently cited prevalence study of autism (Lotter, 1966). In addition, Creak's definition has been used in the construction of several of the most commonly employed autism assessment instruments (e.g., Krug, Arick, & Almond, 1980; Schopler, Reichler, DeVellis, & Daly, 1980).

Rutter's Definition and DSM-III-R

In an extensive review of the literature, Rutter (1978) attempted to clarify the problems surrounding a definition of autism. Thus, he noted that Kanner (1943) considered autism to be a syndrome. By this, Kanner meant two things. First, certain behaviors in his subjects tended to co-occur with *uniformity* across all diagnosed subjects. Second, these behaviors were *specific* to autism and differentiated it from other psychiatric disorders. Rutter proposed that only those behaviors that were both *universal* and *specific* to autism should be considered essential diagnostic criteria.

Rutter (1978) reported three broad bands of symptoms found both in almost all children diagnosed as having autism and, much less frequently, in children who were normal or had other disorders: (a) impaired development of social relations; (b) delayed and deviant language development; and (c) ritualistic, compulsive behavior or insistence on sameness. These three bands of symptoms, with the addition of onset during infancy or childhood, are essentially those adopted by the DSM-III-R (APA, 1987). The DSM-III-R further clarifies the diagnostic criteria for autism by listing specific behavioral symptoms under each of the domains. At present, these definitions are most frequently used for diagnostic classification in research and clinical practice in North America.

The adoption of DSM-III-R criteria for autism should be viewed as a major change, even when compared to DSM-III criteria (APA, 1980). To illustrate, Hertzig, Snow, New, and Shapiro (1990) compared DSM-III and DSM-III-R criteria in a group of 112 children. Subjects were 23 to 66 months of age and attended a therapeutic nursery school. The authors found that children were substantially more likely to be diagnosed as having *autistic disorder* (using DSM-III-R) than *infantile autism* (using DSM-III). Also, just over half of the children diagnosed as having *atypical–pervasive developmental disorder* using DSM-III were classified as having *autistic disorder* using DSM-III-R criteria (see Table 2.1). Similar trends were found in the national field trials of DSM-III-R criteria, suggesting that the new behavioral criteria have resulted in a broader, more liberal definition of autism, accompanied by a large increase in the prevalence of the disorder (Spitzer & Siegel, 1990).

ASA Definition

The Autism Society of America (ASA) has endorsed the definition of autism proposed by Ritvo and Freeman (1978), which has become commonly used in the literature. Similar to Rutter (1978), ASA considers autism a behaviorally defined syndrome. The essential features are typically manifested prior to 30 months of age, including disturbances of (a) developmental rates and/or sequences; (b) responses to sensory stimuli; (c) speech, language, and cognitive capacities; and (d) capacities to relate to people, events, and objects. Disturbances in developmental rates may include delays, arrests, or regressions in motor, cognitive, or social behavior. Disturbances in response to sensory stimuli may include overreactivity or underreactivity to visual, auditory, tactile, or olfactory stimuli.

The DSM-III-R and ASA definitions, in fact, share many more similarities than differences

Table 2.1 DSM-III and DSM-III-R Diagnoses of Autism

	DSM-III-R		
	Autistic Disorder	PDD NOS	Total
DSM-III			
Infantile Autism	30	1	31
Atypical-PDD	23	21	44
Total	53	22	75

SOURCE: From "DSM-III and DSM-III-R diagnosis of autism and pervasive developmental disorder in nursery school children," by M. E. Hertzig, 1990, *Journal of the American Academy of Child and Adolescent Psychiatry, 29*, 124. Copyright © 1990 by American Academy of Child & Adolescent Psychiatry. Reprinted by permission.

(Schopler, 1978). Both acknowledge that their criteria are working definitions. Both consider autism to be a unique diagnostic entity with specific behaviors that categorize the syndrome, but disagree about the criteria essential for diagnosis. Both acknowledge that the behavioral symptomatology varies tremendously from one autistic person to another. Both agree that onset occurs in infancy or childhood. Both consider social skills deficits and language delays to be essential features of autism. There is also general consensus between the two definitions on the *specific* social and language problems thought to characterize the disorder (e.g., poor peer relations, echolalia, and pronomial reversal). However, DSM-III-R includes insistence on sameness as a core feature of autism in keeping with both Kanner's original (Kanner, 1943) and revised diagnoses (Eisenberg & Kanner, 1956). In the ASA definition, insistence on sameness is subsumed under "disturbances in the capacity to relate to people, events, and objects." Also, the ASA definition emphasizes sensory processing abnormalities. Although Rutter (1978) acknowledged sensory abnormalities, he considered them to be a frequently associated feature of autism rather than a universal feature.

Another difference is found in the emphasis on developmental delays. The ASA definition includes developmental delays as a core feature of autism. However, while stressing the use of developmental level as a frame of reference, Rutter (1978) emphasized that it is not enough to base the diagnosis of autism on lack of social responsiveness and impaired language. According to Rutter, these two factors can only be taken as indicators of autism if they are out of keeping with the child's mental age and if the specific behavioral patterns characteristic of autism are evident.

Yet another difference relates to the onset criteria. The ASA definition emphasizes onset prior to 30 months of age, whereas DSM-III-R criteria simply specify that onset must occur in infancy or childhood. Since the adoption of both of these definitions, onset of autism after 36 months has occasionally been reported in the literature (Short & Schopler, 1988; Volkmar, Cohen, & Paul, 1986; Volkmar, Stier, & Cohen, 1985).

Finally, as noted, some important differences between the two definitions can be understood by looking at the purposes for which each was constructed (Schopler, 1978). When constructing his definition, Rutter (1978) worked from a historical perspective, taking into account definitional controversies in the literature and tracing the expansion of the research base on autism. Therefore, he gave close scrutiny to empirical data. The ASA criteria, on the other hand, were compiled out of an urgent need for a definition in order to facilitate political action and distribution of social services to autistic persons. Thus, the individuals who formulated this latter definition were less interested in the research base than in the authority needed for political action.

Core Features

To sum up, four categories of behavioral abnormalities are thought to be universal and specific to autism: (a) qualitative impairment in reciprocal social interactions; (b) qualitative impairment in verbal and nonverbal communication; (c) restricted repertoire of activities or interests, or insistence on sameness; and (d) disturbances in response to sensory stimuli.

Social skills deficits. Impaired social skills are generally viewed as constituting the central feature of autism (Hobson, 1989; Mundy & Sigman, 1989; Ungerer, 1989). In infancy, autistic children typically do not develop normal attachment to parents or caregivers. Children may be stiff or rigid when held (Krug et al., 1980), and in early childhood they tend not to use smiling, gestures, or physical contact to signal social intent. Similarly, eye contact is usually poor, avoidant, or otherwise deviant (Schreibman & Mills, 1983). Imitation skills are usually impaired, and imaginative play is typically absent (Stone & Lemanek, 1990). As children become older, they often fail to develop specific peer friendships; they rarely engage in cooperative peer play (Howlin & Rutter, 1987). Normal displays of affection and demonstrations of empathy are uncommon.

Language deficits. Poor communication abilities are found in nearly all autistic children, and some never acquire functional speech (Rutter, 1978). Even when speech is present, it is much less frequent than in normal peer controls. Further, the content of speech is often unrelated to immediate environmental events, with repetitive and stereotyped utterances being common. Most characteristic of autism, however, is the inability to use speech in a socially communicative fashion (Howlin & Rutter, 1987); for example, the ability to sustain conversations is seldom present, and spontaneous communication is severely limited (Matson, Sevin, Fridley, & Love, 1990; Stone & Caro-Martinez, 1990). However, although delayed, general developmental *sequences* of language acquisition are typically similar to those of normal-age peers (Tager-Flusberg et al., 1990). Other common abnormalities include the presence of delayed or immediate echolalia (Schreibman & Mills, 1983), unusual volume of speech (yelling, whispering, or wide fluctuations in voice volume), and impaired nonverbal communication (Schopler, Reichler, & Renner, 1988).

Insistence on sameness. Insistence on sameness is typically characterized by marked distress over trivial changes in the environment (e.g., a bent fork at the dinner table might induce a tantrum), and many aspects of the daily routine become ritualized. Rituals often extend to patterns of social interaction, verbal dialogue, and play activities (Rutter, 1978). Obsessional interests and attachment to unusual objects or parts of objects are also common (e.g., obsessional interest in carrying a favorite toy or in touching or feeling people's hair or feet), as are intense, narrow ranges of interests in higher-functioning individuals (e.g., obsessional interest in cars or in a particular television show). Stereotyped behaviors such as body rocking, hand flapping, and toe walking are common and may be maintained by their sensory, self-stimulatory properties (Baumeister & Forehand, 1974). Autistic children may also insist that other people in the home and school act in an equally rigid way (Howlin & Rutter, 1987).

Disturbances in responses to sensory stimuli. Strong reactions to sensory stimuli are also listed as core features of autism (Ritvo & Freeman, 1978). Hypersensitivity to visual, auditory, or tactile stimulation is most common; but hyposensitivity is apparent in some children (Schopler et al., 1988).

While these four areas constitute a broad consensus among different definitions of autism, there is still some disagreement over the emphases placed on different symptoms by different authors.

Trends in the Literature

An overview of the development and refinement of conceptualizations of autism brings to light a number of trends. For example, early conceptions tended to see autism as a childhood and infantile disorder that was a precursor of adult schizophrenia. In addition, early conceptions saw the disorder as a global, psychotic disorder. Some authors, other than Kanner, emphasized intellectual disabilities. More recent conceptualizations have presented autism as an emotional, pervasive developmental disorder that evidences multiple, molecular pathologies. A final trend is a change from vague global, clinical descriptions to detailed, specific operational definitions of autism.

Issues That Complicate Diagnosis

Disagreements on definitions of autism mainly relate to distinguishing those features that should be regarded as core to the disorder as opposed to those that are merely commonly associated features. Persons diagnosed with autism exhibit marked heterogeneity of clinical features (Rutter & Schopler, 1988; Schopler, 1978; Wing, 1988). This variability in the clinical presentation of autism has

contributed to problems in diagnosis in three specific areas: (a) heterogeneity of symptoms manifested within the core areas of autism; (b) heterogeneity in presentation of associated features; and (c) etiological heterogeneity. In addition, symptom diversity has prompted several authors to investigate the possibility of homogeneous subtypes of autism. These issues are discussed in greater detail in the following sections.

Heterogeneity of Core Features

Although persons with autism are thought to exhibit similar general patterns of developmental disabilities, clinical presentation significantly varies between individuals. For example, both the DSM-III-R and ASA definitions list communication deficits as important diagnostic criteria. However, while 50% of autistic persons probably never develop functional speech, many autistic persons develop communicative speech patterns (Rutter, 1978). Speech may or may not be characterized by stereotyped use of language, pronomial reversals, and/or immediate or delayed echolalia.

Restricted repertoire of activities, or insistence on sameness, may be manifested in different individuals by stereotyped body movements, attachment to unusual objects, insistence on following routines, distress over trivial environmental changes, or some combination of these.

Severity and types of social deficits also differ across children (Wing & Gould, 1979). For example, some autistic individuals exhibit severe and pervasive social aloofness, while others are socially interactive but exhibit odd mannerisms (Wing & Gould, 1979). Onset of social and language symptoms also varies significantly (Rogers & DiLalla, 1990).

Heterogeneity of Associated Features

Intelligence. Intelligence scores for autistic individuals may range from profoundly mentally retarded to superior. However, it is estimated that approximately 80% of autistic children receive a concurrent diagnosis of mental retardation; approximately 60% have IQs less than 50 (Ritvo & Freeman, 1978). Studies of IQ in autism have shown that IQ tends to remain stable in middle childhood and adolescence (Gittelman & Birch, 1967; Lockyer & Rutter, 1969; Rutter, 1978) and that it is predictive of academic accomplishments (Bartak & Rutter, 1971; Rutter & Bartak, 1973). Both assessment and diagnosis become more difficult with increasing severity of intellectual impairments.

Stimulus overselectivity. Several studies have indicated that autistic individuals often respond to only a component of available sensory information (Schreibman & Mills, 1983). Typically referred to as "stimulus overselectivity," such selective processing of sensory information may contribute to insistence on sameness, problems in generalizing skills (Rincover & Koegel, 1975), and difficulties in initiating language in response to complex social cues (Matson, Sevin, Box, Francis, & Sevin, 1993). Although stimulus overselectivity is frequently discussed in relation to autism, it is not considered a core feature of the disorder and has been found in other populations, such as nonautistic individuals with mental retardation.

Self-injurious behavior. Self-injurious behavior (SIB) consists of any behaviors that result in direct physical harm to the person exhibiting them. Often repetitive and stereotyped, SIB may be one of the most serious and debilitating behavior problems associated with autism. Types of SIB include biting, hitting, head banging, hair pulling, and scratching. Marked individual differences are observed with regard to topography, severity, frequency, and duration of these behaviors. It is estimated that SIB may occur in as many as 40% of autistic individuals (Bernstein, Hughes, Mitchell, & Thompson, 1987). This is significantly greater than estimates of SIB in the nonautistic mentally retarded population (7-22%; Maisto, Baumeister, & Maisto, 1978; Schroeder, Schroeder, Smith, & Dalldorf, 1978; Soule & O'Brien, 1974).

Fears. Although the precise nature of the relationship between anxiety and autism remains unclear, fears and anxiety have been reported in autistic subjects since the earliest conceptualizations of the disorder. The British Working Party listed excessive anxiety as a diagnostic marker for autism (Creak, 1961). Similarly, several current autism assessment devices include items related to fears and anxiety (Krug et al., 1980; Schopler et al., 1988).

Matson and Love (1991) found that childhood fears were more frequent and severe in an autistic sample than in normal age-matched controls. Several fears appeared to be specifically related to symptoms of autism, including social fears (e.g., of strangers or large crowds), sensory-related fears (e.g., of loud noises), and anxiety associated with changes in routines. However, common childhood fears were also frequently reported (e.g., dogs, snakes, storms, and fear of the dark). Thus, although anxiety is frequently reported in autistic individuals, the topography and severity vary from one to another.

Associated organic disorders. Several organic disorders also occur more frequently in autistic persons than in nonautistic controls. For example, fragile-X syndrome (Reiss & Freund, 1990) and other types of genetic fragile sites are more common with autism (Saliba & Griffiths, 1990). Similarly, tuberous sclerosis (Gillberg, Steffenberg, & Jakobsson, 1987), hyperlactosemia (Coleman & Blass, 1985), and neurofibromatosis (Gaffney, Kuperman, Tsai, Minchin, & Hessanein, 1987) are also frequently reported. In addition, it is estimated that one-third of persons with autism develop a seizure disorder by early adulthood (Gillberg, 1991). The co-occurrence of these numerous biological conditions contributes to symptom variability, further complicating diagnosis.

Intelligence, stimulus overselectivity, self-injury, fears, and organic disorders are only a subset of associated features that complicate diagnosis. Numerous other problems, including variations in negativism, attention to the environment, physiognomy, and motor development, also complicate the diagnostic process (Myers, 1989).

Etiological Heterogeneity

The failure to establish common etiological factors for autism further compounds the problem of assessment and diagnosis. Early theories of autism focused primarily on pathogenic parent behaviors. Thus, several early authors attributed autism to poor family relationships (Mohler, 1952) or parent psychopathology (Bettelheim, 1967). Although these factors continue to be examined (e.g., Narayan, Moyes, & Wolff, 1990), they have generally been discredited (Cantwell, Baker, & Rutter, 1977; Coe & Matson, 1989; Rimland, 1964).

Instead, since the early 1970s, etiologic studies have focused on organic causes of autism. Genetic, neuroanatomical, electrophysiological, perinatal-factor, and biochemical studies have been conducted, leading to conflicting results. Twin studies have indicated a significant genetic component to autism (Folstein & Rutter, 1977; Ritvo et al., 1985). Some authors have suggested that abnormalities in the reticular activating system (Hutt, Forrest, & Richer, 1975; Rimland, 1964) or the vestibular system (Ornitz, 1970) may account for the sensory symptoms and abnormal patterns of arousal found with autism. Further, EEG studies have indicated the possible failure in some children to develop normal cerebral lateralization of brain hemispheres (Dawson, Warrenburg, & Fuller, 1982; Small, 1975).

A number of pre- and perinatal factors associated with autism have also been identified, including maternal infections and respiratory distress during birth (Desmond et al., 1967; Gillberg & Gillberg, 1983). Finally, in the last decade, several researchers have focused on possible imbalances in CNS neurotransmitters, and studies have reported increased platelet serotonin levels in autistic children (Piven et al., 1991; Ritvo et al., 1970).

Persons with autism are more likely to exhibit one or more of the biological disorders discussed above. Consequently, it is generally agreed that the primary etiological component of autism is organic (Coe & Matson, 1989). Yet, no single physiological, neurological, or biochemical abnormality or pattern of abnormalities has been consistently associated with autism.

Subtypes of Autism

Given the heterogeneity of behavioral symptoms across individuals, describing a person as autistic provides very little information about the specific nature of his or her problems. Thus, several researchers have begun to look for meaningful ways of subgrouping autistic individuals.

For example, Wing and her colleagues (Wing & Atwood, 1987; Wing & Gould, 1979) presented a typological system for autistic children based on patterns of social interactions. Socially "aloof" children tend to avoid all or most social contact. "Passive" interactors seldom initiate social interactions but participate passively when others initiate contact. "Active but odd" interactors initiate social contact; however, their social interactions are typically odd or stereotyped. Volkmar et al. (1989) found Wing's system to be reliable and related to IQ, with aloof children demonstrating the most severe impairments and active but odd children being the highest functioning.

At least four other typological systems of autism have been widely discussed in the literature. First, given the apparent prognostic significance of IQ (Rutter & Garmezy, 1983), Volkmar (1987) suggested that autistic persons might be subclassified according to level of intellectual functioning. Despite the intuitive appeal of this approach, it has not been widely adopted in the literature.

A second system, offered in DSM-III (APA, 1980), distinguished pervasive developmental disorders (PDDs) based on the temporal onset of symptoms (infantile versus childhood onset). However, empirical studies have often failed to establish a relationship between age of onset and severity of symptoms. Early onset may be more strongly related to severity of mental retardation than to severity of autism (Rogers & DiLalla, 1990).

A third system, offered in DSM-III-R, attempts to subdivide persons with PDDs based on the number and severity of symptoms (autism versus PDD not otherwise specified). Many issues regarding the reliability and validity of this system remain uninvestigated (Spitzer & Siegel, 1990; Szatmari, 1989). For instance, in a signal detection study, Siegel, Vukicevic, Elliott, and Kraemer (1989) found that all but 2 of the 16 DSM-III-R criteria for autism are flawed in terms of their sensitivity or specificity to discriminate autistic from nonautistic children.

A fourth related issue concerns the relationship between autism and Asperger's syndrome. In recent years, several authors have suggested that Asperger's syndrome might best be conceptualized as a form of high-functioning autism (Pomeroy, Friedman, & Stephens, 1991; Szatmari, Bartolucci, & Bremner, 1989; Szatmari, Tuff, Finlayson, & Bartolucci, 1990). This issue is still under preliminary investigation.

In addition, Sevin et al. (1991) offers a preliminary taxonomy based on cluster analyses of the symptom profiles of a sample of children with pervasive developmental disorders. Analyses revealed four homogeneous subtypes of PDDs, which were labeled *atypical, mild, moderate,* and *severe.* The atypical group closely resembled DSM-III-R's PDD NOS category, characterized by less severe and fewer autistic symptoms and higher IQs. The mildly autistic group was characterized by marked but mild social and sameness problems, some functional speech, and mild mental retardation. The moderate group, in turn, included individuals with mixed social responding, severe stereotypy, limited communication skills, and moderate-to-severe mental retardation. Finally, individuals in the severe group were socially aloof; they had no functional communication, severe stereotypy, and severe to profound mental retardation.

Empirically derived taxonomic systems make important contributions to establishing autism subtypes. However, the cluster solution discussed above was explorative and based on a small sample. Therefore, it is in need of further validation.

The identification of behaviorally distinct subtypes of autism may be important for several reasons. First, behaviorally homogeneous groups may share similar etiological conditions. Also, homogeneous subtypes may respond differently to specific behavioral or pharmacological interventions. At the very least, membership in a specific autism subtype might have prognostic significance (i.e., children with late onset of language symptoms and low levels of mental retardation may have a better prognosis). Research on the subtypes of autism is still in its infancy.

Desirable Assessment Characteristics

Procedural Characteristics

For assessment instruments to be widely acceptable, they must be quick and easy to administer, score, and interpret by specialists and non-specialists alike and should be readily usable in a wide range of settings and countries. In addition, tests should be robust across time so that they have a useful clinical life without need for frequent revision.

In addition to being easy to use, assessment instruments should be robust to minor violations of the manner in which they are administered. At the very least, procedural guidelines should be available that give the test administrator enough instructions to administer the test faithfully. These guidelines should be clearly stated and address such questions as these: Should there be a warm-up period prior to the test items being administered? Should the parent(s) be present? Should the administration take place in a familiar or a novel environment? Are the client's toys or standard toys to be used? How should the test administrator deal with disruptive behavior? If the client *refuses* to let the tester take the ball out of the test case does the client fail that item? If the client lies under the table screaming and headbanging does the tester continue to administer items and fail the client on these items if not responded to correctly? All of these factors may be important since novelty and change may especially affect the test scores of autistic individuals. Also, the examiner's responses to such events can significantly affect the subject's performance and scores on the remaining items.

Psychometric Characteristics

A wide array of desirable psychometric properties should be present in assessment instruments. All of them cannot be discussed here at length, but they can be subsumed under three main headings: internal consistency, reliability, and validity.

Internal consistency.   Internal consistency requires that scores on items that make up a test or scale be more closely correlated with each other than with the entire pool of items from which they are drawn. This property can be assessed by statistics such as Cronbach's alpha, split-half reliabilities, item-whole (minus item) point biserial correlations, and inter-item correlations.

However, high internal consistency statistics alone are insufficient. A highly internally consistent test could result from a random sample from a pool of items that are already closely correlated with each other. However, the key idea behind internal consistency is that each item is a partial, if rather poor, measure of some construct (e.g., autism). When items are combined, the composite makes a better measure of the construct than individual items or the total score of the entire pool of items.

The requirement of good internal consistency has implications for the development of subscales within a test. Subscales are only meaningful if they measure different aspects of a characteristic. Thus, subscales should be empirically derived through factor analysis and subsequent analyses of their individual internal consistency.

Reliability.   Reliability is important in that it indicates that extraneous sources of variance in the test scores are trivial compared to important sources of variability. Good reliability also indicates that test results are replicable. For most purposes,

variability due to which day a test was administered, who administered the test, or who acted as informant is regarded as unimportant compared to differences in scores between clients or changes in clients' scores as a result of treatment. The most common indices of reliability, interrater reliability and test-retest reliability, are assessed by Pearson's r.

Most authors regard certain absolute values of reliability coefficients (e.g., .8 or better) as "adequate" or "good." In contrast, a more relativistic approach to reliability has been taken by Shrout and Fleiss (1981), who suggested that reliability requirements change as a function of the goal of assessment. If a crude decision is being made (e.g., comparing autistic with average children), a greater degree of unreliability can be tolerated than if a very fine-grain decision is required (e.g., differentiating profoundly retarded children with autism from those without autism).

This more relativistic approach to reliability is illustrated in Figure 2.1. In part (a), the prevalence of autism is relatively high and might correspond to purposes such as screening hospital or clinical populations. Here poor reliability results in relatively few classification errors. In part (b) of the figure, however, the prevalence of autism is low (e.g., in total community surveys). In contrast to

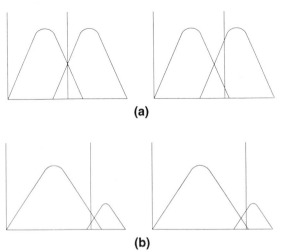

(a)

(b)

Figure 2.1. The effects of prevalence on reliability

the first example, here poor reliability can lead to many classification errors.

Several comments about reliability should be made. First, it is not a fixed commodity. A test may be highly reliable for one purpose and completely useless for another. Consequently, reliability checks *for each use* of the measure should be routinely conducted. Unless there are good reasons to believe that the use of a test is very similar to its use in a previous study, reliability cannot be assumed from previous studies. The effects of restricting ranges of scores on reliability are shown in Figure 2.2. Second, reliability is typically assessed through correlation coefficients, which are measures of association, *not agreement,* between scores. Thus, good reliability can be achieved without good agreement (see Figure 2.3). Third, the reliability of total scores does not guarantee the reliability of scores of individual subscales or test items. Therefore, reliability coefficients should be

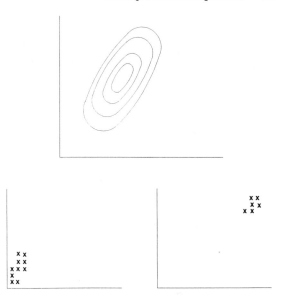

Figure 2.2. The effects of restricting the range of scores on the reliability of a test

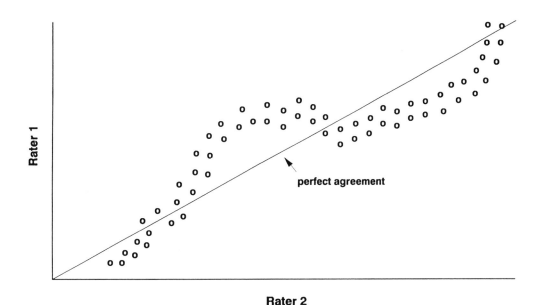

Figure 2.3. Good reliability can arise even when raters are not in perfect agreement.

cited for all levels of scores, items, subscales, and totals.

Validity.   The extent to which a test measures the dimension it purports to measure and performs the functions it was designed to perform represents its validity.   Types of validity include (a) criterion-group validity (autistic clients should score higher on measures of autism than the general population or other nonautistic, pathological groups); (b) predictive validity (results should indicate who will respond to treatment and what the prognosis is for people with high rather than low scores); (c) concurrent validity (correlations between similar measures of autism should be high); and (d) divergent validity (correlations with measures of other pathologies, such as anxiety, should be low).

One kind of validity is the ability of a test to correctly detect cases of the disorder assessed. This can be assessed by the test's *sensitivity*, the propor-tion of true cases scoring above the cutoff for case-ness, and the test's *specificity*, the number of true non-cases scoring below the cutoff; see Figure 2.4 (Shrout & Fleiss, 1981).

Validity is best thought of as a gradually emerg-ing property of a test rather than as an absolute quality (Anastasi, 1986).   One aspect of this idea is illustrated in Figure 2.5.   Considerable dispute surrounds the identification of core versus associa-ted symptoms of autism and related disorders such as mental retardation, childhood schizophrenia, disintegrative psychoses of childhood, and Asperger's syndrome.   Figure 2.5 shows three disorders, each of which has symptoms that are unique as well as symptoms that are pathological but not unique to a given disorder.   Several possible tests are exemplified.   Test 1, a general screen for psychopathology, will distinguish the three pathological groups from the general population but, on the basis of scores alone, will not easily

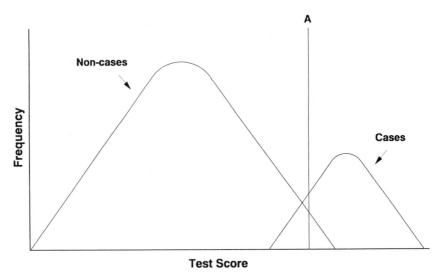

Sensitivity = proportion of cases scoring > A
Specificity = proportion of non-cases scoring < A

Figure 2.4. The sensitivity and specificity of an assessment
SOURCE: *From "Reliability and case detection," by P. E. Shrout & J. L. Fleiss, in* What Is a Case?, *edited by J. K. Wing, P. Bebbington, and L. N. Robbins. Copyright © 1981 by Grant McIntyre. Reprinted by permission.*

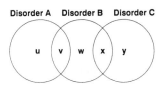

	Disorder A	Disorder B	Disorder C	Population
Test 1 (u,v,w,x,y,)	++	+++	++	0
Test 2 (u,v)	++	+	0	0
Test 3 (v,w,x)	+	+++	+	0
Test 4 (x,y)	0	+	++	0
Test 5 (u)	+	0	0	0
Test 6 (w)	0	+	0	0
Test 7 (y)	0	0	+	0

Figure 2.5. The validity of an instrument changes as a function of the task for which it is employed.

distinguish between the disorders. Tests 2 through 4 can be developed from the general pool of items by selecting items that distinguish each pathological group from the general population. Such tests are sensitive to the overlap between individual disorders; however, they might be seen as having less than ideal criterion-group validity since more than one group will receive high scores. Tests 5 through 7 can be developed by selecting items that are unique to each disorder; they will distinguish each disorder from the general population *and* from other disorders. Although such tests have good criterion-group validity, they are not sensitive to the overlap between the disorders. Thus, the validity of each instrument changes as a function of the task for which it is employed.

Test Rationale and Purpose

Finally, a good test should have a stated rationale and purpose. There should be an adequate concep-

tual foundation for the test itself and how the items were generated and selected. The format of the test and its subscales should be constructed according to some well-defined and empirically meaningful theory and should assist in the development of the theory.

Autism assessments can serve a variety of functions. Two major functions include trait-diagnostic assessments and change/behavioral assessments. Trait-diagnostic assessments should produce scores that are stable across time. In contrast, change/behavioral assessments should be highly sensitive to changes associated with treatments, environmental manipulations, and programming. Finally, autism rating scales can also be used to assess potential target behaviors for intervention and change. Overall, the purpose of the test, such as classification, target behavior identification, or evaluation of treatment efficacy, should be apparent.

Summary

Ideal assessment instruments for autism should be easy and convenient to administer and robust to trivial violations in administration. They should evince good internal consistency, reliability, and validity. The limits to their reliability and validity should be clearly known and used to develop the test further. Finally, they should be firmly based in theory and have an explicit, delimited purpose.

In the next section, we review four current assessments of autism, using the criteria developed in this section. The four assessments are the *Autism Behavior Checklist* (ABC; Krug, Arick, & Almond, 1980), the *Ritvo-Freeman Real Life Rating Scale* (RLRS; Freeman, Ritvo, Yokota, & Ritvo, 1986), the *Childhood Autism Rating Scale* (CARS; Schopler, Reichler, & Renner, 1988), and the *MRC Children's Handicaps, Behavior, and Skills Structured Schedule* (HBS; Wing & Gould, 1978).

A number of scales were excluded from our review. The *Behavior Rating Instrument for Autistic and Atypical Children* (BRIACC; Ruttenburg, Dratman, Franko, & Wenar, 1966) was excluded because of numerous recognized methodological and psychometric shortcomings (Parks, 1983), which have led to it being used less frequently. The *Diagnostic Checklist for Behavior-Disordered Children* (Rimland, 1971) was excluded on similar grounds (Parks, 1983; Parks, 1988). Three other scales, the *Autism Diagnostic Interview* (LeCouteur et al., 1989), the *Autism Diagnostic Observation Schedule* (Lord et al., 1989), and the *Behavioral Summarized Evaluation* (Barthelemy et al., 1990) are still under investigation and need further study before their utility can be fully assessed.

Current Autism Rating Scales

Psychometric data for the four instruments have been summarized in the following tables. Table 2.2 summarizes data on internal consistency,

Table 2.3 data on reliability, and Table 2.4 data on validity.

The Autism Behavior Checklist

The ABC is a 57-item behavior checklist on which parents or teachers rate whether the behavior expressed in an item is exhibited by their child or student. Items, which were selected from diagnostic criteria developed by Kanner (1958) and Creak (1964) and from several early autism scales, are grouped under one of five diagnostic scales: (a) sensory; (b) relating; (c) body and object use; (d) language; and (e) social and self-help skills. Each item has been weighted from 1 to 4. Weighting was determined by expert opinion. Scores within each scale are summed to provide profile scores. These five scores are summed to provide a total score. A score of 67 or above is considered to indicate autism.

Table 2.2 Internal Consistency of Four Autism Assessment Instruments

Scale	Split-Half Reliability	Cronbach's Alpha	Median (Range) Item–Total Point Biserial Correlations	Mean Inter-Item Correlation
ABC	[2].87	—	—	—
	[5].74	—	—	—
		[4].87	.32 (−.10–.67)	.12
RLRS	—	[4].84	.26 (−.24–.71)	.09
CARS	—	[3].94	—	—
	—	[1].79	.50 (−.22–.78)	—
	—	[1].73	.40 (−.17–.73)	—
	—	[4].85	.46 (.29–.71)	.28
HBS	—	—	—	—

[1]Garfin, McCallon, & Cox (1988).
[2]Krug, Arick, & Almond (1980).
[3]Schopler, Reichler, DeVellis, & Daly (1980).
[4]Sturmey, Matson, & Sevin (in press).
[5]Volkmar et al. (1988).

Evaluation of split-half reliability yielded a Pearson product-moment correlation of .87, calculated on 1049 forms completed for five groups: autistic, mentally retarded, deaf/blind, severely emotionally disturbed, and normal children (Krug et al., 1980). Coefficient alpha for the total score is .87 (Sturmey et al., in press). Initial report of whole-scale interrater reliability, based on a small sample ($n = 14$), was .95 (Krug et al., 1980). In a more recent study (Volkmar, Cicchetti, et al., 1988), kappa/k_{max} (used to calculate interrater reliability) was greater than or equal to .40 (indicating fair chance-corrected agreement) for a group of 62 autistic individuals. When ANOVAs were used, the five scale scores and total scores of the autistic standardization sample were significantly higher ($p < .001$) than scores for each of the other four diagnostic groups (listed above), indicating good criterion-group validity. Other checks of criterion-group and concurrent validity have been mixed (Sevin et al., 1991). They are reported in Table 2.4.

Strengths of the ABC include easy completion and scoring (no special training is required to complete the scale) and inclusion of several diagnostic groups in standardization. Initial psychometric data have generally been adequate. In addition, the purpose of the scale is clearly stated: the ABC is meant for use as a general screening instrument. In addition, several of its limitations as a diagnostic instrument are pointed out in Volkmar, Cicchetti, et al. (1988). These include failure to include specific operational definitions of test items, failure to report test-retest data, and lack of empirical justification for the grouping of items into subscales. Another weakness is the ABC's reliance on other-informant data rather than direct observations. Further, it correlates poorly with other measures of autism, and questions have been raised regarding the appropriateness of the proposed cutoff score (Sevin et al., 1991). In general, the ABC is useful as a gross screening instrument for autism, but in clinical work it should be used together with direct observational data.

The Real Life Rating Scale

The RLRS (Freeman et al., 1986) is a behavior observation instrument completed by trained raters following a 30-minute observation of a subject in a naturalistic setting. The scale includes 47 behaviors grouped into five subscales: (a) sensory motor behaviors, (b) social relationship to people, (c) affectual reactions, (d) sensory responses, and (e) language. The 47 items are individually operationally defined.

Raters take behavioral data and score the RLRS at the end of the observation session. Each behavior is scored as follows: 0 = never demonstrated target behavior; 1 = rarely (target behavior was seen only 1–3 times); 2 = frequently (target behavior was seen 4 or more times); or 3 = almost always (target behavior was seen almost constantly throughout the observation period). A mean score for each subscale is determined by adding item scores and dividing by the number of behaviors in that scale. Subscale scores are averaged to yield an overall score. The RLRS was designed primarily to measure behavior changes in patients or groups of

Table 2.3 Reliability of Four Autism Assessment Instruments

Scale	Interrater Reliability
ABC	[1]$r = .95$ [5] $> .40$ (kappa/k_{max})
RLRS	[2]$r = .90$ (.59–.85 for 5 scales) [4]$r = .82$ (.32–.89 for 5 scales)
CARS	[3]$r = .71$ (.55–.93 for 15 scales) [4]$r = .68$ (.10–.85 for 15 scales)
HBS	[6]$r = > .7$ for most scales

[1]Krug, Arick, & Almond (1980).
[2]Ritvo, Freeman, Mason-Brothers, Mo, & Ritvo (1985).
[3]Schopler, Reichler, DeVellis, & Daly (1988).
[4]Sevin, Matson, Coe, Fee, & Sevin (in press).
[5]Volkmar, Cicchetti, Dykens, Sparrow, Leckman, & Cohen (1988).
[6]Wing & Gould (1978).

Table 2.4 Validity of Four Autism Assessment Instruments

Scale	Study	Validity Data
ABC	Krug et al., 1980	*Content*: adequate; item selection based on previous autism scales, definitions, and input from 26 experts in the field.
		Criterion-group: autistic group significantly different from four other diagnostic groups (ANOVAs, $p < .001$). Also, 86% of autistic sample within 1 SD of mean. (*Note*: Raters were not blind to diagnosis.)
	Volkmar et al., 1988	*Criterion-group*: good; significant difference between autistic and nonautistic groups on subscale and total scores.
		Concurrent: good; significant correlation between ABC and relevant Vineland domains.
	Sevin et al. (in press)	*Criterion-group*: poor; 50% of autistic sample scored below cutoff.
		Concurrent: poor; ABC total score correlated .22 and .27 with RLRS and CARS, respectively. (*Note*: These correlations were based on only 24 subjects.)
RLRS	Freeman et al., 1986	*Content*: adequate; items selected from BOS (Freeman et al., 1984).
		Concurrent: significant correlations between RLRS scores and relevant scales of Alpern-Boll. (*Note:* Selection of Alpern-Boll as validation is questionable.)
	Sevin et al., 1991	*Concurrent*: good; correlated .77 with CARS.
CARS	Schopler et al., 1988	*Content*: good; accessed five most frequently used definitions of autism.
		Criterion-group: adequate; CARS scores correlated .80 with expert clinical judgment.
	Sevin et al., 1991	*Criterion-group*: good; 92% of sample correctly diagnosed as autistic or PDD NOS based on cutoff scores.
		Concurrent: good; correlated .77 with RLRS.
HBS		No validity data.

patients over time. The scale is not meant to be a trait-diagnostic instrument; thus, no cutoff score for autism is given.

Initial estimates of the RLRS's interrater reliability calculated with pairs of novice (44 pairs of observations) and experienced raters (50 pairs of observations) appear adequate (Freeman et al., 1986). In two studies, Pearson r's have ranged from .32 to .89 for the five subscales (Freeman et al., 1986; Sevin et al., 1991). Reports of total-score interrater reliability have ranged from .82 to .90. Significant but lower correlations were found between novice raters on the overall, social, affect, sensory, and language scales. With experienced raters, significant correlations were found on all scales as well as on 45 of the 47 individual behaviors. Pearson product-moment correlations between individual subscales are all reported to be significant at the .01 level. In the only study of the scale's internal consistency, Sturmey et al. (in press) found a Cronbach alpha of .84 for the total score. Additional internal consistency data are reported in Table 2.2.

Regarding content validity, the RLRS was developed by modifying the *Behavior Observation System* (Freeman et al., 1984). The RLRS correlates moderately well ($r = .7$) with the CARS (Sevin et al., 1991). Additional validity data are reported in Table 2.4.

The strengths of this scale include easy administration, emphasis on observed behavior in a naturalistic setting, individually operationally defined items, and a focus on discrete behaviors, making the instrument sensitive to small changes in rates of aberrant behaviors. Thus, the RLRS is the only autism assessment scale specifically designed to measure changes in behavior over time. It also shows good concurrent validity with the CARS. Weaknesses include evidence of interrater reliability only with small samples. Although the scale is meant to be sensitive to behavior changes, no validity studies support this function. Also, no test-retest data are included. Since no specific administration instructions are given, nonstandardized examiners' responses may introduce error variance into the scores.

The Childhood Autism Rating Scale

The CARS (Schopler et al., 1980), consisting of 15 general behavior scales/items, is the most thoroughly studied direct observation instrument for measuring autistic behaviors. Children suspected of having autism are observed during psychological testing or classroom participation or in the home setting. Raters are instructed to note the "peculiarity, frequency, intensity, and duration" of scale items. Later, each score is coded 1–4, depending on whether behaviors are within normal limits *for that age group* or are severely abnormal. Methods for scoring each of the 15 scales are operationally defined in the manual, with summary definitions included on rating forms. A total score of 30 is considered indicative of autism.

The CARS contains items from the five most frequently used diagnostic systems for autism (i.e., Kanner's [1943] definition, Creak's [1961] nine points, and the definitions of Rutter [1978], the ASA [1978], and DSM-III-R [1987]). In the manual, rationales for the inclusion of the 15 scales are discussed in the context of these systems. Internal consistency, calculated using coefficient alpha, ranges from .73 to .94 in different studies (Garfin et al., 1988; Schopler et al., 1988; Sturmey et al., in press). Interrater reliability, reported by the authors and based on 280 cases, averaged .71 across the 15 scales (range .55 for intellectual response to .93 for relating to people). Test-retest reliability was calculated for 91 cases measured at a one-year interval. Average correlation was .88, indicating the stability of measured scores over time.

Criterion-group validity was determined by comparing total scores to clinical ratings obtained during the same diagnostic session as the CARS ratings. Correlations of $r = .84$ were found. Total scores were also correlated with independent clinical assessments by child psychologists and psychiatrists, resulting in correlations of $r = .80$. The CARS has been examined for use with children, adolescents, and adults (Garfin et al., 1988; Mesibov, Schopler, Schaffer, & Michal, 1989), and psychometric data for a Japanese version appear promising (Kurita, Miyake, & Katsuno, 1989). Additional psychometric data are reported in Tables 2.2, 2.3, and 2.4.

Strengths of this scale include its emphasis on observed behavior, sampling of a wide variety of behaviors, individually operationally defined items, and good psychometric properties. The CARS is easy to administer by a wide range of professionals with different levels of experience with autism (Schopler et al., 1988). Although it is not explicitly stated, the scale is meant to function primarily as a trait-diagnostic instrument. However, Mesibov et al. (1989) suggested that it may also be used as a longitudinal instrument. Garfin et al. (1988) found that Scale 14 (intellectual response) inversely correlated with the total scores and suggested the scale be dropped. However, this finding has not been replicated in more recent investigations (Sturmey et al., in press). Finally, administration instructions are only loosely specified, resulting in the same problems as discussed for the RLRS.

Children's Handicaps, Behavior, and Skills Structured Interview

The HBS (Wing & Gould, 1978) is intended to survey a wide range of developmental and behavioral strengths and weaknesses in children with developmental disabilities. It includes 42 sections on developmental skills and 21 sections covering behavioral abnormalities. Areas surveyed include self-care, school work, social development, language, stereotyped activities, and many others. The aim of the HBS is to introduce "some structure and consistency into the process of recording clinical descriptions." It takes approximately 45 minutes to 2½ hours to complete the interview.

Specific guidelines for administration are not included, as the HBS is not intended to serve as a standardized questionnaire or checklist. Rather, the informant is encouraged to list specific, easily observed aspects of behavior. Interviewers rate responses based on extensive knowledge of behavioral norms. Therefore, it is recommended that the scale be used only by interviewers who are thoroughly familiar with the scale and have been trained to administer it.

Since the HBS is not intended as a psychometric instrument, few psychometric data are available. Preliminary reports indicate that agreement between interviewers and different informants is adequate for most scales; overall, agreement between parents and professional informants is generally greater than 70% for most of 62 of the 63 sections (Wing & Gould, 1978).

Strengths of the scale include its ability to elicit specific behavioral descriptors or target behaviors for intervention and prioritize these behaviors for treatment. The HBS is also much more comprehensive than the other scales discussed. Weaknesses include lack of psychometric data. Also, administration is difficult and time-consuming, procedures are not spelled out clearly, and scores depend heavily on the skill of the interviewer.

Summary

The four instruments reviewed here can be briefly characterized as follows. The ABC is useful as a preliminary screen, which could be used with large populations to identify atypical children, some of whom may be autistic. The CARS is currently the trait-diagnostic measure of choice for autism. The RLRS is the only available scale ex-

plicitly developed to assess change in this population; however, substantive evidence of this function is lacking. Finally, the HBS provides the broadest array of assessment information, useful for programming and for more broad-based assessment of autistic individuals.

Despite a great deal of data on the development of these scales, a number of important issues have been addressed only infrequently or not at all. For example, test-retest data are almost uniformly lacking. Justification for grouping items into subscales is typically ad hoc, resulting in questionable internal consistency for many of the subscales (Sturmey et al., in press). The validity of interpreting subscale scores is also questionable. No predictive validity studies are available on any of these instruments. In addition, procedures for administering the RLRS, CARS, and HBS are lacking in detail. It is probable that some problems arise when these instruments are used for purposes other than those for which they were intended by the authors. Scales should be used in a manner consistent with the author's explicit instructions regarding function until they are shown to be reliable and valid for additional uses. Future research should attempt to address these issues.

Overview and Emerging Issues

In this chapter, the evolution of definitional systems was traced from Kanner's (1943) original descriptions to present-day taxonomies. Broad consensus regarding the core features of autism has emerged, providing a much clearer picture of the disorder. Further, general acceptance of current definitions and agreement on the nature of autism have stimulated tremendous growth in research and facilitated integration of research findings.

Current diagnostic trends have been influenced by numerous factors. The adoption of more descriptive, molecular, definitional, and taxonomic systems is consistent with theoretical shifts toward behavioral and developmental paradigms. Furthermore, present systems better lend themselves to empirical approaches to the study of autism, which have proliferated in the last two decades. In addition, more ideographic approaches have been mandated by the *necessity* of viewing each client as an individual, given the heterogeneity of clinical features associated with autism.

Despite recent advances in defining and diagnosing autism, numerous issues are in need of further investigation. First and foremost are issues related to the increased prevalence of autism as a result of more liberal diagnostic criteria. Several authors have concluded that the autistic population presently constitutes a significantly larger and more behaviorally diverse group than previously thought (e.g., Factor, Freeman, & Kardash, 1989; Hertzig et al., 1990; Spitzer & Siegel, 1990; Volkmar, Bregman, Cohen, & Cicchetti, 1988). As a consequence, methods of diagnosing and assessing autism, as well as the service delivery system, must adapt to changes in the make-up of the autistic population.

Second, given these changes, empirically and clinically meaningful ways of subclassifying persons with autism are needed (Wing, 1990). The identification of subgroups of autistic individuals who are homogeneous with regard to behavioral and etiological profiles, prognosis, or differential responsiveness to various treatments would represent an important advance in the way autism is defined. Although a few attempts have been made to arrive at such subgroups (e.g., Sevin et al., 1991; Wing & Gould, 1979), the validity of these systems remains questionable. Thus, it is not clear that present systems of subclassification represent improvements over more general nomothetic approaches.

Third, although general consensus has been reached on the core features of autism, researchers should continue to study associated features that complicate diagnosis. The prevalence and severity of associated features need to be defined more clearly. Also, relationships between clinical features (the manner in which various symptoms covary within the autistic population) are in need of further study.

Fourth, the inclusion of standardized measures of autism in the diagnostic process represents a positive step. Initial studies have suggested that standardized assessment scales are useful in providing behavioral norms and in allowing more accurate quantification of pathognomic problems. However, as noted, reliability and validity must be assessed for *each* of the intended uses of a scale. With continued study, autism instruments may constitute a useful standardized manner of gathering information on large samples of autistic individuals. Such information is critical for increasing the understanding of autism and forms the basis for definitional clarifications. Initial reports of the use of standardized scales to help further define the syndrome of autism have appeared in the literature (Freeman, Ritvo, Yokota, Childs, & Pollard, 1988; Jacobson & Ackerman, 1990; Sevin et al., 1991; Volkmar et al., 1987). Given the growing interest and recent advances in defining and assessing autism, the future looks promising.

References

AKERLY, M. (1988). What's in a name? In E. Schopler & G. Mesibov (Eds.), *Diagnosis and assessment in autism* (pp. 59–66). New York: Plenum.

ALFORD, J. D., & LOCKE, B. J. (1984). Clinical responses to psychopathology of mentally retarded persons. *American Journal of Mental Deficiency, 89,* 195–197.

AMERICAN PSYCHIATRIC ASSOCIATION. (1952). *Diagnostic and statistical manual* (2nd ed.). Washington, DC: Author.

AMERICAN PSYCHIATRIC ASSOCIATION. (1980). *Diagnostic and statistical manual* (3rd ed.). Washington, DC: Author.

AMERICAN PSYCHIATRIC ASSOCIATION. (1987). *DSM-III-R. Diagnostic and statistical manual* (3rd ed., revised). Washington, DC: Author.

ANASTASI, A. (1986). Evolving concepts of test validation. *Annual Review of Psychology, 37,* 1–15.

BARTAK, I., & RUTTER, M. (1971). Educational treatment of autistic children. In M. Rutter (Ed.), *Infantile autism: Concepts, characteristics and treatment* (pp. 65–90). London: Churchill-Livingstone.

BARTHELEMY, C., ADRIEN, J. L., TANGUAY, P., GARREAU, B., FERMANIAN, J., ROUX, S., SAUVAGE, D., & LELORD, G. (1990). The behavioral summarized evaluation: Validity and reliability of a scale for the assessment of autistic behaviors. *Journal of Autism and Developmental Disorders, 20,* 189–204.

BAUMEISTER, A., & FOREHAND, R. (1973). Stereotyped acts. In N. R. Ellis (Ed.), *International review of research in mental retardation* (pp. 55–92). New York: Academic.

BERNSTEIN, G. A., HUGHES, J., MITCHELL, J. E., & THOMPSON, T. (1987). Effects of narcotic antagonists on self-injurious behavior: A single case study. *Journal of the American Academy of Child and Adolescent Psychiatry, 26,* 886–889.

BETTELHEIM, B. (1967). *The empty fortress.* New York: Free Press.

CANTWELL, D. P., BAKER, L., & RUTTER, M. (1977). Families of autistic and dysphasic children: I. Family life and interaction patterns. *Archives of General Psychiatry, 36,* 682–687.

COE, D., & MATSON, J. L. (1989). Etiology, incidence, and prevalence of chronic schizophrenia and adult autism. In J. L. Matson (Ed.), *Chronic schizophrenia and adult autism* (pp. 53–88). New York: Springer.

COLEMAN, M., & BLASS, J. P. (1985). Autism and lactic acidosis. *Journal of Autism and Developmental Disorders, 15,* 1–8.

CREAK, M. (1961). Schizophrenia syndrome in childhood: Progress report of a working party. *Cerebral Palsy Bulletin, 3,* 501–504.

CREAK, M. (1964). Schizophrenic syndrome in childhood: Further progress report of a working party. *Developmental Medicine and Child Neurology, 6,* 530–535.

CULBERTSON, F. M. (1977). The search for help of parents of autistic children or beware of professional "group think." *Journal of Clinical Child Psychology, 6,* 63–65.

CUNNINGHAM, C., MORGAN, P., & McGUCKEN, R. (1984). Down Syndrome: Is dissatisfaction with disclosure of diagnosis inevitable? *Developmental Medicine and Child Neurology, 26,* 33–39.

DAWSON, G., WARRENBURG, S., & FULLER, P. (1982). Cerebral lateralization in individuals diagnosed as autistic in early childhood. *Brain Language, 15,* 353–368.

DE SANCTIS, S. (1906). Sopra alcune varieta della demenza precoce. *Rivista Sperimentale Di Freniatra E Di Medicina Legale, 32,* 141–165.

DESMOND, M. M., WILSON, G. S., MELNICK, J. L., SINGER, D. B., ZION, T. E., RUDOLPH, A. J., PINEDA, R. G., ZIAI, M. H., & BLATTNEY, R. J. (1967). Congenital rubella encephalitis. *Journal of Pediatrics, 71,* 311–331.

EISENBERG, T., & KANNER, L. (1956). Early infantile autism 1943-1955. *American Journal of Orthopsychiatry, 26,* 556–566.

FACTOR, D. C., FREEMAN, N. L., & KARDASH, A. (1989). A comparison of DSM-III and DSM-III-R criteria for autism. *Journal of Autism and Developmental Disorders, 19,* 637–640.

FISH, B. (1976). Biological disorders in infants at risk for schizophrenia. In E. R. Ritvo (Ed.), *Autism: Diagnosis, current research and management* (pp. 111–146). New York: Spectrum.

FOLSTEIN, S., & RUTTER, M. (1977). Infantile autism: A genetic study of 21 twin pairs. *Journal of Child Psychology and Psychiatry, 18,* 297–321.

FREEMAN, B. J., RITVO, E. R., & SCHROTH, P. C. (1984). Behavior assessment of the syndrome of autism. Behavior observation system. *Journal of the American Academy of Child Psychiatry, 23,* 588–594.

FREEMAN, B. J., RITVO, E. R., YOKOTA, A., CHILDS, J., & POLLARD, J. (1988). *WISC-R and Vineland adaptive behavior scales* in autistic children. *Journal of the American Academy of Child and Adolescent Psychiatry, 27,* 428–429.

FREEMAN, B. J., RITVO, E. R., YOKOTA, A., & RITVO, A. (1986). A scale for rating symptoms of patients with the syndrome of autism in real life settings. *Journal of the American Academy of Child Psychiatry, 25,* 130–136.

GAFFNEY, G. R., KUPERMAN, S., TSAI, L. Y., MINCHIN, S., & HASSANEIN, K. M. (1987). Midsagittal magnetic resonance imaging of autism. *British Journal of Psychiatry, 151,* 831–833.

GARFIN, D. G., McCALLON, D., & COX, R. (1988). Validity and reliability of the *Childhood autism rating scale* with autistic adolescents. *Journal of Autism and Developmental Disorders, 18,* 367–378.

GILLBERG, C. (1991). The treatment of epilepsy in autism. *Journal of Autism and Developmental Disorders, 21,* 61–78.

GILLBERG, C., & GILLBERG, I. C. (1983). Infantile autism: A total population study of reduced optimality in the pre-, peri-, and neonatal period. *Journal of Autism and Developmental Disorders, 13,* 153–166.

GILLBERG, C., STEFFENBERG, S., & JAKOBSSON, G. (1987). Neurological findings in 20 relatively gifted children with Kanner type autism or Asperger's syndrome. *Developmental Medicine and Child Neurology, 29,* 641–649.

GITTELMAN, M., & BIRCH, H. G. (1967). Childhood schizophrenia: Intellect, neurologic status, perinatal risk, prognosis and family pathology. *Archives of Neurological Psychology, 17,* 16–25.

HERTZIG, M. E., SNOW, M. E., NEW, E., & SHAPIRO, T. (1990). DSM-III and DSM-III-R diagnosis of autism and pervasive developmental disorder in nursery school children. *Journal of the American Academy of Child and Adolescent Psychiatry, 29,* 123–126.

HOBSON, R. P. (1989). Beyond cognition: A theory of autism. In G. Dawson (Ed.), *Autism: Nature, diagnosis, and treatment* (pp. 22–48). New York: Guilford.

HOWLIN, P., & RUTTER, M. (1987). *Treatment of autistic children.* London: Wiley.

HUTT, C., FORREST, S. J., & RICHER, J. (1975). Cardiac arrhythmia and behavior in autistic children. *Acta Psychiatrica Scandinavica, 51*, 361–372.

JACOBSON, J. W., & ACKERMAN, L. J. (1990). Differences in adaptive functioning among people with autism or mental retardation. *Journal of Autism and Developmental Disorders, 20*, 205–219.

KANNER, L. (1943). Autistic disturbances of affective contact. *Nervous Child, 2,* 217-250.

KANNER, L. (1958). The specificity of early infantile autism. *Zeitschrift fur Kinderpsychiatrie, 25,* 108–113.

KRUG, D. A., ARICK, J., & ALMOND, P. (1980). Behavior checklist for identifying severely handicapped individuals with high levels of autistic behavior. *Journal of Child Psychology and Psychiatry, 21,* 221–229.

KURITA, H., MIYAKE, Y., & KATSUNO, K. (1989). Reliability and validity of the *Childhood autism rating scale–Tokyo version* (CARS-TV). *Journal of Autism and Developmental Disorders, 19,* 389–396.

LE COUTEUR, A., RUTTER, M., LORD, C., RIOS, P., ROBERTSON, S., HOLDGRAFER, M., & McLENNAN, J. (1989). Autism diagnostic interview: A standardized investigator-based instrument. *Journal of Autism and Developmental Disorders, 19,* 363–387.

LOCKYER, L., & RUTTER, M. (1969). A five to fifteen year follow-up study of infantile psychosis. *British Journal of Psychiatry, 115,* 865–882.

LORD, C., RUTTER, M., GOODE, S., HEEMSBERGEN, J., JORDAN, H., MAWHOOD, L., SCHOPLER, E. (1989). Autism diagnostic observation schedule: A standardized observation of communicative and social behavior. *Journal of Autism and Developmental Disorders, 19,* 185–212.

LOTTER, V. (1966). Epidemiology of autistic conditions in young children: I. Prevalence. *Social Psychiatry, 1,* 124–137.

MAISTO, C. R., BAUMEISTER, A. A., & MAISTO, A. A. (1978). An analysis of variables related to self-injurious behavior among institutionalized retarded persons. *Journal of Mental Deficiency Research, 22,* 27–36.

MATSON, J. L., & LOVE, S. R. (1991). A comparison of parent-report fear for autistic and normal age-matched children and youth. *Australian and New Zealand Journal of Developmental Disabilities, 16,* 349–358.

MATSON, J. L., SEVIN, J. A., FRIDLEY, D., & LOVE, S. R. (1990). Increasing spontaneous language in three autistic children. *Journal of Applied Behavior Analysis, 23,* 227–234.

MATSON, J. L., SEVIN, J. A., BOX, M. L., FRANCIS, K. L., & SEVIN, B. M. (1993). Evaluation and comparison of two methods for increasing spontaneous language in autistic children. *Journal of Applied Behavior Analysis, 26,* 389–398.

MESIBOV, G. B., SCHOPLER, E., SCHAFFER, B., & MICHAL, N. (1989). Use of the *Childhood autism rating scale* with autistic adolescents and adults. *Journal of the American Academy of Child and Adolescent Psychiatry, 28,* 538–541.

MOHLER, M. S. (1952). On childhood psychosis and schizophrenia: Autistic and symbiotic psychoses. *The Psychoanalytic Study of the Child, 1,* 286-305. [Reprinted in S. I. Harrison and J. F. McDermott (Eds.), *Childhood psychopathology: An anthology of basic reading* (pp. 57–91). New York: International Universities Press.]

MUNDY, P., & SIGMAN, M. (1989). Specifying the nature of the social impairment in autism. In G. Dawson (Ed.), *Autism: Nature, diagnosis, and treatment* (pp. 3–21). New York: Guilford.

MYERS, B. A. (1989). Misleading cues in the diagnosis of mental retardation and infantile autism in the preschool child. *Mental Retardation, 27,* 85–90.

NARAYAN, S., MOYES, B., & WOLFF, S. (1990). Family characteristics of autistic children: A further report. *Journal of Autism and Developmental Disorders, 20,* 523–536.

ORNITZ, E. M. (1970). Vestibular dysfunction in schizophrenia and childhood autism. *Comprehensive Psychiatry, 11,* 159–173.

PARKS, S. L. (1983). The assessment of autistic children: A selective review of available instruments. *Journal of Autism and Developmental Disorders, 13,* 255–267.

PARKS, S. L. (1988). Psychometric instruments available for the assessment of autistic children. In E. Schopler & G. Mesibov (Eds.), *Diagnosis and assessment in autism* (pp. 123–134). New York: Plenum.

PIVEN, J., TSAI, G., NEHMEN, E., COYLE, J. T., CHASE, G. A., & FOLSTEIN, S. E. (1991). Platelet serotonin, a possible marker for familial autism. *Journal of Autism and Developmental Disorders, 21,* 51–60.

POMEROY, J. C., FRIEDMAN, C., & STEPHENS, L. (1991). Autism and Asperger's: Same or different? *Journal of the American Academy of Child and Adolescent Psychiatry, 29,* 152–153.

QUINE, L., & PAHL, J. (1986). First diagnosis of severe mental handicap: Characteristics of unsatisfactory encounters between doctors and parents. *Social Science Medicine, 22,* 53–62.

REISS, A. L., & FREUND, L. (1990). Fragile X syndrome, DSM-III-R, and autism. *Journal of the American Academy of Child and Adolescent Psychiatry, 28,* 885–891.

REISS, S., LEVITAN, G. W., & SZYSZKO, J. (1982). Emotional disturbance and mental retardation: Diagnostic overshadowing. *American Journal of Mental Deficiency, 86,* 567–574.

RIMLAND, B. (1964). *Infantile autism: The syndrome and its implications for a neural theory of behavior.* Englewood Cliffs, NJ: Prentice Hall.

RIMLAND, B. (1971). The differentiation of childhood psychoses: An analysis of checklists for 2,218 psychotic children. *Journal of Autism and Childhood Schizophrenia, 1,* 161–174.

RINCOVER, A., & KOEGEL, R. L. (1975). Setting generality and stimulus control in autistic children. *Journal of Applied Behavior Analysis, 8,* 235–246.

RITVO, E. R., & FREEMAN, B. J. (1978). National Society for Autistic Children definition of the syndrome of autism. *Journal of Autism and Developmental Disorders, 8,* 162–170.

RITVO, E. R., YUWILER, A., GELLER, E., ORNITZ, E. M., SAEGER, K., & PLOTKIN, S. (1970). Increased blood serotonin and platelets in early infantile autism. *Archives of General Psychiatry, 23,* 566–572.

RITVO, E. R., FREEMAN, B. J., MASON-BROTHERS, A., MO, A., & RITVO, A. M. (1985). Concordance for the syndrome of autism in 40 pairs of afflicted twins. *American Journal of Psychiatry, 142,* 174–177.

ROGERS, S. J., & DILALLA, D. L. (1990). Age of symptom onset in young children with pervasive developmental disorders. *Journal of the American Academy of Child and Adolescent Psychiatry, 29,* 863–872.

RUTTENBERG, B. A., DRATMAN, M. L., FRANKO, J., & WENAR, C. (1966). An instrument for evaluating autistic children. *Journal of the American Academy of Child Psychiatry, 5,* 453–478.

RUTTER, M. (1965). The influence of organic and emotional factors on the origins, nature, and outcome of childhood psychosis. *Journal of Developmental Medicine and Child Neurology, 7,* 518–528.

RUTTER, M. (1978). Diagnosis and definition of childhood autism. *Journal of Autism and Developmental Disorders, 8,* 139–161.

RUTTER, M., & BARTAK, I. (1973). Special education treatment of autistic children: A comparative study. II. Follow-up findings and implications for services. *Journal of Child Psychology and Psychiatry, 14,* 241–270.

RUTTER, M., & GARMEZY, N. (1983). Developmental psychopathology. In E. M. Hetherington (Ed.), *Handbook of child psychology* (Vol 4.) (pp. 775–912). New York: Wiley.

RUTTER, M., & SCHOPLER, E. (1988). Autism and pervasive developmental disorders: Concepts and diagnostic issues. In E. Schopler & G. Mesibov (Eds.), *Diagnosis and assessment in autism* (pp. 15–37). New York: Plenum.

SALIBA, J. R., & GRIFFITHS, M. (1990). Brief report: Autism of the Asperger type associated with an autosomal fragile site. *Journal of Autism and Developmental Disorders, 20,* 569–576.

SCHOPLER, E. (1978). On confusion in the diagnosis of autism. *Journal of Autism and Developmental Disorders, 8,* 137–138.

SCHOPLER, E., & MESIBOV, G. (1988a). *Diagnosis and treatment of autism.* New York: Plenum.

SCHOPLER, E., & MESIBOV, G. (1988b). Introduction to diagnosis and assessment of autism. In E. Schopler and G. Mesibov (Eds.), *Diagnosis and assessment in autism* (pp. 1–14). New York: Plenum.

SCHOPLER, E., REICHLER, R. J., DeVELLIS, R. F., & DALY, K. (1980). Toward objective classification of childhood autism: *Childhood autism rating scale* (CARS). *Journal of Autism and Developmental Disorders, 10,* 91–103.

SCHOPLER, E., REICHLER, R. J., & RENNER, B. R. (1988). *The childhood autism rating scale.* Los Angeles: Western Psychological Services.

SCHREIBMAN, L., & MILLS, J. I. (1983). Infantile autism. In T. A. Ollendick and M. Hersen (Eds.), *Handbook of child psychopathology* (pp. 123–150). New York: Plenum.

SCHROEDER, S. R., SCHROEDER, C. S., SMITH, B., & DALLDORF, J. (1978). Prevalence of self-injurious behavior in a large state facility for the retarded: A three year follow-up study. *Journal of Autism and Childhood Schizophrenia, 8,* 261–269.

SELTZER, M. M., & SELTZER, G. B. (1983). Classification and social status. In J. L. Matson & J. A. Mulick (Eds.), *Handbook of mental retardation* (pp. 185–200). New York: Pergamon.

SEVIN, J. A., MATSON, J. L., COE, D., FEE, V., & SEVIN, B. M. (1991). Evaluation and comparison of three commonly used autism scales. *Journal of Autism and Developmental Disorders, 21,* 417–432.

SEVIN, J. A., MATSON, J. L., COE, D., LOVE, S. R., MATESE, M. J., & BENEVIDEZ, D. A. (1991). *Empirically derived subtypes of pervasive developmental disorders: A cluster analytic study.* Unpublished manuscript.

SHORT, A. B., & SCHOPLER, E. (1988). Factors relating to age of onset in autism. *Journal of Autism and Developmental Disorders, 18,* 207–216.

SHROUT, P. E., & FLEISS, J. L. (1981). Reliability and case detection. In J. K. Wing, P. Bebbington, & L. N.

Robbins (Eds.), *What is a case? The problem of definition in psychiatric community surveys* (pp. 117–128). New York: Grant McIntyre.

SIEGEL, B., VUKICEVIC, J., ELLIOTT, G. R., & KRAEMER, H. C. (1989). The use of signal detection theory to assess DSM-III-R criteria for autistic disorder. *Journal of the American Academy of Child and Adolescent Psychiatry, 28,* 542–548.

SMALL, J. G. (1975). EEG and neurophysiological studies of early infantile autism. *Biological Psychiatry, 10,* 385–397.

SOULE, D., & O'BRIEN, D. (1974). Self-injurious behavior in a state center for the retarded: Incidence. In *Research and the Retarded* (pp. 1–8). Goldsboro, NC: O'Berry Center.

SPITZER, R. L., & SIEGEL, B. (1990). The DSM-III-R field trial of pervasive developmental disorders. *Journal of the American Academy of Child and Adolescent Psychiatry, 29,* 855–862.

STONE, W. L., & CARO-MARTINEZ, L. M. (1990). Naturalistic observations of communication in autistic children. *Journal of Autism and Developmental Disorders, 20,* 437–454.

STONE, W. L., & LEMANEK, K. L. (1990). Parental report of social behaviors in autistic preschoolers. *Journal of Autism and Developmental Disorders, 20,* 513–522.

STURMEY, P., MATSON, J. L., & SEVIN, J. A. (in press). Analysis of the internal consistency of three autism scales. *Journal of Autism and Developmental Disorders.*

SZATMARI, P. (1992). A review of the DSM-III-R criteria for autistic disorder. Special issue: Classification and diagnosis. *Journal of Autism and Developmental Disorders, 22,* 507–523.

SZATMARI, P., BARTOLUCCI, G., & BREMNER, R. (1989). Asperger's syndrome and autism: Comparisons on early history and outcome. *Developmental Medicine and Child Neurology, 31,* 709–720.

SZATMARI, P., TUFF, L., FINLAYSON, A. J., & BARTOLUCCI, G. (1990). Asperger's syndrome and autism: Neurocognitive aspects. *Journal of the American Academy of Child and Adolescent Psychiatry, 29,* 130–136.

TAGER-FLUSBERG, H., CALKINS, S., NOLIN, T., BAUMBERGER, T., ANDERSON, M., & CHADWICK-DIAS, A. (1990). A longitudinal study of language acquisition in autistic and Down syndrome children. *Journal of Autism and Developmental Disorders, 20,* 1–21.

TURNBULL, H. R., & WHEAT, M. J. (1983). Legal responses to classification. In J. L. Matson & J. A. Mulick (Eds.), *Handbook of mental retardation* (pp. 157–170). New York: Pergamon.

TURNER, T. H. (1989). Schizophrenia and mental handicap: An historical review, with implications for further research. *Psychological Medicine, 19,* 301–314.

UNGERER, J. A. (1989). The early development of autistic children: Implications for defining primary deficits. In G. Dawson (Ed.), *Autism: Nature, diagnosis, and treatment* (pp. 75–91). New York: Guilford.

VOLKMAR, F. (1987). Diagnostic issues in the pervasive developmental disorders. *Journal of Child Psychology and Psychiatry, 28,* 365–369.

VOLKMAR, F. R., BREGMAN, J., COHEN, D. J., & CICCHETTI, D. V. (1988). DSM-III and DSM-III-R diagnoses of autism. *American Journal of Psychiatry, 145,* 1404–1408.

VOLKMAR, F. R., CICCHETTI, D. V., DYKENS, E., SPARROW, S. S., LECKMAN, J. F., & COHEN, D. J. (1988). An evaluation of the *Autism behavior checklist. Journal of Autism and Developmental Disorders, 18,* 81–97.

VOLKMAR, F. R., COHEN, D. J., & PAUL, R. (1986). An evaluation of DSM-III criteria for infantile autism. *Journal of the American Academy of Child and Adolescent Psychiatry, 25,* 190–197.

VOLKMAR, F., COHEN, D. J., BREGMAN, J. D., HOOKS, M. Y., & STEVENSON, J. M. (1989). An examination of social typologies in autism. *Journal of the American Academy of Child and Adolescent Psychiatry, 28,* 82–86.

VOLKMAR, F. R., SPARROW, S. S., GOUDREAU, D., CICCHETTI, D. V., PAUL, R., & COHEN, D. J. (1987). Social deficits in autism: An operational approach using the *Vineland adaptive behavior scales. Journal of the American Academy of Child and Adolescent Psychiatry, 26,* 156–161.

VOLKMAR, F. R., STIER, D. M., & COHEN, D. J. (1985). Age of recognition of pervasive developmental disorders. *American Journal of Psychiatry, 142,* 1450–1452.

WERRY, J. S. (1988). Diagnostic classification for the clinician. In E. Schopler & G. Mesibov (Eds.), *Diagnosis and assessment in autism* (pp. 49–58). New York: Plenum.

WING, L. (1988). The continuum of autistic characteristics. In E. Schopler & G. Mesibov (Eds.), *Diagnosis and assessment in autism* (pp. 91–107). New York: Plenum.

WING, L. (1990, July). *The diagnostic debate.* Paper presented at the annual meeting of the Autism Society of America, Long Beach, CA.

WING, L., & ATWOOD, A. (1987). Syndromes of autism and atypical development. In D. J. Cohen &

A. Donnelan (Eds.), *Handbook of autism* (pp. 3–19). New York: Wiley.

WING, L., & GOULD, J. (1978). Systematic recording of behaviors and skills of retarded and psychotic children. *Journal of Autism and Childhood Schizophrenia, 8,* 79–97.

WING, L., & GOULD, J. (1979). Severe impairments of social interaction and associated abnormalities in children: Epidemiology and classification. *Journal of Autism and Developmental Disorders, 9,* 11–29.

CHAPTER 3

The Graying of Autism: Etiology and Prevalence at Fifty

Bill J. Locke
TEXAS TECH UNIVERSITY

Joseph A. Banken
TEXAS TECH UNIVERSITY HEALTH SCIENCES CENTER

Charles H. Mahone
TEXAS TECH UNIVERSITY

Over the 50 years since the autism syndrome was first identified (Kanner, 1943), virtually every aspect of this condition has been the subject of some controversy. Certainly this has been the case with etiology and even prevalence. As this field of investigation matures, the alternative causative factors deemed viable by most investigators must still be viewed in equivocal "shades of gray" when their actual contribution to a given instance of autism is being judged. At the same time, there is considerable consensus that the causation of autism lies in the "gray matter," so to speak, of neurobiological functions. This chapter will present the evidence and conceptual considerations that have led to current thought on the causes and incidence of autism as a generic condition.

For the most part, the discussion will not bear directly on management and remediation issues. While treatments of some effectiveness can be offered, knowledge of the syndrome's etiology is not sufficient to allow causal factors to constitute a basis for differential treatment. The limits to what has been learned about the etiology of autism render the discussion of it more relevant to theoretical and research issues than to immediate practical applications. In nearly five decades, conceptualization of autistic phenomena has been subject to such marked and frequent shifts that the time and context within which a given line of speculation was advanced must be taken into account. After some prefacing comments on the varied definitions of the condition, we will briefly summarize the views that have assumed some prominence in the thinking on the causes of autism.

Definitional Conventions and Their Historical Context

As Sturmey and Sevin detailed in the previous chapter, the defining features of autism have been subject to ongoing debate since its initial description. The course of that debate has not only dictated prevalence estimates, but also both reflected and influenced which factors were considered autism's determinants. Thus, by Kanner's original criteria, autism was deemed a relatively rare condition; in contrast, the current broader diagnostic standards have significantly increased its estimated incidence (Shreibman & Charlop, 1987).

Changing definitions tend to reflect emerging changes in the perceived etiology of the syndrome. When Kanner's initial work emerged, the psychoanalytic orientation was predominant, and most investigators were persuaded that all psychiatric conditions had a primary emotional core. This view is reflected in early definitional approaches that emphasize a unitary condition derived from psychogenic sources (a view that can be discerned in Kanner's convention of excluding from the condition children with known central nervous system damage). More recently, there has been increasing recognition of neurophysiological and genetic determinants of other conditions, so it should not be surprising to learn that most scientists now endorse a physical rather than psychological locus of causation for autism (e.g., Gallagher, Jones, & Byrne, 1990). Thus, contemporary definitions generally converge to delineate autism as a behaviorally defined syndrome of neurological impairment with a wide variety of underlying medical etiologies (Gillberg, 1988).

Even when autism is defined in strictly behavioral terms, specialists differ greatly in their views of which manifestations should be deemed primary (Fein, Pennington, Markowitz, Braverman, & Waterhouse, 1986; Goodman, 1989; Rutter, 1983). The symptoms ascribed to autism are extensive and do not present uniformly from one case to the next. As a result, autism is no longer considered a unitary condition by most. Instead, subgroups are posited, with etiologies and differing associated pathologies (e.g., Delong & Dwyer, 1988). The question then becomes what those subtypes should be (Rutter & Schopler, 1987) or, alternatively, what constitutes the differential attributes of each condition in the spectrum of autistic disorders (Bowman, 1988).

Although the definitional question may remain fundamentally unresolved, the ambiguity is mitigated somewhat by the relative reliability with which the generic diagnosis seems to be applied (Rutter & Garmezy, 1983). Moreover, a relatively broad acceptance of a working definition does exist among researchers. The most common definition across investigations (Gillberg, 1988) has viewed autism as a subtype in the DSM-III-R classification of pervasive developmental disorder (American Psychiatric Association, 1987). While the relative empirical validity of this classification may be questioned by some (e.g., Gillberg, 1990a), it does roughly encompass the triad of deficits common to most classifications—impairments of social exchange, communication/imaginative impairments, and marked constriction of activities and interests. The DSM-III-R diagnosis requires that 8 or more of its 16 characteristics be positive, with each element of the triad represented. Given its general acceptance and operational clarity, the DSM-III-R classification will generally apply in our coverage of autism's incidence and etiology.

Psychological Models and Etiology

The state of knowledge about the etiology of autism was indicated at the beginning of this chapter; that is, the specific causes of autism have yet to be identified. In the absence of known determinants, the prevalent etiological views of a given time have often mirrored conceptual approaches dominating other spheres of speculation.

Despite Kanner's (1943) original emphasis on constitutional factors, the early theories of autism tended to emphasize psychodynamic determinants in an era when psychoanalytic accounts of other forms of psychopathology prevailed. Psychoanalytic thought (e.g., Bettelheim, 1959) deemed autism an affective disorder born out of an impoverished, unresponsive parental environment. Comparable lines of speculation developed outside of the psychoanalytic community as well (e.g., Zaslow & Breger, 1969). For example, Ferster's (1961) operant learning model implicated parents who were ill-disposed to provide positive reinforcement but highly reactive in a negative manner to their child's behavioral deficiencies or excesses. The result was seen as an escalating cycle of interdependent reinforcement contingencies operating on both child and parent so as to shape and differentially promote autistic behavior. The emphasis on environmental determinants prevailed until the late sixties. However, more recent variants continue, such as the Tinbergens' (1972) theory emphasizing an ethological focus on the origins of autism in social stress. Despite their environmental emphasis, virtually all these positions accorded some parallel or ultimate instrumentality to underlying organic or constitutional factors.

In the mid- to late sixties, cognitive deficit replaced emotional disorder as the core problem considered to underlie autism and its symptoms. Much of the impetus behind these views derived from the cognitive development research that began to flourish in that period, as its experimental paradigms with normal children were extended to investigations of autism. The most influential extension occurred in Rimland's (1964) cognitive account of autism, which fostered more systematic, empirical explication of dysfunctional cognitive manifestations in attention, perception, and language functions (Hermelin & O'Connor, 1970; Rutter, 1968). Concurrent refutations of parental culpability (e.g., DeMyer et al., 1972) furthered the shift away from the view of autism as environmentally determined emotional pathology.

Thus, for a time, the condition was consensually viewed as a cognitive deficit. However, the effects of autism on social behavior were increasingly noted in comparisons drawn from the emerging developmental research on the social behavior of normal children. As the social impact of the condition was increasingly documented (e.g., Wing, Gould, Yeates, & Brierly, 1977), the near-exclusive emphasis on the cognitive sphere declined. Likewise, as the complexity and alternate manifestations of the syndrome became more widely acknowledged, a number of rival models appeared that emphasized deficits in other spheres.

Many of these models continued the attempt to delineate a primary deficit. Thus, the core difficulty has been variously posited as erratic arousal to sensory stimulation (Delacato, 1974), perceptual dysfunctions (DeMyer, 1976), linguistic difficulties (Churchill, 1972), overselective attentional focus (Lovaas, Koegel, & Schreibman, 1979), sensory integration problems (Ayres, 1979), and undue responsiveness to particular sensory modalities (Hermelin & O'Connor, 1970).

With a burgeoning body of empirical correlates to autism, Rutter's (1983) seminal analysis effectively discounted the fundamental role of some of those factors. In the course of attempting to affirm the relative primacy of cognitive deficits, Rutter noted their recurrent presence across the full spectrum of autistic cases. The functional relation of such deficits to commonly observed social dysfunctions was advanced by reviewing literature that revealed a near-invariant relationship between cognitive difficulties and the deviant processing of certain interpersonal and emotional cues (Langdell, 1978). This included particular consideration of the social cues involved in envisioning and inferring the mental state of others. A convincing linkage of some prominent language correlates to cognitive processes included patterns of verbal IQ score sequencing that were grounded in problems well beyond mere speech failures (Tymchuk, Simmons, & Neafsey, 1977).

The role of age and concomitant disorders was readily discounted in the failure of these factors to accompany the full pattern of deficits. A probable genetic component was well acknowledged in the concordance findings of autistic twin studies (Folstein & Rutter, 1977; Ritvo, Freeman et al., 1985). Further, social-affective symptoms of autism were increasingly noted in various forms (e.g., nonverbal communication) during this period (Loveland & Landry, 1986). In crediting evidence for noncognitive alternatives, Rutter and others (e.g., Howlin, 1978) were essentially acceding to a multidimensional view of autism—cognitive in nature but demonstrating overlapping social and emotional impairments as well. The genetic hypotheses in particular held promise but were largely deferred until technical advances and additional research allowed clarification.

The acuity of Kanner's original observations of autistic phenomena has been widely acknowledged, but his speculations about the etiology of autism seem no less prescient. Both Kanner's original constitutional emphasis (Kanner, 1943) and his subsequent focus on the affective and communicative aspects of autism (Kanner, 1949) would be congruent with many modern variants. Hobson (1989) has presented what is probably the most compatible modern articulation of views Kanner would endorse. Hobson holds that autism stems from constitutional limits on emotional reactivity that alter the necessary sharing of subjective interpersonal experiences. Such limits impede abstraction, symbolic representation of thought/feeling, and empathic recognition of feeling and thought in other persons. Social and affective development is undermined, leading to secondary, lower-order deficits in cognitive and language functions. The direct heuristic impact of the overall formulation of these views has been limited to date, consisting largely of Hobson's own research (e.g., Hobson, Outson, & Lee, 1988). It certainly has not established the core process underlying all autistic difficulties, since some functional affective behavior has been demonstrated in autistic subjects (e.g., Sigman & Mundy, 1984). Yet, Hobson's formulation is among the family of social-affective speculations in the ascendence among contemporary attempts to account for autism in psychological terms.

Deficits akin to the hypothesized empathic deficit constitute a relatively robust finding and appear as alternative but compatible constructs in other theories as well. This general body of positive findings has been reviewed by Baron-Cohen (1988); however, contrary findings have also been reported (Ozonoff, Pennington, & Rogers, 1990; Prior, Dahlstrom, & Squires, 1990).

Building upon these and similar findings, Frith (1989) emphasized deficient functioning in metarepresentational processes. Her "theory of mind" argues for the developmental necessity of learning to infer, on an indirect basis, the content of others' mental states. In this regard, she posits a weakness in the autistic person's cognitive mechanism of "decoupling," a term coined and described by Leslie (1987). This process requires suspension of nonsocial ways of knowing through literal validation of an event and instead development of a belief that takes context into account in such a way that one can attribute beliefs to others that diverge from one's own beliefs about the identical event. This type of belief or metarepresentation is the basis for a theory of mind whereby one surmises mental states in others and utilizes them to predict and account for the behavior of others. This ability is usually developed around age 2 or 3 in normal children, whereas the majority of autistic persons show no evidence of such an ability (Baron-Cohen, Leslie, & Frith, 1985). Some 20–29% of autistic persons do develop a rudimentary attribution of beliefs to others but are delayed years beyond normal children in acquiring this ability (Baron-Cohen, 1989).

Frith (1989) suggested that compromises in metarepresentational ability provide parsimonious evidence of a diversity of autistic phenomena, including the aforementioned empathic deficiency. Without the ability to conceptualize emotions in others, the autistic individual cannot empathetically respond to affective arousal in others confronting events of emotional significance. According to this theory, such autistic difficulties as communication that seems to ignore the impact on the listener, impairment in make-believe play, and the struggle to achieve shared attention all follow from the autistic individual's singular lack of sensitivity to, or even awareness of, others' mental states. As with others advancing largely psychological accounts, Frith noted that these constructs reflect and are compatible with ultimate, more biological, bases of origin in autism.

The Frith and Hobson formulations represent qualities that are emerging in most contemporary accounts of autism. Recent formulations tend to be more readily reconciled with one another as they converge on core phenomena with different but compatible attributions to those processes. For example, Sternberg (1985) proposed an account of autism whereby basic knowledge acquisition (encoding, combination, and comparison) is so misselective that it yields idiosyncratic concepts of what is salient in a given set of stimuli. This shows some commonality with the stimulus overselectivity hypothesis (Lovaas, Schreibman, Koegel, & Rehm, 1971), which ascribes to autistic children the tendency to respond to only one part of a stimulus complex. Sternberg holds still more common theoretical ground, building on Frith and Baron-Cohen, by suggesting that social-cognitive functions are primarily affected in a way that fosters a divergent subjectivity, social withdrawal, and conceptual idiosyncrasies. Many current accounts of autism's causes seem to differ mostly in emphasis among multiple, commonly accepted etiological elements.

Of course, substantive differences do exist among the recent models. First, a more liberal conceptualization of what constitutes autism has led to more diversity of symptoms and the associated conviction that it is a syndrome of etiologically heterogeneous behavioral entities (Cohen, Paul, & Volkmar, 1987). Second, modern thinking is more explicit in its proposed neuropsychological accounts of the syndrome. For example, Hermelin and O'Connor (1985) proposed what they call a logico-affective interpretation emphasizing attentional and orientational dysfunctions jointly determined by cognitive and affective mechanisms. In turn, those mechanisms are explicitly related to subcortical arousal mechanisms in the reticular activating system, right versus left hemisphere filtering of such activation, and ultimate cortical control. While implicit neurobiologic assumptions recur in almost every etiologic model reviewed, Hermelin and O'Connor's model contains a more precise and explicit delineation of the presumed neurophysiological correlates of autism in the research literature.

Apart from the primary character of the functional deficits proposed, the majority of the psychological theories of autism give some weight to neurophysiological difficulties as either ultimately fundamental or collateral, if ill-specified, determinants. These general neurobiologic allusions have pervaded speculations on the etiology of autism since Kanner's observations. This neurobiologic emphasis derives from the numerous genetic or neurophysiological correlates to the conditions identified and from the presumption that enhanced investigative techniques would ultimately allow more precise and comprehensive explication of these as elements underlying the primary psychological difficulties. Before detailing some representative neuropsychological models, we present an overview of the associated empirical work and other neuropsychological speculations.

A Maturing Neurogenetic Movement

Neuroanatomic Imaging

Although neuroanatomic imaging has contributed greatly to the elucidation of many neurological disorders, the findings related to autism have been largely inconclusive. Thus, computerized tomography scans have neither qualitatively (Caraparulo et al., 1981) nor quantitatively (Damasio, Maurer, Damasio, & Chui, 1980) revealed abnormalities that are uniquely associated with autism. Further, although positron emission tomography, magnetic resonance imaging, and other neuroradiologic techniques hold promise, neither these nor autopsies have yielded a characteristic marker of autism when directed toward the central hemispheres, lenticular nuclei, and caudate nucleus (Courchesne, 1991).

Positive findings have been obtained for cerebellar abnormalities in autistic subjects. Neuroanatomic imaging and autopsy findings converge in this regard (Bauman & Kemper, 1985). Such concordance from different procedures and different laboratory studies has not been obtained with any other anatomical structure. These findings have been interpreted as suggesting cerebellar abnormalities resulting from hypoplasia associated with neural maldevelopment (Courchesne, 1991). As techniques become more sophisticated, the role of structural anomalies should become clearer.

Brain Localization

Early theories of brain localization focused on left hemisphere dysfunction and language development. More recent views (e.g., Fein, Humes, Kaplan, Lucci, & Waterhouse, 1984), however, are critical of these localization approaches, seeing them as over-simplistic and lacking appreciation of the autistic syndrome's heterogeneity and complexity. Among others, Edleman (1987) presented a convincing version of that argument. To date, the case has not been made for an explanation of autism via gross abnormalities at the hemispheric level. Minshew (1991) offers a provocative but insufficiently validated account in terms of association cortex dysfunction. This view makes a strong argument that specific autistic manifestations might stem from intrinsic dysfunctions in the association cortex, given recent observations that basic attentional mechanisms and memory functions remain intact in testable autistic individuals (Minshew, 1991). If affirmed, such an account could unify a number of the disparate aspects of the condition.

Structural Brain Abnormalities

Ventricular enlargement with disproportionate widening of the left frontal horn has been found in autistic children (Gillberg & Svendsen, 1983). While some suspect that left medial temporal lobe dysfunction is an important pathogenic feature in autism, there are indications that this is less true of higher-functioning autistic individuals (Prior, Tress, Hoffman, & Boldt, 1984).

Further, the central vestibular system (Ornitz, 1983, 1985) and mesolimbic-striatal abnormalities (Damasio & Maurer, 1978; Maurer & Damasio, 1982) have both been implicated. These involve important hypotheses that will be detailed in a later section.

Pathophysiologic Processes

Seizures

The association of seizure activity with autism has long been established and is thought to have been instrumental in moving causal speculations about autism from psychodynamic to organic views. Seizures frequently develop in childhood, but a second peak of onset occurs in adolescence (Volkmar & Nelson, 1990). Thus, autistic individuals show a significantly increased risk of seizures, approximately one in three, especially at the time of puberty (Deykin & MacMahon, 1979). The condition of a majority of autistic individuals deteriorates around the time of puberty (Gillberg & Steffenburg, 1989; Lockyear & Rutter, 1970) in ways suggestive of epilepsy and other organic pathology.

Taken together, these relationships may implicate other underlying pathophysiologic brain mechanisms in autism, but explanatory models based on such pathology have not yet been presented. This may stem from the absence of a differential relationship between seizures and the development of autism. Thus, there appears to be no seizure type or EEG abnormality specific to the development of autism (Taft & Cohen, 1971; Waldo et al., 1978). The most extensive EEG study of autistic children found abnormalities in approximately 40% of the one-assessment samples (Tsai, Tsai, & August, 1985). Abnormalities were bilateral, nonspecific as to cortex involvement, and varied in wave activity. Still, this finding does point to an underlying but as yet unidentified pathophysiologic process that is exacerbated by the physical changes in puberty.

Hyperarousal

Overactivation as a hypothesized determinant of autism is usually seen as producing hyperselective attention, stereotypical behavior, and other mannerisms that constrict or moderate stimulation (Kinsbourne, 1980). The corollary assumption is made that autistic individuals' arousal is such that they are most comfortable when the range of stimulation is limited. Similarly, the extreme shifts from under- to overactivity have been hypothesized to represent shifts in arousal secondary to endogenous processes (Ornitz, 1971), perhaps related to levels of brain neurotransmitters.

Brainstem involvement has been implicated both in early (Rimland, 1964) and recent (Ornitz, 1978) etiologic theories of autism. There are also indications that ascending activation may be abnormal not only in amount but also in direction (Kinsbourne, 1987). The misdirected or subnormal activation of specific brain structures could account for some of autism's cognitive abnormalities, through an impact on information processing and learning. In keeping with this explanation, Kinsbourne suggested that autism might better be understood as unstable dysregulation secondary to dramatic alterations in frontal dopaminergic activity. This process might be invoked as an explanation of the dramatic alterations in activity among autistic persons.

Neurodevelopmental Influences

A variety of pre- and perinatal factors have been examined as possible etiologic agents. The role of infectious agents in one study (Gillberg & Gillberg, 1983) and of maternal injury, low birth weight, and poorly rated birth condition in another (Deykin & MacMahon, 1980) was seemingly absent in autism. A number of other perinatal factors were similarly discounted as causes of autism. Conversely, an association has been suggested with what Gillberg and Gillberg (1983) call "reduced optimality," a construct involving maternal age of 35 years or more at the time of birth. The precise processes moderated by maternal age are at issue, as is the question of whether the factor's effects are unique to autism. Some speculations revolve around the age-linked production of antibodies associated with the syndrome, but these lack consistent empirical support. More support has been forthcoming for human leukocyte antibodies (HLA) in interaction with the mother's immune system as etiologic agents in autism (Stubbs, Ritvo, & Mason-Brothers, 1985). This relationship does not involve maternal age and does not apply across the full spectrum of autistic cases (Warren et al., 1990).

Genetic Influences

Single-Gene Disorders

A number of autosomal disorders are associated with autism. However, establishing them as causal agents is complicated by the fact that the number of autistic males in general significantly exceeds that of autistic females. Theoretically, the sex ratio of affected persons should be roughly equal. Although it may not be the general case among autistic children, the ratio of males to females who have autosomal disorders may well be roughly equal (Folstein & Rutter, 1987).

The strength of the single-gene relationship with autism remains unclear (Folstein & Piven, 1991), partially as a result of the concomitant presence of mental retardation. Phenylketonuria (PKU) is an inherited metabolic disorder that stems from a recessive gene and is associated with mental retardation and autism when untreated. Delay of the prescribed dietary treatment until after infancy indicates that the autistic symptoms arise out of mechanisms divergent from those producing mental retardation. Under such delay, the treatment sometimes eliminates autistic behavior without improvements in intellectual functioning (Sutherland, Berry, & Shirkey, 1960).

Fragile X is a single-gene X-linked disorder with which autism is associated (Cohen, Sudhalter, Pfadt, Jenkins, & Brown, 1991; McGillivray, Herbst, Dill, Sandercock, & Tischler, 1986). That association has been estimated as high as 25% (Gillberg & Wahlstrom, 1985). More recent studies (Bolton, Pickles, Rutter, & Butler, 1989; Ho & Kalousek, 1989; Payton, Steele, Wenger, & Minshew, 1989) have reported somewhat lower percentages. In contrast to the situation for PKU, autistic and mental retardation influences have not been separated in the fragile-X research to date. Similar confounding of the two also exists with tuberous sclerosis and neurofibromatosis that are inherited as autosomal dominant traits. Some proportion of these children are also autistic (Hunt & Dennis, 1987), and all have brain lesions that vary in severity and location. Systematic comparison of these disorders with and without autism should allow comparisons relevant to the pathophysiology of autistic syndromes.

Family Studies

Concordance for autism in monozygotic twins has been reported consistently in the literature. Early twin studies supported genetic transmission of autism as reflected in language components of the disorder (DeMyer, Hingtgen, & Jackson 1981; Folstein & Rutter, 1977). Later findings (Ritvo, Freeman et al., 1985) based on 65 pairs of twins indicated 95.7% and 23.5% concordance for monozygotic and dizygotic twins, respectively. Ritvo, Spence et al. (1985) also provided evidence compatible with autosomal recessive inheritance of autism. Interpretation of the genetic influences is complicated in such studies by the possibility of a phenotype of autism that extends beyond clear diagnostic boundaries (Bolton & Rutter, 1990).

Approximately 3% of autistic probands have autistic siblings (Smalley, Asarnow, & Spence, 1988), which is approximately 50 to 100 times higher than expected in the general population (Steffenburg & Gillberg, 1986). Moreover, the siblings of autistic children seem to demonstrate a higher rate of cognitive deficits than do controls (August, Stewart, & Tsai, 1981). Although these findings strongly suggest that autistic genotypes may aggregate in families, Bolton and Rutter (1990) caution that familial loading lacks consistency across studies.

Genetic Models

While new and more sophisticated methods of investigation are being used to explore genetic influences underlying autism, many questions remain. Polygenetic and multifactorial genetic mechanisms exist only for some aspects of autism (Spence, 1976), and it may be that genetic effects exert general rather than specific forms of influence (Prior, 1989). Nonspecific genetic influences may well be the key in clarifying the heterogeneity of

autistic manifestations. Folstein and Rutter (1977) cautioned against the assumption of genetic homogeneity in these studies. Also, symptoms such as language disorders that are increasingly linked to autism tend to support the role of nonspecific factors (Reichler & Lee, 1987). Moreover, no clear genetic etiology has been established for the majority of autistic individuals (Bolton & Rutter, 1990). Thus, it would be premature to assume the primacy of a genetic etiology. Nevertheless, few would disagree with the need for continuing pursuit of one or more genetic factors as more sophisticated investigative methods evolve.

Neurochemical Influences

Serotonin

Some investigations (Young, Kavanagh, Anderson, Shaywitz, & Cohen, 1982; Yuwiler, Geller, & Ritvo, 1985) have indicated more elevated blood serotonin levels among autistic subjects than among nonautistic subjects. However, blood serotonin is also associated with other conditions. Among these, mental retardation has been considered more at issue by some (Gillberg, 1988), and serotonin levels relate more closely to intellectual capacity than to psychiatric disorder (DeMyer et al., 1981). Increased whole blood serotonin does not necessarily reflect brain serotonin metabolism (Yuwiler et al., 1985). Nonetheless, a number of provocative correlations with autistic phenomena have been reported. For example, decreased central serotonergic responsivity was found in male autistic adults (McBride et al., 1989), and platelet serotonin levels were higher in probands with autistic siblings than those without (Piven et al., 1991). In a manipulative study that indirectly bears on this issue, the autistic symptoms of roughly one-third of autistic subjects were moderated by Fenfluramine, an agent that depletes serotonin levels (Campbell et al., 1986; Ritvo et al., 1986). However, neither reliable correlates of autism nor amelioration of its symptoms by a pharmacological agent conclusively implicates the underlying processes or structures as direct causes of the condition.

Dopamine

Cortical dopamine projections are involved in processes of attention and cognitive integration. Although not yet empirically supported, the possibility of dysfunctional dopamine being involved in autism has been advanced but considered unlikely to be a function of mental retardation (Gillberg, 1988). Less speculatively, Haloperidol-produced decrements in autistic hyperactivity and stereotyped behavior have been taken as suggestive of dopamine involvement in the motoric abnormalities of autism (Yuwiler et al., 1985).

Endorphins

With only limited empirical support, the work of Gillberg and associates on endorphins constitutes much of the impetus for considering them a possible causal agent in autism. Thus, endorphin fraction II may be increased in the central nervous system of some autistic persons (Gillberg, 1988), and increased endorphins have been reported among autistic persons who exhibit self-injury (Gillberg, 1989). Further, beta-endorphins are lower among individuals with both autism and Rett syndrome (Gillberg, 1990b). Spinal endorphins have been reported in the majority of individuals with Rett syndrome, and treatment with an opiate antagonist has produced behavioral improvement (Percy, Gillberg, Hagberg, & Witt-Engerstrom, 1990).

Neurodevelopmental Models of Autism

The interaction of intrinsic and extrinsic influences on neurological development is considered a likely etiologic element in the autistic syndrome. Factors affecting neural development might impact on connective integrity between different brain sites and subsequently modify brain functioning at a variety of different levels. Within this view at least, diverse etiologic mechanisms may each influence a final common pathway that results in the manifestation of autism. However, the timing and onset of the neurodevelopmental disturbances that result in autism are not clear (Courchesne, 1991). Behavioral experiences and learning also play a prominent role.

The more widely endorsed models of autism tend to implicate neurodevelopmental dysfunctions at a system level rather than discretely localized structures and/or processes. This follows from current knowledge of brain function correlates of autism, including the consistent association of autism with brainstem pathology and an enlarged fourth ventricle (Gillberg & Svendsen, 1983). The prolongation of brainstem transmission time (Ornitz, 1985), along with the sheer complexity of other autistic manifestations, points to a system of brainstem pathology. Three representative models will be described in this section.

Mesolimbic Model

Damasio and Maurer considered autism to derive from dysfunctions of the older cortex, located in the mesial aspect of the frontal and temporal lobes along with dysfunctions in the neostriatum (Damasio & Maurer, 1978; Maurer & Damasio, 1982). Both of these structures, which could be susceptible to diverse etiologic agents, consist of terminating dopamine neurons that arise in the midbrain. Importantly, the mesocortex serves as a relay point for information arriving from the perceptual neocortex on the way to allocortical structures. These areas are important in affective and learning processes as well as for stimulus recognition in subsequent developmental periods. Thus, labeling, learning, and recognition functions depend on the connective integrity of this cortical way station.

Damasio and Maurer explained disturbances of motility as reflecting dysfunction of the basal ganglia, particularly in the neostriatum and closely related frontal lobe structures. Communication disturbances relate to similar regions of the mesial surface of the frontal lobes and supplementary motor areas that are implicated in language and motility disturbances (Maurer & Damasio, 1982).

Other autistic characteristics are similarly linked to disturbance in the implicated brain structure systems.

Sensory and Information-Processing Model

Ornitz (1983, 1985) proposed a neuro-physiological model in which disturbances of modulation and motility are considered primary and dysmodulated sensory input produces disturbances in socialization and communication. Unique to this model is the hypothesis of an autistic etiology that involves the neural network of brainstem and diencephalic structures in dysfunctional initial processing of sensory information. The dysfunction begins prior to the sensory information and acquires "informational value" as it moves toward processing at the more complex and elaborative cortical levels.

In the Ornitz model, brainstem and diencephalic structures may account for the sensory and language disturbances of autism through subcortical and cortical structures, respectively. Specifically, a neurophysiologic dysfunction is suggested that involves merging loops in the brainstem and diencephalon associated with the process of sensory input. A number of neuroanatomic structures are implicated, including the brainstem reticular formation, substantia nigra, thalamic nuclei, and rostral projections from these structures to neocortical and cortical structures.

According to this model, autism is explained as a dysfunction of the brainstem and related diencephalic systems, in consort with the cascading impact of these dysfunctions on higher and more complex neural structures that modulate and elaborate the information from lower centers (Ornitz, 1989). In short, autism is a neurobehavioral dysfunction at the interface of sensory and information-processing functions.

This dynamic, complex model provides a cogent explanation of many aspects of autism. However, as with other models, the testing of these hypotheses is difficult. The model does appear to allow for differing levels of autistic disturbance as a function of differing levels of neuropathology in subcortical and cortical functions.

Neural Interference Model

Courchesne (Courchesne, 1987; Courchesne, Yeng-Courchesne, Press, Hesselink, & Jernigan, 1988) hypothesized that erratic functioning in nervous system mechanisms undermines ongoing attention as well as memory and learning development among autistic individuals. Such interference derives from intermittent "static" associated with dysfunctional neurotransmitter systems, which causes the integrity of nervous system processes in autistic persons to fluctuate. The resulting "on-again, off-again" interference with attention undermines the acquisition, storage, and retrieval of the intact units of information that would ordinarily be developed. Fragmented elements of information do build if sufficiently extensive periods of functional awareness are allowed by the intermittent "on" phases of the systems. Even so, the result is a piecemeal foundation of knowledge about the world, as well as an insufficient basis for subsequent mastery of complex language and social concepts. Courchesne speculated that strong affective arousal may allow more effective attention through compensatory facilitation of other neural systems as a way to override the "static" interference.

Courchesne argued that multiple neural systems—reticular, thalamic, and cortical—may be involved, probably reflecting the absence of an established, specific pathway by means of which the hypothesized neural agents produce such a diverse range of autistic manifestations. Thus, a range of alternate systems and pathways becomes part of the formulation. Neurotransmitter system "static" is obviously a global construct rather than a specific, empirically established neurological agent. Certainly, validation of the model awaits evidence of a linkage between attention and social relatedness, which has yet to be established even in normal development. Nonetheless, the heuristic impact of these formulations along with independent programs of brain-behavior research promises to advance the understanding of the neurobiological underpinnings of autism at a rate comparable to the burgeoning pace of recent psychological research in the area.

Course of Development

Manifestations of the autism syndrome vary at different stages of development, but etiological variants may or may not underlie these differences. Some generalizations about the developmental nature of the condition will be offered here without direct reference to hypothesized etiological subtypes within the autistic spectrum. That omission does not imply the absence of such subgroups but reflects the difficulty in establishing their differential character at this time. Although some of the age-linked diversity among autistic persons seems to be no more than the result of the evolution of syndrome attributes in a maturing organism, other aspects may well reflect differing etiologies. For example, the prognosis for adolescent and adult stages of autistic development is clearly linked to measured intelligence in childhood and the preschool level of language development. Taken singly or together, these important prognostic indicators may well constitute marker variables for identifying subtypes for which a theoretical relation to neurophysiologic or genetic etiologies can be established.

Such leads notwithstanding, we will generalize across possible subtypes in order to give the most parsimonious account of autism as it develops across the lifespan. Given the diversity of developmental perspectives and the limits of relevant empirical findings, a conservative approach seems warranted. Accordingly, we will accept the traditional emphasis on social dysfunctions as the standard for inclusion, since that feature is common to all concepts of autism and constitutes the most important characteristic that distinguishes it from mental retardation (Fein et al., 1986). We now turn to findings and views linked to specific developmental stages.

Infancy (The First 30 Months)

At least through the publication of DSM-III (American Psychiatric Association, 1980), traditional diagnosis emphasized identification of the symptoms in early childhood as the hallmark of autism. When comparable symptoms emerged after 30 months of age, alternative diagnoses such as childhood schizophrenia were more likely. An early diagnosis on the basis of sensory deficits and pre-verbal communication patterns was taken as a matter of course by some authorities (Gillberg et al., 1990; Litrownik & McInnis, 1982). Others (Frith, 1989; Hermelin & O'Connor, 1970) concluded that reliable means do not exist for accurately differentiating autistic from other developmentally disabled children. Reliability does improve after 30 months, with the normal onset of meaningful language. Some investigators (Frith, 1989; Hoshino et al., 1987; Losche, 1990) noted a "setback course phenomenon" in many autistic children, where the first two years of life are unremarkable but individuals subsequently exhibit clear autistic symptoms. Partly because of the dispute over the requisite age of onset, DSM-III-R (APA, 1987) omitted the requirement that age of onset occur before 30 months.

Such diagnostic controversy makes it difficult to offer an assured account of autism and its course during infancy. To the extent that the condition can be identified this early, the signs are those associated with (a) suspected sensory defects (abnormalities of hearing, gaze, and vestibular functions), and (b) pre-verbal deficits in communication (particularly in "joint attention behavior" wherein an adult attempts to direct the infant's attention) (Mundy, Sigman, Sherman, & Ungerer, 1986; Sigman, Ungerer, Mundy, & Sherman, 1987). The very young autistic child seems to lack the ability to interact successfully and thus relates in a manner qualitatively different from that associated with retardation of intellect.

Preschool Period (Ages 2½ through 5)

There is clear agreement that all autistic children exhibit profound deficits not only in social behavior but also in cognition, language, and affect in the preschool period. The preschooler's ineptitude with the pragmatics of verbal communication reflects failure to acquire empathic understanding of the "other" (Frith, 1989; Hermelin & O'Connor,

1985; Olley, 1985), in addition to retardation in acquisition of more mechanical language skills (Goodman, 1989). These language problems contribute substantially to the child's feeling of social isolation in adult and, to a lesser extent, peer interactions. As Paul (1987) noted, "the classic picture of the autistic child—aloof, mute or echolalic, with a great need to preserve sameness and stereotypic motor behaviors—is really most characteristic of the preschool period" (p. 121). At this age, the child typically fits well the "aloof" pattern described by Wing and Gould (1979), in which the signs of normal attachment behavior are minimal or absent. By the end of this period, however, some of the brighter autistic children may begin to resemble Wing's "passive" pattern, which is characterized chiefly by the absence of spontaneous social interaction and nonverbal communication rather than by utter indifference to others. The third of Wing's typologies, the "active but odd" pattern, may also appear prior to the beginning of the school period. Children in this group are noteworthy for their spontaneous but awkward approach to others and higher incidence of psychiatric complications.

Elementary School Years
(Age 6 through Preadolescence)

In the initial years of this period, the autistic child's isolation is increasingly reduced (Frith, 1989), and so greater attention is drawn to the more disturbing behaviors that emerged during the preschool years. For example, echolalia abates, with improved language comprehension and speech beginning in about half of those who were previously nonverbal (Rutter, 1970). Improvement becomes most apparent in interactions with adults, evidenced as greater willingness to adjust to adult demands and expectations (Lotter, 1974).

However, social relationships with peers remain seriously impaired (Garfin & Lord, 1986). Howlin's review (1986) noted four general deficits in peer relations at this age: (a) impoverished play, (b) lack of cooperation, (c) failure to initiate contact, and (d) absence of reciprocity. Even so, the isolation effects of these limitations may be lessened by

the introduction of nonhandicapped children into the classroom and play environment of the autistic child. Some research suggests that such contact fosters increased social interaction and cooperative behavior (McHale, Simeonsson, Marcus, & Olley, 1980). Such effects were even more pronounced when age peers were given special training and took initiative in prompting and reinforcing the social behavior of autistic children (Lord, 1984). Although the increased social responsiveness generalized to less contrived situations, social initiatives from others were not imitated by the autistic children.

Adolescence

Both Kanner (1971) and Rutter (1970) reported adolescent follow-up data indicating an increased interest in peers and, with a few children, definite improvement in social relationships. For those few, this improvement in relationships is usually maintained into adulthood. However, even high-IQ autistic adolescents sustain only rudimentary social relationships (Volkmar, 1987) and seem to retain the characteristic lack of empathy and the shallow affect. Mesibov (1983) indicated that the general improvement occurs in the areas of self-help, group participation, initiative, and self-control. In addition, the activity level moderates, and behavior becomes more manageable. Notwithstanding such general improvements, episodic acting out tends to occur in the adolescent years. For example, Gillberg and Steffenburg (1987) reported that over half their sample of autistic adolescents exhibited at least transient aggravation of symptoms that were often manifested in aggressive or destructive behavior. Given the increased social stimulation, pressure to learn new social skills, and/or heightened interest in social relations at this age, Wing (1983) considered the observed acting out to be the result of social arousal that exceeds the autistic adolescent's tolerance. Not surprisingly, the newly pubescent autistic individual's emergent acting out takes a sexual form on occasion, though typically the sexual expression is regressive (Corbett, 1976).

Other negative symptoms that tend to be exaggerated during this period include the loss of some language skills, intellectual deterioration, inertia, and intensified concern for environmental sameness (Gillberg, 1991). Most prominent among the adolescent-onset difficulties is the emergence of epilepsy, estimated at between 11% (Gillberg, 1991) and 30% (Deykin & MacMahon, 1979). Clearly, adolescent deterioration is common among autistic individuals. Because of such decline, roughly half of autistic teens reside in long-term treatment institutions by mid-adolescence (Adams & Sheslow, 1983). Institutional treatment for this age group should focus on expressive language difficulties such as repetition, literalness, obsession with details, and irrelevancy. Additional attention should be given to dialogue difficulties in differentiating between old and new information, using pronouns, and responding to personal or emotional content. Mesibov (1983) suggested that the formality and pedantic quality of autistic speech constitute a common core to these problems.

Even though there will be the inevitable intermittent episode of acting out, Lettick (1983) offered the optimistic prospect of effective adolescent residential programs. To be successful, such programs should contribute to the acquisition of functional communication skills, increased independence in daily living skills, and movement from one-on-one to group supervision and even to part-time work.

Adulthood

Paul's (1987) summary of adult follow-up studies indicates poor outcomes for roughly two-thirds of the cases. While marked deficits in intellectual level and linguistic abilities remain, the most distinctive adult deficiency lies in the inability to establish close, intimate personal relationships. Further, ritualistic and mechanical repetitive behaviors improve but remain part of what others perceive to be an oddness or quirkiness that sets the autistic adult apart from others with comparable chronological or mental age levels.

Roughly half of autistic adults currently live in residential care, compared to nearly all (95%) only a few years ago (Hitzing, 1987). Many consider this to be essentially a movement from custodial care to responsive environments affording active treatment and training (Simonson & Simonson, 1987). Whether or not that optimistic view is true, no ceiling is clearly established on the gains autistic adults may realize in many areas of functioning. At the same time, two-thirds of autistic adults are unable to lead independent lives and only about 5% are employed in nonsheltered jobs (Adams & Sheslow, 1983). Thus, it is vitally important that the opportunities for acquisition of self-care and everyday living skills occur in consort with assistance toward improved social skills and orientation.

One study (Rumsey, Rapaport, & Sceery, 1985) noted that even among high-functioning autistic adults, 89% lacked identifiable friends and 56% exhibited flat affect in relating to others. These deficits alone constitute major barriers to long-term relationships (i.e., close friendship and marriage). As Rutter (1970) put it, there is a general deficit in the skills needed to proceed from acquaintanceship to friendship.

At lower intellectual levels, 43% of autistic adults require assistance with toileting, 46% have inadequate self-feeding skills, and only 24% can dress and groom themselves (Janicki, Lubin, & Friedman, 1983). Little wonder that the overall prospects are considered poor for some two-thirds of autistic adults.

Still, the natural course of autism in adulthood can be considered one of gradual symptomatic improvement, albeit with persistent residual social impairment (Rumsey et al., 1985). This means that the 15% of autistic individuals who improve during adolescence are likely to exhibit continued increments in social adaptability, provided that programs enhancing self-management and independent living skills remain in place.

Prevalence

Until recently, the autism syndrome was generally estimated to occur with a frequency of roughly 4 to

6 per 10,000 children. Recent estimates have generally fallen in the higher range of 7 to 14 cases per 10,000, but Ritvo et al. (1989) note the extraordinary range among findings—between 2 and 21 cases per 10,000. The operation of factors other than true base rates would seem likely in the face of such marked differences. As noted at the outset of this chapter, definitional variations can and have led to differences in the assumed prevalence of autism. The relative rarity of autism under early restrictions to classical Kanner symptoms has been rendered less applicable with more liberal definitional conventions that respect a spectrum of autistic disorders (Wing & Gould, 1979). Beyond divergent defining operations, other aspects of method and procedure have been culpable in the range of frequency estimates for the condition. A lack of common diagnostic criteria has plagued attempts to compare various assessments. Thus, studies vary with respect to the ages sampled, and the ease of diagnosis varies at different age levels. Optimal detection appears likely for children between 4 and 10 years of age (Hoshino, Kumashiro, Yashima, Tachibana, & Watanabe, 1982, cited in Zahner & Pauls, 1987). As a result, some have discouraged epidemiological studies involving samples above age 10 (Zahner & Pauls, 1987). While more expensive, the use of an entire population in a given area as a basis for inferring prevalence yields higher frequency estimates and seems less subject to selective biases than the more common utilization of treatment clinic records (Wing, Yeates, Brierly, & Gould, 1976). Such methodological divergence may account for some of the variability in prevalence estimates. Further, some of the discrepancies have been ascribed to ethnic changes in recent samples (Gillberg, 1990a), and, with greater sensitivity and better methods of detection, most surveys in the last 10 years indicate higher prevalence figures (Gillberg, Steffenburg, & Schaumann, 1991).

In such a context, then, any given estimate must be qualified with respect to the procedural conventions as well as the time and pattern of sampling from which its database was derived. Among the studies to date, the most comprehensive was that conducted in the 1960s by Lotter (1966, 1967). Conducted in England, this survey applied a multistage screening process to all 8- to 10-year-old children in a county adjacent to London. The survey yielded a rate of 4.5 per 10,000. The most extensive epidemiologic surveys in the United States have been those by Treffert (1970) and Ritvo's group (Ritvo et al., 1989), yielding estimates of 3.1 and 4.0 per 10,000, respectively. The U.S. surveys have been somewhat vague in describing their procedures and are considered less thorough than other major surveys. Nonetheless, the U.S. estimates are comparable to other early findings and to the most commonly cited findings: Lotter's 4.5 per 10,000, or roughly half that level when sampling is restricted to cases meeting classic Kanner criteria. Where nuclear, or Kanner-defined, autism has been differentiated from more amorphous cases, frequencies for it have fallen by between .7 (Treffert, 1970) and 2.3 per 10,000 (Hoshino et al., 1982, cited in Zahner & Pauls, 1987), while non-nuclear autism rates were estimated at roughly twice those levels in most surveys. Those frequencies have been replicated in surveys conducted not only in England and the United States but also in Japan (Hoshino et al., 1982, cited in Zahner & Pauls, 1987), Denmark (Brask, 1970, cited in Gillberg, 1990a), and West Germany (Steinhausen, Gobel, Breinlinger, & Wohlleben, 1983). Most of the surveys to date have been conducted in Europe or Japan, and, as indicated earlier, those since 1980 often tend to indicate elevations over earlier study estimates in well-controlled studies. These findings cannot be readily discounted as artifacts of biased sampling or procedural insensitivity. Gillberg's group performed two surveys in the same Swedish urban area of Gothenburg and an adjacent rural area. Incidence rates ranging from 6.6 (Steffenburg & Gillberg, 1986) to 11.6 per 10,000 (reported in Gillberg, 1990a) were obtained. These changes seem linked to recent generations as Gillberg (1984) screened the total population of children born between 1962 and 1976 in the same Gothenburg area and did not obtain rates elevated over earlier epidemiological studies of autism. Similarly elevated prevalences were reported in Canada (Bryson, Clark, & Smith, 1988), the United States (Burd, Fisher, & Kerbeshian, 1987), France (Cialdella & Mamelle, 1989), and Japan (Sugiyama & Abe, 1989; Tanoe, Oda, Asano, & Kawashima, 1988). These trends are even more marked for Asperger syndrome, which may or may not be considered an autistic disorder (Gillberg & Gillberg, 1989). Whether or not these increments also reflect such factors as more liberal diagnostic standards, autism can no longer be considered a rare condition.

Overview

What has been learned about the etiology of autism in the past 50 years? There is increased sophistication to the investigative techniques available for empirical pursuit of the neurobiology long considered the key to the condition's origins. With few exceptions, however, findings from the different techniques are often negative and sometimes hard to compare, and when there are positive outcomes, they seldom converge. While investigators have yet to establish the biological markers of autism and its source defect(s), there is tantalizing if fragmentary evidence of numerous correlates of the condition in at least some of its manifestations. Moreover, recent conceptual models hold the promise of being able to account for many of the unique features of autism in terms not only of its molecular, biological substrates but also in the molar manifestations of behavior development.

Thus, an ostensibly neurophysiological model like that of Fein's group (Fein et al., 1986) assigns primary weight to a social deficit. The neurodevelopmental models allow a blend of etiological specificity with alternate pathways that accommodate differing levels and sequencing of the condition and its symptoms. The Ornitz model (1983, 1985) incorporates disturbance at subcortical levels that contribute to distorted cortical output. Distorted output

might explain the cognitive deficit, while subcortical dysregulation might account for the sensory dysfunctions evident with autistic persons. The model does not preclude an underlying neurochemical contribution since neurotransmitter activity has also been accommodated as a contributing factor. Theorists such as Rutter, Schopler, and Courchesne seem to rapidly accommodate new developments in this period of accelerated activity. Models of general promise are emerging and, in many instances, are being revised based on a burgeoning body of empirical findings resulting from a flux of activity that reflects a responsive cross-fertilization of research, theory, and clinical practice.

Unfortunately, the more elegant the model, the more difficult it is to test its hypothesized relationships. Conversely, models that are readily testable fail to account for the heterogeneity and full range of autistic manifestations. For example, in spite of substantial empirical support, the genetic models explain only a segment of the autistic population. Many of the questions facing us today are similar to those of an earlier time. Indeed, the argument could be made that the present neurodevelopmental models are simply recapitulations of earlier localization models.

Although there is some truth to the argument that investigators are still addressing the same issues as 50 years ago, this need not be a regressive or merely repetitive process. They are steadily acquiring new information about brain systems and when and how they operate, so the issues in the altered context are hardly the same. A review and update of the cumulative knowledge about different central nervous system and brain structures should ultimately yield a useful and even necessary perspective on the central locus of the autistic syndrome's genesis. The body of information is changing and, reverting to the "graying" metaphor used at the outset of this chapter, the "old gray mare" of autistic etiology "ain't what she used to be." She has learned a few new tricks that both clarify and muddle our comprehension of the gray areas in the continuing enigma of autism.

Note

The authors express gratitude to Gail Ditmore, M.D., for her critical review of earlier drafts of this chapter.

References

ADAMS, W. V., & SHESLOW, D. V. (1983). A developmental perspective of adolescence. In E. Schopler & G. B. Mesibov (Eds.), *Autism in adolescence and adults* (pp. 11–36). New York: Plenum.

AMERICAN PSYCHIATRIC ASSOCIATION. (1980). *Diagnostic and statistical manual of mental disorders* (3rd ed.). Washington, DC: Author.

AMERICAN PSYCHIATRIC ASSOCIATION. (1987). *Diagnostic and statistical manual of mental disorders* (3rd ed., rev.). Washington DC: Author.

AUGUST, G. J., STEWART, M. A., & TSAI, L. (1981). The incidence of cognitive disabilities in the siblings of autistic children. *British Journal of Psychiatry, 138,* 416–422.

AYRES, A. J. (1979). *Sensory integration and the child.* Los Angeles: Western Psychological Services.

BARON-COHEN, S. (1988). Social and pragmatic deficits in autism: Cognitive or affective? *Journal of Autism and Developmental Disorders, 18,* 379–402.

BARON-COHEN, S. (1989). The autistic child's theory of mind: A case of specific developmental delay. *Journal of Child Psychology and Psychiatry, 30,* 285–297.

BARON-COHEN, S., LESLIE, A., & FRITH, U. (1985). Does the autistic child have a "theory of mind"? *Cognition, 21,* 37–46.

BAUMAN, M., & KEMPER, T. L. (1985). Histoanatomic observations of the brain in early infantile autism. *Neurology, 35,* 866–874.

BETTELHEIM, B. (1959). Joey: A mechanical boy. *Scientific American, 200,* 116–127.

BOLTON, P., PICKLES, A., RUTTER, M., & BUTLER, L. (1989, August). *Fragile X and autism.* Paper presented at the First World Congress on Psychiatric Genetics, Churchill College, Cambridge, England.

BOLTON, P., & RUTTER, M. (1990). Genetic influences in autism. *International Review in Psychiatry, 2,* 67–80.

BOWMAN, E. (1988). Asperger syndrome and autism: The case for a connection. *British Journal of Psychiatry, 152,* 377–382.

BRYSON, S., CLARK, B., & SMITH, I. (1988). First report of a Canadian epidemiological study of autistic syndromes. *Journal of Child Psychology and Psychiatry and Allied Disciplines, 29,* 433–445.

BURD, L., FISHER, W., & KERBESHIAN, J. (1987). A prevalence study of pervasive developmental disorders in North Dakota. *Journal of the American Academy of Child and Adolescent Psychiatry, 26,* 700–703.

CAMPBELL, M., DEUTSCH, S. I., PERRY, R., WOLSKY, B. B., & PALIJ, M. (1986). Short-term efficacy and safety of fenfluramine in hospitalized preschool-age autistic children: An open study. *Psychopharmacology Bulletin, 22,* 141–147.

CARAPARULO, B. K., COHEN, D. J., ROTHMAN, S. L., YOUNG, J. G., KATZ, J. D., SHAYWITZ, S. E., & SHAYWITZ, B. A. (1981). Computerized tomographic brain scanning in children with developmental neuropsychiatric disorders. *Journal of the American Academy of Child Psychiatry, 20,* 338–357.

CIALDELLA, P., & MAMELLE, M. (1989). An epidemiological study of autism in a French department (Rhone): A research note. *Journal of Child Psychology and Psychiatry and Allied Disciplines, 30,* 165–175.

CHURCHILL, D. (1972). The relationship of infantile autism and early childhood schizophrenia to developmental language disorders of childhood. *Journal of Autism and Childhood Schizophrenia, 2,* 182–197.

COHEN, D. J., PAUL, R., & VOLKMAR, F. R. (1987). Issues in the classification of pervasive developmental disorders and associated conditions. In D. J. Cohen, A. M. Donnellan, and R. Paul (Eds.), *Handbook of autism and pervasive developmental disorders* (pp. 20–40). New York: Wiley.

COHEN, I. L., SUDHALTER, V., PFADT, A., JENKINS, E. C., & BROWN, T. (1991). Why are autism and the fragile-X syndrome associated? Conceptual and methodological issues. *American Journal of Human Genetics, 48,* 195–202.

CORBETT, J. (1976). Medical management. In L. Wing (Ed.), *Early childhood autism* (2nd ed., pp. 271–286). Oxford: Pergamon.

COURCHESNE, E. (1987). A neurophysiological view of autism. In E. Schopler & G. B. Mesibov (Eds.), *Neurobiological issues in autism: Current issues in autism* (pp. 285–324). New York: Plenum.

COURCHESNE, E. (1991). Neuroanatomic imaging in autism. *Pediatrics, 87* (Suppl. 2), 781–790.

COURCHESNE, E., YENG-COURCHESNE, R., PRESS, G. A., HESSELINK, J. R., & JERNIGAN, T. L. (1988). Hypoplasia of cerebellar verbal lobules VI and VII in autism. *New England Journal of Medicine, 318,* 1349–1354.

CORBETT, J., HARRIS, R., TAYLOR, R., & TRIMBLE, M. (1977). Progressive disintegrative psychosis of childhood. *Journal of Child Psychology and Psychiatry, 18,* 211–219.

DAMASIO, A. R., & MAURER, R. G. (1978). A neurological model for childhood autism. *Archives of Neurology, 35,* 777–786.

DAMASIO, H., MAURER, R. G., DAMASIO, A. R., & CHUI, H. C. (1980). Computerized tomographic scan findings in patients with autistic behavior. *Archives of Neurology, 37,* 504–510.

DELACATO, C. (1974). *The ultimate stranger: The autistic child.* Garden City, NY: Doubleday.

DELONG, G., & DWYER, J. (1988). Correlation of family history with specific autistic subgroups: Asperger's syndrome and bipolar affective disease. *Journal of Autism and Developmental Disorders, 18,* 593–600.

DEMYER, M. K. (1976). Motor, perceptual-motor, and intellectual disabilities of autistic children. In L. Wing (Ed.), *Early childhood autism* (2nd ed., pp. 169–193). Oxford: Pergamon.

DEMYER, M. K., HINGTGEN, J. N., & JACKSON, R. K. (1981). Infantile autism reviewed: A decade of research. *Schizophrenia Bulletin, 7,* 388–451.

DEMYER, M., PONTIUS, W., NORTON, J., BARTON, S., ALLEN, J., & STEELE, R. (1972). Parental practices and innate activity in normal, autistic, and brain-damaged infants. *Journal of Autism and Childhood Schizophrenia, 2,* 49–66.

DEYKIN, E. Y., & MacMAHON, B. (1979). The incidence of seizures among children with autistic symptoms. *American Journal of Psychiatry, 136,* 1310–1312.

DEYKIN, E. Y., & MacMAHON, B. (1980). Pregnancy, delivery, and neonatal complications among autistic children. *American Journal of Diseases of Children, 134,* 860–864.

EDLEMAN, G. (1987). *Neural Darwinism. The theory of neuronal group selection.* New York: Basic Books.

FEIN, D., HUMES, M., KAPLAN, E., LUCCI, D., & WATERHOUSE, L. (1984). The question of left hemisphere dysfunction in infantile autism. *Psychological Bulletin, 95,* 258–281.

FEIN, D., PENNINGTON, B., MARKOWITZ, P., BRAVERMAN, M., & WATERHOUSE, L. (1986). Toward a neuro-psychological model of infantile autism: Are the social deficits primary? *Journal of the American Academy of Child Psychiatry, 25,* 198–212.

FERSTER, C. B. (1961). Positive reinforcement and behavioral deficits of autistic children. *Child Development, 32,* 437–456.

FOLSTEIN, S. E., & PIVEN, J. (1991). Etiology of autism: Genetic influences. *Pediatrics, 87* (Suppl. 2), 767–773.

FOLSTEIN, S., & RUTTER, M. (1977). Infantile autism: A genetic study of 21 twin pairs. *Journal of Child Psychology and Psychiatry, 18,* 297–321.

FOLSTEIN, S., & RUTTER, M. (1987). Autism: Familial aggregation and genetic implications. In E. Schopler and G. B. Mesibov (Eds.), *Neurobiological issues in autism* (pp. 83–104). New York: Plenum.

FRITH, U. (1989). *Autism: Explaining the enigma.* Oxford: Basil Blackwell.

GALLAGHER, B. J., JONES, B. J., & BYRNE, M. M. (1990). A national survey of mental health professionals concerning the causes of early infantile autism. *Journal of Clinical Psychology, 46,* 934–939.

GARFIN, D. G., & LORD, C. (1986). Communication as a social problem in autism. In E. Schopler & G. B. Mesibov (Eds.), *Social behavior in autism* (pp. 133–152). New York: Plenum.

GILLBERG, C. (1984). Infantile autism and other childhood psychoses in a Swedish urban region: Epidemiological aspects. *Journal of Child Psychology and Psychiatry and Allied Disciplines, 25,* 35–43.

GILLBERG, C. (1988). The neurobiology of infantile autism. *Journal of Child Psychology and Psychiatry, 29,* 257–266.

GILLBERG, C. (1989). The role of endogenous opioids in autism and possible relationships to clinical features. In L. Wing (Ed.), *Aspects of autism: Biological research* (pp. 31–37). London: Gaskell/The National Autistic Society.

GILLBERG, C. (1990a). Autism and pervasive developmental disorders. *Journal of Child Psychology and Psychiatry, 31,* 99–119.

GILLBERG, C. (1990b). CSF beta-endorphins in child neuropsychiatric disorders. *Brain and Development, 12,* 88–92.

GILLBERG, C. (1991). Outcome in autism and autistic-like conditions. *Journal of the American Academy of Child and Adolescent Psychiatry, 30,* 375–382.

GILLBERG, C., EHLERS, S., SCHAUMAN, H., JAKOBSSON, G., BAHLGREN, S. O., LINDBLOM, R., BAGENHOLM, A., TJUUS, T., & BLIDNER, E. (1990). Autism under age 3 years: A clinical study of 28 cases referred for autistic symptoms in infancy. *Journal of Child Psychology and Psychiatry, 31,* 921–934.

GILLBERG, C., & GILLBERG, I. (1983). Infantile autism: A total population study of reduced optimality in the pre-, peri-, and neonatal period. *Journal of Autism and Developmental Disorders, 13,* 153–166.

GILLBERG, C., & STEFFENBURG, S. (1987). Outcome and prognostic factors in infantile autism and similar conditions. *Journal of Autism and Developmental Disorders, 17,* 271–285.

GILLBERG, C., & STEFFENBURG, S. (1989). Autistic behavior in Moebius syndrome. *Acta Paediatrica Scandinavica, 78,* 314–316.

GILLBERG, C., STEFFENBURG, S., & SCHAUMANN, H. (1991). Is autism more common now than 10 years ago? *British Journal of Psychiatry, 158,* 403–409.

GILLBERG, C., & SVENDSEN, P. (1983). Childhood psychosis and computed tomographic brain scan findings. *Journal of Autism and Developmental Disorders, 13,* 19–32.

GILLBERG, C., & WAHLSTROM, J. (1985). Chromosome abnormalities in infantile autism and other childhood psychoses: A population study of 66 cases. *Developmental Medicine and Child Neurology, 27,* 293–304.

GILLBERG, I., & GILLBERG, C. (1989). Asperger syndrome—some epidemiological considerations: A research note. *Journal of Child Psychology and Psychiatry, 30,* 631–638.

GOODMAN, R. (1989). Infantile autism: A syndrome of multiple primary deficits? *Journal of Autism and Developmental Disorders, 19,* 409–424.

HERMELIN, B., & O'CONNOR, N. (1970). *Psychological experiments with autistic children* (pp. 283–310). Oxford: Pergamon.

HERMELIN, B., & O'CONNOR, N. (1985). Logico-affective states and nonverbal language. In E. Schopler & G. B. Mesibov (Eds.), *Communication problems in autism* (pp. 283–310). New York: Plenum.

HITZING, W. (1987). Community living alternatives for persons with autism and related severe behavioral problems. In D. J. Cohen, A. M. Donnellan, & R. Paul (Eds.), *Handbook of autism and pervasive developmental disorders* (pp. 396–417). New York: Wiley.

HO, H., & KALOUSEK, D. (1989). Brief report: Fragile X syndrome in autistic boys. *Journal of Autism and Developmental Disorders, 19,* 343–347.

HOBSON, R. P. (1989). Beyond cognition: A theory of autism. In G. Dawson (Ed.), *Autism: New perspectives on diagnosis, nature and treatment* (pp. 22–48). New York: Guilford.

HOBSON, R., OUTSON, J., & LEE, A. (1988). Emotion recognition in autism: Coordinating faces and voices. *Psychological Medicine, 18,* 911–923.

HOSHINO, Y., KANEKO, M., KUMASHIRO, H., VOLKMAR, F. R., & COHEN, D. J. (1987). Clinical features of autistic children with setback course in their infancy. *Japanese Journal of Psychiatry and Neurology, 41,* 237–246.

HOWLIN, P. (1978). The assessment of social behavior. In M. Rutter & E. Schopler (Eds.), *Autism: A reappraisal of concepts and treatment* (pp. 63–69). New York: Plenum.

HOWLIN, P. (1986). An overview of social behavior in autism. In E. Schopler & G. B. Mesibov (Eds.), *Social behavior in autism* (pp. 103–132). New York: Plenum.

HUNT, A., & DENNIS, J. (1987). Psychiatric disorder among children with tuberous sclerosis. *Developmental Medicine and Child Neurology, 29,* 190–198.

JANICKI, M. P., LUBIN, R. A., & FRIEDMAN, E. (1983). Variations in characteristics and service needs of persons with autism. *Journal of Autism & Developmental Disorders, 13,* 73–85.

KANNER, L. (1943). Autistic disturbances of affective contact. *The Nervous Child, 2,* 217–250.

KANNER, L. (1949). Problems of nosology and psychodynamics in early infantile autism. *American Journal of Orthopsychiatry, 19,* 416–426.

KANNER, L. (1971). Follow-up of 11 autistic children originally seen in 1943. *Journal of Autism and Childhood Schizophrenia, 1,* 119–145.

KINSBOURNE, M. (1980). Do repetitive movement patterns in children and animals serve a dearousing function? *Journal of Developmental and Behavioral Pediatrics, 1,* 39–42.

KINSBOURNE, M. (1987). Cerebral-brainstem relations in infantile autism. In E. Schopler & G. B. Mesibov (Eds.), *Neurobiological issues in autism* (pp. 107–125). New York: Plenum.

LANGDELL, T. (1978). Recognition of faces: An approach to the study of autism. *Journal of Clinical Psychology and Psychiatry, 8,* 255–268.

LESLIE, A. (1987). Pretense and representation: The origins of "theory of mind." *Psychological Review, 94,* 412–426.

LETTICK, A. L. (1983). Benhaven. In E. Schopler & G. B. Mesibov (Eds.), *Autism in adolescents and adults* (pp. 355–379). New York: Plenum.

LITROWNIK, A. J., & McINNIS, E. T. (1982). Cognitive and perceptual deficits in autistic children: Model of information processing. In J. Steffen & P. Karoly (Eds.), *Autism and severe psychopathology* (pp. 103–158). Lexington, MA: D. C. Heath.

LOCKYEAR, L., & RUTTER, M. (1970). A five to fifteen year follow-up study of infantile psychosis: IV. Patterns of cognitive ability. *British Journal of Social and Clinical Psychology, 9,* 152–163.

LORD, C. (1984). The development of peer relations in children with autism. In F. J. Morrison, C. Lord, & D. P. Keating (Eds.), *Applied Developmental Psychology* (Vol. I, pp. 165–229). New York: Academic.

LOSCHE, G. (1990). Sensorimotor and action development in autistic children from infancy to early childhood. *Journal of Child Psychology and Psychiatry, 31,* 749–761.

LOTTER, V. (1966). Epidemiology of autistic conditions in young children: I. Prevalence. *Social Psychiatry, 1,* 124–137.

LOTTER, V. (1967). Epidemiology of autistic conditions in young children: II. Some characteristics of the parents and children. *Social Psychiatry, 1*, 163–173.

LOTTER, V. (1974). Social adjustment and placement of autistic children in Middlesex: A follow-up. *Journal of Autism and Childhood Schizophrenia, 4*, 11–32.

LOVAAS, I., KOEGEL, R., & SCHREIBMAN, L. (1979). Stimulus overselectivity in autism: A review of research. *Psychological Bulletin, 86*, 1236–1254.

LOVAAS, O., SCHREIBMAN, L., KOEGEL, R., & REHM, R. (1971). Selective responding by autistic children to multiple sensory input. *Journal of Abnormal Psychology, 77*, 211–222.

LOVELAND, K., & LANDRY, S. (1986). Joint attention and language in autism and developmental language delay. *Journal of Autism and Developmental Disorders, 16*, 333–349.

MAURER, R. G., & DAMASIO, H. (1982). Childhood autism from the viewpoint of behavioral neurology. *Journal of Autism and Developmental Disorders, 12*, 195–205.

McBRIDE, P. A., ANDERSON, G. M., HERTZIG, M. E., SWEENEY, J. A., KREAM, J., COHEN, D. J., & MANN, J. J. (1989). Serotonergic responsivity in male young adults with autistic disorder. *Archives of General Psychiatry, 46*, 213–221.

McGILLIVRAY, B. C., HERBST, D. S., DILL, F. J., SANDERCOCK, H. J., & TISCHLER, B. (1986). Infantile autism: An occasional manifestation of fragile (X) mental retardation. *American Journal of Medical Genetics, 23*, 353–358.

McHALE, S. M., SIMEONSSON, R. J., MARCUS, L. M., & OLLEY, J. F. (1980). The social and symbolic quality of autistic children's communication. *Journal of Autism and Developmental Disorders, 10*, 299–310.

MESIBOV, G. B. (1983). Current perspectives and issues in autism and adolescence. In E. Schopler & G. B. Mesibov (Eds.), *Autism in adolescents and adults* (pp. 37–53). New York: Plenum.

MINSHEW, N. J. (1991). Indices of neural function in autism: Clinical and biologic implications. *Pediatrics, 87* (Suppl. 2), 774–780.

MUNDY, P., SIGMAN, M., SHERMAN, T., & UNGERER, J. (1986). Defining the social deficit of autism: The contribution of nonverbal measures. *Journal of Child Psychology and Psychiatry, 27*, 657–669.

OLLEY, J. G. (1985). Social aspects of communication in children with autism. In E. Schopler and G. B. Mesibov (Eds.), *Communication problems in autism* (pp. 311–328). New York: Plenum.

ORNITZ, E. M. (1971). Childhood autism: A disorder of sensorimotor integration. In M. Rutter (Ed.), *Infantile autism: Concepts, characteristics and treatment* (pp. 50–68). London: Churchill-Livingstone.

ORNITZ, E. M. (1978). Neurophysiology of infantile autism. In M. Rutter & E. Schopler (Eds.), *Autism: A reappraisal of concepts and treatment* (pp. 117–139). New York: Plenum.

ORNITZ, E. M. (1983). The functional neuroanatomy of infantile autism. *International Journal of Neuroscience, 19*, 85–124.

ORNITZ, E. M. (1985). Neurophysiology of infantile autism. *Journal of the American Academy of Child Psychiatry, 24*, 251–262.

ORNITZ, E. M. (1989). Autism as the interface between sensory and information processing. In G. Dawson (Ed.), *Autism: Nature, diagnosis and treatment* (pp. 174–207). New York: Guilford.

OZONOFF, S., PENNINGTON, B. F., & ROGERS, S. J. (1990). Are there emotion perception deficits in young autistic children? *Journal of Child Psychology and Psychiatry, 31*, 343–361.

PAUL, R. (1987). Natural history. In D. J. Cohen, A. M. Donnellan, & R. Paul (Eds.), *Handbook of autism and pervasive developmental disorders* (pp. 121–132). New York: Wiley.

PAYTON, J. B., STEELE, M. W., WENGER, S. L., & MINSHEW, N. J. (1989). The fragile X marker and autism in perspective. *Journal of American Academy of Child and Adolescent Psychiatry, 28*, 417–421.

PERCY, A., GILLBERG, C., HAGBERG, B., WITT-ENGERSTROM, I. (1990). Rett syndrome and the autistic disorder. *Pediatric Neurology, 8*, 659–676.

PIVIN, J., TSAI, C. G., NEHME, E., COYLE, J., CHASE, G., & FOLSTEIN, S. (1991). Platelet serotonin, a possible marker for familial autism. *Journal of Autistic and Developmental Disorders, 21*, 51–59.

PRIOR, M. (1989). Biological factors in childhood autism. *NIMHANS Journal, 7*, 91–101.

PRIOR, M., DAHLSTROM, B., & SQUIRES, T. (1990). Autistic children's knowledge of thinking and feeling states in other people. *Journal of Child Psychology and Psychiatry, 31*, 587–601.

PRIOR, M. R., TRESS, B., HOFFMAN, W. L., & BOLDT, D. (1984). Computed tomographic study of children with classic autism. *Archives of Neurology, 41*, 482–484.

REICHLER, R. J., & LEE, E. M. C. (1987). Overview of biomedical issues in autism. In E. Schopler & G. B. Mesibov (Eds.), *Neurological issues in autism* (pp. 14–41). New York: Plenum.

RIMLAND, B. (1964). *Infantile autism: The syndrome and its implications for a neural theory of behavior.* Englewood Cliffs, NJ: Prentice Hall.

RITVO, E. R., FREEMAN, B. J., MASON-BROTHERS, A., MO, A., & RITVO, A. M. (1985). Concordance for the syndrome of autism in 40 pairs of afflicted twins. *American Journal of Psychiatry, 43*, 74–77.

RITVO, E., FREEMAN, B., PINGREE, C., MASON-BROTHERS, A., JORDE, O. L., JENSON, W., McMAHON, W., PETERSEN, P., MO, A., & RITVO, A. (1989). The UCLA–University of Utah epidemiologic survey of autism: Prevalence. *American Journal of Psychiatry, 146*, 194–199.

RITVO, E. R., FREEMAN, B. J., YUWILER, A., GELLER, E., SCHROTH, P., YOKOTA, A., MASON-BROTHERS, A., AUGUST, G. J., KLYKYLO, W., LEVENTHAL, B., LEWIS, K., PIGGOTT, L., REAL-MUTTO, G., STUBB, E. G., & UMANSKY, R. (1986). Fenfluramine treatment of autism: UCLA collaborative study of 81 patients at nine medical centers. *Psychopharmacology Bulletin, 22*, 133–140.

RITVO, E. R., SPENCE, M. A., FREEMAN, B. J., MASON-BROTHERS, A., MO, A., & MARAZITA, M. L. (1985). Evidence for autosomal recessive inheritance in 46 families with multiple incidence of autism. *American Journal of Psychiatry, 142*, 187–192.

RUMSEY, J. M., RAPAPORT, J. L., & SCEERY, W. R. (1985). Autistic children as adults: Psychiatric, social, and behavioral outcomes. *Journal of American Academy of Child and Adolescent Psychiatry, 24*, 465–473.

RUTTER, M. (1968). Concepts of autism: A review of research. *Journal of Child Psychology and Psychiatry and Allied Disciplines, 9*, 1–25.

RUTTER, M. (1970). Autistic children: Infancy to adulthood. *Seminars in Psychiatry, 2*, 435–450.

RUTTER, M. (1983). Cognitive deficits in the pathogenesis of autism. *Journal of Child Psychology and Psychiatry, 24*, 513–531.

RUTTER, M., & GARMEZY, N. (1983). Developmental psychopathology. In E. M. Hetherington (Ed.), *Socialization, personality and social development. Vol. 4, Mussen's handbook of child psychology* (4th ed.) (pp. 775–911). New York: Wiley.

RUTTER, M., & SCHOPLER, E. (1987). Autism and pervasive developmental disorders: Concepts and diagnostic issues. *Journal of Autism and Developmental Disorders, 17*, 159–186.

SCHREIBMAN, L., & CHARLOP, M. (1987). Autism. In V. B. Van Hasselt & M. Hersen (Eds.), *Psychological evaluation of the developmentally and physically disabled*. New York: Plenum.

SIGMAN, M., & MUNDY, P. (1984). Attachment behaviors in autistic children. *Journal of Autism and Developmental Disorders, 14*, 231–244.

SIGMAN, M., UNGERER, J. A., MUNDY, P., & SHERMAN, T. (1987). Cognition in autistic children. In D. J. Cohen, A. M. Donnellan, & R. Paul (Eds.). *Handbook of autism and pervasive developmental disorders* (pp. 384–395). New York: Wiley.

SIMONSON, L. R., & SIMONSON, S. M. (1987). Residential programming at Benhaven. In D. J.

COHEN, A. M. DONELLAN, & R. PAUL (Eds.), *Handbook of autism and pervasive developmental disorders* (pp. 384–395). New York: Wiley.

SMALLEY, S. L., ASARNOW, R. L., & SPENCE, M. A. (1988). Autism and genetics: A decade of research. *Archives of General Psychiatry, 45*, 958–961.

SPENCE, M. A. (1976). Genetic studies. In E. Ritvo (Ed.), *Autism: Diagnosis, current research and management* (pp. 169–174). New York: Halstead-Wiley.

STEFFENBURG, S., & GILLBERG, C. (1986). Autism and autistic-like conditions in Swedish rural and urban areas: A population study. *British Journal of Psychiatry, 149*, 81–87.

STEINHAUSEN, J., GOBEL, D., BREINLINGER, M., & WOHLLEBEN, B. (1986). *Journal of the American Academy of Child Psychiatry, 25*, 186–189.

STERNBERG, R. J. (1985). A unified theoretical perspective on autism. In D. J. Cohen & A. M. Donnellan (Eds.), *Handbook of autism and pervasive developmental disorders* (pp. 690–696). New York: Wiley.

STUBBS, E. G., RITVO, E. R., & MASON-BROTHERS, A. (1985). Autism and shared parental HLA antigens. *Journal of the American Academy of Child Psychiatry, 24*, 182–185.

SUGIYAMA, T., & ABE, T. (1989). The prevalence of autism in Nagoya, Japan: A total population study. *Journal of Autism and Developmental Disorders, 19*, 87–96.

SUTHERLAND, B. S., BERRY, H. K., & SHIRKEY, H. C. (1960). A syndrome of phenylketonuria with normal intelligence and behavioral disturbances. *Journal of Pediatrics, 57*, 521–525.

TAFT, L. T., & COHEN, H. J. (1971). Hypsarrhythmia and infantile autism. *Journal of Autism and Childhood Schizophrenia, 1*, 327–336.

TANOE, Y., ODA, S., ASANO, F., & KAWASHIMA, K. (1988). Epidemiology of infantile autism in southern Ibarki, Japan: Differences in prevalences in birth cohorts. *Journal of Autism and Developmental Disorders, 18*, 155–166.

TINBERGEN, E., & TINBERGEN, N. (1972). Early childhood autism: An ethological approach. In *Advances in ethology, 10* (Supplement to *Journal of Comparative Ethology*), 9–53.

TREFFERT, D. (1970). Epidemiology of infantile autism. *Archives of General Psychiatry, 22*, 431-438.

TSAI, L. Y., TSAI, M. C., & AUGUST, G. J. (1985). Brief report: Implications of EEG diagnoses in the subclassification of infantile autism. *Journal of Autism and Developmental Disorders, 15*, 339–344.

TYMCHUK, A., SIMMONS, J., & NEAFSEY, S. (1977). Intellectual characteristics of adolescent childhood psychotics with high verbal ability. *Journal of Mental Deficiency Research, 21*, 133–138.

VOLKMAR, F. R. (1987). Social development. In D. J. Cohen, A. M. Donnellan, & R. Paul (Eds.), *Handbook of autism and pervasive developmental disorders* (pp. 41–60). New York: Wiley.

VOLKMAR, F. R., & NELSON, D. S. (1990). Seizure disorders in autism. *Journal of the American Academy of Child and Adolescent Psychiatry, 1*, 127–129.

WALDO, M., COHEN, D., CAPARULO, E., YOUNG, J., PARICHARD, J., & SHAYWITZ, B. (1978). EEG profiles of neuropsychiatrically disturbed children. *Journal of the American Academy of Child Psychiatry, 17*, 656–670.

WARREN, R. P., COLE, P., ODELL, D., PINGREE, C. B., WARREN, W. L., WHITE, E., YONK, J., & SINGH, V. K. (1990). Detection of maternal antibodies in infantile autism. *Journal of the American Academy of Child Psychiatry, 29*, 874–877.

WING, L. (1983). Social and interpersonal needs. In E. Schopler & G. B. Mesibov (Eds.), *Autism in adolescents and adults* (pp. 337–354). New York: Plenum.

WING, L., & GOULD, J. (1979). Severe impairments of social interaction and associated abnormalities in children: Epidemiology and classification. *Journal of Autism and Developmental Disorders, 9*, 11–30.

WING, L., GOULD. J., YEATES, S., & BRIERLY, L. (1977). Symbolic play in severely mentally retarded and autistic children. *Journal of Child Psychology and Psychiatry, 18*, 167–178.

WING, L., YEATES, S. R., BRIERLY, L. M., & GOULD, J. (1976). The prevalence of early childhood autism: Comparison of administrative and epidemiological studies. *Psychological Medicine, 6*, 89–100.

YOUNG, J. G., KAVANAGH, M. E., ANDERSON, G. M., SHAYWITZ, B. A., & COHEN, D. J. (1982). Clinical neurochemistry of autism and associated disorders. *Journal of Autism and Developmental Disorders, 12*, 147–165.

YUWILER, A., GELLER, E., & RITVO, E. (1985). Biochemical studies in autism. In A. Lajtha (Ed.), *Handbook of neurochemistry: Pathological neurochemistry* (2nd ed.) (pp. 671–678). New York: Plenum.

ZAHNER, G., & PAULS, D. (1987). Epidemiological surveys of infantile autism. In D. Cohen, A. Donnellan, & R. Paul (Eds.), *Handbook of autism and pervasive developmental disorders* (pp. 199–207). New York: Wiley.

ZASLOW, R. W., & BREGER, L. (1969). A theory and treatment of autism. In L. Breger (Ed.), *Clinical-cognitive psychology*. Englewood Cliffs, NJ: Prentice-Hall.

CHAPTER 4

Autism, Facilitated Communication, and Future Directions

John W. Jacobson
NEW YORK STATE OFFICE OF MENTAL RETARDATION
AND DEVELOPMENTAL DISABILITIES

Michael Eberlin
DEVELOPMENTAL DISABILITIES INSTITUTE

James A. Mulick
THE OHIO STATE UNIVERSITY

Allen A. Schwartz
NEW YORK STATE OFFICE OF MENTAL RETARDATION
AND DEVELOPMENTAL DISABILITIES

Joseph Szempruch
ROME (NEW YORK) DEVELOPMENTAL DISABILITIES
SERVICES OFFICE

Douglas L. Wheeler
O. D. HECK/ELEANOR ROOSEVELT DEVELOPMENTAL
SERVICES AUTISM PROGRAM

Language function has been a central concern in the treatment of autism. Not only has disordered language been considered a diagnostic hallmark of autism (American Psychiatric Association, 1987; Wing, 1976), but improved language function portends increased opportunities for functional skill development and, in particular, offers a modality for interpersonal skill enhancement. In this chapter, we will review the current context of services for people with developmental disabilities, summarize new perspectives on language development, and critique the most recent and fashionable zeitgeist. In great part, this will involve discussing a technique known as "facilitated communication" (FC) and consideration of relevant research.

The Context of Developmental Disabilities Services

The field of developmental disabilities has some important features that distinguish it from other fields of social and human services. Some of these characteristics involve the nature of the disabilities present among people who are served; others involve the qualities and motivations of the people—staff and professionals—who serve these individuals. A dominant characteristic of people diagnosed with mental retardation, or autism and mental retardation, is that they generally learn at rates that are appreciably slower than those of the average individual. In fact, this characteristic can be used to define mental retardation from the standpoint of applied behavior analysis (Bijou & Dunitz-Johnson, 1981). Consequently, intensive and precise instruction is necessary to help these people learn how to communicate and function more independently. Such instruction is time-consuming, slow-paced, highly individualized, and repetitive because quality instruction must, of necessity, be tailored to the learning style of the person being instructed.

At the same time, it is acknowledged that mental retardation has many, many etiologies, and that there are a variety of ways in which individuals come to function in a manner that is diagnosed as indicating the presence of mental retardation as a chronic condition. The etiologies of autism remain more poorly understood than those of mental retardation, and much less is known about the nature of autism itself than about the nature of mental retardation. Past research, although clearly providing a wealth of information about general and specific characteristics of the behavior (and adaptation) of people with autism, has not uncovered the neurological factors that result in autism.

This is not to suggest that past research has been of no value. Extensive knowledge of the condition has evolved with continuing study, as we will show elsewhere in this chapter. Studies have indicated that (a) although behavioral and social growth can be expected for most people with mental retardation and autism, appropriately developed and implemented training for these people will result in relatively slow progress (much effort is required to achieve small, albeit important, improvements in skills); and (b) critical gaps exist in the understanding of the conditions of mental retardation (in specific cases) and autism.

Added to these realities is the consideration that the field of developmental disabilities has evidenced incredible dynamism of philosophical change during the past 25 years. Practices that were considered ideal at one time, such as group community living, have often been accepted as the state of the art very rapidly, only to be outmoded as new concepts of care have overtaken them. As improved practices are achieved, standards and aspirations are set higher, escalating the expectations of consumers, parents, professionals, and program administrators.

Implications for Therapists

The lack of a precise and fully developed understanding of autism and related conditions, coupled with volatile philosophical dynamics, has important implications for staff and professionals working in the field of developmental disabilities. Professional conduct, terms used in conversation, valuation of treatment goals, and methods of treatment and training are continuously subjected to scrutiny not only with regard to technical merit, but also for philosophical propriety. Unfortunately, like a large segment of the American population, many people who work in the field of developmental disabilities are relatively uninformed about the nature, strengths, and limits of science and scientific methods (Blackmore, 1992; Miller, 1992). For example, social scientists attribute small but steady increases in the share of the population believing in paranormal phenomena (e.g., telepathy) to relative ignorance of science (Frazier, 1992; Lett, 1992), and indeed, some parents have attributed paranormal abilities to their children with autism (McMullen, 1991). In the absence of the ability to fully understand and benefit directly from scientific reports, many staff members and professionals must rely extensively on secondhand "expert" perspectives on many practice issues.

Existing knowledge gaps make it possible for experts to set forth highly speculative, but essentially plausible, explanations of the everyday behavior of people with mental retardation and autism. When, however, professionals act on what are basically commonsense notions that have not been adequately proven, they run the danger of being ineffective (by using an ineffective treatment), doing harm (through forgoing use of an established and effective treatment), or concluding wrongly that a treatment is effective when it isn't. Rapidly shifting sands of philosophical sentiment, intense motivation of staff members to produce meaningful improvement in the skills and abilities of people with developmental disabilities, and lack of general comprehension of science increase the likelihood that some treatments may be adopted or overused when in fact their use is not well justified. This is certainly a possibility if a procedure has great face validity (i.e., meets the test of satisfying commonsense notions) (Jacobson & Mulick, 1991).

Lessons from the Past

If this perspective appears too extreme in its portrayal of the susceptibility of staff and professionals to poorly validated treatment practices, one needs only to consider the events of the past. Probably the most important treatment fad in the field of developmental disabilities in the past 30 years was "patterning" (Delacato, 1966; Doman, 1974). Patterning was a movement-based treatment intended to stimulate the adaptive and intellectual development of people with developmental disabilities through constant manual manipulation of their physical position. Patterning was time-consuming, expensive, long-term, and continuous and (after hopeful adoption by thousands of families and many practitioners) ultimately found to be of no appreciable benefit.

At the same time, instruction based on principles of behavior analysis and learning was demonstrating widespread success. Given the right circumstances, people with mental retardation could learn a good deal more than previously expected. Despite these promising results, behavioral approaches were forgone as people were put through repetitive movement exercises for days, weeks, even years on end. If, however, the leap had not been made precipitously from theory to practice, and if appropriate and illuminating quantitative research had been conducted, patterning would not have become so widely adopted. Unfortunately, treatments that have some characteristics of fads seem to remain all too common today in developmental disabilities and other human services. Possibly the greatest failure in preparing staff and professionals for careers in developmental disabilities services lies in teaching them adequately about the important promising therapeutic efforts of the past and where these efforts fell short of hopes and expectations.

The philosophical dynamism of recent times also increases the likelihood that unjustified or ineffective practices may be adopted. For example, current beliefs emphasize the appropriateness of involving people with severe disabilities in their own treatment and life planning. The presence of well-developed language skills makes it easier for people with disabilities to realize effective participation in the planning process. For people who have poorly developed language skills, however, the achievement of participation can be more difficult. Although parents or siblings can represent the interests of the individual in planning, clinical experience shows many instances when the basis for surrogate decision making is highly ambiguous. Obviously, in this climate, any treatment that appears to produce unexpected literacy among people with poorly developed language skills would be prone to uncritical and widespread acceptance. We suggest that this may be the case with facilitated communication.

Facilitated Communication as a Treatment Approach

Facilitated communication (FC) is a technique developed during the 1970s in Australia by Rosemary Crossley. Initially used primarily with individuals having cerebral palsy and motor disorders, this technique has recently become increasingly used in the treatment of communication disorders among people with autism, mental retardation, or both conditions (Biklen, 1991; Crossley & Remington-Gurney, 1992; Intellectual Disability Review Panel, 1989). Although the literature on FC emphasizes treatment of people with autism, large numbers of people with mental retardation who do not have autism also receive this treatment (Interdisciplinary Working Party, 1988). Recent publications confirm that this is a common practice in Australia (Crossley & Remington-Gurney, 1992).

Facilitated communication is defined as

a means by which many people with major speech difficulties type or point at letters on an alphabet board or typing device to convey their thoughts. It involves a facilitator who provides physical support to help stabilize the arm, to isolate the index finger if necessary, to pull back the arm after each selection, to remind the individual to maintain focus, and to offer emotional support and encouragement; the facilitator progressively phases out the physical support. (Biklen, 1992c, p. 243)

Crossley and Remington-Gurney (1992) have stressed that facilitated communication was developed for the "purpose of teaching the hand skills needed to use communication aids effectively to individuals whose severe communication impairment (SCI) is compounded by impaired hand function" (p. 29). They identify hand-use problems as including poor eye-hand coordination, low muscle tone, high muscle tone, index finger isolation and extension problems, perseveration, impulsivity, tremor, radial/ulnar muscle instability, initiation problems, impaired proximal stability, reduced proprioception, using both hands for a task requiring only one, and lack of confidence (Crossley & Remington-Gurney, 1992). Clearly, factors other than manual dexterity (e.g., sensory processes, motivation, and disinhibition) are considered germane in the clinical decision to attempt FC as a preferred treatment.

Biklen (1991) delineates 25 principal elements, principles, or processes that are central to the performance of FC training. Most of these are ramifications or elaborations of the definition presented by Biklen (1992c). Some do bear specific mention, however. First, facilitators are advised not to test individuals for competence in a formal manner that would be challenging to them, thereby undermining their confidence and resulting in test results that severely underestimate their actual performance ability.

According to Biklen, Morton, Gold, Berrigan, and Swaminathan (1992), evidence that facilitated communications are genuine is based upon these findings:

1. Style, speed, and accuracy of students' fine motor control movement to the letters or keys are fairly constant across facilitators.
2. Individuals make typographical errors that are unique to them. Some individuals fairly consistently hit more than one key at a time when typing.
3. Many individuals produce phonetic or invented spellings that are unique to them and do not appear in the work of others, despite the fact that several individuals sometimes share a common facilitator.
4. Some individuals type phrases or sentences that are unusual and would not be expected from the facilitators.
5. Individuals sometimes produce content that is not known to the facilitator.
6. Through facilitated communication, individuals reveal their personalities. (pp. 19–20)

We will comment on each of these sources of confirmation for the validity of FC in a later section of this chapter. Both Crossley and Remington-Gurney (1992) and Biklen (1992c) have stipulated further that evidence of validation is provided by the person's progress in producing more extensive and varied FC messages, doing so with more people in a wider range of contexts, and becoming less dependent upon physical support.

A second factor expected to be especially important in practical terms is that the ability to communicate orally and, in fact, to engage in skilled voluntary movements, is inhibited by the presence of global apraxia. In this context, *apraxia* is understood to be a condition that prevents integration of motor routines such that it results in an inability to speak or difficulty in speech and in awkwardness of movement, specifically as it relates to the ability of a person to initiate a movement. Limited apraxias and adult traumatic onset apraxias have been discussed in some detail by Luria (1980) and Heilman and Gonzalez-Roth (1985), respectively. Speech impairments of people with autism are said to be evinced by word-finding difficulties (Biklen, 1992; Crossley & Remington-Gurney, 1992; DEAL Communication Centre, 1992b). According to

Crossley and Remington-Gurney (1992), word-finding problems "were generally less severe in clients' written language than in the same clients' spoken language" (p. 37). Crossley (1992) and DEAL (1992a) more specifically refer to noun-finding problems, to which the findings of Szempruch and Jacobson's (1992) message-passing study of FC, and possibly of the Wheeler et al. (in press) experimental study (both discussed later in this chapter) have also been attributed (R. Crossley, personal communication, October 5, 1992).

A third process that is important is the provision of a highly supportive context. Biklen (1992c) stresses that prior to attempting FC, "the reading abilities and thinking abilities undoubtedly were already present" (p. 244). "By saying that the person with autism has a problem with praxis we do not presume a deficit in understanding, but rather in expression (speaking or enacting words or ideas)" (Biklen, 1991, p. 303). Therefore, FC is understood to be a means of accessing the existing language abilities in people with autism or other disabilities, rather than a means of teaching language. Contrasting with this perspective is the statement that "facilitated communication is, as its name implies, a training method" (DEAL, 1992a). Acting in an accepting, positive, and supportive manner with the person with autism helps establish a context that is motivating for the person. In addition, it indicates that, despite past failures to communicate, communication is possible and expected (Kurtz, 1992).

The above provides a brief description of some aspects of FC. Interested readers are referred to Biklen (1991, 1992a, 1992b, 1992c, 1992d), Biklen and Schubert (1991), Biklen, Morton, Gold, Berrigan, and Swaminathan (1992), Biklen et al. (1991), Crossley (1992), and Crossley and Remington-Gurney (1992) for further details. Biklen (1992a) describes the major features of the FC process as involving physical support, initial training and introduction, maintaining focus, avoiding testing for competence, generalizing, and fading. Initial training proceeds from simple key presses in response to verbal requests, through "set work," to eventual spontaneous conversational interactions.

There is no apparent pace of process. Some people evidence literacy upon initial assessment (Biklen et al., 1992d; Crossley, 1992). However, "facilitators reported that they usually had to go through a process lasting from an hour to several weeks or even months to move individuals from structured work to open-ended typed discourse" (Biklen, 1992d, p. 9). Crossley and Remington-Gurney (1992) report that achievement of discourse can occur in from six months to six years, and DEAL (1992a) states, "Training in non-speech communication takes time—6 years is the time suggested for basic competence to be achieved in communication aid use" (p. 49). In contrast, Biklen et al. (1991) report that one student began open-ended discourse after five months of single-word responses and statements. Biklen and Schubert (1991) present information on 21 students, all with autism, with 19 requiring support at wrist or hand to communicate, but it is unclear how long each had been taking part in FC.

Thus, at this time, qualitative reports have described unexpected literacy and language progress by people with autism who take part in FC. However, the degree of language ability implied by these individuals' initial or longer-term typing is inconsistent with performance that would be expected, based on their past language performance. These factors have stimulated interest in this area of study on the part of a small number of other researchers. Further interest has been fueled by extremely rapid proliferation of the use of FC in settings serving people with mental retardation or autism and popular acceptance of the treatment. These trends have been stimulated by the video media and businesses seeking profits (e.g., Anonymous, 1991, 1992a, 1992b; Bagan, 1992; Barron & Barron, 1992; Crestwood Company, 1992). As this brief review indicates, the assertions and contradictions of the Australian originators and the American purveyors of FC present sufficient grounds for serious research.

Recent Research on FC

In this section, we will present summaries of the quantitative studies of facilitated communication. Five studies conducted in Australia will be presented first. Four other studies have been submitted for peer-reviewed publication or publication as letters in journals. Although three of these studies were conducted in New York state, they were spontaneously and independently initiated by their respective principal investigators. Technical reports of each are available upon request to the authors.

Previous research.   The first five studies included work by the Interdisciplinary Working Party (1988), the Intellectual Disability Review Panel (1989), and Hudson, Melita, and Arnold (in press). The first two studies were summarized, from differing perspectives, by Biklen (1990) and Cummins and Prior (1992). The Interdisciplinary Working Party (1988) identified and verified instances where FC or similar techniques were being inappropriately employed. These involved individuals with paralysis or who were surviving injury in persistent vegetative states and were unable to make the types of movements required. That report concluded that "'assisted communication' as practiced and taught by D.C.C. (DEAL Communication Centre) personnel has led, on some occasions, to communications being imposed upon nonspeaking persons" (p. 60).

The report also presented a study conducted at another center (not DEAL), with other supervising personnel, where FC was in use. The study involved four students with cerebral palsy (or similar disorders) and suspected or psychometrically diagnosed mental retardation. In three experimental conditions, both student and facilitator were shown stimulus cards (test patterns) to be labeled or described. The student was presented with stimuli not seen by the facilitator, or the student and facilitator were shown different stimuli and were unable to see the other stimulus. The results reported were as follows:

1. When the material was seen by both the communication assistant and the student, the responses were always correct.
2. When the communication assistant did not see the material presented, the responses were mostly wrong and those correct occurred at below chance level.
3. When different material was presented to the student and the communication assistant, the response given by the student was the same as the correct answer expected from the material presented to the communication assistant on 28 out of 30 test trials. (Interdisciplinary Working Party, 1988, p. 80

Although the above report (cited as the Catanese study by Cummins & Prior, 1992) does not present full procedural details, its results are consistent with findings of other quantitative studies using similar methodologies. The significance of this study is that it provided a basis for identifying facilitator influence over participants' typed content. As Cummins and Prior (1992) have noted, in all instances where communications via FC were disputed, evidence showed that facilitators were influencing the content.

Research reported by the Intellectual Disability Review Panel (1989) was also reviewed by Cummins and Prior (1992), and, as in the instance of the Interdisciplinary Working Party (1988) report, the original report was available as well. One study involved three participants who were asked questions under four conditions: (a) facilitator and participant were asked the same question without headphones; (b) facilitator and participant were asked the same question, facilitator wearing headphones; (c) facilitator and participant were asked different questions, facilitator wearing headphones; (d) facilitator wore headphones with music screening conversation and the participant was asked questions.

Cummins and Prior (1992) consider the criterion used for correctness of response in this study to be too inclusive; that criterion was that the response must be "systematically relevant" to the question, as defined by the facilitator. The Intellectual Disability Review Panel (1989) concluded that the communication of one of three participants had been validated. However, we believe Cummins and Prior's (1992) reasoned reinterpretation of the data is more consistent with the results and with the presence of facilitator influence on FC content for all three participants.

A third study reported by the Review Panel involved message-passing. The participant received a gift in the absence of the facilitator and thereafter communicated the nature of the gift to the facilitator using FC. The study used participants selected by DEAL Communication Centre who were presumably among those people whom DEAL personnel expected to be able to perform the message-passing *and* who were willing to participate. All three participants were considered by the Review Panel to have validated their communications, and facilitator influence was not indicated. However, among the Review Panel's conclusions was that "some communications were valid and reliable through 'assisted communication' without influence by the assistant. On the other hand, some communications were influenced by the assistants" (Intellectual Disability Review Panel, 1989, p. 41).

In a fourth study, Hudson (1992) and Hudson et al. (in press) have reported on their findings on the communications of a person who was believed to have made allegations of abuse using FC. The results of psychometric measures that were administered separately from the validation procedure were consistent with participant intellectual functioning in the range of severe to profound mental retardation, and there was no mention of a diagnosis of autism. They used four conditions: (a) facilitator and participant were asked the same questions without headphones; (b) facilitator and participant were asked the same questions over headphones; (c) facilitator and participant were asked different questions over headphones; and (d) facilitator heard music over headphones and participant was asked questions over headphones.

In the first condition, 8 of 10 questions were answered correctly; in the second condition, 4 of 10.

Under the third condition, there were no correct responses to the participant's questions, and 4 of 10 "accurate" responses were to the facilitator's questions. Finally, there were no accurate responses under the fourth condition. These findings are similar to those reported in the Interdisciplinary Working Party (1988) report: only questions that were heard by the facilitator were answered correctly, including questions never heard by the participant.

In an extension of the Hudson et al. (in press) study, Moore, Donovan, Hudson, Dykstra, and Lawrence (under submission) report on eight additional cases of FC use. Subjects had participated in FC training for 17 to 33 months. None was able to demonstrate independent and valid communication via FC when their facilitator, who wore earphones with masking music, was unable to hear the question asked of the individual. Therefore, four of the five studies from Australia indicate facilitator influence, if not control, of FC typed content. As a result, it is not surprising that FC has not received general support from the professional human services community in Australia (Prior & Cummins, 1992).

The most recent research. Szempruch and Jacobson (1992) used a quasi-experimental message-passing procedure to assess the validity of the facilitated communications of people with mental retardation, a small number of whom were diagnosed with autism. In this procedure, a participant was shown the picture of a common object while his or her facilitator was out of the room. In addition, the object was identified to the participant verbally, and the participant was instructed to touch the picture, with physical assistance to do so if necessary. The facilitator was then allowed back into the room and permitted to assist the individual in communicating the identity or nature of the object that had been presented. During the 10 minutes provided for identifying the object, the person being evaluated was permitted to have the object presented a second time in the absence of the facilitator if he or she requested this via FC.

Although the participant did not need to use the correct term for the object, he or she did need to describe it in a manner that would enable an observer, other than the examiner who had presented the picture of the object, to correctly identify it. An observer was present for each trial; altogether, two different professionals served as observers. Three-trial blocks were conducted with each participant on two different days. The blocks were conducted in the participants' normal FC settings with their facilitators of choice. No special apparatus was used.

The 10 male and 13 female participants ranged from 21 to 75 years of age and were classified as having intellectual skills within the range of severe to profound mental retardation. They included people served by public and private agencies. Each participant was believed by facilitators to be validly engaging in simple or extended conversational interactions via FC. Informed consent was obtained for each participant as stipulated by the requirements of the agencies that served them.

No participant was able to label or describe any of the everyday objects shown to them. An important factor in this study was the inclusion of people with mental retardation who did not have a diagnosis of autism. There were no apparent quantitative or qualitative differences in participants' performance based on whether or not they had a diagnosis of autism.

The results of this evaluation process raise a number of concerns with respect to FC. Although no participant correctly identified an object, there were numerous instances in which erroneous objects or entire scenes were described in some detail. These included communications of a personal nature that were not relevant to the task. In addition to the obvious ethical considerations, this raises some very practical concerns regarding treatment when the person is participating in the individual program planning process via FC.

Several of the participants were able to correctly identify the objects to the examiner, either verbally or through pantomime, without the benefit of facilitation. Although at least one of the facilitators

indicated that an individual's verbal communication should be disregarded as the facilitated typing was really the valid communication, there were more instances in which the participants were able to communicate more accurately through verbalization or pantomime than through FC.

These findings raise serious concerns about the validity of these participants' facilitated communications, but one significant benefit of the FC process was evident. Both the observers and the examiner reported that the majority of participants seemed to greatly enjoy, and even look forward to, their FC sessions. Two of the facilitators, who were experienced therapists, indicated that they had found individuals who were responsive to FC despite their lack of participation in other therapies due to inattentiveness and behavior problems. The quality of the attention that the participants received from the therapists in this evaluation was observed to be somewhat unique in that it was individualized, involved physical proximity, and was characterized by apparently heightened expectations of individual performance on the part of the therapists.

The second study (Eberlin, McConnachie, Ibel, & Volpe, 1992) was conducted at a private agency that provides educational and habilitative services to children and adults with autism and other developmental disabilities. Twenty-one students aged 11-20 years participated. The experiment was designed to test hypotheses based on claims that autistic individuals show unexpected literacy and communication skills through the process of FC. Reliable diagnoses were established for all the students: 20 received a diagnosis of autistic disorder, and 1 a diagnosis of pervasive developmental disorder, according to DSM-III-R criteria (American Psychiatric Association, 1987). Recent psychological assessments employing standardized individual assessment instruments indicated a range of intellectual and adaptive functioning consistent with additional diagnoses of mild to profound mental retardation.

Ten facilitators were trained according to the guidelines produced and disseminated by Biklen and associates (e.g., Schubert, 1991). Training included a presentation of the philosophy underlying the FC technique and the necessity for assuming literacy is present in all students. In addition, procedures for working through Crossley's "communication ladder," set work, methods for determining handedness, optimal positioning, and level of physical assistance necessary for finger isolation were presented. Two individuals who were familiar to the students and experienced with FC provided ongoing supervision of facilitators and observation of FC sessions.

The vocabulary subtest of the *Stanford-Binet Intelligence Scale* (4th ed.) (Thorndike, Hagen, & Sattler, 1986) and a personal interview designed by the experimenters were administered at baseline, pretest, and posttest. The personal interview started with simple personal identification and preference questions and progressed to more complex questions regarding feeling states. Baseline testing was conducted prior to the students' exposure to FC. During baseline, the students used any and all communicative modalities in their repertoire to answer questions. A pretest was conducted the next day after 30 minutes of exposure to the Canon Communicator and FC process. During the pretest, students used FC exclusively. Posttest followed 40 half-hour training sessions that use the Canon Communicator and followed Crossley's communication ladder approach (Schubert, 1991). During pre- and posttest, the facilitator was screened from seeing pictorial stimuli or hearing test questions. This was accomplished by using a wooden T approximately 18 inches high and 36 inches wide and white noise (at 90 db measured on a C-scale) through stereo headphones. Training was carried out in an environmental context that was as similar as possible to the testing contexts.

To test for facilitator influence on facilitated responses, an alternative form of the personal interview and the *Expressive One-Word Vocabulary Test—Revised* (EOWVT-R) (Gardner, 1990) were administered after training, prior to the posttest. Alternative measures were used to prevent the facilitators from discovering the content of the dependent measures employed during posttest.

During administration of the alternative form of the interview and the EOWVT-R, the facilitator was not screened.

Some facilitators reported new and surprising communicative abilities for their students during training. However, no student showed unexpected literacy or communicative abilities at pretest or posttest. After 20 hours of training, only two students showed the ability to communicate via facilitation at or near their initial, nonfacilitated levels. It is noteworthy that these two students had typing or writing abilities *before* exposure to FC. Fifteen students could type only gibberish (i.e., random letters or perseverative patterns of letters, such as parts of the alphabet) at the screened posttest. Four students were able to type a correct response when asked, "Is your name _____? Type 'y' if your answer is yes and 'n' if your answer is no" at posttest, but not at pretest. Three of these students were able to answer this question verbally at baseline. The fourth reliably indicated yes or no with words and gestures as part of his observed communicative repertoire, but did not do so at baseline.

Comparisons between the screened posttest and the unscreened administration of the EOWVT-R and alternative form of the personal interview indicated that six of the facilitators unknowingly influenced the communicative output of the students they were facilitating. Nine students who worked with these facilitators answered more questions correctly when the facilitator was unscreened than when the facilitator was screened. Because the tasks were comparable in difficulty and content in the screened posttest and the unscreened test session, these facilitators apparently aided these students in responding accurately on the unscreened tasks.

Additional measures showed that the students in this study were highly cooperative with the testing procedures, countering claims by FC proponents that the act of testing inherently destroys a person's willingness to communicate (Biklen, 1990, 1992c). Specifically, at least 11 of the participants gave correct simple one-word responses verbally or with sign language during the FC posttest, but did not produce correct responses via facilitation. In addition, only 2 of the 84 testing sessions were terminated because of lack of cooperation with the assessment procedures.

The third study involved 12 people with autism who were served by the O. D. Heck Developmental Center Autism Program (in Schenectady, New York) and 9 people who provided FC support to them and worked at the program (Wheeler, Jacobson, Paglieri, & Schwartz, in press). The 12 individuals were selected because they were the most competent producers of FC in the program at the time. Specifically, all were reported by facilitators to be typing valid communications, including words, phrases, sentences, and extended conversation. The procedure consisted of three conditions, all involving showing pictures of everyday objects to the participants. Standard research randomization methods were used in the presentation of pictures.

In the first condition, only the people with autism (and not the facilitators) were shown a picture and asked to type out a label or description for the object shown, and they were provided with facilitation. In the second condition, participants were shown a picture (again, their facilitators were not shown the picture) and asked to type out a label or description for the object without facilitation or other physical contact. In the third condition, both the facilitators and participants were shown pictures. Neither group was able to see (as verified by review of videotapes) what picture the other had been shown; on one-half of the trials the pictures were the same, and on the other half the pictures were different. Facilitators were aware that their picture might be the same or different. Responses were coded as correct or incorrect based on independent reviews by panels of five judges, each panel consisting of four impartial professionals and each respective facilitator.

The findings showed that the participants were unable to produce correct labels or descriptions, by either typing independently or being facilitated, in the absence of a picture's being shown also to the facilitator. When the facilitator was shown a stimulus picture at the same time, the performance of 10 of 12 participants improved (two continued to label the pictures completely unsuccessfully). However, on trials when the facilitators and participants saw different cards, the only "correct" labels were for the cards shown to the facilitators, not for the cards shown to the participants. This finding demonstrated that facilitators were not only influencing (unknowingly) but, in fact, determining what was typed.

One unplanned but fortunate aspect of the study was that three facilitators were paired with two subjects each. Several variables were compared across these pairs and provided compelling evidence for facilitator influence. Rates of idiosyncratic word usage, occurrences of category responses and nonsense responses, and numbers of words and sentences were highly and significantly correlated across pairs of facilitators and participants, further validating facilitator influence or control.

There were other qualitative findings that bear mention. One very consistent observation was that facilitators stared continuously at the keyboard. In contrast, participants often were not looking at the keyboard during typing. This pattern was observed to be the norm. Second, at least three staff members involved with FC in the autism program reported what they referred to as "mind-reading." During facilitation, participants appeared to type out information that was so highly personal to their facilitator that the facilitator was shocked. Because facilitators were confident that they were not influencing the typing, they concluded that some telepathic phenomenon must have been occurring. Third, many of the center's staff involved with FC observed that facilitators often translate or decode the FC output immediately and with little apparent difficulty, even if the output is produced very rapidly on a letter board or contains a great number of excess spaces or characters, whereas others take much longer. In addition, other staff sometimes disagree about the content of the FC output. Trained facilitators explain ease of translation based on rapport and familiarity with the person's idiosyncracies. For all three phenomena, facilitator influence is a more plausible and more direct explanation.

In reacting to the findings of this study, Biklen (National Public Radio, 1992, September 28) stated:

> The study that was done in New York state was terribly flawed, most centrally in how it was designed. What it asked people to do was label pictures. Well, one of the things that we've discovered through the facilitated communications is that's probably the most difficult task that one could ask the person with autism [to do], given the kind of word retrieval or word finding problems that people have. They will go to label an object but give it a wrong but often related name. Here was a study that ran the risk of undermining the confidence of the individuals doing the test and then gave them a task that plays into their disabilities. So, here you have a study that basically discovers how disabled people are and gives very little insight into the nature of facilitated communication.

Regarding the inarguable findings of facilitator control in this study, Biklen stated: "What that shows is influence, which I've stated does occur." What these passages fail to reveal is that if the content of FC is being controlled or determined by the facilitators, word-finding problems (which have not been experimentally determined to be the key issue in communication by people with autism) are irrelevant. Additionally, if word-finding presents an immense challenge for people with autism, why are conceptually equivalent tasks (e.g., filling in a blank in a sentence with a required word) core elements in the set work that FC proponents recommend as initial orientation and training in the facilitation process?

Even if one were to entertain the possibility that some people with autism in the study had specific word-finding problems, one would expect the labeling of the pictures to include (as Biklen stated above) names of descriptions related to the stimuli. This was not the case in either the Wheeler study or the Szempruch study, where the typed and transcribed responses showed no pattern of such responses. Additionally, in these studies, most of the incorrect responses were subsequently "confirmed" by the typing of a "y" for yes in response to the facilitator's questioning the correctness of the response. There is a disturbing inclination among proponents of FC to view the issue of validity as a secondary concern that is an annoyance to be defended against, rather than the central concern about the technique.

Another recent research report (in the form of a letter to the editor) in *Topics in Language Disorders* (Calculator & Singer, 1992) documents a facilitation effect (i.e., benefit) in the performance by four of five students when they were tested with and without FC assistance using two forms (L and M) of the *Peabody Picture Vocabulary Test—Revised* (PPVT-R) (Dunn & Dunn, 1981). The PPVT-R is a test of receptive language that requires the individual being tested to point to one of four pictures (with four pictures on a page) that is accurately described by a spoken word. Scores for these students were significantly higher with facilitation with the facilitator wearing ear plugs and earphones with masking white noise. However, several factors hinder clear interpretation of these findings. Apparently, the examiners were within the field of vision of the facilitators; hence, facilitators may have been unknowingly cued by the examiners' mouth movements (e.g., number of apparent syllables). Second, this was not a communication task, as responses were limited to four choices rather than the greater response complexity presented by a keyboard; besides, responses were consequent to verbal and visual cues presented together. In contrast to all the other studies reviewed here, no expressive skills or abilities were tested by Calculator and Singer (1992), and no evidence was presented that would indicate that, in day-to-day activities without facilitation, there was any suspected discrepancy between the students' receptive language skills and their social or adaptive behavior. Given such considerations, these findings merit replication with better procedural controls (i.e., more careful control of masking and blinding) before they can be interpreted unambiguously.

The findings from these four recent studies can be summarized as follows:

1. One study demonstrated that FC content was being controlled by the facilitators, not the participants.
2. One study failed to show the validity of FC for over 20 people believed by facilitators (and others) to be truly communicating, without the experimental use of special apparatus.
3. One study failed to detect "unexpected" literacy or to promote superior written over verbal communication performance following systematic use of the recommended sequence of treatment procedures and standardized psychometric measures; it also demonstrated facilitator influence.
4. One study offered preliminary support for the perspective that some people with autism or mental retardation demonstrate unexpected receptive language skills if assisted via FC.

We suggest that the findings from the first three studies converge with those generally obtained in the Australian studies to indicate that the generality of FC effects and benefits may be less extensive than had been previously portrayed or expected. In addition, we suggest that the typical facilitator, based on the O. D. Heck Developmental Center, Developmental Disabilities Institute, and Rome Developmental Disabilities Services Offices findings, is unable to determine whether a person is validly communicating with FC or whether the facilitator is influencing the FC content. The key to understanding the parameters of valid communication within an FC framework rests upon the nature and extent of facilitator influence or control in the individual instance. Therefore, stringent controls must be employed to identify and prevent such influence.

The Rationale for Facilitated Communication: Flawed Concepts?

Biklen (1990, 1992c) and Biklen et al. (1992) cite a number of behavioral observations that indicate to them that participants in facilitation are producing valid communicative typing. None of these methods for validating the communications of people with severe communication deficits have been studied or reported systematically. Rather, proponents of FC tend to cite these arguments in anecdotal fashion, ignoring basic rules of scientific proof by using imprecise or undefined terms, unconfirmed observation, self-report by untrained individuals, and idiosyncratic references to single cases. Each of the indicators offered by Biklen et al. (1992, pp. 19–20) will be considered.

1. *Style, speed, and accuracy of fine motor control movement to the letters or keys are fairly constant across facilitators.* To our knowledge, no one has provided quantitative or otherwise objective evidence that this assertion is true. Therefore, this finding can only be accepted on the basis of informal observation and self-report. This sort of evidence is, of course, highly subjective and can be influenced by the beliefs and expectations of facilitators. It is not immediately clear how one would even go about demonstrating the constancy of "style" or "accuracy" of fine motor control toward individual keys. If facilitators watch each other work with a person, share their experiences in facilitating the same person, or offer advice to a new facilitator, clearly the independence of the facilitators' observations is tainted.

2. *Individuals make typographical errors that are unique to them. Some individuals fairly consistently hit more than one key at a time when typing.* Again, these observations remain undocumented except for the few instances cited anecdotally. Further, this claim suffers from a number of problems. First, there is no way of knowing to whom the observation refers and to what proportion of those facilitating it applies. Few critics of FC deny that the technique has utility for some persons with impaired communication, at least at some stage of nonspeech communication training. Some reports (again anecdotal) allege that certain individuals graduate from assisted to independent typing; perhaps it is these individuals who generate unique typographical errors during facilitation. Alterna-

tively, mechanical errors that are repeated in typing may result from person-specific neuromotor deficits or tendencies. These individuals, therefore, may contribute to the systematic variation in movement toward letters or keys without any comprehension of the symbolic or communicative dimension of their actions. For example, a constant visual displacement or directional motor weakness may produce a particular type of keyboard error regardless of the person's awareness of the meaning that others may ascribe to the act.

3. *Many individuals produce phonetic or invented spellings that are unique to them and do not appear in the work of others, despite the fact that several individuals sometimes share a common facilitator.* The first point in the preceding paragraph applies here as well. If valid, these observations may apply only to more competent persons who go on to type without assistance. Because individuals generally facilitate with the same assistants, certain error tendencies may become ingrained or habitual as part of the facilitator/facilitated dyad (e.g., the facilitator comes to associate a specific idiosyncratic spelling or phrase with a particular person and so is more likely to influence future communications along these lines). Furthermore, facilitators seeking to confirm their belief in the validity of the individuals' typed communications would tend unwittingly to repeat these unique inventions, thereby building a repertoire of student-specific error tendencies over time. The development of such a repertoire may be common to highly motivated facilitators.

4. *Some individuals type phrases or sentences that are unusual and would not be expected from the facilitators.* This line of reasoning is circular. It assumes the communication originates with the person being facilitated and that facilitators are unimaginative or otherwise incapable of determining unusual responses. If indeed (as virtually all quantitative studies of FC have indicated) there is significant, measurable facilitator influence over communications, it would be erroneous to consider any facilitated statements to be unusual or unexpected in the judgment of facilitators, *because they are their likely source.* There is no objective evidence to support the claim of "unusualness" or "unexpectedness," and no clearly defined method for identifying what constitutes an unusual or unexpected statement.

5. *Individuals sometimes produce content that is not known to the facilitator.* This is perhaps the most frequently cited piece of evidence supporting the validity of FC, but like eyewitness accounts of a crime, it may prove the least reliable. Once again, there are no quantitative findings reported by which to assess how often, or under what circumstances, such content is supposedly produced. Therefore, one must rely only on the reports of the facilitators themselves that they were not privy to the information communicated. Among our own research subjects (Wheeler et al., in press), this sort of evidence was offered by facilitators. When one of the researchers attempted to validate these accounts, most failed to stand up to careful scrutiny, while others could be neither proved nor disproved but had other more plausible explanations. In most cases, the facilitator's fervent FC belief system resulted in cognitive construction of actual events or selective perception that allowed the belief system to be maintained and reinforced.

A typical example is as follows: A facilitator claimed that an individual, through FC, typed out the number of his male and female siblings and the names of his family members. The facilitator said that this information was surprising in its accuracy and that he did not know the information beforehand. This anecdote was shared with others and helped to support the mutual FC belief system. Upon examination, however, the typed information was only fairly accurate (none of it was fully correct), was readily available in the person's records, had almost certainly been read by the facilitator in the past, and had most likely been reviewed in past treatment team meetings. When confronted with these facts, the facilitator acknowledged that he had almost certainly remembered parts of the information at a low level of awareness and, therefore, had possibly influenced the typing unknowingly.

An opposite but related line of support for FC derives from the claim that individuals on occasion type out information that is *only* known to the facilitator. This observation has given rise to the so-called mind-reading phenomenon reported by facilitators in both Australia and the United States. That is, individuals supposedly "read the mind" of their facilitator and produce information that is available to the facilitator only. The problem with this line of "evidence" is that both information sets are under the control of the facilitator, who presumably has private knowledge and then facilitates another person's expression of that knowledge. Clearly, such situations carry the potential for a facilitator-controlled phenomenon. As note, nearly all quantitative studies of FC have unequivocally established the potential for facilitator influence over pointing and typing. Most of these researchers also note that facilitators appear to be *unaware* of their influence over the students' typing. It is more parsimonious to explain mind-reading as a situation in which the facilitator, outside of awareness, has determined the production of a message that contains private information.

6. *Through facilitated communication, individuals reveal their personalities.* Apart from the obvious subjectivity of this observation, several of the previous arguments also apply to this claim. Facilitators with a strong belief in the validity of FC are likely to influence communications from their students in ways that produce recognizable, student-specific response tendencies. For example, a facilitator who works with several individuals could come to associate one with humor, another with brashness, and yet another with timidity. Because our explanation for mind-reading relies on the assumption that facilitator control of output more directly explains the phenomenon than telepathy does, it seems reasonable to assume that communication response tendencies that reveal aspects of "personality" could also be the product of facilitator control.

Nevertheless, the strongest case for facilitation benefits can be made with respect to demonstration of consistent progress toward more independent typing (Crossley & Remington-Gurney, 1992). Certainly, individuals who have progressed to apparently productive typing with a "touch" to the shoulder especially bear scrutiny through scientific methods and controlled studies in order to appraise possible benefits.

Most of the above propositions for demonstrating the validity of facilitated communications are amenable to post-hoc quantitative analysis without affecting the interpersonal aspects of the procedure. However, as we have noted, these analyses have not been forthcoming. Basic considerations of research methodology have been generally ignored. For example, although FC proponents have published a number of articles on American samples of FC participants, objective subject selection criteria have not been stated. Thus, it is unknown whether these individuals are representative of others, as a whole, with whom FC has been attempted or what the nature of the larger sampling frame might be (e.g., Biklen et al., 1992). It also is not consistently clear whether the larger American samples have included the smaller American samples reported in other articles supporting FC (i.e., whether the same sample is reported repeatedly). As a result, these samples should be considered most likely biased and probably nonrepresentative. Even if they represent the most successful individuals, and these people are in fact truly communicating in the absence of independent validation, this does not portend well for dramatic benefit from use of FC. The modal individual described to date, when data are provided, continues to require support at the hand or wrist to participate in FC.

As indicated in the beginning of this chapter, there is an extensive literature on language and autism, some of which is consistent with claims for the relative integrity of receptive language skills among people with autism. Closer scrutiny, however, suggests that the receptive language skills of people with autism are probably not normative, but rather are generally consistent with assessed developmental and cognitive level. Recent reports have also included use of FC with people with mental retardation but no apparent autism (e.g., Crossley, 1992). Current knowledge of language functioning of people with mental retardation indicates that their language development is generally consistent with the level of their general cognitive development, making people with severe or profound mental retardation de facto poor prospects for benefiting from FC.

The following data analysis, drawn from the New York state database of the Developmental Disabilities Profile (DDP) (Brown et al., 1986, 1987, 1990), illustrates the relationship we have described. Within the DDP, five indices, or item clusters, are employed to characterize communication skills (receptive and expressive in combination), self-care skills, cognitive (practical problem-solving) skills, motor skills, and community living skills. Table 4.1 shows the correlation of each of these standardized skill summary scores with the standardized communication score, separately for people either having or not having autism. We have also included summary scores for problem behavior frequency (rated summed frequencies of 10 behaviors) and clinical behavioral response (the extent to which presence of problem behaviors stimulates a programmatic response).

Although index scores for other areas of adaptive functioning correlate marginally higher for individuals with mental retardation than for individuals with both autism and mental retardation, it appears that, for both groups, language perfor-

Table 4.1 Correlations of Communication Skills with Other Skills

Skill Ratings	Autism	MR
Motor skills	.61	.66
Cognitive skills	.77	.78
Self-care skills	.66	.75
Community living skills	.70	.74
Problem behavior frequency	.26	.17
Clinical behavioral response	.25	.22
N	2,777	67,221

Note: All correlations, $p \le .01$ (to .0001), two-tailed; all scores are standardized.

mance is closely related to level of cognitive performance (a measure that, here, excludes IQ score). Furthermore, for both groups, the correlation between cognitive and language performance is significantly greater than the correlation between motor and language performance. This latter correlation is the benchmark against which the explanatory premise of global dyspraxia (i.e., a generalized volitional motor-initiation deficit considered a rationale for deficient verbal expressive language) may reasonably be assessed. If dyspraxia accounts for expressive language deficits among people with autism, we should expect that the correlation between language performance and motor performance measures would be significantly greater than that between language performance and cognitive performance measures. The findings shown here challenge the sensibility of the "apraxia hypothesis."

Other elements of the rationale for FC also appear not to rest on an entirely sound base. In particular, these include observations about hyperlexia (oral recitation of printed materials with skill that is disproportionately advanced compared to other developmental or cognitive attainments) and issues of continuity of communicative and adaptive development. Several sources on FC (e.g., Biklen, 1992c; Biklen et al., 1992) have cited the occurrence of hyperlexia as convergent evidence of the integrity of the receptive language of people with autism. However, one epidemiological study estimated that hyperlexia occurred among only 6.6% of people with autism (Burd, Kerbeshian, & Fisher, 1985).

Among people with hyperlexia, only the more able people with mental retardation and hyperlexia use sentence context in a normal way to pronounce homographs (in tests of reading comprehension) (Snowling & Frith, 1987), as would be expected if their language skills are consistent with their developmental level. These individuals show greater than expected ability to retain sound-symbol associations (Kistner, Robbins, & Haskett, 1988), but not necessarily to use them in functional language. Although these people read fluently, their comprehension of both spoken and *written* language is limited (Huttenlocher & Huttenlocher, 1973), and although they have an excellent stored vocabulary that can be used with written words, their expressive language is impoverished (Whitehouse & Harris, 1984). Taken in combination, such findings imply that hyperlexia does not provide straightforward and convergent evidence for high developmental potential of expressive written language (i.e., typing) in people with autism.

Issues that involve developmental continuity and the condition of autism present further challenges to the premises of FC. For example, Jacobson and Ackerman (1990) compared the adaptive skills of people with both autism and mental retardation and people with mental retardation in three age cohorts (5–12, 13–21, and 22–35 years; $N = 25,490$). The authors found that the language skills of children with autism approached those of children with mental retardation, but for adolescents and adults with autism, such skills were considerably more delayed than in their peers with mental retardation. This relationship was evident when biases due to age, intellectual level, and residential setting were controlled statistically. In substance, although the findings suggested that people with autism show developmental progress in language, greater developmental progress could be inferred for their peers with mental retardation alone. Differences among individuals' language function were more closely related to intellectual level than to age, type of residence, or diagnosis of autism. Complementary findings have been reported by Loveland and Kelley (1991) for comparisons of the adaptive behavior and communication skills of children with Down syndrome or autism and by Waterhouse and Fein (1984) regarding cognitive skill development of children and adolescents with autism.

Other literature challenges the observations of facile conversational interaction through FC by people with autism. Transcripts of FC interactions are often rich in emotion and demonstrate perspective-taking via FC. Yet, extensive experimental evidence has demonstrated the difficulty with which people with autism take another's perspec-

tive or assume a "metacognitive" perspective (Baron-Cohen, 1988, 1989; Dawson & Fernald, 1987; Oswald & Ollendick, 1989). The speech of people with autism is characterized by deficits in syntax, semantics, and pragmatics, creativity and generativity, and integration of emotional states (DeLong, 1992). Although children with autism demonstrate patterns of vocalization and body-movement development that are qualitatively similar to those of normal children, development of communication, reception of sounds and speech, and social responsiveness is delayed (Wenar, Ruttenberg, Kalish-Weiss, & Wolf, 1986). Observed forms of delay are consistent with such factors as lack of social responsiveness (which would affect attentional processes and resulting learning) (Klin, 1991) and cognitive deficits. Although autistic children can learn some word meanings (Eskes, Bryson, & McCormick, 1990), insensitivity to the inherent pattern of auditory input and a tendency to impose simple patterns on more complex patterns affect their comprehension (Hermelin & Frith, 1971), as do difficulties in accurately identifying others' feeling states (Prior, Dahlstrom, & Squires, 1990), reading for meaning (Frith & Snowling, 1983), recognition of emotional adjectives compared to concrete nouns and nonemotional adjectives (Van Lancker, Cornelius, & Needleman, 1991), and labeling of emotional intonations (Van Lancker, Cornelius, & Kreiman, 1989).

Some indications of cognitive biases related to autism have a bearing on language function. Autistic children do not appear to have a specific cognitive deficit in the ability to categorize and form abstract concepts (Tagler-Flusberg, 1985a). However, previous findings that suggested such deficits (Bartolucci & Albers, 1974; Bartolucci, Pierce, & Streiner, 1980; Pierce & Bartolucci, 1977), especially semantic or syntactic ones, may reflect an inability to use cognitive representations in an appropriate and flexible manner (Tagler-Flusberg, 1985b; Ungerer & Sigman, 1987). This may be attributed, in part, to the failure of many individuals with autism to develop imitative skills (Yates, 1986).

Given the presence of receptive and cognitive biases, it should not be surprising to find that the expressive language of people with autism is characterized by distinctive common features. Although the vocal articulation of people with autism has been found to be superior to that of language-matched controls and receptive dysphasic controls (Boucher, 1976), these distinctive features of expressive language involve both pragmatic use of language and characteristics of its content. People with autism exhibit individual abnormalities in length of utterance, echoing, syntactic disturbance, semantic concreteness, context inappropriateness, and disorders of prosody (Shapiro & Huebner, 1976). Furthermore, they are more noncontingent in discourse (Tagler-Flusberg & Anderson, 1991), are more likely to use words inappropriately that have no phonological or semantic similarity to an intended word (and the frequency of idiosyncratic language increases with language complexity) (Volden & Lord, 1991), and make poor use of prosodic cues in others' language when responding conversationally (Frankel, Simmons, & Richey, 1987). In addition, there are direct parallels between verbal and nonverbal communication: autistic people are less likely than matched controls to make spontaneous remarks (Cantwell, Baker, & Rutter, 1978). They are less able than others to respond correctly to language or gestures used to direct their attention and use attention-directing (pointing or showing) less frequently when making requests (Landry & Loveland, 1988). They make use of instrumental gestures but very little use of expressive gestures (Attwood, Frith, & Hermelin, 1988), and generally demonstrate deficits in nonverbal indicating behaviors (Mundy, Sigman, Ungerer, & Sherman, 1986).

Adolescents or adults with autism have been reported to demonstrate persistent peculiar uses of speech and language (Rumsey, Rapoport, & Sceery, 1985). For example, adolescents with autism and near-normal intelligence typically use nonreciprocal speech, have recurrent problems of failing to listen, interpret words too literally, or make comments that are irrelevant to context

(Dewey & Everard, 1974). Others have continuing difficulties perceiving prosodic features of speech (Simmons & Baltaxe, 1975) or demonstrate relative impairments in appreciation and production of emotional expressions (MacDonald et al., 1989). Proponents of FC who report sophisticated conversational interactions by people with autism must account for the evident qualitative differences in perspective-taking abilities indicated by this conversational content, in contrast with the persisting expressive language biases demonstrated in the literature for adolescents and adults with autism and normal or near-normal intelligence.[1]

The Overriding Importance of Authenticity

Despite the absence of scientific research to support the use of FC and to confirm the rationale for its use, some have argued that it should, nevertheless, be used. For example, one article suggests that "the danger of not offering the option of facilitation to an individual is far greater than the danger of raising false hopes for families" (Donnellan, Sabin, & Majure, 1992, p. 71). We strongly oppose such a position and believe it is misguided. Many other scientists and practitioners in the field of developmental disabilities also would disagree with the perspective of Donnellan et al., arguing that people with autism and their families have already been subjected to a sufficient number of misguided and fruitless therapeutic endeavors that were initially presented to them as extremely promising.

We have also become aware of many instances throughout the United States where family members and staff have been accused through FC of physical or sexual abuse of people with disabilities. In many of these cases, there is no physical evidence but only facilitated communications as support for the allegations. Yet, characteristically, the in-

---

[1] Although discussion of neurological factors related to language function of people with autism is beyond the scope of this chapter, interested readers are referred to the following sources: Balottin et al. (1989), Courchesne et al. (1989), Darby & Clark (1992), Dawson (1983), Dawson, Warrenburg, & Fuller (1982), Hoffman & Prior (1982), James & Barry (1983), Maurer (1986), Narita & Koga (1987), and Yeterian (1987).

dividuals who have purportedly made allegations are removed from their lifelong family homes, or their caregivers are arrested and jailed, at least temporarily. This poses a great danger to caregivers because there often is no confirmation of abuse from other sources.

We have been involved in situations where accusations of physical and sexual abuse have been made through FC. While U. S. courts are reluctant to admit testimony based only on FC, some people have been arrested, incarcerated, and required to spend significant sums in their own defense based upon accusations originating through FC. We know of one situation where, because of an accusation of sexual abuse that had been made through FC, a direct care worker in an educational setting was relieved of his position and asked to relocate to another school, even though an investigation of the incident failed to confirm any wrongdoing and no charges were ever brought.

Another case dramatizes the importance of validation in instances of great emotional consequence to families. A 10-year-old boy who is profoundly retarded, physically impaired, and medically frail had severe health problems persisting for months, which required several hospitalizations. His health was deteriorating, and his mother and doctors believed he might be dying. He had never communicated beyond a few simple gestures and facial expressions until he began working, for several months, with a facilitator. Although the mother was unable to facilitate with her son, the facilitator reported progress in the boy's communication ability. The boy is purported recently to have indicated that he believed he was dying, was in distress, and wanted his mother to stop worrying about him. This information caused great alarm to the boy's family and grave concern about how his medical condition should be managed. Scenes like these, involving family members, workers, and the people whom they serve, are being repeated all over the country, creating distress, anger, sorrow, and confusion.

Those who are responsible for making decisions about the use of FC should be especially wary of superficially reasoned rhetoric. Donnellan et al. (1992) pose the apparent quandary that "those who dismiss facilitated communication out of hand [with suggestions of facilitator influence] must explain why learners with autism would consent to giving other people's messages day after day for years" (p. 71). If one assumes that FC and its rationale are valid, this question makes sense. However, scientific evidence does not support the general validity of FC. Considerable scientific evidence indicates that severe or profound retardation occurs at disproportionately high rates among people with autism and involves severe expressive and receptive language impairments. Therefore, there is a far more parsimonious explanation: the great majority of participants in FC are *unaware* that their typing is being treated as communication by others. The reality may be that the procedures thought to be producing communication are actually shaping situation-specific compliance. Such an explanation would be consistent with an existing body of scientific information in fields such as learning, psychometrics, neuroscience, and epidemiology. Whether "communication" is also being shaped remains open to question but has so far received little scientific support.

Wide-scale adoption of poorly supported therapeutic procedures is a valid concern for the responsible and ethical clinician. As Brown (1982) noted:

> There are ... retreats to which both scientists and nonscientists are vulnerable. The retreat from fact, from established knowledge, too often is a retreat into folklore, faith healing, spiritualism, faddism, or outright charlatanism. ... In some areas of pseudoscience it almost seems that conviction and enthusiasm grow in inverse relationship to the factual support for the proposed idea. (p. 89)

Adoption of poorly supported procedures threatens the quality of clinical services provided to foster developmental and social growth of people with disabilities. Attribution of competence to an individual as a consequence of FC-assisted psychological testing could result in termination of eligibility for developmental services (Crossley, 1992), because the intellectual criteria for mental retardation would no longer be met. Apparent, but invalid, representation of one's interests and preferences could even be life-threatening, as when consent for surgical procedures is rendered through FC.

With the maturation of advocacy and self-advocacy efforts for people with disabilities, self-determination has become a watchword of the developmental disabilities community. But individual and parental interests and preferences may differ, and so a fully adequate approach to assuring self-determination for people with severe disabilities that prevent conventional forms of expression or clear and consistent interpretation of nonverbal, possibly communicative, behavior has resisted definition. FC provides a particularly seductive means to resolve this problem (Prior & Cummins, 1992; Schopler, 1992). As argued elsewhere (Wheeler et al., in press), nothing could be more relevant today than discriminating between communications that represent true self-expression and those representing the imposed views and preferences of others.

If the findings of initial quantitative studies indicating pervasive facilitator influence are borne out, proponents of FC will have advocated for an intervention that has subjugated thousands of people to the control of others. Wheeler et al. (in press) identify three particularly sensitive types of communications that are currently produced through facilitation: (a) expressions of personal choice or preference, (b) allegations of abuse or mistreatment, and (c) reports of inner states, relating to mental or physical sensations such as pain. To this list, we add a fourth: (d) statements revealing abilities and competencies. The damage that can result from false statements in any of these categories can be enormous.

Conclusions

In the end, FC is important for two rather different reasons. First, it is important as a social or psychological phenomenon in developmental disabilities services because of what it reveals about the values and motives of the people who rely on the service system and those who provide the services. Second, it is important in the social and behavioral sciences because it points up the need for a reappraisal of the role of science and scientific methods in answering questions that have applied significance in differentiating between science and pseudoscience.

When consumers of developmental disabilities services and service providers abandon past practices and embrace a new, time-consuming alternative approach, it says something about their perception of the utility of the old approaches and their desire for effective solutions to problems. What problems? Although the obvious problem solved by FC is that of communication, it also solves the problem of participation in socially defined normative roles that have been created for people with handicaps. The two problems are related. If no one were listening, if people with handicaps were isolated, segregated, and kept away from mainstream society (as many once were), there would be no problem for FC to solve—no ready context for widespread adoption. The normalization, valorization, deinstitutionalization, communitization, participation, self-advocacy, mainstreaming, and total inclusion movements—widespread ideologies based on common social values—have created the conditions that made the developmental disabilities community ripe for an effective solution to the problem that emerged: facilitating adaptation to social contexts defined, in part, by communicative participation.

Context is a powerful element in deciding among alternative courses of action. If no one were listening to people with disabilities or demanding the fullest possible participation from them, the urgency of deciding on a communication modality would be diminished. It was in *this* context that other systems requiring greater expertise, effort, planning, and cost to implement, such as sign language, independent keyboard use, vocal speech, picture or pictographic systems, and so forth, were rejected by those who readily embraced FC. In addition, these more conventional communication systems (a) have yielded few astonishing individual communication breakthroughs, (b) generally are cumbersome, and (c) often result in reduced intelligibility when judged against normative expectations. These factors made segments of the developmental disabilities community vulnerable to the appeal of FC with its reported rapid gains and easy methods.

Service providers are under considerable pressure from increasingly empowered and expectant consumers. Their resources are stretched thin in a community-based service system that is increasingly regulated. Their best efforts often have yielded only limited effectiveness when conventional methods have been used. The growing deprofessionalization of direct service provision in "communitized" and "integrated" settings has resulted in few workers at the level of program planning and direct service delivery who can evaluate treatment alternatives according to scientific criteria. As a result, new intervention approaches that fit with nonscientific and widely accepted value-based criteria are seldom critically evaluated for validity or consistency with scientific knowledge. Such conditions open a door to pseudoscientific practices and rationales.

To stem the growing vulnerability of consumers and paraprofessionals to pseudoscientific intervention strategies, greater discussion of scientific standards for treatment evaluation must become commonplace. This is difficult, because the dividing line is not neat and simple, and there is confusion between pseudoscience (i.e., the erroneous confirmation of false descriptions, false causal relations, and ineffective practices) and nonscience (i.e., esthetics, beliefs about rights, and literary criticism). Thagard (1988) suggested that the best method for detecting pseudoscience is to list the differences between obviously scientific and pseudoscientific systems and then see which side best fits a given field. If this advice is followed for FC, it emerges as pseudoscience.

First, practitioners of a scientific field are concerned about empirical confirmations and discon-

firmations of their principles and practices, while practitioners of a pseudoscience are oblivious to such activities. Practitioners of a pseudoscience explain away empirical disconfirmations and alternative explanations and tend to be selective in the admission of evidence. Practitioners of a science generally reserve judgment about disconfirming evidence until the relation of the evidence to established observations, methods, and theories is understood and disconfirming data are replicated and extended.

Second, practitioners of pseudoscience rely on a natural but deficient form of reasoning that Thagard (1988) referred to as *resemblance thinking*, while scientific practitioners use *correlation thinking*. In resemblance thinking, people make the mistake of inferring that two things are causally related if they are similar to each other (e.g., form without verified substance). An example of resemblance thinking in a pseudoscience is the belief that the red planet Mars governs influences over people that are associated with blood, war, and aggression. In correlation thinking, two things are inferred to be causally related if they are correlated with one another. This is a powerful tool, because causally related things are always correlated (despite the obvious fact that all correlated things are not always causally related). Correlation thinking is understood to include established methods of generalization from examples, statistical reasoning, and other kinds of inductive tests of causality.

Among supporters of FC, resemblance thinking is rampant. One example is the inference that because independent communication during conversation between two verbal humans often resembles transcripts of FC sessions (and because independently communicating people only rarely converse via question-and-answer format), FC is valid. Likewise, because FC training superficially resembles conventional valid training methods such as graduated assistance and fading of manual prompts (Hugenin, Weidenman, & Mulick, 1991), it too must be a valid training method.

Third, in scientific practice, apparent causal relations and theories are always tested empirically in a systematic effort to rule out the influence of spurious correlations. In pseudoscience, on the other hand, tests are discouraged and alternative theories are ignored.

Fourth, science uses compatible and simple theories to explain and predict phenomena; pseudoscience uses complex and ad-hoc theories and explanations.

Finally, science progresses over time as theories are modified to explain new facts, while pseudoscience tends to stagnate in its doctrine and field of application.

Of these proposed characteristics of pseudoscience (Thagard, 1988), the third and fourth can be discerned in the FC literature and in records of remarks of FC practitioners (e.g., National Public Radio, 1992, September 28). It would be premature to apply the last characteristic in the case of FC, because if it stabilizes and begins to be supported by empirical evidence, it could emerge as a scientific field (or be recognized as part of an existing scientific field) despite early characteristics of a pseudoscience.

Researchers especially, but also practitioners, should recognize that although it is possible that some individuals with autism may benefit from treatment that incorporates FC, this practice is based on faith and not on science at this time. Indeed, "these procedures seem to require immediate decisions by the facilitator that are extraordinarily demanding" (McLean, 1992, p. 25). Proponents of FC have not yet produced research that satisfies conventional standards of scientific evidence (Calculator, 1992a, 1992b; Jacobson & Mulick, 1992; Rimland, 1991; Silliman, 1992).

It is widely recognized that people with severe disabilities are especially vulnerable as a group to neglect, and it should be understood that ineffective therapies present the jeopardy of benign neglect, at the very least. Recognizing this, the "debate" and rhetoric surrounding FC are not a matter of autism orthodoxy versus free speech, or of the stirring of passions that this juxtaposition may evoke. It is a matter of whether people with autism will be protected from unproductive and socially harmful therapeutic endeavors by an insistence that therapies meet the same standards of objective clinical merit that are expected to underpin and confirm the value of any medical, surgical, or behavioral treatment in general use.

Note

Other than the principal author, authors are listed in alphabetical order. Development of this chapter was supported in part by the New York State Office of Mental Retardation and Developmental Disabilities, Rome Developmental Disabilities Services Office, Developmental Disabilities Institute, Ohio State University, and O. D. Heck/Eleanor Roosevelt Developmental Services Autism Program. The perspectives and conclusions presented here do not necessarily reflect the policies of these organizations.

References

AMERICAN PSYCHIATRIC ASSOCIATION. (1987). *DSM-III-R: Diagnostic and statistical manual* (3rd ed., revised). Washington, DC: Author.

ANONYMOUS. (1991, Almanac Edition). Defeating the silence. *The Anderson School Express, 2,* 1–9.

ANONYMOUS. (1992a, May 22). Facilitative communication: Finding the words. *NYSARF Rehabilitation News Digest,* 7–8.

ANONYMOUS. (1992b, January). Facilitated communication: Old theories challenged, new hopes generated. *Futurity,* 2.

ATTWOOD, A., FRITH, U., & HERMELIN, B. (1988). The understanding and use of interpersonal gestures by autistic and Down's syndrome children. *Journal of Autism and Developmental Disorders, 18,* 241–257.

BAGAN, M. (1992, January). New way of talking from down under. *Wilton Wire, 3,* 5.

BALOTTIN, U., BEJOR, M., CECCHINI, A., MARTELLI, A., PALAZZI, S., & LANZI, G. (1989). Infantile autism and computerized tomography brain-scan findings: Specific versus nonspecific abnormalities. *Journal of Autism and Developmental Disorders, 19,* 109–117.

BARON-COHEN, S. (1988). Social and pragmatic deficits in autism: Cognitive or affective? *Journal of Autism and Developmental Disorders, 18,* 379–402.

BARON-COHEN, S. (1989). Are autistic children "behaviorists"? An examination of their mental-physical and appearance-reality distinctions. *Journal of Autism and Developmental Disorders, 19,* 579–600.

BARRON, J., & BARRON, S. (1992, August). The boy within. *Parenting,* pp. 83–90.

BARTOLUCCI, G., & ALBERS, R. J. (1974). Deictic categories in the language of autistic children. *Journal of Autism and Childhood Schizophrenia, 4,* 131–141.

BARTOLUCCI, G., PIERCE, S. J., & STREINER, D. L. (1980). Cross-sectional studies of grammatical morphemes in autistic and mentally retarded adults. *Journal of Autism and Developmental Disorders, 10,* 39–50.

BIJOU, S. W., & DUNITZ-JOHNSON, E. (1981). Interbehavior analysis of developmental retardation. *The Psychological Record, 31,* 305–329.

BIKLEN, D. (1990). Communication unbound: Autism and praxis. *Harvard Educational Review, 60,* 291–314.

BIKLEN, D. (1992a, January). Typing to talk: Facilitated communication. *American Journal of Speech and Language Pathology, 1,* 15–17, 21–22.

BIKLEN, D. (1992b, March 15). DEAL: Achievements are of international importance [letter to the editor]. *The Sunday Age,* Melbourne, Victoria, Australia.

BIKLEN, D. (1992c). Autism orthodoxy versus free speech: A reply to Cummins and Prior. *Harvard Educational Review, 62,* 242–256.

BIKLEN, D. (1992d, Summer). Questions and answers on facilitated communication. *The Advocate: Newsletter of the Autism Society of America,* pp. 16–18.

BIKLEN, D., MORTON, M. W., GOLD, D., BERRIGAN, C., & SWAMINATHAN, S. (1992). Facilitated communication: Implications for individuals with autism. *Topics in Language Disorders, 12,* 1–28.

BIKLEN, D., MORTON, M. W., SAHA, S. N., DUNCAN, J., GOLD, D., HARDARDOTTIR, M., KARNA, E., O'CONNOR, S., & RAO, S. (1991). "I AMN NOT A UTISTIVC OH THJE TYP" ("I'm not autistic on the typewriter"). *Disability, Handicap & Society, 6,* 161–180.

BIKLEN, D., & SCHUBERT, A. (1991). New words: The communication of students with autism. *Remedial and Special Education, 12*(6), 46–57.

BLACKMORE, S. (1992). Psychic experiences: Psychic illusions. *Skeptical Inquirer, 16,* 367–376.

BOUCHER, J. (1976). Articulation in early childhood autism. *Journal of Autism and Childhood Schizophrenia, 6,* 297-302.

BROWN, C. B., HANLEY, A. T., NEMETH, C., EPPLE, W., BIRD, W., & BONTEMPO, A. (1986). *The developmental disabilities profile: Final report—The design, development, and testing of the core instrument.* Albany: New York State Office of Mental Retardation and Developmental Disabilities.

BROWN, C. B., HANLEY, A. T., NEMETH, C., EPPLE, W., BIRD, W., & BONTEMPO, A. (1987). *The developmental disabilities profile: User's guide.* Albany: New York State Office of Mental Retardation and Developmental Disabilities.

BROWN, C. B., NEMETH, C., HANLEY, A. T., BONTEMPO, A., & BIRD, W. (1990). *Scoring the DDP.* Albany: New York State Office of Mental Retardation and Developmental Disabilities.

BROWN, G. W. (1982). A loss of nerve. *Developmental and Behavioral Pediatrics, 3,* 88–95.

BURD, L., KERBESHIAN, J., & FISHER, W. (1985). Inquiry into the incidence of hyperlexia in a statewide population of children with pervasive developmental disorder. *Psychological Reports, 57,* 236–238.

CALCULATOR, S. N. (1992a). Perhaps the emperor has clothes after all: A response to Biklen. *American Journal of Speech and Language Pathology, 1,* 18–20.

CALCULATOR, S. N. (1992b). Facilitated communication: Calculator responds. *American Journal of Speech and Language Pathology, 1,* 23–24.

CALCULATOR, S. N., & SINGER, K. M. (1992). Letter to the editor: Preliminary validation of facilitated communication. *Topics in Language Disorders, 12*(5), ix-xvi.

CANTWELL, D. P., BAKER, L., & RUTTER, M. (1978). A comparative study of infantile autism and specific developmental receptive language disorder. IV. Analysis of syntax and language function. *Journal of Child Psychology and Psychiatry and Allied Disciplines, 19,* 351–362.

COOK, T. D., & CAMPBELL, D. T. (1979). *Quasi-experimentation: Design and analysis issues for field settings.* Chicago: Rand McNally.

COURCHESNE, E., LINCOLN, A. J., YEUNG-COURCHESNE, R., ELMASIAN, R., & GRILLION, C. (1989). Pathophysiologic findings in nonretarded autism and receptive developmental language disorder. *Journal of Autism and Developmental Disorders, 19,* 1–17.

CRESTWOOD COMPANY. (1992). New road to communications. *Communication Aids for Children and Adults* (catalog), 1.

CROSSLEY, R. (1992). Getting the words out: Case studies in facilitated communication training. *Topics in Language Disorders, 12,* 46–59.

CROSSLEY, R., & REMINGTON-GURNEY, J. (1992). Getting the words out: Facilitated communication training. *Topics in Language Disorders, 12,* 29–45.

CUMMINS, R. A., & PRIOR, M. P. (1992). Autism and facilitated communication: A reply to Biklen. *Harvard Educational Review, 62,* 228–241.

DARBY, J. K., & CLARK, L. (1992). Autism syndrome as a final common pathway of behavioral expression for many organic disorders. *American Journal of Psychiatry, 149,* 146.

DAWSON, G. (1983). Lateralized brain dysfunction in autism: Evidence from the Halstead-Reitan neuropsychological battery. *Journal of Autism and Developmental Disorders, 13,* 269–286.

DAWSON, G., & FERNALD, M. (1987). Perspective taking ability and its relationship to the social behavior of autistic children. *Journal of Autism and Developmental Disorders, 17,* 487–498.

DAWSON, G., WARRENBURG, S., & FULLER, P. (1982). Cerebral lateralization in individuals diagnosed as autistic in early childhood. *Brain and Language, 15,* 353–368.

DEAL COMMUNICATION CENTRE. (1992a). *Facilitated communication training.* Caulfield, Australia: Author.

DEAL COMMUNICATION CENTRE. (1992b). *Getting the message.* Caulfield, Australia: Author.

DELACATO, C. H. (1966). *Neurological organization and reading.* Springfield, IL: Thomas.

DELONG, G. R. (1992). Autism, amnesia, hippocampus, and learning. *Neuroscience and Biobehavioral Reviews, 16,* 63–70.

DEVELOPMENTAL LEARNING MATERIALS. (1982). *All-purpose photo library sets 1 and 2.* Allen, TX: Author.

DEWEY, M. A., & EVERARD, M. P. (1974). The near-normal autistic adolescent: Nonreciprocal speech. *Journal of Autism and Childhood Schizophrenia, 4,* 348–356.

DOMAN, G. (1974). *What to do about your brain-injured child.* Garden City, NY: Doubleday.

DONNELLAN, A. M., SABIN, L. A., & MAJURE, L. A. (1992). Facilitated communication: Beyond the quandary to the questions. *Topics in Language Disorders, 12,* 69–82.

DUNN, L., & DUNN, L. (1981). *Manual for forms L and M of the Peabody Picture Vocabulary Test—revised.* Circle Pines, MN: American Guidance Service.

EBERLIN, M., McCONNACHIE, G., IBEL, S., & VOLPE, L. (1992, October). *A systematic investigation of "facilitated communication": Is there efficacy or utility with children and adolescents with autism?* Paper presented at the Annual Conference of Region X, AAMR, Albany, NY.

ESKES, G. A., BRYSON, S. E., & McCORMICK, T. A. (1990). Comprehension of concrete and abstract words in autistic children. *Journal of Autism and Developmental Disorders, 20,* 61–73.

FRANKEL, F., SIMMONS, J. Q., & RICHEY, V. E. (1987). Reward value of prosodic features of language for autistic, mentally retarded, and normal children. *Journal of Autism and Developmental Disorders, 17,* 103–113.

FRAZIER, K. (1992). NORC knocks Gallup trend claim. *Skeptical Inquirer, 47,* 347–348.

FRITH, U., & SNOWLING, M. (1983). Reading for meaning and reading for sound in autistic and dyslexic children. *British Journal of Developmental Psychology, 1,* 329–342.

GARDNER, M. (1990). *The expressive one-word vocabulary test—revised.* Novato, CA: Academic Therapy Publications.

HEILMAN, K. M., & GONZALEZ-ROTH, L. J. (1985). Apraxia. In K. M. Heilman & E. Valenstein (Eds.), *Clinical neuropsychology* (2nd ed.) (pp. 131–150). New York: Oxford University Press.

HERMELIN, B., & FRITH, U. (1971). Psychological studies of childhood autism: Can autistic children make sense of what they see and hear? *Journal of Special Education, 5,* 107–117.

HOFFMAN, W. L., & PRIOR, M. R. (1982). Neuropsychological dimensions of autism in children: A test of the hemispheric dysfunction hypothesis. *Journal of Clinical Neuropsychology, 4,* 27–41.

HUDSON, A. (1992, August). *Evaluating the validity of facilitated communication.* Paper presented at the Ninth World Congress of the International Association for the Study of Mental Deficiency, Gold Coast, Australia.

HUDSON, A., MELITA, B., & ARNOLD, N. (in press). Assessing the validity of facilitated communication: A case study. *Journal of Autism and Developmental Disorders.*

HUGENIN, N. H., WEIDENMAN, L. E., & MULICK, J. A. (1991). Programmed instruction. In J. L. Matson & J. A. Mulick (Eds.), *Handbook of mental retardation* (2nd ed.) (pp. 451–467). New York: Pergamon.

HUTTENLOCHER, P. R., & HUTTENLOCHER, J. (1973). A study of children with hyperlexia. *Neurology, 23,* 1107–1116.

INTELLECTUAL DISABILITY REVIEW PANEL. (1989). *Report to the director-general on the validity and reliability of assisted communication.* Melbourne, Australia: Victoria Community Services.

INTERDISCIPLINARY WORKING PARTY ON ISSUES IN SEVERE COMMUNICATION IMPAIRMENT. (1988). *DEAL communication centre operations: A statement of concern.* Melbourne, Australia: Author.

JACOBSON, J. W., & ACKERMAN, L. J. (1990). Differences in adaptive functioning among people with autism or mental retardation. *Journal of Autism and Developmental Disorders, 20,* 205–219.

JACOBSON, J. W., & MULICK, J. A. (1991). Common sense and the crisis of confidence. *Psychology in*

Mental Retardation and Developmental Disabilities, 17(2), 6–9.

JACOBSON, J. W., & MULICK, J. A. (1992). Speak for yourself, or . . . I can't quite put my finger on it! *Psychology in Mental Retardation and Developmental Disabilities, 17*, 3–7.

JAMES, A. L., & BARRY, R. J. (1983). Developmental effects in the cerebral lateralization of autistic, retarded, and normal children. *Journal of Autism and Developmental Disorders, 13*, 43–56.

KISTNER, J., ROBBINS, F., & HASKETT, M. (1988). Assessment and skill remediation of hyperlexic children. *Journal of Autism and Developmental Disorders, 18*, 191–205.

KLIN, A. (1991). Young autistic children's listening preferences in regard to speech: A possible characterization of the symptom of social withdrawal. *Journal of Autism and Developmental Disorders, 21*, 29–42.

KURTZ, A. (1992, March). Testing for validity. *New England Newsletter on Facilitated Communication, 1, 3.*

LANDRY, S. H., & LOVELAND, K. A. (1988). Communication behaviors in autism and developmental language delay. *Journal of Child Psychology and Psychiatry and Allied Disciplines, 29*, 621–634.

LETT, J. (1992). The persistent popularity of the paranormal. *Skeptical Inquirer, 47*, 381–388.

LOVELAND, K., & KELLEY, M. L. (1991). Development of adaptive behavior in preschoolers with autism or Down syndrome. *American Journal of Mental Retardation, 96*, 13–20.

LURIA, A. R. (1980). *Higher cortical function in man.* New York: Basic Books.

MacDONALD, H., RUTTER, M., HOWLIN, P., RIOS, P., LECOUTEUR, D., EVERED, C., & FOLSTEIN, S. (1989). Recognition and expression of emotional cues by autistic and normal adults. *Journal of Child Psychology and Psychiatry and Allied Disciplines, 30*, 865–877.

MAURER, R. G. (1986). Neuropsychology of autism. *Psychiatric Clinics of North America, 9*, 367–380.

McLEAN, J. (1992, January). Facilitated communication: Some thoughts on Biklen's and Calculator's interaction. *American Journal of Speech and Language Pathology, 1*, 25–27.

McMULLEN, T. (1991). The savant syndrome and extrasensory perception. *Psychological Reports, 69*, 1004–1006.

MILLER, N. E. (1992). Introducing and teaching much-needed understanding of the scientific process. *American Psychologist, 47*, 848–850.

MOORE, S., DONOVAN, B., HUDSON, A., DYKSTRA, J., & LAWRENCE, J. (under submission). *Evaluation of facilitated communication: Eight case studies.*

MUNDY, P., SIGMAN, M., UNGERER, J., & SHERMAN, T. (1986). Defining the social deficits of autism: The contribution of non-verbal communication measures. *Journal of Child Psychology and Psychiatry and Allied Disciplines, 27*, 657–669.

NARITA, T., & KOGA, Y. (1987). Neuropsychological assessment of childhood autism. *Advances in Biological Psychiatry, 16*, 156–170.

NATIONAL PUBLIC RADIO. (1992, September 28). Discussion regarding facilitated communication with Douglas Biklen and Bernard Rimland. *Talk of the Nation* (radio broadcast).

OSWALD, D., & OLLENDICK, T. (1989). Role taking and social competence in autism and mental retardation. *Journal of Autism and Developmental Disorders, 19*, 119–128.

PIERCE, S., & BARTOLUCCI, G. (1977). A syntactic investigation of verbal autistic, mentally retarded, and normal children. *Journal of Autism and Developmental Disorders, 7*, 121–134.

PRIOR, M., & CUMMINS, R. (1992). Questions about facilitated communication and autism. *Journal of Autism and Developmental Disorders, 22*, 331–337.

PRIOR, M., DAHLSTROM, B., & SQUIRES, T. L. (1990). Autistic children's knowledge of thinking and feeling states in other people. *Journal of Child Psychology and Psychiatry and Allied Disciplines, 31*, 587–601.

RIMLAND, B. (Ed.). (1991). Facilitated communication reports generate heated controversy. *Autism Research Review International, 5*, 1–6.

RUMSEY, J., RAPOPORT, J. L., & SCEERY, W. R. (1985). Autistic children as adults: Psychiatric, social, and behavioral outcomes. *Journal of the American Academy of Child Psychiatry, 24*, 465–473.

SCHOPLER, E. (1992). Editorial commentary. *Journal of Autism and Developmental Disorders, 22*, 337–338.

SCHUBERT, A. (1991). *Facilitated communication resource guide.* Brookline, MA: Adrianna Foundation.

SHAPIRO, T., & HUEBNER, H. F. (1976). Speech patterns of five psychotic children now in adolescence. *Journal of the American Academy of Child Psychiatry, 15*, 278–293.

SILLIMAN, E. R. (1992). Three perspectives of facilitated communication: Unexpected literacy, Clever Hans, or enigma? *Topics in Language Disorders, 12*, 60–68.

SIMMONS, J. Q., & BALTAXE, C. (1975). Language patterns of adolescent autistics. *Journal of Autism and Developmental Disorders, 5*, 333–351.

SNOWLING, M., & FRITH, U. (1987). Comprehension in "hyperlexic" readers. *Journal of Experimental Child Psychology, 42*, 392–415.

SZEMPRUCH, J., & JACOBSON, J. W. (1992). *Evaluating facilitated communications of people with developmental disabilities.* Rome, NY: Rome Developmental Disabilities Services Office.

TAGLER-FLUSBERG, H. (1985a). Basic level and superordinate level categorization by autistic, mentally retarded, and normal children. *Journal of Experimental Child Psychology, 40,* 450–469.

TAGLER-FLUSBERG, H. (1985b). The conceptual basis for referential word meaning in children with autism. *Child Development, 56,* 1167–1178.

TAGLER-FLUSBERG, H., & ANDERSON, M. (1991). The development of contingent discourse ability in autistic children. *Journal of Child Psychology and Psychiatry and Allied Disciplines, 32,* 1123–1134.

THAGARD, P. (1988). *Computational philosophy of science.* Cambridge, MA: The MIT Press.

THORNDIKE, R., HAGEN, E., & SATTLER, J. (1986). *The Stanford-Binet intelligence scale* (4th ed.). Chicago: Riverside.

UNGERER, J. A., & SIGMAN, M. (1987). Categorization skills and receptive language development in autistic children. *Journal of Autism and Developmental Disorders, 17,* 3–16.

VAN LANCKER, D., CORNELIUS, C., & KREIMAN, J. (1989). Recognition of emotional-prosodic meanings in speech by autistic, schizophrenic, and normal children. *Developmental Neuropsychology, 5,* 207–226.

VAN LANCKER, D., CORNELIUS, C., & NEEDLEMAN, R. (1991). Comprehension of verbal terms for emotions in normal, autistic, and schizophrenic children. *Developmental Neuropsychology, 7,* 1–18.

VOLDEN, J., & LORD, C. (1991). Neologisms and idiosyncratic language in autistic speakers. *Journal of Autism and Developmental Disorders, 21,* 109–130.

WATERHOUSE, L., & FEIN, D. (1984). Developmental trends in cognitive skills for children diagnosed as autistic and schizophrenic. *Child Development, 55,* 236–248.

WENAR, C., RUTTENBERG, B. A., KALISH-WEISS, B., & Wolf, E. (1986). The development of normal and autistic children: A comparative study. *Journal of Autism and Developmental Disorders, 16,* 317–333.

WHEELER, D. L., JACOBSON, J. W., PAGLIERI, R. A., & SCHWARTZ, A. A. (in press). An experimental assessment of facilitated communication. *Mental Retardation.*

WHITEHOUSE, D., & HARRIS, J. C. (1984). Hyperlexia in infantile autism. *Journal of Autism and Developmental Disorders, 14,* 281–289.

WING, L. (1976). *Autistic children: A guide for parents and professionals.* New York: Brunner/Mazel.

YATES, J. (1986). Communication and intentionality in autism. *Educational and Child Psychology, 3,* 55–60.

YETERIAN, E. H. (1987). Childhood autism as a forebrain disorder: Review of a neural model and selected brain imaging and drug therapy studies. In J. A. Mulick & R. F. Antonak (Eds.), *Transitions in mental retardation* (pp. 235–253). Norwood, NJ: Ablex.

CHAPTER 5

A Comprehensive Program for Serving People with Autism and Their Families: The TEACCH Model

Gary B. Mesibov
SCHOOL OF MEDICINE,
UNIVERSITY OF NORTH CAROLINA AT CHAPEL HILL

Autism is a complex disability, affecting communication as well as social, cognitive, and behavioral functioning (Rutter & Schopler, 1978). The most severe of the developmental disabilities, autism causes stress, confusion, and frustration among both people with autism and their families (Schopler & Mesibov, 1984). Programs to serve this population appropriately must be as comprehensive as the disability itself.

Division TEACCH, North Carolina's statewide program serving people with autism and their families, began over 25 years ago (Schopler, 1986) with the mission of assuring the full array of services needed by people with autism and their families throughout their lives. A mandate of this magnitude requires multiple approaches, complex administrative structures, and comprehensive services. Division TEACCH continues to develop such strategies in response to the many challenges presented by autism.

This chapter outlines the evolution of the Division TEACCH program. After tracing the early history, the chapter describes the program's organization, philosophy, services, research, and training efforts. The importance of having a comprehensive, integrated, and coordinated program effort is emphasized throughout.

History

The TEACCH program originated in a psycho-analytic group for children with autism and their parents at the University of North Carolina at Chapel Hill in the early 1960s. The original intervention offered psychodynamic group therapy for the children, allowing them total freedom to express their feelings, and intensive group therapy for the parents, who were the suspected cause of their children's severe handicaps. A university faculty member, and later Division TEACCH's founder, Eric Schopler, and his colleague Robert Reichler recognized the substantial limitations of this therapeutic approach: it did not appear to help the children; in fact, it made their inappropriate behaviors more frequent and intense.

Based on their experiences and observations, Schopler and Reichler adopted the radical proposition that autism is not caused by parent pathology, but by an unidentified organic brain abnormality. Thus, they changed their focus from providing psychotherapy for parents and children to developing environments conducive to the cognitive needs of people with autism, based on an understanding of brain pathology. This approach dramatically altered the parental role. Rather than being blamed as the cause of autism, parents were viewed as both its victims and the major vehicle for their child's improved adaptation.

In 1966, Schopler and Reichler tested their innovative notions about autism empirically. In their grant proposal to the National Institutes of Mental Health (NIMH), they suggested an intervention consisting of training parents as co-therapists for their children with autism. Their proposal advocated parent-professional collaboration designed to pool information and resources in order to develop and implement individualized treatment programs for each child. After determining appropriate plans for the children, the project proposed to implement them by training parents in specific intervention techniques and helping them improve their interactions with their handicapped children. Troublesome behavioral problems, such as temper tantrums and toileting difficulties, were another focus of these collaborative parent-professional treatment sessions.

This innovative treatment approach was successful beyond even the participants' high expectations (Schopler & Reichler, 1971). Parents enthusiastically embraced the training. Many contributed to the intervention programs with innovative ideas of their own. Around 1970, word of this exciting experiment spread beyond North Carolina as the federal grant approached completion.

The parents and professionals who had struggled to create this new approach were not deterred by the end of the federal grant. During the project, the parents had formed a North Carolina chapter of the National Society for Autistic Children (NSAC). The state chapter endorsed the continuation of the project as its priority and worked tirelessly to obtain the North Carolina state legislature's support. As a result, in 1972, Division TEACCH was established by the North Carolina legislature as the United States' first statewide program for diagnosis, treatment, training, research, and education of autistic children and their families. A rare example of a federally funded program being adopted and expanded by a state, Division TEACCH had a legitimate mandate to serve people with autism and their families throughout North Carolina.

Organizational Structure

The TEACCH program consists of six regional centers around the state, each housed near three important resources: (a) a campus of the University of North Carolina system, (b) a developmental evaluation clinic (DEC) mandated to evaluate young handicapped children, and (c) an area health education center (AHEC) designed to provide up-to-date health care to all areas of the state.

The role of each TEACCH center is to coordinate services for people with autism and their families in its region. The centers provide diagnostic and family training services for children referred because of characteristics that might be related to autism. They also provide such direct services as social skills training, vocational training, and case management.

In addition to direct services, the regional centers collaborate with other agencies involved in service provision. The largest collaboration is with the Department of Public Instruction. North Carolina has over 100 self-contained classrooms for people with autism located in regular public school facilities. Although the classrooms are administered by local education agencies, Division TEACCH trains the teachers, provides regular consultation, and organizes annual in-service training. Since many children with autism attend educational programs outside of TEACCH classrooms (e.g., in learning disabilities resource rooms or regular classrooms), the TEACCH centers also provide assistance, support, and training to these programs. In addition, collaborative relationships also exist between

TEACCH centers and agencies providing early intervention services, residential services, vocational services, and other assistance to children with autism and their families.

The regional TEACCH centers are administered and coordinated by an administrative and research (A&R) unit. Directed by Schopler and myself, full professors of psychology and psychiatry in the School of Medicine at the University of North Carolina at Chapel Hill, this unit is responsible for overall program administration, direction, and coordination. The TEACCH A&R unit also serves as the main liaison with the North Carolina state legislature and the statewide parent group, the chapter of the Autism Society of North Carolina.

Each regional center is directed by a doctoral-level psychologist, licensed by the state of North Carolina to provide clinical services. Each clinical director supervises a staff of four to six therapists with backgrounds in serving people with handicaps and especially those with autism. Therapists come from many disciplines: special education, speech and language, social work, psychology, occupational therapy, child development, recreational therapy, and rehabilitation counseling. Although most TEACCH therapists have concentrated professional training in a specific discipline, they function as generalists in the TEACCH program, providing the full range of services needed by people with autism and their families.

Philosophy

As the TEACCH program has matured, certain philosophical principles about the nature of autism and its treatment have emerged. Although constantly reexamined in light of current developments, these principles have remained useful and effective guidelines for program efforts. Enduring principles directing the TEACCH program emphasize the organically based perceptions and world views of people with autism; parent-professional collaboration; the generalist model; comprehensive, coordinated, lifelong, community-based services;

and individualization. Each of these principles will be briefly discussed.

Organically Based Perceptions and World Views of People with Autism

Although most professionals today accept autism as an organic disability, they often ignore the most obvious implications of this reality. That is, organically impaired people with autism often process information and understand the world differently than their nonhandicapped peers do. Concepts such as normalization, therefore, are less applicable to this group than to others. People with autism do not simply need normal treatment; they need others to understand their different ways of viewing the world and to help bridge the gap between their perceptions and those shared by the rest of society.

The TEACCH program accepts that there are differences between people with autism and the general population. Without diminishing the rights of those with autism or sacrificing their dignity, the program aims to understand the implications of their cognitive impairments and to use this information to reduce the gap between the way they think and what is necessary for them to function adequately in adult society. Consequently, the key concepts in the TEACCH approach are tolerance, compromise, acceptance, and personal enhancement rather than normalization.

Parent-Professional Collaboration

Acknowledging that parents know more about their children and realizing that professionals understand more about the autism syndrome, parents and professionals in North Carolina have joined to create a partnership that has become larger and more effective than either group alone. This collaborative effort has continued for the past two decades and is responsible for many advances in services for people with autism in North Carolina (Schopler, Mesibov, Shigley, & Bashford, 1984).

Parent-professional collaboration is important for several reasons. First, it assures the best possible services for each child with autism by combining parental concern and experience with professional expertise and perspective. Parent-professional collaboration also encourages mutual support and growth. Children with autism generally are incapable of giving much emotional feedback to those who help them. Thus, parents and professionals working separately often find themselves emotionally isolated. However, working together as partners, they can offer each other the emotional support that neither receives directly from the children.

The parent-professional collaborative alliance is also politically potent. Parents of handicapped children can be influential with state governments when organized and determined. With access to the knowledge, vision, and expertise of professional partners, they can be formidable advocates for the services that they need.

Parent-professional collaborative relationships represent a sensible way to build strong programs for people with autism. Unfortunately, they are difficult to achieve as they require the ability to see the other group's perspective as clearly as one's own and a willingness to subordinate personal pride and goals to the welfare of the larger whole.

Generalist Model

When the TEACCH program began, most of the families had already contacted professionals from a variety of disciplines. Chief among their complaints was the professionals' tendency to view their children narrowly through the eyes of their specific disciplines. Rather than seeing a child, many professionals saw a behavior problem, a speech deficit, family turmoil, or a new medical syndrome. Few saw the whole child in the context of a family.

Adopting a holistic approach, the TEACCH program considers children in the context of their aggregate skills, overall deficits, and unique family situations. Such a holistic approach requires a broad view of autism, of the needs of these children, and of the role of their families. The generalist model was developed to assure an appropriate emphasis on the central concerns—the needs of the children with autism and their families.

Thus, the generalist model avoids too much concentration on a single aspect of the child or the problem. TEACCH staff are trained as generalists, prepared to address all aspects of the problems of autism and the needs of the families; their roles are not determined by professional disciplines. Instead, all TEACCH staff are asked to focus on either the family's or the child's needs and to organize their information and recommendations around those central priorities.

Comprehensive, Coordinated, Lifelong, Community-Based Services

Because autism is a lifelong disability for which no cure has yet been found, people with autism and their families require comprehensive services across the life span (Mesibov, 1983). Such services must be coordinated so that there is consistency in teaching strategies and priorities throughout each child's life. Consistency over time and setting is important for students with autism because of their difficulties with learning and applying what they know in different situations. If demands and expectations are generally uniform throughout each child's life, later teaching can build on what has already been learned, optimizing his or her possibilities.

Because so many aspects of their functioning are impaired, people with autism require consistent approaches that target the many different areas of their functioning. Autism is not just a social or communication problem; it involves cognitive, sensory, behavioral, organizational, and planning difficulties as well. Each of these requires attention and treatment from a person knowledgeable about the disability and its effects on overall functioning.

Comprehensive programs and services are also crucial for people with autism because of the state of knowledge in this area. Autism is a poorly understood, low-incidence disability. Few disciplines have adequate training programs for students interested in helping these clients. Research and scholarly information are lacking at best and inaccurate in many cases. Thus, policy makers on the local, state, and national levels often make important decisions affecting the lives of people with autism based on inadequate information.

Given the unfortunate state of current information, programs for this population must take a broad view of their mission. Division TEACCH defines its role as not only providing exemplary and comprehensive services to people with autism and their families, but also developing appropriate preservice and in-service training programs, initiating and disseminating research, and participating in policymaking on the local, state, national, and international levels.

Individualization

Although the program follows general principles such as structured teaching and community-based instruction, the key to the effectiveness of Division TEACCH is the application of these principles based on the individual needs of each client and family. Although there are general strategies and techniques that have proven useful for all people with autism and their families, the specific implementations differ for each individual situation. For example, a teaching task for one child might use words because the child is verbal, whereas a task for a child who does not understand words might use pictures or objects. Similarly, some families work hard with their children in structured teaching sessions each evening. For other families, their lack of skills and their other commitments make it undesirable and impossible for them to assume these daily obligations.

The TEACCH program works hard to find the unique applications of its principles, philosophies, and services to each family. The key concept is a balance—having the uniformity and consistency to systematically provide what is needed, yet offering sufficient individualization for the specific skills, strengths, and interests of each individual client and family.

Services

The goal of Division TEACCH has always been to provide the full array of services needed by people with autism and their families throughout their lives. Starting with diagnostic and parent-training opportunities when the children are first identified, these services branch out to include public school classrooms and, ultimately, local community vocational and residential programs when the children become adults. The comprehensiveness of these lifelong services is essential to ensure that people with autism reach their potentials and that family members have the support and assistance that they need.

Clinic Diagnostic Services

Contact with a TEACCH center usually begins with a referral. Each of the six regional centers accepts referrals from physicians, preschool programs, public school programs, early intervention programs, child evaluation clinics, and the families themselves. Following a determination that the referral is appropriate (the child has primary problems in areas related to autism, i.e., communication, socialization, resistance to change, and sensory functions), the first visit to a TEACCH center is generally on the diagnostic and assessment day. Although both a diagnosis and an assessment are completed during the same full-day initial evaluation, each emphasizes different aspects. Diagnostic classification refers to identification of characteristics that are similar among people with autism. The purpose of diagnosis is primarily administrative: a decision is being made whether the referred child fits generally accepted criteria for autism. To facilitate this process, Division TEACCH has developed the *Childhood Autism Rating Scale* (CARS) (Schopler, Reichler, & Renner, 1988).

While the diagnostic process seeks out characteristics that people with autism have in common, the assessment process targets each person's and family's uniqueness. Although a diagnostic label is important to help a family understand its child's difficulty, it does not identify specific teaching goals. Knowing that a child has autism does not tell parents or professionals how that child learns or what to teach. Although there are commonalities among people with autism, each person has unique learning styles, needs, and strategies. Division TEACCH has developed two assessment instruments to identify this uniqueness: the *Psychoeducational Profile—Revised* (PEP-R) (Schopler, Reichler, Bashford, Lansing, & Marcus, 1990) for young children, and the *Adolescent and Adult Psychoeducational Profile* (AAPEP) (Mesibov, Schopler, Schaffer, & Landrus, 1988) for adolescents and adults. Information from these instruments is combined with extensive parent interviews and discussions with teachers and other relevant community professionals. Together, this information forms the basis of the next phase of the program, the extended diagnostic process.

Clinic Extended Diagnostic Services

After completing an evaluation and interpreting the results to the family, Division TEACCH offers extended diagnostic sessions to assist families in developing skills and increasing their understanding of their children. The extended diagnostic phase includes weekly sessions for as long as the family wishes, typically from 6 to 8 weeks. During this phase, two therapists are assigned to each family, one to work primarily with the child (child therapist) and the other to work with the parents (parent consultant).

The child therapist works directly with the child, trying to identify strengths, interests, and appropriate teaching strategies. Using results from the assessment, information from the parents and appropriate professionals, and observations from direct work with the child in the clinic, the child therapist proposes appropriate goals and suggests strategies for implementing them. Goals are discussed and mutually agreed upon by the family and the therapists to assure that they are feasible and useful. Once goals are established, the child therapist helps the family reach the goals by writing home programs for them to practice, modeling teaching strategies behind a one-way mirror in the clinic, and providing feedback to the parents after observing their direct work with their child.

The parent consultant works in collaboration with the child therapist to develop and implement appropriate teaching strategies. The parent consultant's other role is to help improve the family's understanding of its child's disability. Thus, these consultants review the results of the full-day evaluation with the family as often as necessary during the extended diagnostic process. They also support the family emotionally, helping it cope with the child's disability and the issues it raises in the extended family and community. The parent consultant also helps the family organize its priorities so that the selected intervention goals are the most beneficial.

Classroom Programs

Although the main focus of the extended diagnostic process is training parents to manage and understand their children, that process also offers an opportunity to review the child's current schooling and suggest possible changes. Parents in North Carolina have several models of school programs to choose from. The first and most popular are the special classes for children with autism, located in regular public schools with same-aged nonhandicapped peers. Approximately 110 classrooms throughout the state follow this model. Classes have from five to nine students with a teacher plus enough assistants to make a student-to-adult ratio of 3:1. For example, classrooms with six students or fewer have one teacher and one assistant, and classrooms with from six to nine students have an additional assistant.

Other classroom models are as varied as the school systems in the state. For example, some children with autism, generally the higher-functioning group, are mainstreamed into regular classes for certain periods of the day. Some of these children receive no extra assistance; some have one-to-one assistance throughout the school day; others are mainstreamed without assistance but spend extensive time in resource rooms. Some children with autism are placed in learning disabilities programs; others are placed in programs for moderately mentally retarded students. The goal in educational placement is to find the situation or combination of programs that will meet the needs of each individual child. Parent-teacher collaborative efforts, initiated during the diagnostic process, are essential for finding the best available school programs.

Although Division TEACCH plays an important role in North Carolina's public school programs, it does not administer the programs. Instead, each program is administered by the local public school system. Division TEACCH works in collaboration with these agencies in locating appropriate teachers, consulting about the student's placement and classroom management, and coordinating teacher training.

Division TEACCH conducts intensive 1-week preservice training programs for all teachers and assistants who are hired to work in the state. The training emphasizes the unique aspects of autism and provides practicum experiences in classroom settings to demonstrate how to implement TEACCH philosophies and techniques. This training is followed immediately by two days of orientation by the teacher's or assistant's regional clinic. These two days familiarize teachers and assistants with the local TEACCH resources and help them prepare for working with their students. Although the teachers and assistants are new to their children, Division TEACCH generally has worked with the children and families and has useful information about them.

Following the preservice training and follow-up orientation, each new teacher and assistant is visited by a consultant from the TEACCH center on a regular basis. These visits are usually monthly at first, becoming less frequent. The consultation visits are designed to help implement the TEACCH techniques and discuss problems or concerns. Consultants are available for crisis intervention whenever the need arises.

Division TEACCH also provides ongoing in-service training to all teachers and assistants of students with autism in North Carolina, consisting of two statewide meetings annually plus several regional activities. The comprehensive in-service training program assures that teachers have access to up-to-date information and approaches.

Residential Programs

Division TEACCH collaborates with the North Carolina Department of Human Resources to provide residential services to people with autism and their families. This collaborative arrangement is similar to TEACCH's relationship with the public schools; that is, the State Department of Human Resources administers the programs while TEACCH provides consultation in program development, program implementation, and preservice and in-service training of staff.

The philosophy behind residential services is to provide a continuum of opportunities to allow for individual needs and family preferences. Although recent trends in the field have been to limit residential options to small-group normalized settings, Division TEACCH does not define its role as dictating what families should want for their children. Instead, it uses the collaborative process and listens to families so that a range of services that are consistent with their wishes and appropriate for their children can be developed.

The most common residential service in North Carolina is the small, community-based, group home for adults. Serving from five to six residents, these year-round programs provide for the full range of needs and skills, are viewed as permanent homes, and are staffed according to the clients' needs.

When clients are capable of functioning in less restrictive settings, they are moved to sheltered apartments, where two or three adults with autism live together. These apartments usually have responsible staff nearby but not living in the same dwelling. Clients in these programs work in their community, shop, cook, and generally function independently with a minimum of assistance and supervision. As TEACCH clients mature, a growing number of them are becoming capable of this semi-independent lifestyle.

A new and exciting residential option is the Carolina Living and Learning Center (CLLC). Inspired by similar programs in England (Somerset Court) and Ohio (Bittersweet Farms), this is a rural alternative to the group home. Whereas group homes are generally situated in more urban parts of the state where there is access to transportation and downtown shopping facilities, the CLLC is a farm where people with autism can have the rural lifestyle so common in North Carolina. The day program encourages residents to carry out the daily responsibilities of managing a farm. Clients are engaged in typical farming activities such as harvesting crops, managing land, and caring for animals. An important difference between the CLLC and typical residential models is the integration of the living and working environments. When completed, the CLLC is projected to serve 25–30 clients.

Because North Carolina's residential programs are costly, the number of available residential units is limited and does not meet the compelling demand. As a result, priorities must be set. Most of the residential programs are reserved for adults, because adults with autism have fewer other opportunities.

Vocational Programs

The goal of the vocational programs is to identify a continuum of services appropriate for people with autism who have different yet overlapping needs. A particular program for an individual is selected based on the person's strengths and needs, informed choices by the person, family, and other caretakers, the appropriateness and intensity of the person's educational preparation, and the realities of the local job market.

Division TEACCH has developed a range of vocational models to meet the needs of adults with autism in North Carolina, ranging from those requiring minimal supervision to those requiring intensive support. These models are the job coach, the enclave, the small business, the mobile crew, the sheltered workshop, and the rural residential program.

Job coach. The job coach model has been highly successful. Designed for higher-functioning individuals capable of vocational independence after a period of intensive training, this model has led to placement of clients in many employment settings around the state. Division TEACCH has placed approximately 70 people with autism in jobs using this model and expects to add about 15 more per year.

The job coach assists a client in identifying appropriate jobs and doing what is necessary to get hired (make telephone calls, participate in job interviews, etc.). Once a client is hired, the job coach goes to the job setting daily to help the client learn the responsibilities of the job and to assure adequate adjustment to the employment setting. The job coach also helps management and nonhandicapped employees understand and work with the person with autism. The amount of time spent on the job by the job coach varies, ranging from 20 to 300 hours, depending on the needs of the client and the job setting; the average is 150 hours.

While it is not necessarily the best vocational model, the job coach model is cost effective and has been adequately funded by the North Carolina Division of Vocational Rehabilitation through a collaborative plan with Division TEACCH.

Enclave. Enclaves have evolved out of TEACCH's experiences with the job coach model. Although most clients served by job coaches have successfully maintained their placements, a few encountered problems on the job that made continued employment impossible. These clients were almost ready for competitive employment, but once or twice each week an incident occurred requiring special intervention and assistance. Although one or two incidents a week may not seem like much, the severity of the clients' handicaps and their inability to be totally independent at their jobs were significant enough to prompt even the most supportive employers to dismiss them.

Based on these experiences, TEACCH brought several of these clients together into two large food-service operations, one at a university and the other at a nursing home. From five to eight people with autism work in each of these settings with a full-time job coach employed by TEACCH to help avoid and manage disruptions. Thus, appropriate assistance is provided without reverting to the costly one-on-one or one-on-two supervision models that are typical for people with autism.

These enclave programs have been highly successful. Management is able to tolerate clients' brief improprieties because there is a trained professional available on site who can intervene immediately. Thus, the enclave model has made competitive employment possible for people with autism who cannot function successfully in a job unless assistance and support are available continuously.

Enclaves have been unfairly criticized by some professionals who stereotype them as separate rooms attached to industries where handicapped people earn 20 cents an hour and receive no benefits to do monotonous and repetitive jobs. This is not an accurate portrayal of the TEACCH enclaves. Clients work in different parts of the food services, busing tables, washing dishes, serving food, taking inventory, and operating equipment. They are employees of the organization managing the business, not of a workshop or Division TEACCH. Working in the same business but not doing the same job gives them the choice of interacting with nonhandicapped employees, with customers, or with one another. As a result, most of them choose to divide even their free time among the available options. In addition, as employees of large corporations, the clients earn more than the minimum wage and receive the same benefits as anyone else working for the same corporations at their level.

Small business. The small business model is similar to the enclave, except the organization operating the business is established to employ handicapped workers. Rather than hiring handicapped workers to supplement their staff, programs following this model hire nonhandicapped people to supplement the efforts of their handicapped clients. As owners and operators of the business, advocates for handicapped people have more control over factors that might facilitate or inhibit the handicapped clients' adaptation to the work setting. They also have more leverage with nonhandicapped workers and can require them to provide more support and supervision than is possible from nonhandicapped workers in enclaves.

Mobile crew. The mobile crew is a model further along the continuum, offering even greater support, supervision, and structure than enclaves or small businesses. A mobile crew is a group of supervised handicapped people providing a single service in several different settings. The TEACCH mobile crew cleans houses with one to three handicapped people working under the supervision of a coach. The work is typically done in individual houses where there is less noise and there are fewer distractions than in less sheltered businesses. The presence of a job coach assures additional structure, assistance support, and training. Clients in TEACCH mobile crews do real work for which they are paid at least the minimum wage.

Sheltered workshop. Sheltered workshops are harshly criticized by many professionals today. Designed as self-contained work environments for handicapped people, these programs are viewed by some as segregated, stagnant, and unproductive. The subcontract work typically performed in these settings is considered limiting, and the programs are often described as demeaning.

In spite of obvious limitations, sheltered workshops offer an option on the continuum of vocational services that meets important needs of some people with autism. Division TEACCH opposes the elimination of any options that adequately serve some people with autism. The experiences of Division TEACCH suggest that sheltered workshops can serve a useful role for some adults with autism. Intensive applications of TEACCH's structured teaching techniques (Mesibov, Schopler, & Hearsey, in press) have made several sheltered workshops in North Carolina into productive vocational settings.

Rural residential program. The final option on the vocational continuum is the CLLC discussed previously. This combination residential and vocational center provides numerous work options and experiences for people with autism. The close integration of outdoor farm work and residential services is well suited to the needs and skills of certain clients with autism. Although this program is mentioned last, it is not the least independent nor do the clients require the most supervision and support. This program cuts across the continuum of vocational options, allowing considerable independence for some clients and intensive support and assistance to others.

Other Agency Collaborations

Most of Division TEACCH's interagency collaboration is for school, residential, and vocational programs. However, TEACCH assists other agencies when their services and the needs of people with autism coincide. An example is North Carolina's early intervention program that provides in-home parent training. Although most of the needs met by this program are addressed in TEACCH's extended diagnostic sessions with families, sometimes further help is needed in their homes. TEACCH collaborates with the early intervention program to assure that the services provided are appropriate for people with autism and their families.

Research

Although there tends to be a dichotomy between research and practice in the mental health fields, this is neither inevitable nor desirable. It is, however, understandable. The demands of research and clinical practice are different, requiring considerable time and energy to reconcile. For example, a research project on diagnosis and assessment requires everyone to administer the identical test battery to each child who comes to the clinical center. In contrast, exemplary clinical practice individualizes for each child and family, administering different test batteries to different children depending on their needs and the referral questions.

Both clinical practice and research are demanding in their own right. Combining them involves increasing the already pressing demands on overloaded staff and families. However, we believe this extra effort is justified by the benefits of integrating research and clinical efforts. Ongoing productive research enhances clinical efforts; exemplary clinical practice makes research more relevant, important, and effective.

A vigorous research orientation has enhanced Division TEACCH in many ways. Active involvement in research activities requires staff to be fully informed about current developments in the field. Innovative ideas and ways of thinking are constantly challenging assumptions and procedures. Research puts the staff in contact with professionals from all over the world. Associations with others doing similar and important work add energy, ideas, and a sense of a larger mission.

Researchers in the TEACCH program, in turn, are richer because of their clinical involvement. They are constantly challenged with real-life problems and regularly questioned about the implications of their work for clinical practice.

As a result of Division TEACCH's dual mandate of innovative research and exemplary clinical practice, most of the research has focused on applied issues, such as intervention approaches. TEACCH research has stimulated important advances in diagnostic and assessment techniques, social skills training, and structured teaching. Research projects on family needs and concerns, early identification of children, and effectiveness of the extended diagnostic process have also supplemented and enhanced service delivery efforts.

Training

For several reasons, comprehensive training is essential for programs serving people with autism and their families. The severity of the disability and the variability among people with autism require special professional preparation. Sometimes the severe behaviors that occur can be serious and even life-threatening. Consequently, professionals have to know how to avoid such problems and how to manage them when prevention fails. Further, children with autism are diverse; IQs of clients in a single program can range from 20 to 140. Educating these children and assisting their families require a solid understanding of the disability and of different intervention strategies. Autism also places extra training demands on programs because of the inadequacy of preservice training preparation in most disciplines. The interdisciplinary focus required to adequately serve individuals with autism leads to a diffusion of responsibility; thus, no particular discipline recognizes autism as its priority. Therefore, this frequently misunderstood, low-incidence disorder is inadequately covered in virtually all university programs.

Recognizing the importance of training and acknowledging the inadequacies of preservice preparation programs, Division TEACCH has developed its own comprehensive training program to meet the compelling need for improved professional preparation. The program includes strong preservice and in-service components to address the needs of students and professionals at all levels.

Preservice Training

The three goals of Division TEACCH's preservice training program are (a) to familiarize undergraduate students with autism, (b) to provide specialized training to students in professional programs, and (c) to prepare teachers and group-home staff for careers in working with people with autism. Preservice training programs are intensive, providing students with the depth of information that serving people with autism demands.

The first preservice training component for undergraduate university students assumes that they have not selected an area of specialization. Although most of the students involved in these activities will not work with autistic people in their professional capacities, they are an important target nevertheless. As future citizens of the state and country, their attitudes toward handicapped people will affect programs and possibilities. Thus, the better they understand the compelling needs and exciting potential of clients with autism, the better informed they will be when making important decisions. Talented undergraduate students are also important because some may choose to work

professionally in the field of autism if their interest and commitment can be captured.

Lectures in general psychology and courses in special education are one way of reaching these undergraduate students. TEACCH staff are available for as many of these lectures as possible. Division TEACCH also provides direct experiences with autistic people. Appropriate opportunities for interacting with people with autism expose students to the excitement and challenges that the field offers. Babysitting for children with autism is one such opportunity. TEACCH also encourages undergraduates to participate in recreational social groups. Its social skills programs for adolescents and adults offer excellent opportunities for volunteers without sophisticated training to learn about autism by serving as peers who model appropriate social behavior. Several of TEACCH's successfully employed adults have student advocates who take them on community outings. This is another positive way for undergraduate students to learn about autism.

Intensive preservice training is also offered to advanced students majoring in areas related to autism. Division TEACCH provides practicum and internship experiences to students who are majoring in psychology, special education, rehabilitation counseling, recreation, speech and language, and social work. Opportunities range from brief part-time placements to full-time, yearlong rotations in the program. Such placements provide good opportunities for intensive involvement in the field of autism and help many students decide if it is to be their career choice. Similar training opportunities also are available for foreign students interested in studying the TEACCH program.

The third type of preservice training activity is for professionals beginning their careers. Although many of them had decided to work in autism while students in university programs, their academic departments did not offer concentrated training in this specialty. The TEACCH 1-week intensive preservice training model combines a thorough theoretical orientation with an opportunity to practice the principles at a training site with autistic students. This intensive training model has been effective in preparing teachers and group-home staff for their responsibilities.

The 1-week preservice training includes presentation of didactic material outlining basic information about autism, TEACCH's theoretical orientation, teaching strategies, curriculum, and classroom organizational systems. This information becomes more meaningful to trainees when practiced in the training classroom with autistic children. For example, a didactic lecture focusing on a specific aspect of autism is followed by an opportunity to implement activities with autistic children based on the principles from the lecture. An experienced TEACCH trainer guides trainees in the classroom. Finally, after hearing and applying the principles, trainees are encouraged to discuss the theories and their applications to better understand their scope and limitations. Each important concept essential for working with children with autism is presented and followed up in this way.

In-Service Training

Programs serving people with autism also need strong in-service training components. Because preservice training opportunities in autism are so limited, most professionals begin working with this population without adequate preparation. In-service training, therefore, is essential to compensate for limitations in most training programs.

In-service training is also important if professionals are to maintain state-of-the-art knowledge in this complex and rapidly changing area. Because the field of autism is truly interdisciplinary, advances in many disciplines affect theory and practice, making a comprehensive in-service training program particularly essential.

Finally, the intensity of the jobs and the isolation of those working with autistic clients are further reasons for in-service training. *Burnout* is a word commonly used to describe the tendency for many professionals to lose the enthusiasm and intensity required to work with children with autism. Solid in-service training has been documented as an effective way of dealing with such burnout, energizing professionals with fresh outlooks and promising new techniques.

Division TEACCH arranges local and statewide in-service training. Locally, each TEACCH clinic organizes in-service opportunities for professionals in its region. Models vary but include daylong presentations on topics of interest, opportunities for teachers to gather for informal discussions, and chances to visit other programs.

Division TEACCH also sponsors two major statewide in-service training activities each year. One occurs each February when over 300 professionals from all around North Carolina gather for 2½ days of seminars, lectures, and discussions. An outside speaker is generally invited to provide new and fresh perspectives. The core of the program, however, is presentations by TEACCH professionals describing successful techniques or innovative solutions to some of the difficulties that many staff confront. Small group discussions on topics of interest are another exciting part of this winter in-service program.

The other major in-service activity is the annual TEACCH conference each May. Now in its thirteenth year, this conference attracts professionals from around the world who gather for two days of lectures and discussions on major topics of interest in autism. North Carolina professionals also attend this important meeting.

Summary

Division TEACCH is in its third decade of providing comprehensive services to people with autism and their families. The TEACCH system has evolved into a program as all-inclusive as the disability demands. A comprehensive clinical, research, training, and service delivery system is essential for providing people with autism and their families with what they need to cope with the most severe of the developmental disabilities. Evidence suggests that a comprehensive approach of such scope can substantially improve the life situation of those with autism and their families (Schopler, Mesibov, & Baker, 1982).

References

MESIBOV, G. B. (1983). Current perspectives and issues in autism and adolescence. In E. Schopler & G. B. Mesibov (Eds.), *Autism in adolescents and adults* (pp. 37–53). New York: Plenum.

MESIBOV, G. B., SCHOPLER, E., & HEARSEY, K. (in press). Structured teaching. In E. Schopler & G. B. Mesibov (Eds.), *Assessment and treatment of behavior problems in autism*. New York: Plenum.

MESIBOV, G., SCHOPLER, E., SCHAFFER, B., & LANDRUS, R. (1988). *Individualized assessment and treatment for autistic and developmentally disabled children. Vol. 4: Adolescent and adult psychoeducational profile (AAPEP)*. Austin, TX: PRO-ED.

RUTTER, M., & SCHOPLER, E. (Eds.). (1978). *Autism: A reappraisal of concepts and treatment*. New York: Plenum.

SCHOPLER, E. (1986). Relationship between university research and state policy: Division TEACCH—Treatment and education of autistic and related communication handicapped children. *Popular Government, 51*, 23–32.

SCHOPLER, E., & MESIBOV, G. B. (Eds.). (1984). *The effects of autism on the family*. New York: Plenum.

SCHOPLER, E., MESIBOV, G. B., & BAKER, A. (1982). Evaluation of treatment for autistic children and their parents. *Journal of the American Academy of Child Psychiatry, 21*, 262–267.

SCHOPLER, E., MESIBOV, G. B., SHIGLEY, R. H., & BASHFORD, A. (1984). Helping autistic children through their parents: The TEACCH model. In E. Schopler & G. B. Mesibov (Eds.), *The effects of autism on the family* (pp. 65–81). New York: Plenum.

SCHOPLER, E., & REICHLER, R. J. (1971). Parents as co-therapists in the treatment of psychotic children. *Journal of Autism and Childhood Schizophrenia, 1*, 87–102.

SCHOPLER, E., REICHLER, R., BASHFORD, A., LANSING, M., & MARCUS, L. (1990). *Individualized assessment and treatment for autistic and developmentally disabled children. Vol. 1: Psychoeducational profile revised (PEP-R)*. Austin, TX: PRO-ED.

SCHOPLER, E., REICHLER, R. J., & RENNER, B. R. (1988). *The childhood autism rating scale (CARS)*. Los Angeles: Western Psychological Services.

CHAPTER 6

Autism: Differential Diagnosis

Raymond G. Romanczyk
Stephanie B. Lockshin
Carryl Navalta
STATE UNIVERSITY OF NEW YORK
AT BINGHAMTON

It is critical to stress that autism is a behavioral syndrome, not a disease entity, and that it is defined by a clustering of behaviors. Further, it is expressed in a heterogeneous manner and has multiple biological (as opposed to psychogenic) etiologies. The current standard for diagnosis, DSM-III-R, includes the general category of pervasive developmental disorders (PDDs), which are characterized by qualitative impairment in reciprocal social interaction, verbal and nonverbal communication skills, and imaginative activities and a restricted repertoire of interests and activities. Autistic disorder currently is the only recognized subtype of PDD. Problems of overlapping clinical descriptions have delayed agreement on additional subtypes. The diagnosis pervasive developmental disorder not otherwise specified (PDDNOS) is made when symptomatology is consistent with pervasive developmental disorder but does not meet the specific criteria of autistic disorder.

With respect to diagnoses of PDDs, definitions and recognition of their varied presentations pose major difficulties. Burd and Kerbeshian (1988) stated that "clearly, diagnostic criteria need to be refined when the majority of children classified are typically atypical" (p. 275). With respect to the diagnostic process, they commented that "it is not possible to make a definite diagnosis from the data generated from neuroradiological procedures, neuropathologic investigations, or other laboratory procedures as these methods cannot successfully link symptoms to actual brain dysfunction" (p. 276). Further, while autism, like mental retardation, has historically been associated with certain medical disorders (e.g., congenital rubella, infantile spasms, tuberous sclerosis, and cerebral lipoidosis), it has rarely been associated with other distinct disorders (e.g., Down's syndrome and cerebral palsy) (Rutter & Schopler, 1988).

Rutter and Schopler (1988), in distinguishing autistic from nonautistic children of similar mental age, viewed inability to discriminate socioemotional cues and cognitive deficits involving impaired language, sequencing, abstraction of meaning, and coding functions as most important. Although such deficits also occur with mental retardation, evidence suggests that they are consistent with the individual's mental age (i.e., delays in motor, social, and cognitive abilities are coordinated) (Ritvo & Freeman, 1978).

In contrast, research on cognitive deficits associated with autism has indicated that individuals with autism demonstrate large variability in intellectual functioning (Rutter & Lockyer, 1967). Performance is best for nonverbal tasks that utilize visual-spatial skills and immediate-memory verbal tasks. Rutter and Schopler (1988) offered the perspective that the abnormalities of language and social behavior with autism differ qualitatively from those observed with mental retardation and may be seen as deviant from normative behavior rather than delayed behavior.

Diagnostic Issues

Autism was first included in DSM-III (American Psychiatric Association, 1980), where it was grouped under the broad class of pervasive developmental disorders, with an emphasis on early onset, pervasive social unresponsiveness, language deficits and deviance, and bizarre responses to the environment. Volkmar and Cohen (1988) noted that "the considerable overlap and variability in symptom expression prove problematic in attempts to develop criteria which differentiate diagnostic groups on the basis of exclusive, necessary, and sufficient findings" (p. 76). In DSM-III-R, 16 items clustered in three categories must be present in a specific distribution across categories in order for the diagnosis of autism to be made. In a break with DSM-III and Kanner's original criteria, early onset is not a necessary criterion.

In support of the position that autism is a specific disorder, Rutter and Schopler (1988) found it improbable that autism and schizophrenia constitute subvarieties of the same basic condition. Rather, the authors concluded that autism constitutes a valid and meaningfully different psychiatric syndrome, suggesting that the evidence for its validity is stronger than for any other psychiatric condition in childhood. Most recently, it has come to be realized that what differentiates autism from other developmental disorders is the deviance, rather than the delay, in the developmental process. Therefore, diagnostic assessment should include a careful and systematic cognitive evaluation.

With regard to diagnostic rating systems, Rutter and Schopler (1988) suggested a combination of a detailed standardized parental interview designed to elicit key diagnostic features and a standardized observation system. Features that have differentiated autistic from nonautistic children of comparable mental age include (a) abnormalities in the appreciation of socioemotional cues, (b) cognitive deficits in the abstraction of meaning, (c) differential association with particular medical syndromes, (d) association with seizures that develop in adolescence rather than in early childhood, (e) concordance in monozygotic pairs of twins, and (f) familial loading on language-related cognitive impairments.

Differentiation of autism is most problematic in the case of children with severe mental retardation (mental age of 2 years). Another area of difficulty concerns the differentiation between autism and autistic-like disorders (e.g., Asperger's syndrome) in individuals of normal intelligence. The third difficulty in differential diagnosis occurs when there is a profound regression and behavioral disintegration following 3–4 years of apparently normal development (e.g., Heller's dementia infantilis). The fourth problem concerns conditions arising in early or middle childhood in which there is grossly disturbed behavior together with abnormalities in language and thought processes (e.g., early-onset schizophrenia). Finally, uncertainty also concerns the overlap between autism and severe developmental disorders of receptive language.

Rapin (1991) commented:

> If the definition of autism is behavioral, all persons who fulfill the behavioral criteria for autism should be considered autistic, whatever the etiology, associated symptomatology, severity, and course of their encephalopathy. . . . [Further,] as biologic markers for various conditions causing autistic symptomatology are defined, autism will gradually be partitioned into a number of subtypes due to specific etiologies or to the dysfunction of specific brain systems. (p. 752)

Also according to Rapin (1991), "the major differential diagnosis in the preschool child, once hearing loss has been ruled out, is between autism and mental deficiency in low-functioning children, and autism and developmental language disorder in higher-functioning ones" (p. 756). In the older child, adolescent, and young adult, the major choice is often between autism and mental deficiency for low-functioning persons or among autism, schizophrenia, and schizotypal personality disorder for higher-functioning persons. "The term disintegrative psychosis is used by some for children whose autistic symptomatology follows an acute encephalopathy, for example, an encephalitis, Reye's Syndrome, or a severe skull injury" (p. 752)

Gillberg (1990) emphasizes subtleties of diagnosis and has stated that "the diagnosis of autism is clinical and should not be made purely on the basis of some rating scale" (p. 99). While this stance is understandable in light of the perceived heterogeneity of autism and the current lack of a widely agreed-upon set of objective diagnostic criteria, it perpetuates an interpretive approach that serves to delay more exacting criteria that will permit needed research advances.

Wing (1989) described a "triad" of social impairments, which differentiates autism from other disorders: (a) social interaction, (b) social communication, and (c) imaginative development. Associated abnormalities or problems are often found in the areas of language, motor coordination, responses to sensory stimuli, cognitive skills, behavior, and psychiatric profile. Wing asserted that differential diagnosis rests essentially upon identifying the triad of social impairments. While this focus is interesting, it is not clear whether it aids accurate differential diagnosis.

One very important aspect of social development—play—remains understudied, particularly with respect to quantification. The research of Stone, Lemanek, Fishel, Fernandez, and Altemeier (1990) was designed to address two questions: (a) What characterizes the play behaviors and imitation skills of young autistic children during the preschool years? (b) How do the play behaviors and imitation skills of young autistic children differ from those of children with handicapping conditions that have overlapping symptoms?

The following children served as subjects: 22 with autism, 15 with mental retardation, 15 with hearing impairment, 14 with language impairment, and 20 with typical development. The sample consisted of 57 males and 34 females, aged 3 to 6 years old (mean age of 4 years, 6 months). For a diagnosis of autism, children were required to meet DSM-III diagnostic criteria. For the group of autistic children, CARS (*Childhood Autism Rating Scale*) scores were all within the autism range. No child in any other group obtained a CARS score in the autism range. The diagnosis of mental retardation required IQ scores at least 2 standard deviations below the mean (≤ 70 based on the *Merrill Palmer Scale of Mental Abilities*). The language-impaired children were required to demonstrate receptive or expressive language delays and no significant impairment in intellectual function (IQ > 70). Finally, the hearing impaired children all had documented bilateral hearing loss within the severe-to-profound range and no significant impairment in intellectual functioning.

Each subject was videotaped in a free-play situation for 8 minutes. The following play behaviors were scored: total number of toys used, total time spent playing with toys, time spent playing with toys appropriately, and level of toy play. For assessment of imitation skills, 12 motor imitation tasks were presented, and each child's responses were recorded "live." The tasks were derived from DeMyer, Barton, and Norton (1972). The children with mental retardation obtained significantly lower IQ scores than all the others, and their scores did not differ from one another's. The children with autism used fewer toys than the language-impaired, hearing-impaired, and nonhandicapped children, and they spent less total time playing with toys compared to children in all other groups. Also, the children with autism demonstrated few functional play acts compared with all other groups, and their imitation skills were significantly lower than those of children in all other groups.

A three-variable model was obtained, with a stepwise discriminant function analysis where appropriate toy play, functional play, and imitation accounted for 70% of the variance in group membership (autism versus nonautism). The imitation score accounted for 65% of the variance. Eighty-two percent of the children with autism and 100% of the children without autism were classified correctly with the three-variable model. A second discriminant-function analysis was conducted to determine the extent to which play and imitation variables differentiated the autism group from the mental retardation group. Imitation accounted for 56% of the variance, and functional play for 5%. "The results of this study suggest that weak imitation skills and low levels of functional play constitute important early features of autism, whereas deficits in symbolic play may be less critical for diagnosis in the preschool years" (DeMyer et al., 1972, p. 272). The relative importance of play and imitation skills remains to be determined.

Myers (1989) observed that there may be unevenness of intellectual abilities, which "is particularly striking in children with mental retardation and autism" (p. 85). Therefore, professionals must be aware of possible biases. Evidence suggests that a major proportion of children with autism are also mentally retarded and that intelligence testing can be predictive of future functioning. Certain common misconceptions may lead to erroneous diagnoses (Myers, 1989):

1. Negativism—a response to demands beyond ability to comply
2. Bright, alert look—people commonly judge intelligence based on apparent alertness to the environment, which may be misleading
3. Normal physiognomy—"a child does not need to 'look retarded' to be retarded . . ." (p. 87)
4. Normal motor development—"has no implication for future mental development" (p. 87)
5. Isolated areas of apparently normal intellectual functioning
   a. Good mechanical abilities
   b. Normal puzzle-solving abilities

   c. Ability to "read"
   d. Unusual speech characteristics
   e. Unitary approach to differential diagnosis—a single explanation for a number of signs and symptoms
   f. Erroneous post hoc, ergo propter hoc reasoning
   g. Greater acceptability of the diagnosis of infantile autism than of that of mental retardation

Asperger's Syndrome

Asperger's syndrome has received increasing attention in recent years and is a controversial topic. Wing (1981, 1989) described characteristics of Asperger's syndrome, such as "odd, naive, egocentric style of social interaction; long-winded, pedantic, repetitive speech; a limited range of circumscribed interests pursued to the exclusion of other activities; poor coordination of movements; and a conspicuous lack of common sense" (p. 6). Green (1990) stated:

> On most tests of social functioning and neurobiological investigations, including physical disorders, chromosome analysis, and brain imaging, Asperger syndrome and infantile autism differ in degree rather than kind, and a number of family pedigrees have been reported in which both Asperger syndrome and infantile autism have been clearly present. All this evidence, along with the clinical similarities, make a strong case for Asperger syndrome being a mild variant of infantile autism. (pp. 744–745)

However, there are developmental differences, particularly the absence of early language disorder, in Asperger's syndrome. There are also differences in current functioning (even when groups are matched for intelligence), including a greater incidence of psychiatric disorder, better educational outcome, a tendency to greater sociability, and the presence of clumsiness.

Comparing Asperger's syndrome, as described by Asperger and as modified by Wing (1981), with the syndrome of autism, as currently defined, makes it increasingly difficult to reconcile the claim that autism is significantly different from other syndromes unless Asperger's syndrome is admitted to the same diagnostic category. Bowman (1988) described a family of four boys and their father that provides some support for the connection between the two conditions. The youngest boy exhibited the features of Asperger's syndrome, two brothers satisfied the diagnostic criteria for autism, and the fourth did not have any clinical symptomatology. All four were of normal intelligence (WISC-R or WAIS). "This evidence supports Wing's (1981) hypothesis that the variation in the two conditions could be explained on the basis of severity . . . and suggests that Asperger's syndrome, with its apparently normal verbal intelligence, may be autism in its most pure form" (p. 381). All four boys showed the cognitive and psycholinguistic profile associated with autism.

In contrast, Pomeroy, Friedman, and Stephen (1990) stated:

> With regard to subgroups in PDD, it seems premature to conclude that there are no significant differences between children diagnosed as having high-functioning autism and those considered to have Asperger Syndrome, since we are unable to assess whether either group is truly homogeneous and the boundaries of selection are dictated by clinical referral (and, presumably, by the researcher's preconception of the disorder being studied). Potential subgroups could be missed. (p. 832)

Szatmari, Bartolucci, and Bremner (1989) examined the diagnostic validity of Asperger's syndrome by determining to what extent children with this syndrome differ in early history and present status from two comparison groups of (a) nonretarded children with autism and (b) children referred to a psychiatric clinic with nonspecific problems in getting along with other children as part of their presenting complaint. The inclusion criteria for the Asperger's syndrome (AS) group was adapted from Wing (1981). Of 38 children referred for the AS group, 10 were eliminated upon assessment. The final AS sample of 28 children comprised 5 females and 23 males, with an average age of 14 years. The high-functioning autism (HFA) sample consisted of 25 individuals (6 females, 19 males) whose average age was 23 years. The mean IQ of the HFA group was 85. The outpatient control (OPC) group consisted of 42 children (34 males and 8 females) whose average age was 14 years. To be included in the study, these children had to present a problem in getting along with other children of the same age, for whatever reason. They also had to match the AS group on age and sex and could not have a history of brain damage.

Early history data were available for 27 of the 28 Asperger's syndrome children and for all but 1 of the 25 autistic children. These data were gathered from parent and child interviews and school history forms. Early history information from the parent interview included social responsiveness, deviant language, bizarre behavior, impairments in nonverbal communication, clumsiness, and age at onset. An assessment of current psychiatric symptoms was made from the parent and child versions of the *Diagnostic Interview for Children and Adolescents* (DICA) (Herjanic & Reich, 1982).

The three groups differed significantly on all measures of social responsiveness. The HFA and AS groups differed in early history of bizarre preoccupations, motor stereotypies, and symptoms of insistence. There was no difference in the two PDD groups' ability to use or understand nonverbal means of communication. There also was no difference among the three groups in performing fine-motor activities. Further, differences in age at onset were not significant. On the DICA, the autism group had fewer schizotypal symptoms than either the AS or the OPC group. All three groups differed with respect to history of special education, with the HFA group having spent more time in special education than the AS group. A cluster analysis of early history variables revealed that the autism group had high scores on all of these variables, while the AS group obtained low scores on all of them. The main finding of this report is that no substantive, qualitative differences were found between the AS and HFA groups. Based on these results, the authors suggested that "it may be best to think of AS a mild form of HFA" (p. 717).

Issues of Onset

Burd, Fisher, and Kerbeshian (1988) presented detailed case reports of two individuals with a clear age of onset later than 30 months from a geographically defined population of 59 DSM-III–defined PDD individuals. These subjects were compared with other childhood-onset PDD individuals (COPDD) in the literature and with individuals described as demonstrating the later-onset disorders referred to as "dementia infantilis" and "disintegrative psychosis." The authors argued that individuals who meet strict DSM-III criteria for COPDD do not have a developmental disorder but rather a disintegrative disorder that results in functional muteness, severe autistic symptoms, and profound mental retardation with an extremely poor prognosis. The authors suggested that "these children should be differentiated from children with PDD in classification systems" (p. 156) and recommended the use of the diagnostic term 'pervasive disintegrative disorder,' which points to the symptomatic similarities with PDD, but which also highlights the disintegrative course of such children" (p. 161).

In an extension of their work, Burd, Fisher, and Kerbeshian (1989) presented data and discussed similarities and differences between males and females with acquired autism symptoms. According to the authors, there are sufficient differences between the sexes to warrant separate classification. "In the main, male children with acquired autistic conditions tend to have a late onset and females a much earlier onset" (p. 610). Various diagnoses for acquired autism conditions include (a) Heller's disease, (b) dementia infantilis, (c) disintegrative psychosis, (d) Rett syndrome, (e) childhood-onset pervasive developmental disorder, and (f) autistic disorder, late onset. The authors "believe that dementia infantilis and Rett Syndrome are not synonymous, but rather are separate conditions which can be distinguished on the basis of sex, age at onset, motor impairments and types of stereotypic behavior when specific diagnostic criteria are rigorously applied" (p. 612).

Volkmar and Cohen (1989) conducted a study to determine (a) whether cases of disintegrative disorder could be identified among a large group of individuals diagnosed as autistic and (b) which features of clinical presentation or course could differentiate these cases from those of more "typical" autism. A total of 165 (136 males and 29 females) were selected from consecutive cases that had been assessed for autism during a 10-year period. Subjects were included if they met Rutter's (1978) behavioral criteria of autism. Cases were reviewed by one or both of the authors to determine whether the child met ICD-10 criteria for disintegrative disorder and the age of onset. Age of onset or recognition was typically determined from copies of previous evaluations and early medical records. Ten cases (all males) met ICD-10 criteria for disintegrative disorder. All 10 cases appeared to have experienced a prolonged period (at least 2 years) of normal development, including the use of communicative speech, before the onset of developmental regression. The remaining 155 cases were divided into an early-onset group ($N = 136$, 109 males and 27 females), with onset prior to 24 months of age, and a later-onset group ($N = 19$, 17 males and 2 females), with onset after 24 months of age. Onset for the later-onset group was between 2 and 4 years of age.

The three groups differed in IQ, with the disintegrative disorder group exhibiting the lowest mean IQ and the later-onset autism group the highest mean IQ. Subjects with disintegrative disorder were significantly more likely than the late-onset subjects to be mute and significantly more likely to be in residential placement than either the early-onset or the late-onset subjects. Volkmar and Cohen (1989) concluded:

> Despite behaviorally exhibiting features of autism, the cases in this series differed from more typically autistic children in both the clinical presentation of their disorder and its course; these differences were particularly marked when such cases were compared to "late onset" autistic ones. This difference provides support for providing a separate diagnostic category for disintegrative disorder. (p. 723)

However, it is important to note that these authors also stated that "the distinction between autism and disintegrative disorder may be less important for the practical clinical management of such children than for research studies" (p. 723). Whitehouse (1990) reinforced this important perspective by stating that "grouping Rett Syndrome and the 'Heller type' together, and apart from childhood autism, might cloud the complex phenomenology for non-experts, implying an as yet unfounded understanding, rather than clarify the issues" (p. 556).

Diagnostic Instruments

A wide range of diagnostic instruments are used for clinical and research purposes to assist in the diagnosis of autism. The relationship between these instruments and DSM-III-R criteria and also among the instruments themselves is far from adequate, highlighting the difficulty of achieving consensus on diagnostic criteria. Newsom, Hovanitz, and Rincover (1988) reviewed a number of important instruments, including Rimland's *Diagnostic Checklist for Behavior Disturbed Children*, Krugg's *Autism Behavior Checklist* (ABC), Schopler's *Childhood Autism Rating Scale* (CARS), Rutter's *Behavior Rating Instrument for Autistic and Other Atypical Children* (BRIAAC), and Freeman's *Behavior Observation Scale* (BOS). Based on their review, Newsom et al. conclude that "the attempt to define autism objectively is a relatively active area of research, but much more work remains to be done before a generally satisfactory instrument is available" (p. 374). However, these authors do recommend that Krugg's ABC is useful for making the diagnosis of autism and that Rimland's Form E2 is most appropriate for identifying those who are often referred to as "Kanner syndrome children" to indicate a core, low-incidence group that reflects Kanner's original syndrome.

Several new instruments are of interest. For example, Barthelemy et al. (1990) conducted a study to determine if the *Behavioral Summarized Evaluation* (BSE) could be used in a reliable and valid manner with autistic children involved in neurophysiological studies and therapeutic programs. The BSE consists of 20 items on a single sheet, which supplies information about the child's actual clinical state. Each of the 20 items is scored on a scale from 0 to 4 (0 = never, 1 = sometimes, 2 = often, 3 = very often, 4 = always). Items consist of symptoms most frequently observed in autistic as well as in mentally retarded children. A total score (global score was 65) can be obtained by summing the 20-item scores. Analyses were carried out to determine content validity, criterion-related validity, age and IQ effects, and interrater reliability. The sample consisted of 90 autistic children (56 boys and 34 girls) aged from 2 to 15 years ($\overline{X}$ = 8.2 years), diagnosed by two independent psychiatrists according to DSM-III criteria. IQs ranged from 20 to 75 ($\overline{X}$ = 36). Interrater reliability was determined using 31 children (22 boys and 9 girls) ages 2 to 11.2 years ($\overline{X}$ = 5.7 years). IQs ranged from 10 to 60 ($\overline{X}$ = 40). Seven items correlated highly with factor I (found with factor analysis), both with and without varimax rotation. The authors labeled this factor "autism." Age had no influence on the global score. The significant negative correlations found between the global score of 65 and IQ suggest that the BSE items are mainly found in severely affected autistic children with additional mental retardation. Interrater reliability was .6 or better for 15 items of the scale and for the global score of 65. For the other five items, revision of the definitions in the glossary appears necessary.

The authors listed the following potential uses of the BSE: (a) to provide an actual portrait of the child from the observation of current behaviors, (b) to provide information for making and executing educational programs and/or therapeutic studies, (c) to provide information to determine possible effects of treatment by studying the covariations of BSE ratings and biological markers, and (d) to lead to better identification of bioclinical profiles and subtypes of autistic subjects.

Le Couteur et al. (1989) developed a research interview to assess older, intellectually more able subjects. The result was the behavioral differentiations required for current systems of diagnostic classification. The *Autism Diagnostic Interview* (ADI), designed to be used with the subject's principal caregiver, aims at providing a lifetime assessment of the range of behaviors relevant to the differential diagnosis of PDD in individuals of any chronological age from 5 years to early adulthood and with any mental age level from 2 years upward. Three main areas are emphasized: (a) the qualities of reciprocal social interaction, (b) communication and language, and (c) repetitive, restricted, and stereotyped behaviors. The interview also covers a variety of behaviors that frequently occur with PDDs and are important in planning treatment. The ADI focuses on the age range of 4–5 years for many ratings, clearly specifying the qualities that indicate deviance rather than delay. The ADI includes items still likely to show abnormalities in older, higher-functioning subjects and requires that coding refer to the behavior that was most abnormal during the specified age period. The ADI is a standardized investigator-based interview, for which standardization lies in the specifying of the behavioral criteria used for each rating. The ADI relies on skilled interviewers who are trained both on how to question effectively and on the conceptual distinctions involved in each coding. The approach of the ADI is to get the informant engaged in the task of remembering real incidents.

For the Le Couteur et al. study, interrater reliability was assessed on the basis of 32 videotaped interviews, with raters kept blind to the clinical diagnosis of the subjects whose mothers were being interviewed. The diagnostic validity was assessed by determining the degree to which coding differentiated autism from nonautistic mental retardation. The autism subjects all met the criteria for autism/PDD as set out in ICD-9 (World Health Organization, 1977) and DSM-III (APA, 1980). The kappa level for 10 of the 14 reciprocal social interaction items exceeded .70. The kappa level for 9 of the 12 communication/language items

exceeded .75. Five of the 6 items on repetitive, restricted, and stereotyped behaviors had kappas in excess of .75. Further, all kappas exceeded .75 for measures of abnormal development both in the first 30 and in the first 36 months. The interclass correlations for the scores of each of the three diagnostic areas were .94 or higher. There was complete agreement when the diagnosis was not autism. In 15 of 16 cases, raters agreed that all four criteria were met and that the diagnosis was autism. All 16 individuals in the autism group and no subject in the nonautism group met the full criteria. What differentiated the autism group most clearly was the pattern of multiple indicators of specific types of deviance in social reciprocity, communication, and play. The authors concluded that "the application of the ADI to children below the age of 5 years remains an important task for the future" (p. 381).

Another recent instrument is the *Autism Diagnostic Observation Schedule* (ADOS), which is intended to provide a standard series of contexts for observation of communicative and social behavior of persons with autism and related disorders. Lord et al. (1989) described the ADOS and provided a preliminary report of its psychometric properties. One of the instrument's underlying purposes is to facilitate observation of social and communicative features specific to autism rather than those accounted for or exacerbated by severe mental retardation. In the ADOS, the contexts that provide the background for all observations and the behaviors of the examiner are standardized, not the sample.

The ADOS is an attempt to combine aspects of previous scales by emphasizing the nature of social and communicative behavior in autism and by evaluating the qualities of autistic interactions and communication interns of specific behaviors. The ADOS consists of eight tasks presented by an examiner, which generally require 20–30 minutes to administer. Behaviors targeted for observation in each task are coded as the interview proceeds. Immediately after the interview, general ratings are made for four areas: (a) reciprocal social interaction, (b) communication/language, (c) stereotyped/restricted behaviors, and (d) mood and nonspecific abnormal behaviors. An overall autism rating is included to facilitate comparisons with CARS results.

Differential Diagnosis: Cognitive Functioning

The obvious and at times intense behavior anomalies associated with autism have drawn particular attention with respect to differential diagnosis. However, the more difficult to measure aspects of cognitive functioning deserve special focus. Empirical investigation of cognitive abilities in individuals with autism has provided overwhelming evidence contrary to Kanner's (1943) original belief that individuals with autism are endowed with good cognitive potential. Specifically, the data consistently indicate that although a minority of the population performs at or near normative levels on standardized tests of intellectual abilities, the majority of testable individuals fall within the subnormal range. Estimates indicate that as many as 70–90% score below 70 on standardized IQ tests (Rutter & Lockyer, 1967; Schopler, Reichler, DeVellis, & Daly, 1980; Shah & Holmes, 1985). Thus, a large proportion of the population meet current diagnostic criteria for a dual diagnosis of autism and mental retardation. Given the focus on differential diagnosis in this chapter, the question of interest is to what extent autism is associated with specific cognitive deficits that differentiate it from other diagnostic categories.

An extensive body of literature has explored the nature of the cognitive deficits in autism via the study of perceptual, coding, memory, and symbolic processes, discrimination and cross-modal learning, organization and planning abilities, and differential performance patterns on tests of intellectual functioning. However, interpretation of the findings with respect to differential diagnosis has been complicated by several factors. For example, given the overlap between autism and mental retardation, it is not surprising that many of the deficits initially thought to be autism-specific are associated with mental retardation as well. Thus, many aspects of task performance in individuals with autism are heavily influenced by mental retardation or developmental delay and, hence, are not syndrome-specific (Prior, 1979, 1984).

Moreover, both task and sample characteristics strongly influence experimental outcomes. It is perhaps for this reason that specification of cognitive deficits does not appear in current diagnostic criteria. In the most recent edition of the *Diagnostic and Statistical Manual* (DSM-III-R), for example, specific reference to cognitive skills appears within the context of associated features. Rather than identifying specific areas of relative strength or deficit, the manual highlights as a correlate of autism irregularities in the pattern of cognitive abilities, independent of overall level of intellectual functioning.

In an effort to explore syndrome-specific impairments in cognitive functioning without the confound of general developmental delay associated with mental retardation, a number of researchers have advocated restricting samples to individuals with normal or near-normal levels of general intellectual functioning (Prior, 1979, 1984; Rutter, 1983). Others have argued that the study of young children is most appropriate, as the learning process might be less distorted, making it possible to investigate primary deficits as opposed to those that develop secondarily (Sigman, Mundy, Sherman, & Ungerer, 1986). Yet others have argued for the study of adults, reasoning that such samples would enable an examination of those deficits that endure over time (Rumsey, 1985).

Such diversity of approach, along with methodological problems of appropriate subject match to controls, makes definitive conclusions impossible at present. However, several areas of cognitive functioning merit discussion. While consensus on specific categorization of function types has not been achieved, the following categories serve to structure diverse research findings.

Perception and Attention

Perceptual difficulties become evident early in life (Prior & Gajzago, 1974). Hermelin and

O'Connor (1970) found that the level of intellectual functioning is a major determinant of task performance, with abnormalities in response to perceptual stimuli, particularly in the auditory modality. Subjects categorized as having autism differed from typical and mentally retarded control subjects in their lack of response to auditory stimuli and greater response to tactile stimuli. The authors concluded that these individuals' ability to process and integrate information from multiple sources is impaired.

In an effort to elucidate deficits in symbolic processing and representational thought associated with autism, Hermelin and O'Connor (Hermelin & O'Connor, 1975; O'Connor & Hermelin, 1971, 1973) conducted a series of experiments that compared the performance of autistic, blind, and deaf subjects on a variety of visual, spatial, and tactile-kinesthetic tasks. In an immediate-recall experiment where three uppercase letters were displayed successively, O'Connor and Hermelin (1973) found that while autistic, deaf, and typical subjects did not differ on the number of letter sequences correctly recalled, typical subjects differed from both autistic and deaf subjects in their pattern of recall. While typical subjects tended to recall letters in the same temporal-sequential order in which they were presented, the autistic and deaf subjects tended to recall the letters with reference to their spatial location on the stimulus display (from left to right).

O'Connor and Hermelin interpreted these findings as indicating that the typical subjects had used a temporally ordered recall code, transposing the visual material into an auditory-verbal code, whereas the deaf and autistic subjects employed a visual, spatially organized code, storing a visual representation of the display. The results of a subsequent recognition manipulation that utilized the same method of stimulus presentation supported this interpretation. Following each trial, subjects were required to identify the sequence just viewed on a response card with one three-digit sequence printed on the upper half and another three-digit sequence on the lower half of the same card. One set of digits corresponded either to the temporal or the sequential order of digits just displayed, while the other set comprised a random ordering of the same digits. Consistent with earlier results, the typical subjects recognized only the temporally arranged digits successfully, whereas the autistic and deaf subjects recognized only the spatially organized digits successfully. Typical subjects guessed whenever presented with spatially organized or random digits, as did autistic and deaf subjects when presented with temporally organized or random digits.

In a similar test, Hermelin and O'Connor (1971) taught a tactile-verbal association to blindfolded typical and autistic subjects and blind subjects by assigning a spoken word to each of four fingers via touch. Two fingers of each hand were held up and placed one in front of the other to provide a spatial reference. After training the associations to criterion, the position of the hands was reversed. As above, the results indicated that the typical subjects' response pattern differed from that of the autistic and blind subjects, who performed similarly. Specifically, while the typical subjects tended to associate specific words with a fixed spatial location, both the autistic and the blind subjects tended to retain an association between the finger touched and the corresponding word. Hence, while the typical children showed evidence of a fixed absolute organization of space, the performance of the autistic and blind subjects was suggestive of a relative, movable organization of space.

Again comparing blind, blindfolded autistic, and blindfolded typical subjects, O'Connor and Hermelin (1975) found no group differences on the ability to determine on the basis of tactile exploration alone whether or not two pieces of a puzzle mounted on opposite ends of a flat board could fit together to form a square. As one set of test materials was designed so that the smaller puzzle piece would have to be rotated 180 degrees to complete the puzzle, mental rotation was required to solve the problem. However, for another spatial task involving tactile exploration, blind children and blindfolded autistic children were found to differ from blindfolded typical children on the ability to determine whether a model hand positioned in various spatial orientations and rotations was a right or a left hand. Subjects in the typical group responded more quickly and more often correctly than subjects in both comparison groups. It was speculated that this group's superior performance was due to the existence of a spatial reference frame that includes visual dimensions and, therefore, enables them to draw on stored information originally derived from the visual modality to help solve the tactile discrimination task. By way of contrast, blind and autistic subjects have to rely on touch alone.

In summarizing the results of the findings obtained from studies involving spatial motor tasks, Hermelin (1978) noted that the similarities in the performance of autistic and blind subjects suggest that the two impairments—the absence of sight and the inability to make cognitive references from a visual reference system—can have similar effects. While visually and cognitively impaired individuals are able to perform adequately on tasks that can be solved by means of the directly available kinesthetic data, they are disadvantaged on tasks requiring inferences based on perceptual reference systems.

Hermelin (1978) also compared groups of children classified as having autism, mental retardation, and hearing loss. Based on this study, the author concluded that the central problem of autism does not lie in processing particular sensory modalities, but in reorganizing incoming information to take advantage of redundancy in organizing a manageable information load. Thus, higher-order processing is deficient although basic input and simple memory may be unimpaired (for mid- to high-functioning children). When combined with an inability to reduce information by extracting crucial features (i.e., rules and redundancies), this explains the presence of well-remembered, stereotyped, and restricted behavior patterns, which become increasingly inappropriate as the requirements for complex, flexible codes increase.

Language Disturbance

Although a variety of abnormalities in nonverbal communication, such as a paucity of nonverbal communication, poverty of facial expression and bodily gestures, difficulties in comprehending nonverbal communication (Ricks & Wing, 1976), and limited production of spontaneous gesture (Bartak, Rutter, & Cox, 1975), have been consistently associated with autism, a surprisingly limited amount of research has focused on the extent and nature of these deficits.

Yirmiya, Kasari, Sigman, and Mundy (1989) described a study by Langdell that found that children with autism have greater difficulty than controls in producing expressions of happiness and sadness on request. Yirmiya et al. further reported that, relative to children with mental retardation, children with autism are more flat/neutral in their expression of affect and display a variety of ambiguous expressions not observed in children with mental retardation or in typical children. Further, MacDonald et al. (1989) found that, compared to normal controls matched for nonverbal IQ, high-functioning autistic men are impaired in both their ability to accurately produce facial expressions of emotions and their ability to convey emotions vocally.

Attwood, Frith, and Hermelin (1988) reported the results of two experiments designed to explore the gestural competence of adolescents diagnosed with autism. The researchers studied two classes of gestures: instrumental (function is to alter behavior) and expressive (function is to express feeling). In the first experiment, Attwood et al. compared the abilities of autistic and Down's syndrome adolescents and normal young children (between the ages of 3 and 6) to comprehend and exhibit simple instrumental gestures upon request within simulated situations designed to elicit the gesture. The autistic subjects were subgrouped on the basis of intellectual functioning. One subgroup was composed of subjects whose measured IQ scores fell within the normative range, while the other two subgroups included individuals with moderate or severe retardation. Subjects with Down's syndrome were the same age and had IQ scores comparable to the latter two autistic subgroups.

The major finding was that the developmentally disabled groups did not respond differentially to instrumental gestures and general performance levels indicated that the majority of the gestures were understood by the subjects. The only group to demonstrate notable difficulty with the comprehension task were the normal 3- to 4-year-olds. On the task requiring the production of instrumental gestures, performance did not differentiate the more able autistic adolescents from either the moderately and severely retarded Down's syndrome adolescents or the normal 6-year-old controls. However, compared to the aforementioned groups, autistic adolescents classified as moderately and severely retarded demonstrated significant impairments in the ability to produce a situationally appropriate instrumental gesture on request. Surprisingly, the normal 4- and 5-year-olds demonstrated a degree of impairment comparable to that of autistic children with moderate to severe mental retardation.

Attwood et al. (1988) also compared the frequency and type of spontaneous social interaction observed in the severely mentally retarded Down's syndrome group and the three subgroups of autistic adolescents in two naturalistic settings: on the school playground and at the dinner table. Results showed that degree of mental retardation within the autistic sample was not related to either the frequency or the type of interaction.

As a group, the adolescents with Down's syndrome were more socially interactive than the combined autistic group, with 100% of the former and only 61% of the latter observed to engage in at least one peer interaction. Comparing only subjects who interacted socially, Down's syndrome adolescents were significantly more interactive than autistic adolescents both on the playground and at mealtime. The mean number of gestures per interaction did not differentiate between the autistic and Down's syndrome groups; neither did the frequency of spontaneous use of deictic (simple pointing) or instrumental gestures (relative to the frequency of social interaction). However, significant differences were found between autistic and Down's syndrome subjects' use of expressive gestures.

Whereas 10 of the 15 Down's syndrome subjects displayed at least one such gesture, none of the autistic subjects were observed to produce expressive gestures spontaneously. Moreover, Attwood et al. (1988) observed that the majority of instrumental gestures used spontaneously by autistic adolescents served to reduce or terminate social interaction.

With respect to verbal language, Hermelin and O'Connor (1971) found that subjects with autism recalled random strings of words as effectively as meaningful sentences. By way of contrast, normal children used syntactic and semantic redundancies of language to facilitate recall process. These findings provide evidence that individuals with autism may be unable to use meaning to aid in recall and support the claim that they are unable to encode language and language-like stimuli in meaningful ways. Yet, Fyffe and Prior (1978) observed that higher-functioning children with autism did use meaning to aid in recall and performed at their mental age level. Further, low-functioning children, although they performed poorly in recall of word strings, did demonstrate use of strategies.

Language disturbance is viewed as the most universal symptom of autism (Prior, Gajzago, & Knox, 1976), with more than half of individuals with autism remaining mute. For those who acquire speech, many facets of language are impaired, with the impairment being stable and specific even when other areas of functioning improve (Prior, 1984). Churchill (1972) asserted that a central language deficit—more severe and global than that of developmental aphasia—might be the necessary and sufficient cause of autism. Similarities do exist between autism and developmental aphasia: similar sex ratios, evidence for neurobiological impairment, similar performance on psychometric tests (language subtests almost universally below nonverbal tests), deviant use of language (e.g., pronominal reversal and peculiar syntax), and stability of communication disturbance and reduction of symptoms when language develops successfully.

Bartak et al. (1975) found that the language of children with autism and aphasia differs in four ways. Autism produces (a) a greater frequency of deviant language (echolalia, pronominal reversal), (b) more severe deficits in comprehension, (c) more severe deficits in comprehension and use of gestures, and (d) more inappropriate social language. Distinct differences were noted between autism and dysphasic groups in the use of language, parallel level of spoken language production, and deviance (frequency of undue sensitivity to sounds, echolalia, pronominal reversal, metaphorical language, inappropriate remarks, lack of spontaneous social speech, poor use and understanding of gesture, lack of symbolic play, and deficient comprehension of written language). This implies more extensive cognitive involvement for the children with autism than is apparent in the dysphasic children.

Ricks and Wing's (1975) review of experimental and clinical data highlighted deficits in verbal and nonverbal communication, such as idiosyncratic or absent facial expression, lack of gestural communication, abnormal vocalization (control of pitch and volume), odd prosody, and impaired comprehension of nonverbal communication, which persist even when there is considerable development of other cognitive and language skills. Ricks (1975) also identified abnormal babbling, immediate and delayed echolalia, stereotyped repetitions of phrases or words, immature or abnormal use of syntax, pronunciation difficulties, lack of an "inner" language, failure to develop symbolic play in young children, an impoverished or absent inner life in higher-functioning older children and adolescents, and specific difficulty in the use of symbols that pervades language and other areas of cognitive and social functioning.

According to Rutter (1983), language cannot be viewed in isolation, as it is a complex skill dependent upon many perceptual and cognitive functions that develop in a social context. The question, therefore, is not whether language dysfunction is a necessary and sufficient variable for the development of autism, but rather which specific cognitive functions have to be impaired for autism to follow (Bartak & Rutter, 1976; Lotter, 1974; Rutter, 1974).

Performance Patterns on Tests of Intellectual Functioning

One of the most consistent findings reported in the literature concerned with the intellectual functioning of individuals with autism is a significant discrepancy between measures of verbal and performance IQ, favoring the latter. Convergence of data occurs from study of samples across age and IQ range (DeMyer, 1975; Lincoln, Courchesne, Kilman, Elmasian, & Allen, 1988; Lockyer & Rutter, 1970; Ohta, 1987). This pattern is found in some control groups (Lincoln et al., 1988), but not in others (Ohta, 1987). Generally, individuals with autism who are capable of performing on the Wechsler scales demonstrate their best performance on subtests measuring visual-spatial abilities (block design and object assembly) and poorest on tasks requiring verbal abstraction and social reasoning, with comprehension being the lowest of the verbal subtests (Asarnow, Tanguay, Bott, & Freeman, 1987; Lincoln et al., 1988). Although exceptional skill on tasks involving rote memory is typically associated with autism, performance on such subtests is subject to great variation (Lincoln et al., 1988).

In an examination of psychometric scatter in young children with autism (mean chronological age of 48 months), McDonald, Mundy, Kasari, and Sigman (1989) compared the performance of autistic subjects on the *Cattell Infant Intelligence Scale* to that of normal, Down's syndrome, and mentally retarded (unspecified etiology) subjects who were matched on performance mental age. The principal finding was that significantly more psychometric scatter was present in the profiles of the subjects with autism than those of the three comparison groups.

While significantly more autistic subjects demonstrated statistically meaningful scatter than subjects in the normal and the Down's syndrome groups, no differences were found between the autistic and the mentally retarded groups. Additional analyses revealed that the autistic subjects demonstrated a relative weakness in language-related skills (including nonverbal communication, vocalization, use of words, language comprehension, and rote repetition of verbal utterances) and a relative strength in nonlanguage skills (i.e., motor and perceptual-spatial abilities).

Recently, Lincoln et al. (1988) found similar patterns of performance on the *Wechsler Intelligence Scales* in two distinct samples of noninstitutionalized, relatively high-functioning individuals with autism. The first sample was comprised of 33 autistic subjects ranging in age from 8 years, 6 months to 29 years, 2 months (mean age of 17 years, 6 months) with a mean full-scale Wechsler IQ of 75.66. Discrepancies between scores on Wechsler verbal and performance scales indicative of higher performance IQ scores were found for 27 of the 33 subjects, and the difference between verbal IQ and performance IQ scores was significant for the sample. Group means indicated that performance was lowest on the two Wechsler subtests that require the greatest degree of verbal reasoning and judgment (comprehension and vocabulary), with mean-scaled scores falling 2 or more standard deviations below the mean. The two subtests with the highest group means were those that load heavily on visual-motor ability, namely block design and object assembly. The majority of the autistic sample performed within 1 standard deviation of the mean for the normative sample (79% and 64% for block design and object assembly, respectively). The results of a principal component analysis that included all the Wechsler subtests supported the dichotomy of poor verbal and nonverbal comprehension of social and context-relevant information from the nonverbal processing of asocial and noncontextual information.

In a second investigation that compared the *Wechsler Intelligence Scale for Children—Revised* (WISC-R) performance of autistic children to that of children diagnosed with receptive developmental dysphasia, oppositional disorder, and dysthymic disorder, Lincoln et al. (1988) found that, although the four groups of children differed significantly on measures of verbal, performance, and full-scale IQs, the autistic sample obtained the lowest scores on all three scales. Three of the four groups (dys-

phasic, oppositional disorder, and autistic disorder) displayed a pattern of performance IQ being greater than verbal IQ; however, the autistic group had the highest mean within-subject differences, and its performance differed significantly from the performance of the other three groups on the four subtests of interest (i.e., comprehension, vocabulary, block design, and object assembly). Despite the autistic sample's overall depressed performance relative to that of the other groups, its mean scores on block design and object assembly were within 1 standard deviation of those of the other groups.

The results of a discriminant analysis indicated that the autistic subjects' significantly impaired performance on the comprehension subtest best differentiated the groups of children studied. This pattern was so robust and autism-specific that some have suggested that it may be used to substantiate a diagnosis of autism (Lincoln et al., 1988). It is interesting to note that individuals with schizophrenia typically have higher verbal IQ than performance IQ scores (Aylward, Walker, & Bettes, 1984).

Asarnow et al. (1987) compared the performance of normally intelligent children diagnosed with autism or schizophrenia, matched for chronological age and full-scale IQ, on three factors of WISC-R: verbal comprehension, perceptual organization, and freedom from distractibility. Contrary to expectation, the two groups did not differ on verbal IQ, but the autistic group achieved significantly higher performance IQs. While no group differences were found on the verbal comprehension and perceptual organization factors, the autistic group obtained significantly higher scores on the freedom-from-distractibility factor than the schizophrenic subjects did. Not only were the freedom-from-distractibility factor scores for the schizophrenic group lower than those of the autistic sample, they were also below the range of normal children and significantly lower than the scores obtained on the other two factors.

Asarnow et al. (1987) interpreted these results as supporting recent hypotheses that implicate problems in recruitment and allocation of processing capacity as the core impairment in schizophrenia. Consistent with previous research, analysis of performance patterns for the autistic sample indicated that scores on the perceptual organization factor were superior to those obtained on both the verbal comprehension and the freedom-from-distractibility factors.

With respect to individual subtests, the children with autism performed better than the children with schizophrenia on block design, object assembly, coding, and arithmetic. The only subtest on which the autistic children demonstrated inferior performance was comprehension. Asarnow et al. (1987) concluded that impairments in verbal abstraction and social reasoning are found in autistic children even when gross language impairment and global retardation are absent. Of special interest, however, was the finding that a subgroup of children diagnosed with residual autism scored significantly higher on both the verbal comprehension and the freedom-from-distractibility factors and the comprehension subtest than did those children who met diagnostic criteria for autism at the time of the investigation. Thus, the impaired performance on the comprehension subtest was due to the relatively poorer performance of the latter subgroup. Because of the cross-sectional nature of the research, it could not be determined whether the subgroup with residual autism had made gains in verbal abstraction and social reasoning over time or were initially less impaired in these areas.

Despite considerable debate about whether Asperger's syndrome is most appropriately considered the equivalent of high-functioning autism or whether it is sufficiently different to warrant a distinct label within the autistic continuum (Gillberg, 1985; Schopler, 1985; Szatmari, Bartolucci, Finlayson, & Krames, 1986; Volkmar, Paul, & Cohen, 1985), two recent investigations have compared children with high-functioning autism and children with Asperger's syndrome to each other and to nonautistic controls on cognitive abilities (Ozonoff, Rogers, & Pennington, 1991; Szatmari, Tuff, Finlayson, & Bartolucci, 1990).

Szatmari et al. (1990) administered a comprehensive battery of intellectual, achievement, and neuropsychological measures to children with Asperger's syndrome or high-functioning autism who were matched on Wechsler verbal, performance, and full-scale IQ. Despite the broad range of skills assessed, group differences were found on only two measures. Subjects with Asperger's syndrome scored significantly higher on the similarities subtest of WISC-R while the high-functioning autistic children scored higher on the grooved pegboard test, a test of motor speed and coordination, when performed with the non-dominant hand.

In the Ozonoff et al. (1991) study, high-functioning autistic and Asperger's syndrome groups did not differ on Wechsler full-scale IQ. However, the Asperger's group had significantly higher verbal IQ scores than the autistic group, who scored higher (although not significantly higher) on the performance scale. A significant discrepancy between verbal and performance IQ, favoring performance IQ, was found for the high-functioning autistic group but not for the subjects with Asperger's syndrome.

Neither autistic nor Asperger's syndrome subjects differed from their respective nonautistic controls (comprised of children diagnosed with attention deficit–hyperactivity disorder, developmental reading disorder, developmental expressive language disorder, or mild mental retardation), who were individually matched on age, sex, and verbal IQ. Consistent with the literature previously cited, the autistic subjects achieved their best scores on a composite measure of spatial ability. Interestingly, while the composite spatial scores of the Asperger's syndrome group did not differ significantly from those of the autistic group, spatial ability was one of the least developed domains in this group's performance profile.

Interpretations of the superior nonverbal, visual-spatial abilities have been varied. In accordance with the view that autism is the result of some as yet unidentified brain dysfunction, some have posited that superior performance on visual-spatial tasks represents areas of competence, islets of special ability (Shah & Frith, 1983), or spared function. Frith (1989) offered an alternative interpretation, which views these alleged strengths as further evidence of syndrome-specific anomalies in information-processing. Specifically, she suggested that individuals with autism demonstrate a greater degree of detachment from normally powerful context effects (Frith, 1985, 1989).

The results of several investigations aimed at examining the nature of the visual-spatial abilities provide support for Frith's contention. For instance, Shah and Frith (1983) demonstrated that autistic children (rough IQ estimates between 50 and 70) were more proficient at locating embedded figures than both normal and nonautistic mentally retarded controls who were mental age–matched (*Raven's Coloured Progressive Matrices*). Not only did the autistic children achieve significantly higher scores than the control subjects, but they performed at a level that was consistent with that expected on the basis of their chronological age. Shah and Frith noted that this level of performance was exceptional, even relative to performance on other visual-spatial tasks (i.e., block design and object assembly) where performance is typically superior to that on other subtests but still below levels expected for chronological age. Hence, they argued that individuals with autism demonstrate uneven ability on two aspects of spatial skills: the ability to comprehend the arrangement of elements within a stimulus pattern (orientation) and the ability to mentally rotate, twist, and invert visual stimuli (visualization). Within this framework, the exceptional performance on embedded figures is related to good orientation skills being applied to a task that primarily involves orientation, while the relatively inferior performance on block design and object assembly is related to these tasks' involvement of both orientation and visualization.

Problem Solving

Using three-dimensional stimuli (blocks differing on dimensions of shape, size, and color) in a learning-set acquisition task, Prior and Chen (1975) found that children with autism (mean chronological age of 9 years, 7 months and mean mental age of 4 years, 3 months) were superior to typical children (matched for nonverbal mental age) and control children with mental retardation (matched on nonverbal mental age) in their ability to abstract simple rules in order to solve a series of problems. Specifically, the autistic group required fewer trials to criterion, and a greater proportion of autistic subjects reached the criterion compared to both control groups.

Subsequently, Prior (1977) found that autistic subjects were inferior to mentally retarded subjects (matched for chronological age, mental age, and IQ) on a more complex task that necessitated the use of conditional cues or symbols for problem solution. On two-dimensional symbolic stimuli that required a flexible approach involving thinking about alternative outcomes, autistic subjects' performance deteriorated notably, and they were unable to solve conditional problems.

Prior and McGillivray (1980) compared the performance of autistic subjects to that of mentally retarded and normal controls (normal subjects were matched to autistic subjects on verbal mental age and retarded subjects were matched on the basis of verbal mental age and IQ) on three separate tasks: object-discrimination learning set, matching learning set, and conditional matching learning set. The finding that autistic subjects performed at least as well as controls matched for mental age in the acquisition of object-discrimination learning set replicated Prior and Chen's (1975) results with concrete stimuli. On the matching task, although the autistic group did not differ from either control group with respect to trials to criterion, fewer autistic subjects acquired the set compared to normals (8 of 12 versus 12 of 12 subjects, respectively) but not to mentally retarded subjects, who did not differ from either group. On the conditional matching task, the majority of autistic subjects were able to acquire the concept required to achieve criterion for single-problem learning. The autistic group differed from the normal group but not from the mentally retarded group on the number of subjects reaching criterion. Although autistic subjects required more trials to reach criterion, suggesting that they were slower to learn, the autistic group did not differ from either comparison group in number of subjects achieving the criterion of solving two consecutive problems in the conditional matching task.

Executive Function

Rumsey (1985) compared the conceptual problem-solving ability of nine autistic men of average intelligence to that of nine control subjects matched on highest level of education completed and explored the relationship between conceptual problem solving (as measured by the *Wisconsin Card Sort Test*) and social functioning. Although the two groups did not differ significantly in age, level of education, or performance IQ, the autistic subjects' mean verbal IQ differed significantly from that of the control group, resulting in a marginal group difference in full-scale IQ. The results indicated that, as a group, high-functioning autistic males demonstrated significant deficits in conceptual problem-solving skills compared to normal controls. Specifically, when differences in IQ were statistically controlled, the autistic subjects differed from controls on the number of categories completed, the total number of errors made, and percentage of conceptual-level responses (reflective of the ability to formulate rules or concepts). Perseverative tendencies were also found in the autistic sample.

Rumsey (1985) also found significantly greater heterogeneity on the large majority of dependent measures within the autistic group. The degree of within-group performance variability is exemplified by the finding that three of the autistic subjects completed the maximum number of categories (six), while the remaining six subjects completed zero to three categories. The results pertaining to the relationship between level of social functioning and conceptual problem-solving indicated that although the *Vineland Social Maturity* social quotients of the autistic subjects were indicative of social-adaptive deficits, they did not correlate with conceptual problem-solving scores measured by the *Wisconsin Card Sort Test*. In fact, of the three subjects who completed all categories, one was described as the most independent of the sample, while two ranked relatively low in social functioning.

Ozonoff et al. (1991) found that while children with high-functioning autism and children with Asperger's syndrome differed with respect to the number and types of deficits identified relative to controls, the two groups scored lower than their respective controls and did not differ from each other on a composite measure of executive function.

Concept Formation

Hobson (1983) investigated whether autistic and matched nonautistic mentally retarded children differed in their ability to sort pictures of people, animals, and nonpersonal things according to age-related characteristics. Children with autism were slightly better than nonautistic controls in sorting geometric figures and demonstrated equal ability in sorting drawings of items on the basis of whether they were new or worn-out. However, compared to controls, autistic children were significantly less consistent in sorting photographs of people and dogs on the basis of age (young versus adult). Differences in the quality of the stimuli did not permit assessment of the degree of specificity of this deficit.

To further investigate whether a deficit in the ability to recognize age characteristics is specific to autism, Hobson (1987) studied the ability of 17 individuals with autism (estimated mean performance IQ of 73.2 as measured by *Raven's Progressive Matrices* and estimated mean verbal IQ of 52.2 as measured by the *Peabody Picture Vocabulary Test* [PPVT]) to match schematic drawings of faces differing on dimensions of age and gender (i.e., boy, girl, man, and woman) to video- or audiotaped segments of faces, voices, and stereotyped age and gender-related gestures and contexts depicted in videotaped segments where the actors' faces were not visible. In order to control for task requirements, a similar procedure was conducted using nonpersonal objects (i.e., bird, train, dog, and car). The videotaped sequences comprising the nonpersonal counterpart to the experimental task included appearance, movements (blurred image moving across screen), sounds, and contexts (bird's nest, empty dog basket, etc.). Hobson compared the responses of the autistic group to those of three distinct control groups: normal controls matched on *Raven Progressive Matrices* scores, nonautistic mentally retarded controls matched on chronological age and performance IQ, and normal controls with chronological ages corresponding to the verbal mental ages of the autistic sample as measured by the PPVT.

The results indicated that the autistic group did not differ significantly from any of the three comparison groups on tasks involving the identification of nonpersonal stimuli. By contrast, although the majority of children in each of the three control groups performed at near-ceiling levels on the tasks requiring identification of faces that corresponded with the taped presentations, the autistic subjects displayed significant impairments. Correlational analyses indicated that within the autistic group, performance on the people task was positively and significantly related to scores on the *Raven Progressive Matrices*, verbal mental age, and chronological age. At 1-year follow-up, it was found that the performance of the autistic children was stable over time and that there was no improvement in the identification of faces when photographs of faces were used (experiment 2) instead of schematic drawings (experiment 1).

Since the children had demonstrated the ability to match schematically drawn faces to videotaped faces early in the experimental sequence and since analyses of performance indicated that the majority of autistic children were performing above chance levels, Hobson (1987) concluded that the observed deficit could not be explained in terms of an inability to extract meaning from schematic drawings of faces, but rather seemed related to a failure to learn the conventional cues that correspond to each category of person (differing with respect to age and sex). As a few of the most intellectually advanced

autistic subjects performed well on this task, the deficit appeared to be relative, not absolute.

Ohta (1987) assessed size comparisons, spatial relationships, and gestural imitation skills and found performance comparable to those typical of children less than 3 years of age. The mean verbal mental age of the autistic group was higher than that of the 3-year-olds, suggesting that delays in size comparisons and spatial relationships are not simply a function of overall delays in language development.

Imitation.   Dawson and McKissick (1984) examined imitative behavior in a sample of young children with autism characterized by a wide range of intellectual functioning. Imitative tasks assessed were derived from the Piagetian stages of imitative behavior, including imitation of single and multiple (two) actions involving object use that were highly familiar to the children (e.g., banging a hammer and stirring a spoon in a pot) as well as novel gestures. The novel gestures were of two types: actions that were visible to the child when imitated (e.g., finger and hand movements) and actions that the child could not see when imitated (e.g., facial gestures).

The results indicated that only half the subjects demonstrated good imitation skills. That is, they were able to imitate actions beyond two familiar routines (a skill level consistent with stage V or VI on the Piagetian imitative scales); the remaining subjects demonstrated skills at or below stage III. These findings support the notion of significant deficits in motor imitation.

Using two different tests of gestural imitation (one involving pointing, the V sign, and waving, the other "bull's horns" and the T sign), Ohta (1987) found impaired imitative abilities in high-functioning, older autistic children compared to nonverbal, IQ-matched normal and hyperactive controls and preschool controls.

A proportion of the autistic children were found to engage in "partial imitation"; that is, they reproduced only part of the modeled behavior on imitative tasks. In contrast to the nonverbal IQ-matched controls, none of whom demonstrated partial imitation, 3 of 16 and 8 of 16 of the autistic children produced partial responses on the first (one task) and second (two tasks) series of imitative tasks, respectively. Similar to the first control group, none of the preschool control group demonstrated partial imitation on the first series of tasks. On two of the tasks in the second series, autistic children did not differ from the 3- to 3½-year-olds on frequency of partial imitation but demonstrated partial imitation more frequently than 3½-to 4-year-olds. Autistic children who engaged in partial imitation did not differ from subjects who did not engage in partial imitation in terms of IQ or ability to make size comparisons and spatial relationships. As a result, Ohta (1987) concluded that the presence of partial imitation in the autistic group was suggestive of a disorder in gestural imitation.

Perspective taking. In an effort to clarify the relationship among visual-spatial perspective taking, cognitive functioning (as measured by Piagetian tasks of operational thinking), and social competence, Hobson (1984) found that relatively high-functioning children with autism were no more impaired in their appreciation of visual-spatial perspectives than normal children matched on levels of operational thinking. The results suggested that measures of cognitive ability, not the diagnosis of autism, are related to visual-spatial perspective-taking abilities. Additional comparisons indicated that autistic subjects and a small group of subjects with Down's syndrome matched on verbal mental age performed similarly. Hence, Hobson concluded that the cognitive functions involved in coordinating visual-spatial perspectives do not explain the social deficits associated with autism.

More recently, Dawson and Fernald (1987) provided evidence contrary to Hobson's conclusions. In a correlational study that examined the relationship of two separate measures of social competence, measures of verbal and nonverbal mental age, severity of autistic symptoms, and performance on three types of role-taking (perceptual, conceptual, and affective), the researchers found that a composite score representing the three types

of perspective-taking ability predicted levels of social behavior, whereas measures of mental and chronological age failed to do so. Of the three types of perspective-taking tasks, conceptual role-taking (the ability to make inferences about others' thoughts/intentions) was most consistently related to social behavior and autistic symptoms. Further, a significant relationship was found between perceptual role-taking and a measure of social behavior that was specifically designed to measure social relationships (e.g., proximity, initiative, responsiveness, sharing, avoidance, and sensitivity to social cues).

However, Baron-Cohen, Leslie, and Frith (1986) demonstrated that autistic children may fail to understand or focus upon the "beliefs" of others. Failure to understand related intentional and emotional events may contrast with a grasp of other aspects of events involving people (Baron-Cohen et al., 1986; Hobson, 1986b).

Ozonoff et al. (1991) found that children with high-functioning autism performed more poorly than controls on both first- and second-order theory-of-the-mind composite scores, while children with Asperger's syndrome did not differ from controls on these measures. Initial comparisons between autistic and Asperger's syndrome subjects resulted in group differences indicative of superior performance for the Asperger's syndrome group on these measures. However, when verbal IQ was statistically controlled (mean verbal IQ of the Asperger's syndrome group was significantly higher than that of the autistic group), marginal group differences were found on first-order theory-of-the-mind composite scores, whereas no differences were found for second-order composite scores.

Person/face identification/recognition. Lack of self-awareness has historically been viewed as a common feature of autism. One method commonly used to assess self-awareness in normal young children is to place a small amount of rouge on the nose of a child and observe the child's reaction. Self-directed hand-to-nose contact as opposed to mirror-directed contact is interpreted as a demonstration of self-recognition. Mirror recognition has been viewed as a developmental phenomenon (Bertenthal & Fischer, 1978) and has been associated with mental age in Down's syndrome children (Mans, Cicchetti, & Sroufe, 1978).

In an effort to explore the question of whether a deficit in self-recognition is specific to autism or is associated with developmental delay (mental age), Ferrari and Matthews (1983) assessed self-recognition in 15 children diagnosed with autism (age range from 3 years, 5 months to 10 years, 4 months). The level of intellectual functioning for all subjects was reported to be within the severe to profound range of mental retardation. Eight of the 15 subjects demonstrated self-recognition (recognizers), while the remaining 7 failed to do so (nonrecognizers). Recognizers and nonrecognizers were compared on standardized measures of mental age and teacher ratings of school-related and interpersonal behaviors (i.e., attentional skills, behavioral excess, cognitive skills, language skills, social skills, emotional responsiveness, affection, and self-care).

The results indicated that while there were no between-group differences in chronological age, recognizers had significantly higher mental ages than did nonrecognizers. In addition, recognizers were almost unanimously described by their teachers as functioning higher than nonrecognizers on cognitive, affective, and behavioral indices. By contrast, behaviors such as absence of eye contact, infrequent social relationships, and reacting to people as if they were inanimate objects were more common among the nonrecognizers. The degree to which the group differences on mental age biased the findings regarding the behavioral ratings could not be determined within this sample. Ferrari and Matthews (1983) concluded that the inability to recognize oneself is best conceptualized as reflecting a general developmental delay rather than a deficit specific to autism.

Langdell (1978) compared the ability of autistic individuals, individuals with mental retardation, and normal controls variously matched for chronological and mental age to recognize the faces of familiar peers when shown photographs in which

(a) only isolated facial features were visible, (b) the whole face was visible, or (c) the face was inverted. In an effort to examine changes in processing facial stimuli that might occur as a function of age, each diagnostic group was represented by two different age groups—younger and older.

Langdell (1978) found that the performance of the normal and mentally retarded subjects was similar with respect to the percentage of errors and that both groups found it easier to identify photographs when they were shown the upper half of the face than when they were shown the lower half. By contrast, the younger autistic subjects performed significantly better when presented with the lower half of the face than when presented with the upper. While the older autistic subjects performed similarly to their younger counterparts on trials in which the lower portion of the face was visible, their performance on trials involving the upper portion of the face did not differ from that of age-matched controls, and their error scores did not differ as a function of the two types of stimuli. In other words, they appeared to use both the upper and the lower parts of the face for recognition. Lastly, Langdell found that while the younger autistic subjects did not differ from controls on their ability to recognize inverted faces, the older autistic subjects performed significantly better on recognition of inverted faces compared to their controls. The older autistic subjects' superior performance on the inverted stimuli was attributed to the finding that this group demonstrated a less circumscribed strategy for scanning faces than did the other two groups. Langdell interpreted the anomalous findings for both groups of autistic subjects as being consistent with the notion of a cognitive deficit that affects the manner in which both verbal and non-verbal communication is processed.

Volkmar, Sparrow, Rendes, and Cohen (1989) employed a novel task to assess autistic individuals' ability to utilize the human face as a source of information. The task required subjects to complete a series of puzzles constructed from photographs of human faces that varied along dimensions of complexity (number of pieces), familiarity, and configuration (assembled puzzle either resulted in facial gestalt or did not). Average time to complete each of the puzzles failed to differentiate between autistic youths and nonautistic mentally retarded controls who were matched on nonverbal mental age.

Volkmar et al. (1989) found that both groups of subjects completed puzzles with less complexity, greater familiarity, and normal configuration more quickly than those with greater complexity, less familiarity, and scrambled configuration. Similarly, both subject groups experienced greater difficulty with unfamiliar and scrambled faces as the complexity (number of pieces) of the puzzle increased. Given that effects of familiarity and configuration were found, the authors interpreted the findings as supporting the premise that individuals with autism are capable of utilizing at least some aspects of information provided by the human face.

Social Cognition

Converging data from a number of sources suggest that most individuals with autism are specifically impaired in their ability to process information with emotional content. Thus, the manner in which autistic individuals attend to, discriminate, and understand bodily expressions of emotion in other people may differentiate them from individuals with normal development as well as individuals with other developmental disabilities. However, it would be premature to conclude that impairments in the appreciation of emotional content are both universal and specific to autism.

Hobson (1986a) examined the comparative abilities of autistic individuals (mean estimated performance IQ based on *Raven's Progressive Matrices* of 72.0, mean estimated verbal IQ based on *Peabody Picture Vocabulary* of 50.1, mean verbal mental age of 7 years, 1 month), nonautistic mentally retarded individuals, and two groups of normal controls (matched for chronological age and performance IQ, and performance IQ and verbal IQ, respectively) to comprehend feeling states when conveyed through facial expression, bodily gesture, voice, and situational contexts. He demonstrated

that while the autistic subjects did not differ from the control subjects in their ability to identify schematic drawings of common objects when presented with audio- or videotaped stimuli depicting the sounds, movements, or contexts of these inanimate objects, they were significantly impaired in their ability to identify the schematic drawings of faces depicting the emotions portrayed in the audio- and videotaped sequences.

The only notable exception was that the autistic subjects did not differ from the nonautistic mentally retarded controls in their ability to identify emotions on the basis of situational contexts. For the autistic group, a significant relationship was found between performance on the emotions task and performance on *Raven's Progressive Matrices* and the PPVT. Despite the generally poor performance of the autistic children, a small group of six autistic children with relatively high mental ages were successful on the emotions task. The results of a 1-year follow-up study using the emotions stimuli and substituting photographs for schematic drawings replicated the earlier findings.

In a subsequent experiment, Hobson (1986b) compared the ability of autistic children and nonautistic mentally retarded controls (matched for chronological age and *Raven's Progressive Matrices* scores, with a mean chronological age of 15 years, 4 months and a mean verbal mental age of 7 years, 8 months) to match schematic drawings of faceless figures depicting gestures to taped examples of gestures, faces, and voices representing happy, unhappy, angry, and frightened emotional states. To eliminate the possibility that subjects performed poorly because of an inability to derive meaning from schematic drawings, subjects were preselected on the basis of their ability to identify the appropriate schematic drawing to complete a sequence of events enacted by human actors in videotaped sequences. Furthermore, the majority of subjects were able to select the correct drawing to complete a temporal sequence of events portrayed in a series of drawings (9 of 13 and 11 of 13 subjects for the autistic and nonautistic groups, respectively). Thus, the majority of subjects also demonstrated the ability to anticipate subsequent events involving nonemotional sequelae. On the experimental tasks, the two groups did not differ with respect to their ability to match emotionally laden gestures observed on videotape to schematic drawings of the same. By way of contrast, the performance of the autistic subjects was significantly inferior to that of the matched controls on taped presentations of voice and face. The autistic subjects' performance on the voices and faces tasks was positively and significantly correlated with scores on the PPVT.

Additional evidence for a syndrome-specific deficit in the ability to comprehend emotion-related concepts has been presented by Hobson and Lee (1989), who analyzed and compared the response patterns produced by autistic and nonautistic mentally retarded adolescents and young adults on the *British Picture Vocabulary Scale* (BPVS). The control subjects were individually matched to the autistic subjects on chronological age and overall performance on the BPVS. In order to compare content-related performance, the BPVS items were grouped into the following four categories based on the ratings of independent judges: emotional content, abstract content, social content, and human content. The autistic subjects performed significantly lower on emotion-related items compared to nonemotional items than did the controls, and this difference was independent of the social content of the items. While preliminary analyses indicated that the autistic subjects performed more poorly than controls on BPVS items with human content, removing the emotion-related and social-related items from the analysis eradicated the between-group differences. Interestingly, the two groups did not differ in their response accuracy on the social/nonsocial or abstract/concrete dichotomies. In fact, with respect to the latter, the authors found little evidence to suggest that subjects within either group found abstract items more difficult than concrete items.

Several independent investigations lend empirical support to Hobson and Lee's (1989) findings. For example, Tantam, Monaghan, Nicholson, and Stirling (1989) found that youths with autism (mean performance IQ of 67.3) demonstrated impaired performance relative to nonautistic controls matched for chronological age, gender, and nonverbal mental age on tasks involving the ability to (a) identify the unique emotion in an array of photographs with different individuals displaying the same emotional expression, (b) identify the photograph of an individual who differs from the individual portrayed in the remaining photographs, and (c) match written adjectives describing emotions to the correct photograph. By way of contrast, the autistic youths performed as well as the controls on tasks requiring them to match written adjectives to pictures of common objects and to match emotion words to upside-down photographs of emotional expressions.

Similarly, in one of the few investigations of emotional recognition and expression of emotional cues, MacDonald et al. (1989) compared the ability of high-functioning autistic men to that of normal male controls matched for chronological age and nonverbal IQ. The results indicated that autistic subjects were relatively impaired on a number of measures. Specifically, the normal controls performed better than the autistic subjects on (a) matching an emotional expression to a picture portraying an appropriate context that might elicit a particular affect, (b) labeling emotional expressions in faces, and (c) correctly identifying the emotion conveyed in unfiltered speech. Interestingly, while normal subjects experienced a significant performance decrement when required to interpret the emotion in filtered speech (in which the frequency bands were altered in such a way as to render the words unintelligible but preserve the emotional tone of the utterance), only 40% of the subjects with autism responded similarly. The remainder did not experience a performance decrement.

In a recent attempt to replicate Hobson (1986a), Prior and her colleagues (Prior, Dahlstrom, & Squires, 1990) studied autistic children (mean age of 9 years, 11 months and mean verbal mental age of 7 years, 2 months as measured by the PPVT) and a control group comprised primarily of children classified as learning-disordered or learning-delayed, who were pairwise-matched for chronological age, gender, and verbal mental age. Little support was found for an autism-specific deficit in the perception of emotion. Similar to Hobson's findings, none of the autistic or control subjects failed the things tasks. However, in contrast to Hobson's findings, the autistic and control groups did not differ in composite performance on the emotions tasks (11 of 20 autistic subjects versus 10 of 20 control subjects succeeded), nor did the two groups differ in performance across the three experimental conditions (sounds, gestures, and contexts). Of importance is the finding that for the sample as a whole, verbal mental age discriminated between subjects who were successful on the emotions task and those who were not. Specifically, Prior et al. found that with one exception, subjects with a verbal mental age greater than 6 years were successful, whereas all but one subject with a verbal mental age below 6 met with failure. Success was also associated with a higher chronological age. Finally, although the autistic and control groups differed significantly on ratings of social behavior, these scores were only weakly associated with task performance.

Additional support for the pervasiveness of a deficit in comprehending and expressing emotions across the autistic continuum was provided by Scott (1985), who found that adults with Asperger's syndrome demonstrated more general impairments in nonverbal communication skills than controls matched on chronological age, IQ, and sex. Of particular interest in the current context is that within the domain of nonverbal communication, subjects with Asperger's syndrome were impaired on tasks requiring recognition and production of emotional expression. However, Ozonoff et al. (1991) reported that while children with Asperger's syndrome performed more poorly than controls on a composite measure of emotion perception, children with high-functioning autism performed as well as controls. No differences between the Asperger's syndrome group and the autistic group were found on this measure.

Conclusion

Diagnostic criteria for autism, and thus differential diagnosis issues, remain controversial with no clear basis for resolution and consensus in sight. However, the proposed DSM-IV (American Psychological Association Task Force on DSM-IV, 1991) may provide some assistance in clarifying the diagnostic confusion. The current DSM-IV working document states, "The literature review and data reanalysis indicate that the DSM-III-R criteria for Autistic Disorder provide a different and broader definition than do DSM-III, ICD-10, and clinicians' judgment (all three of which are in better agreement with one another than with DSM-III-R)." It is encouraging that the document goes on to state, "An important goal of the field trial is an attempt to foster convergence between the DSM-IV and ICD-10 criteria sets for Autistic Disorder" (p. 3). In addition to changes in diagnostic criteria for autism, DSM-IV may add Rett syndrome, childhood disintegrative disorder, and Asperger's syndrome to autistic disorder as specific disorders under the category of pervasive developmental disorder. This may assist in the differential diagnosis process by providing appropriate choices that help subdivide the heterogeneous population that has received the diagnosis of pervasive developmental disorder.

The most important advance, however, will be the development of quantitative assessment instruments. A number of rating scales and observation systems exist, but these need to be combined with other assessments, particularly with respect to cognitive and language functioning. As described, an emerging research base is detailing the quantifiable response patterns of individuals with autism in comparison to other groups. Findings of such investigations need to be replicated and extended to permit construction of objective measurement procedures that can be used to establish firm quantitative criteria in conjunction with other measures. Such procedures will facilitate the tasks of reliably reporting subject characteristics in research studies, categorizing clinical observations, and identifying the subgroups that exist in the heterogeneous population of individuals with autism.

References

AMERICAN PSYCHIATRIC ASSOCIATION. (1980). *Diagnostic and statistical manual of mental disorders* (3rd ed.). Washington, DC: Author.

AMERICAN PSYCHOLOGICAL ASSOCIATION TASK FORCE ON DSM-IV. (1991). *DSM-IV Options Book: Work in progress.* Washington, DC: Author.

ASARNOW, R. F., TANGUAY, P. E., BOTT, L., & FREEMAN, B. J. (1987). Patterns of intellectual functioning in non-retarded autistic and schizophrenic children. *Journal of Child Psychology and Psychiatry and Allied Disciplines, 28,* 273–280.

ATTWOOD, A., FRITH, U., & HERMELIN, B. (1988). The understanding and use of interpersonal gestures by autistic and Down's syndrome children. *Journal of Autism and Developmental Disorders, 18,* 241–257.

AYLWARD, E., WALKER, E., & BETTES, B. (1984). Intelligence in schizophrenia: Meta-analysis of the research. *Schizophrenia Bulletin, 10,* 430–459.

BARON-COHEN, S., LESLIE, A. M., & FRITH, U. (1986). Mechanical, behavioral and intentional understanding of picture stories in autistic children. *British Journal of Developmental Psychology, 4,* 113–125.

BARTAK, V., & RUTTER, M. (1976). Differences between mentally retarded and normally intelligent autistic children. *Journal of Autism and Childhood Schizophrenia, 6,* 109–120.

BARTAK, L., RUTTER, M., & COX, A. (1975). A comparative study of infantile autism and specific developmental receptive language disorder. I. The children. *British Journal of Psychiatry, 126,* 127–145.

BARTHELEMY, C., ADRIEN, J. L., TANGUAY, P., GARREAU, B., FERMANIAN, J., ROUX, S., SAUVAGE, D., & LELORD, G. (1990). The behavioral summarized evaluation: Validity and reliability of a scale for the assessment of autistic behaviors. *Journal of Autism and Developmental Disorders, 20,* 189–204.

BERTENTHAL, B. I., & FISCHER, K. W. (1978). Development of self-recognition in the infant. *Developmental Psychology, 14*(1), 44–50.

BOWMAN, E. P. (1988). Asperger's syndrome and autism: The case for a connection. *British Journal of Psychiatry, 152,* 377–382.

BURD, L., FISHER, W., & KERBESHIAN, J. (1988). Childhood onset pervasive developmental disorder. *Journal of Child Psychology and Psychiatry and Allied Disciplines, 29,* 155–163.

BURD, L., FISHER, W., & KERBESHIAN, J. (1989). Pervasive disintegrative disorder: Are Rett syndrome and Heller dementia infantilis subtypes? *Developmental Medicine and Child Neurology, 31,* 609–616.

BURD, L., & KERBESHIAN, J. (1988). Diagnosis of autism and other pervasive developmental disorders. *Neuroscience and Biobehavioral Reviews, 12,* 275–282.

CHURCHILL, D. W. (1972). The relation of infantile autism and early childhood schizophrenia to developmental language disorders of childhood. *Journal of Autism and Childhood Schizophrenia, 2,* 182–197.

DAWSON, G., & FERNALD, M. (1987). Perspective-taking ability and its relationship to the social behavior of autistic children. *Journal of Autism and Developmental Disorders, 17,* 487–498.

DAWSON, G., & McKISSICK, F. C. (1984). Self-recognition in autistic children. *Journal of Autism and Developmental Disorders, 14,* 383–394.

DEMYER, M. K. (1975). The nature of the neuropsychological disability in autistic children. *Journal of Autism and Childhood Schizophrenia, 5,* 109–128.

DEMYER, M. K., BARTON, S., & NORTON, J. A. (1972). A comparison of adaptive, verbal and motor profiles of psychotic and non-psychotic subnormal children. *Journal of Autism and Childhood Schizophrenia, 2,* 359–377.

FERRARI, J., & MATTHEWS, W. (1983). Self-recognition deficits in autism: Syndrome-specific or general developmental delay? *Journal of Autism and Developmental Disorders, 13,* 317–324.

FRITH, U. (1985). The usefulness of the concept of unexpected reading failure: Comments on "Reading retardation revisited." *British Journal of Developmental Psychology, 3,* 15–17.

FRITH, U. (1989). A new look at language and communication in autism. Special issue: Autism. *British Journal of Disorders of Communication, 24,* 123–150.

FYFFE, C., & PRIOR, M. (1978). Evidence for language recoding in autistic, retarded and normal children: A reexamination. *British Journal of Psychology, 69,* 393–402.

GILLBERG, C. (1985). Asperger's syndrome and recurrent psychosis—A case study. *Journal of Autism and Developmental Disorders, 15,* 389–397.

GILLBERG, C. (1990). Autism and pervasive developmental disorders. *Journal of Child Psychology and Psychiatry and Allied Disciplines, 31,* 99–119.

GREEN, J. (1990). Is Asperger's a syndrome? *Developmental Medicine and Child Neurology, 32,* 743–747.

HERJANIC, B., & REICH, W. (1982). Development of a structured psychiatric interview for children:

Agreement between child and parent on individual symptoms. *Journal of Abnormal Child Psychiatry, 10,* 307–324.

HERMELIN, B. (1978). Images and language. In M. Rutter & E. Schopler (Eds.), *Autism: A reappraisal of concept and treatment* (pp. 141–154). New York: Plenum.

HERMELIN, B., & O'CONNOR, N. (1970). *Psychological experiments with autistic children.* Oxford, England: Pergamon.

HERMELIN, B., & O'CONNOR, N. (1971). Spatial coding in normal, autistic and blind children. *Perceptual and Motor Skills, 33,* 127–132.

HERMELIN, B., & O'CONNOR, N. (1975). The recall of digits by normal, deaf and autistic children. *British Journal of Psychology, 66,* 203–209.

HOBSON, R. P. (1983). The autistic child's recognition of age-related features of people, animals and things. *British Journal of Child Psychology and Psychiatry, 1,* 343–352.

HOBSON, R. P. (1984). Early childhood autism and the question of egocentrism. *Journal of Autism and Developmental Disorders, 14,* 85–104.

HOBSON, R. P. (1986a). The autistic child's appraisal of expressions of emotion. *Journal of Child Psychology and Psychiatry, 27,* 321–342.

HOBSON, R. P. (1986b). The autistic child's appraisal of expressions of emotion: A further study. *Journal of Child Psychology and Psychiatry, 27,* 671–680.

HOBSON, R. P. (1987). The autistic child's recognition of age–sex-related characteristics of people. *Journal of Autism and Developmental Disorders, 17,* 63–79.

HOBSON, R. P., & LEE, A. (1989). Emotion-related and abstract concepts in autistic people. Evidence from the *British Picture Vocabulary Scale. Journal of Autism and Developmental Disorders, 10,* 23–32.

KANNER, L. (1943). Autistic disturbances of affective contact. *Nervous Child, 2,* 217–250.

LANGDELL, T. (1978). Recognition of faces: An approach to the study of autism. *Journal of Child Psychology and Psychiatry, 19,* 255–268.

LE COUTEUR, A., RUTTER, M., LORD, C., RIOS, P., ROBERTSON, S., HOLDGRAFER, M., & McLENNAN, J. (1989). Autism diagnostic interview: A standardized investigator-based instrument. *Journal of Autism and Developmental Disorders, 19,* 363–387.

LINCOLN, A. J., COURCHESNE, E., KILMAN, B. A., ELMASIAN, R., & ALLEN, M. (1988). A study of intellectual abilities in high-functioning people with autism. *Journal of Autism and Developmental Disorders, 18,* 505–524.

LOCKYER, L., & RUTTER, M. (1970). A five to fifteen year follow-up study of infantile psychosis. IV. Patterns of cognitive ability. *British Journal of Social and Clinical Psychology, 9,* 152–163.

LORD, C., RUTTER, M., GOODE, S., HEEMSBERGEN, J., JORDAN, H., MAWHOOD, L., & SCHOPLER, E. (1989). Autism diagnostic observation schedule: A standardized observation of communicative and social behavior. *Journal of Autism and Developmental Disorders, 19,* 185, 212.

LOTTER, V. (1974). Factors related to outcome in autistic children. *Journal of Autism and Childhood Schizophrenia, 4,* 263–277.

MacDONALD, H., RUTTER, M., HOWLIN, P., RIOS, P., LE COUTEUR, A., EVERED, C., & FOLSTEIN, S. (1989). Recognition and expression of emotional cues by autistic and normal adults. *Journal of Child and Adolescent Psychology and Psychiatry and Allied Disciplines, 30,* 865–877.

McDONALD, M., MUNDY, P., KASARI, C., & SIGMAN, M. (1989). Psychometric scatter in retarded, autistic preschoolers as measured by the Cattell. *Journal of Child and Adolescent Psychology and Psychiatry and Allied Disciplines, 30,* 599–604.

MANS, L., CICCHETTI, D., & SROUFE, A. L. (1978). Mirror reactions of Down's Syndrome infants and toddlers: Cognitive underpinnings of self-recognition. *Child Development, 49,* 1247–1250.

MYERS, B. A. (1989). Misleading cues on the diagnosis of mental retardation and infantile autism in the pre-school child. *Mental Retardation, 27,* 85–90.

NEWSOM, C., HOVANITZ, C., & RINCOVER, A. (1988). Autism. In E. J. Mash & L. G. Terdal (Eds.), *Behavioral assessment of childhood disorders* (pp. 355–401). New York: Guilford.

O'CONNOR, N., & HERMELIN, B. M. (1971). Cognitive deficits in children. *British Medical Bulletin, 27,* 227–232.

O'CONNOR, N., & HERMELIN, B. M. (1973). The spatial or temporal organization of short-term memory. *Quarterly Journal of Experimental Psychology, 25,* 335–343.

O'CONNOR, N., & HERMELIN, B. (1975). Modality specific spatial coordinates. *Perception and Psychophysics, 17,* 213–216.

OHTA, M. (1987). Cognitive disorders of infantile autism: A study employing the WISC, spatial relationship conceptualization, and gesture imitations. *Journal of Autism and Developmental Disorders, 17,* 54–62.

OZONOFF, S., ROGERS, S. J., & PENNINGTON, B. F. (1991). Asperger's syndrome: Evidence of an empirical distinction from highly functioning autism. *Journal of Child Psychology and Psychiatry and Allied Disciplines, 32,* 1107–1122.

POMEROY, J. C., FRIEDMAN, C., & STEPHEN, S. L. (1990). Further thoughts on autistic tendencies. *Developmental Medicine and Child Neurology, 32,* 832–833.

PRIOR, M. R. (1977). Conditional matching learning set performance in autistic children. *Journal of Child Psychology and Psychiatry and Allied Disciplines, 18,* 183–189.

PRIOR, M. (1979). Cognitive abilities and disabilities in infantile autism: A review. *Journal of Abnormal Child Psychology, 52,* 4–17.

PRIOR, M. (1984). Developing concepts of childhood autism: The influence of experimental cognitive research. *Journal of Consulting and Clinical Psychology, 52,* 4–17.

PRIOR, M. R., & CHEN, C. S. (1975). Learning set acquisition in autistic children. *Journal of Abnormal Psychology, 84,* 701–708.

PRIOR, M., DAHLSTROM, B., & SQUIRES, T. (1990). Autistic children's knowledge of thinking and feeling states in other people. *Journal of Child and Adolescent Psychology and Psychiatry and Allied Disciplines, 31,* 587–601.

PRIOR, M. R., & GAJZAGO, C. (1974). Two cases of "recovery" in Kanner syndrome. *Archives of General Psychiatry, 31,* 264–268.

PRIOR, M. R., GAJZAGO, C., & KNOX, D. T. (1976). An epidemiological study of autistic and psychotic children in the far eastern states of Australia. *Australian and New Zealand Journal of Psychiatry, 10,* 173–184.

PRIOR, M. R., & McGILLIVRAY, J. (1980). The performance of autistic children on three learning set tasks. *Journal of Child Psychology and Psychiatry and Allied Disciplines, 21,* 313–323.

RAPIN, I. (1991). Autistic children: Diagnosis and clinical features. *Pediatrics, 87,* 751–760.

RICKS, D. M. (1975). Vocal communication in preverbal, normal and autistic children. In N. O'Conner (Ed.), *Language, cognitive deficits and retardation* (pp. 75–83). London: Butterworths.

RICKS, D. M., & WING, L. (1975). Language, communication, and the use of symbols in normal and autistic children. *Journal of Autism and Childhood Schizophrenia, 5,* 191–221.

RICKS, D. M., & WING, L. (1976). Language, communication and the use of symbols. In L. Wing (Ed.), *Early childhood autism* (pp. 93–134). Oxford, England: Pergamon.

RITVO, E. R., & FREEMAN, B. J. (1978). National Society for Autistic Children, definition of autism. *Journal of Autism and Developmental Disorders, 8,* 162–167.

RUMSEY, J. M. (1985). Conceptual problem solving in highly verbal nonretarded autistic men. *Journal of Autism and Developmental Disorders, 15,* 23–26.

RUTTER, M. (1974). The development of infantile autism. *Psychiatric Medicine, 4,* 147–163.

RUTTER, M. (1978). Language disorder and infantile autism. In M. Rutter & E. Shopler (Eds.), *Autism: A reappraisal of concepts and treatment* (pp. 85–104). New York: Plenum.

RUTTER, M. (1983). Cognitive deficits in the pathogenesis of autism. *Journal of Child Psychology and Psychiatry, 24,* 513–531.

RUTTER, M., & LOCKYER, V. (1967). A 5–15 year follow-up study of infantile psychosis. I. Description of sample. *British Journal of Psychiatry, 113,* 1169–1182.

RUTTER, M., & SCHOPLER, E. (1988). Autism and pervasive developmental disorders: Concepts and diagnostic issues. In E. Schopler & G. B. Mesibov (Eds.), *Diagnosis and assessment in autism* (pp. 15–36). New York: Plenum.

SCHOPLER, E. (1985). Convergence of learning disability, higher-level autism, and Asperger's syndrome. *Journal of Autism and Developmental Disorders, 15,* 359–360.

SCHOPLER, E., REICHLER, R. J., DEVELLIS, R. F., & DALY, K. (1980). Toward objective classification of childhood autism: *Childhood autism rating scale* (CARS). *Journal of Autism and Developmental Disorders, 10,* 91–103.

SCOTT, D. W. (1985). Asperger's Syndrome and nonverbal communications: A pilot study. *Psychological Medicine, 15,* 683–687.

SHAH, A., & FRITH, V. (1983). The islet of ability in autistic children: A research note. *Journal of Child Psychology and Psychiatry and Allied Disciplines, 24,* 613–620.

SHAH, A., & HOLMES, N. (1985). The use of the *Leiter international performance scale* with autistic children. *Journal of Autism and Developmental Disorders, 15,* 195–203.

SIGMAN, M., MUNDY, P., SHERMAN, T., & UNGERER, J. (1986). Social interactions of autistic, mentally retarded, and normal children and their caregivers. *Journal of Child Psychology and Psychiatry, 27,* 647–656.

STONE, W. L., LEMANEK, K. L, FISHEL, P. T., FERNANDEZ, M. C., & ALTEMEIER, W. A. (1990). Playing and imitation skills in the diagnosis of autism in young children. *Pediatrics, 86,* 267–272.

SZATMARI, P., BARTOLUCCI, G., & BREMNER, R. (1989). Asperger's syndrome and autism: Comparison of early history and outcome. *Developmental Medicine and Child Neurology, 31,* 709–720.

SZATMARI, P., BARTOLUCCI, G., FINLAYSON, A., & KRAMES, L. (1986). A vote for Asperger's Syndrome. *Journal of Autism and Developmental Disabilities, 16*, 515–517.

SZATMARI, P., TUFF, L., FINLAYSON, M., & BARTOLUCCI, G. (1990). Asperger's syndrome and autism: Neurocognitive aspects. *Journal of American Academy of Child and Adolescent Psychiatry, 29*, 130–136.

TANTAM, D., MONAGHAN, L., NICHOLSON, H., & STIRLING, J. (1989). Autistic children's ability to interpret faces: A research note. *Journal of Child and Adolescent Psychology and Psychiatry and Allied Disciplines, 30*, 623–630.

VOLKMAR, F. R., & COHEN, D. J. (1988). Classification and diagnosis of childhood autism. In E. Schopler and G. B. Mesibov (Eds.), *Diagnosis and assessment in autism* (pp. 71–89). New York: Plenum.

VOLKMAR, F. R., & COHEN, D. J. (1989). Disintegrative disorder or "late onset" autism. *Journal of Child Psychology and Psychiatry and Allied Disciplines, 30*, 717–724.

VOLKMAR, F. R., PAUL, R., & COHEN, D. J. (1985). The use of "Asperger's syndrome." *Journal of Autism and Developmental Disorders, 15*, 437–439.

VOLKMAR, F. R., SPARROW, S. S., RENDES, R. D., & COHEN, D. J. (1989). Facial perception in autism. *Journal of Child Psychology and Psychiatry and Allied Disciplines, 30*, 591–598.

WHITEHOUSE, W. (1990). Pervasive disintegrative disorder? *Developmental Medicine and Child Neurology, 32*, 556.

WING, L. (1981). Asperger's syndrome: A clinical account. *Psychological Medicine, 11*, 115–130.

WING, L. (1989). "Diagnosis of autism." In C. Gillberg (Ed.), *Diagnosis and treatment of autism* (pp. 5–22). New York: Plenum.

WORLD HEALTH ORGANIZATION. (1977). *International statistical classification of diseases, injuries and causes of death* (9th rev.). Geneva: Author.

YIRMIYA, N., KASARI, C., SIGMAN, M., & MUNDY, P. (1989). Facial expressions of affect in autistic, mentally retarded and normal children. *Journal of Child and Adolescent Psychology and Psychiatry and Allied Disciplines, 30*, 725–735.

YIRMIYA, N., SIGMAN, M. D., KASARI, C., & MUNDY, P. (1992). Empathy and cognition in high functioning children with autism. *Child Development, 63*, 150–160.

CHAPTER 7

Behavioral Assessment of Autistic Disorder

Sandra L. Harris
Jill Belchic
Lisa Blum
David Celiberti
RUTGERS, THE STATE UNIVERSITY OF NEW JERSEY

Diagnosing the person with autism is a critical step in treatment. Knowing that an individual exhibits the symptoms of autistic disorder alerts the clinician or educator to the importance of examining the social, communication, and behavioral domains as areas of potential deficit. Nonetheless, for autistic disorder, as for most psychological disorders, the ways in which these symptoms manifest themselves vary considerably from person to person. Consequently, effective treatment is a highly individualized process, not one dictated by diagnosis alone. As Van Houten and his colleagues (1988) argued, behavioral assessment and ongoing evaluation comprise a basic right of every recipient of treatment.

Behavioral assessment calls upon the clinician to consider each client as a unique person whose biological capacities, learning history, and present environment combine to create a set of strengths, behavioral deficits, and special needs. An effective behavioral assessment grapples with questions such as "When does this maladaptive behavior occur?" "What environmental events may bear upon the expression of that symptom?" and "How can con-

textual events be manipulated to enable this client to function more effectively?"

This chapter provides an overview of approaches to behavioral assessment of the person with autism. Following an examination of general issues in behavioral assessment, we will review some of the most common rating scales and checklists for autistic behavior and consider the problems involved in assessing behavioral excesses such as self-injury, aggression, and self-stimulation. We will also address the assessment of common behavioral deficits in communication, social skills, activities of daily living, and vocational skills.

General Issues in Behavioral Assessment

Although this chapter focuses on behavioral assessment of the person with autism, many problems confronted in assessments of persons with this diagnosis hold true in other areas of behavior therapy. How to set goals, collect data, assess generalization and maintenance, and evaluate consumer responses are issues addressed by most therapists concerned with behavioral assessment.

Setting Goals

A myriad of potential points of intervention present themselves for each client. For example, the person with autism may be engaging in stereotyped behavior, show major deficits in self-care skills, fail to sleep through the night, or exhibit a profound indifference to the presence of other people. How does one decide which behaviors merit immediate attention, which can be deferred until later, and which are socially or developmentally inappropriate for intervention?

According to Mash and Terdal (1988), among the behaviors usually considered of highest priority for intervention are those that (a) are physically dangerous, (b) would enable the client to have better access to naturally reinforcing events, (c) provide a positive rather than problem-focused approach, (d) play an important developmental role, (e) are precursors to later, more complex skills, (f) increase flexible adaptation, or (g) alter the perceptions of others and thus have long-term positive implications.

This sequence is not a rigid hierarchy, but a set of guidelines. The decision about whether and where to intervene does not rest with the behavior therapist alone. Parents, teachers, and direct care staff often have priorities for treatment. These goals must be respected by the clinician, although families and teachers may need help in setting realistic objectives and understanding how skill acquisition is sequenced.

Assessment as an Ongoing Process

Behavioral assessment is not simply conducted at the beginning of a treatment plan and never again. Effective treatment depends on a continual process of feedback from the intervention process. Thus, regular plotting of data concerning skill acquisition or reduction of intrusive behaviors is an on-going aspect of behavioral assessment, because the client's response to treatment provides

new hypotheses about controlling variables. These hypotheses are then tested as part of the assessment/treatment feedback loop.

Performance versus Skill Deficits

Powers and Handleman (1984) advised that a behavioral assessment should examine whether the client is exhibiting a performance deficit or a skill deficit. Sometimes a client has a certain skill in his or her repertoire but fails to provide the desired response under specific conditions. An example of a performance deficit is exhibited by the child who is toilet-trained at home but consistently has "accidents" at school. In this situation, the relevant environmental stimuli in the school have not gained control over the desired toileting behavior. By contrast, a child who has never achieved continence at home or school is likely to be exhibiting a skill deficit. The approach to dealing with the latter child would differ from that used with the child who has the skill but fails to emit it under some conditions.

Both interview and observational data may be important in discriminating between these deficits. Careful natural observations may be essential to identify those events that facilitate the child's generalization of skills from one setting to the next. For example, observation in the child's home may reveal that the parents follow a set of behaviors that always precede placing their child on the toilet, including checking his pants, going with him to the kitchen to select a reinforcer, and so forth. By contrast, the teacher might be taking the child to the lavatory and standing him in front of a urinal. These variations in stimuli and instructional styles could lead to very different behaviors on the part of the child.

Methods of Data Collection

The words "idiographic" and "nomothetic" are used to describe two different approaches to assessment. Nomothetic assessment focuses on the use of norm-based, standardized assessment tools such as achievement tests and diagnostic checklists, which enable one to identify where a client's performance falls in relation to a larger group of persons. Thus, standardized tests, including measures of intelligence and achievement, are useful in determining how the client compares to a specific norm group. However, these normative measures are of limited value in identifying the client's specific deficits.

Idiographic assessment is an individualized approach to data collection involving direct observation of the client in the natural environment or in specially created analogs of these settings designed to examine the impact of specific variables on behavior. Collection of idiographic data may begin with interviews of the parents, teacher, direct care workers, and others who know the client. Depending upon the severity of the deficits exhibited by the person with autism, he or she may also participate in an interview. Higher-functioning persons with autism may be capable of talking about their behavior and collaborating in a data collection process, while those persons with severe cognitive deficits may not be able to do so.

Powers and Handleman (1984) urged a sensitive approach by the interviewer, especially in the early stages. One must establish rapport with the family, conveying an openness to understanding their experiences with their child and the young person's impact on their lives. An important aspect of the interview is to assess to what extent the family members are partners in the assessment and change process. Although typically lacking the professional's expertise in behavioral assessment, family members can be valuable collaborators in providing expert information about the child. Most parents are eager to assume this role. Nonetheless, a family in which members are disorganized or severely disturbed may be unable or unwilling to share this process (Harris, in press). Consequently, plans must be made for alternative interventions.

Once an initial rapport is established, it is possible to move to the detailed interview, in which the clinician explores what the family members or other informants see as the problems, under what conditions the problem behaviors occur, what interventions they have tried in the past, and so forth

(Powers & Handleman, 1984). It is also helpful to identify what they believe to be the cause of the problem and their goals for the client.

Interview data enable the behavior analyst to formulate hypotheses about where to begin observations. If, for example, the parents report that their child's self-injury usually happens when she has been asked to do something, or that episodes of aggression are most common in the morning, such a description would suggest areas for further observations. Nonetheless, the opinions of family and friends about "why" or "when" a person engages in target behaviors may not be related to the environment or the biological events that control the responses. Systematic observation is essential to making those determinations.

Direct observation can be done with paper and pencil using a shorthand code to note the occurrence of target behaviors or with the assistance of a handheld computer to record and analyze data as they are entered (e.g., Paggeot, Kavale, Mace, & Sharkey, 1988; Repp, Karsh, Felce, & Ludewig, 1989). Regardless of the recording modality, the basic process remains the same in that one records behaviorally defined target behaviors, such as acts of aggression, self-injury, or stereotyped behavior, as well as environmental phenomena, including time of day, day of week, activity being performed, persons present, and antecedent and consequent events.

Supplements to interviews and direct observation include the use of checklists to structure the collection of information. For example, an autism reinforcers checklist, to be completed by caretakers or clients, taps the potential range of reinforcers for a client (Atkinson et al., 1984). Similarly, the *Motivation Assessment Scale* addresses situational determinants of self-injurious behavior by persons with autism and related disorders (Durand & Crimmins, 1983, 1988) and can be filled out by parents or other concerned adults.

Developmental Considerations

A behavioral assessment of the person with autism should consider both the chronological and mental age of the individual. The standards by which behavior analysts judge behavior vary according to age. If behavior analysts are to set realistic goals for clients and determine to what extent their behaviors merit professional attention, such decisions need to incorporate the individual's present level of development (Harris & Ferrari, 1983).

Although the thrust toward normalization has heightened the awareness of the importance of using age-appropriate materials and teaching age-appropriate skills, cognitive deficits cannot be ignored in setting goals. For example, a teenager with autism who has severe or profound mental retardation may never learn to play adolescent video games in spite of many lessons and the fact that his peer group plays these games. Not only must goals be normalized, they must be developmentally appropriate as well. Normative data about the child's targeted peer group can be helpful in determining appropriate treatment goals. For example, in identifying desirable social and play behaviors for young children with autism, Hendrickson, Strain, Tremblay, and Shores (1982) began by observing the social initiation strategies of 60 normally developing 3-, 4-, and 5-year-old youngsters.

Social Validity

In addition to being concerned with meeting the specific needs of the person with autism and being developmentally appropriate, a behavioral assessment should also consider how the treatment goals and means of change are viewed by others. Parents and behavior therapists may differ in their opinions of appropriate treatment goals (Runco & Schreibman, 1987). Such differences heighten the importance of considering consumer goals and values when developing interventions.

Wolf (1978) urged behavior analysts to consider how acceptable a program's goals and methods are to the consumers intended to benefit from the services. In fact, measures of social validity are commonly included in published studies of behavioral assessment and treatment (Schwartz &

Baer, 1991). Although the consumers of a service are usually the direct recipients, others, including, for example, neighbors of a group home or parents of children in a school program, may also be asked their opinions about the program.

Generalization and Maintenance

Skill acquisition is of little value if the new behaviors are not applied in the contexts in which they are appropriate or are not maintained over time. Assessment of generalization and maintenance is, therefore, an integral aspect of behavioral assessment. This component of the assessment examines the recipient's use of a skill in multiple settings with different people and various stimuli and tests for the continuing use of the skill over time. Examples of assessing for generalization include sampling a child's play skills at home after she has learned to initiate play at school and observing the ability of a man with autism to use at the job site the assembly skills he initially mastered in a training facility.

When assessing generalization and maintenance, it is important to include the full range of settings in which the client or student must function. Whether a person is living at home or in a group home or supervised apartment, is attending school or a job training program, or is working, the particular context needs to be part of the assessment process. Since the expectations and opportunities in each social unit will vary, effective behavioral treatment and education need to consider these contextual, ecological variables.

Rating Scales and Checklists

Several rating scales and checklists have been developed to aid in the diagnostic assessment of people with autism. We will focus on five of the most prominent. Although objective in nature and based primarily on direct behavioral observation, these checklists use varying definitions of autism and will, therefore, discriminate differently among children.

The *Childhood Autism Rating Scale* (CARS) (Schopler, Reichler, DeVellis, & Daly, 1980) is based on the criteria of the British Working Party (Creak, 1964), Rutter (1978), and the National Society for Autistic Children (NSAC, 1978). The 15 scales of the CARS assess autistic behavior, including relationships with other people, affective responses, body awareness, receptive and expressive language, uses of communication, nonverbal communication, and adaptation to change. During administration of the CARS, a person's behavior in a structured setting is rated on a 4-point scale ranging from 1 (age-appropriate) to 4 (severely abnormal). There are specific behavioral criteria for each of the 15 scales. The total score places the child on a spectrum ranging from nonautistic to mildly to moderately involved to severely autistic.

Another instrument used to assess autism is the *Behavior Observation Scale for Autism* (BOS) (Freeman, Ritvo, Guthrie, Schroth, & Ball, 1978), based on the criteria of the NSAC (1978). The BOS, a checklist of 67 objectively defined behaviors, was developed to examine behaviors independent of a theoretical framework. During administration of the BOS, the child is observed playing with age-appropriate toys, and the frequency of specific behaviors is scored in nine 3-minute intervals. The examiner attempts to interact with the child during one interval, but remains passive throughout the rest of the observation period. Freeman and her associates noted the importance of a developmental perspective when using the BOS.

Rimland's (1971) *E-2 Checklist*, a revised form of the *Diagnostic Checklist for Behavior Disturbed Children* (Form E-1), is based on Kanner's (1943) definition of autism. The *E-2 Checklist,* which can be completed by parents, consists of a checklist of items regarding the child's developmental and medical history and the presence or absence of specific behavioral symptoms and patterns of speech. The total score is comprised of a behavior score and a language score.

Another instrument that adheres strongly to Kanner's classic criteria for autism is the *Behavior Rating Instrument for Autistic and Atypical Children* (BRIACC) (Ruttenberg, Dratman, Franknoi, & Wenar, 1966; Ruttenberg, Kalish, Wenar, & Wolf, 1977). The BRIACC's eight scales are scored by direct observation and consist of: (a) the child's relationship to an adult, (b) communication, (c) the child's "Drive for Mastery," including insistence on sameness, (d) expressive language, (e) receptive language, (f) responsiveness to social situations, (g) body awareness, and (h) developmental history (Ruttenberg et al., 1977). These scales are similar to and overlap with some of those on the CARS. Like the CARS, the BRIACC has a scoring spectrum that ranges from behaviors that are characteristic of a "normal" 3½- to 4½-year-old to behaviors that identify a child who is severely autistic (Morgan, 1988).

The *Autism Screening Instrument for Educational Planning* (ASIEP) (Krug, Arick, & Almond, 1978) is a comprehensive assessment tool consisting of five independent subtests designed to measure the child's autistic behavior, language skills, and social skills. The ASIEP also assesses educational skills and ability to learn a new task (Krug et al., 1978; Morgan, 1988).

The *Autism Behavior Checklist* (ABC) (Krug et al., 1978), intended to be completed by teachers, is the first subtest of the ASIEP. In assessing the autistic behavior of the child, it includes five areas: sensory, relating body/object use, language, and social and self-help skills.

These five instruments, although not substitutes for clinical experience and individualized behavioral assessment, are of potential value for providing norm-based summary data about the extent of a person's autistic involvement.

Assessment of Behavioral Excesses

Some of the most impressive technological gains in the behavioral assessment of persons with autism and related disorders have come about in the management of behavioral excesses such as self-injury, aggression, and stereotypic behavior. This research examines contextual and organismic variables to determine whether it is possible to manipulate environmental events, such as teacher demands, attention, and physical context, to alter a disruptive behavior; whether there is a communicative component to the problem behavior that can be addressed; and/or whether medical factors, such as infection or illness, might be involved. In general, this research indicates that careful assessment, subsequent teaching of alternative modes of communication, and modification of environmental factors can reduce the frequency of a variety of disruptive behaviors, including self-injury, stereotyped behavior, and aggression (Cowdery, Iwata, & Pace, 1990; Durand & Carr, 1991; Wacker et al., 1990).

Conducting a Functional Assessment

A wide range of contextual events have been connected to disruptive behavior. Among the many factors that have been found to influence the frequency of such behavior are visual stimulation in a classroom (Duker & Rasing, 1989), familiarity of the teacher to the child (Runco, Charlop, & Schreibman, 1986), content of the curriculum (Dunlap, Kern-Dunlap, Clarke, & Robbins, 1991), opportunities to make choices among activities and reinforcers (Dyer, Dunlap, & Winterling, 1990), level of physical exercise (Kern, Koegel, & Dunlap, 1984), presence of protective clothing (Silverman, Watanabe, Marshall, & Baer, 1984); and use of varying punishers (Charlop, Burgio, Iwata, & Ivancic, 1988). Medical factors such as middle-ear infections, allergies, and urinary tract infections can also lead to disruptive behavior and, therefore, must be considered in a comprehensive evaluation (O'Neill, Horner, Albin, Storey, & Sprague, 1990).

Much of the research on the functional relationship between environmental events and disruptive behavior has focused on escape and attention-seeking responses. Carr and Durand (1985) suggested that disruptive behavior is often either an escape response that is negatively reinforced or an attention-seeking response that is positively reinforced. Identifying whether one of these two patterns is in effect may make it possible to teach the student

appropriate alternative means of communicating the desired message. For example, attempts to escape from work by having a tantrum can be replaced by asking for a break; seeking attention by throwing papers on the floor can be replaced by asking for feedback on one's work. The combination of functional assessment and functional communication training has effectively addressed such behaviors as aggressive, disruptive behavior (Carr & Durand, 1985), stereotyped behavior (Durand & Carr, 1987), and psychotic language (Durand & Crimmins, 1987).

A functional analysis of variables that may be related to disruptive behavior can be conducted by observing clients in their natural environment, by paper-and-pencil assessment devices, or by creating analog settings in which variables of interest are manipulated systematically to determine whether they have a functional relationship to the target behavior. Analog studies are particularly powerful because they permit direct manipulation of variables of interest. This technology has been useful in the functional analysis of self-injury (Iwata, Dorsey, Slifer, Baumann, & Richman, 1982), aggression (Mace, Page, Ivancic, & O'Brien, 1986), stereotyped behavior (e.g., Mace, Browder, & Lin, 1987), and pica (Mace & Knight, 1986).

By sequentially combining these assessment tools, the behavior therapist is able to conduct an efficient and complete evaluation. Mace, Lalli, and Lalli (1991) propose that in a comprehensive methodology for assessment of aberrant behavior, the behavior therapist would: (a) conduct a descriptive analysis of the behavior under natural conditions, (b) formulate hypotheses about functional relationships based on this natural assessment, and (c) perform an experimental analysis under analog conditions.

A functional assessment should extend across settings because the events that control a behavior in one setting may not hold true in another. In a demonstration of this, Haring and Kennedy (1990) showed that during an instructional task, differential reinforcement of other behavior (DRO) led to a reduction in disruptive behavior and an increase in on-task behavior, while time-out did not have any effect. However, for the same persons during a leisure activity, time-out reduced disruptive behavior, while DRO had no impact. It appears that the leisure activity was reinforcing and that removal, therefore, was aversive. In the classroom, however, removal was not punishing.

Self-injurious behavior.   One of the most compelling and dangerous behaviors of persons with autism is self-injury. These life-threatening behaviors historically have led to institutionalization, chronic physical restraint, or the use of highly aversive punishers. Functional analysis has been especially effective in dealing with these dangerous behaviors in less intrusive ways.

A notable early functional analysis of self-injury by Iwata et al. (1982) used four analog conditions to assess the impact of (a) social disapproval, (b) being alone, (c) academic demand, and (d) unstructured play. Recording the occurrence of self-injury by nine participants in each of these settings, the investigators found that seven children showed a distinctive differential response to the analog conditions. The highest rates of self-injury occurred in the alone condition for four of the children, in the academic context for two, and in the social disapproval condition for one. Two children showed no differential response to the analog settings.

For many persons with autism and other developmental disabilities, self-injury may have a communicative function. For example, Bird, Dores, Moniz, and Robinson (1989) used the *Motivation Assessment Scale* (Durand & Crimmins, 1983, 1988) to identify the communicative intent linked to aggression and self-injury in two nonverbal men with mental retardation. The assessment revealed that both men were motivated by escape from demands. As a consequence of these findings, one was taught to exchange tokens for breaks from work, while the other learned to manually sign the word "break." Using communicative responses that were functionally equivalent to their disruptive behaviors enabled both men to learn more adaptive responses, thereby diminishing their self-injury.

Wacker and his colleagues (1990) conducted an elegant component analysis of functional communication training of three persons with developmental disabilities, each of whom had a topographically different and severe behavior problem—self-injury, stereotyped behavior, or aggression. A functional analysis of the maintaining conditions for each person's behavior was conducted in four analog conditions like those described by Iwata and his colleagues (1982). Based on their response to the analog assessment, participants were trained to emit an alternative response that solicited reinforcement. In addition, for two of the participants, it was important that a consequence of time-out or graduated guidance following disruptive behavior also be included.

Although demand conditions are often linked to self-injury (Iwata, Pace, Kalsher, Cowdery, & Cataldo, 1990), this is not always true. A case study involving a 9-year-old self-injurious boy revealed that his behavior was a stereotypic, automatically reinforcing response (Cowdery et al., 1990). Analog assessment showed that neither contingent attention nor contingent escape were reinforcers for his behavior. Rather, self-injury was confined to those times when he was alone. It was concluded that the behavior was a form of self-stimulation maintained by reinforcement from the behavior itself.

Stereotyped behavior.   Stereotyped or self-stimulatory behavior, such as body-rocking, hand-flapping, or light-gazing, has been of considerable interest to persons developing the technology of functional analysis. For example, in an early study, Aiken and Salzberg (1984) examined the effects of masking auditory stimuli on the aberrant vocalizations of two children with autism. They found a decrease in stereotypic vocalizations when these sounds were masked by white noise, but no change in hand-flapping or object-dropping, suggesting that these stereotyped behaviors were maintained by different reinforcement.

Although stereotyped behaviors are often considered inherently reinforcing, functional analysis reveals that other variables may maintain these behaviors. For example, Durand and Carr (1987) examined the hypothesis that, for some persons, stereotyped behavior may be socially mediated. They studied four children with developmental disabilities who engaged in hand-flapping and body-rocking. Results showed that stereotyped behavior increased for all four children when difficult demands were imposed and that teaching the alternative functional communication of saying "help me" led to a decrease in this behavior. Such findings highlight the risk in assuming that all stereotyped behavior is self-stimulatory and argue, once again, for careful assessment prior to intervention.

Assessment of Behavioral Deficits

Although control of dangerous, disruptive behavior is an important component of treatment, teaching clients new, adaptive behaviors is at the heart of the educational enterprise. People with autism are able to master a broad range of self-sufficiency skills when properly taught. We will review the assessment of communication, social skills including play, adaptive behaviors, and vocational skills.

Communication: Speech and Language

Disturbances of speech, language, and communication are defining symptoms of autism. While some people with autism develop adequate language, many exhibit deviations of form including immediate or delayed echolalia and pronoun reversal. In addition, approximately half of children with autism do not speak at all (Schreibman, 1988). Further, individuals with autism may have little understanding of symbolic gestures such as waving "bye-bye" or abstract concepts such as prepositions. Clients may also have idiosyncratic speech, in which certain words and phrases are repeatedly used out of context or in a nonsensical manner and seem to have no communicative intent. A

monotonous tone and flat intonation are also common.

No assessment for an individual with autism would be complete without a thorough evaluation of communication. A combination of nomothetic and idiographic methods assesses the client's range of verbal and nonverbal function. Voluntary and involuntary motor function is examined to rule out the existence of impairments in the client's ability to produce speech. For example, the client's involuntary motor movements during eating and swallowing are observed, as are voluntary motor movements such as the ability to imitate mouth positions and stick out the tongue. The general skill of imitation is assessed to determine the client's ability to mimic gestures and imitate sounds and sound combinations. A hearing test is also necessary to rule out hearing impairment (Powers & Handleman, 1984).

After preverbal skills are evaluated, the client's functional communication is assessed. "Functional communication" refers to the use of verbal and nonverbal communication to express needs and wants and to comprehend messages from others. The client is assessed for both receptive and expressive abilities in labeling a wide range of relevant objects and actions: body parts, pictures of common items, verb actions, plural nouns, subject-verb agreement, pronouns, agent-action-object combinations, negatives, "wh" questions (who, what, where, when, and why), colors, shapes, numbers, size, and prepositions (Powers & Handleman, 1984).

The clarity of articulation and degree of spontaneous speech are important dimensions of the language assessment. In addition, skills of greater complexity are assessed: the abilities to request items, ask information questions, request help, describe pictures, and answer social questions. For highly verbal individuals, advanced language skills are also assessed, including interactive conversation, oral reading, abundance of ideas, complexity of sentence structure, and appropriate vocabulary. Finally, language skills such as intonation and voice quality can also be evaluated.

A number of standardized language assessments are available for evaluating language abilities, including receptive and expressive speech, auditory processing, semantic processing, syntax, and articulation. Swanson and Watson (1982) provided an extensive review of language assessment instruments. While many sound instruments are available, evaluating an individual with autism requires special considerations. For some clients, the severity of the disability precludes the use of standardized tests. Furthermore, standardized evaluations alone do not adequately assess the client's unique language problems, nor do they adequately identify the client's communication strengths (Kristoff, 1991; Peins, 1983). In order to determine a client's level of competence, therefore, the communication specialist must use a combination of formal and informal assessment procedures.

Use of standardized tests for assessment of persons with autism presents other problems. A lack of attending behaviors, interfering stereotyped behaviors, and general difficulties in task compliance may significantly compromise the test administration. Additionally, many test items require fine-tuned visual discriminations and verbal responses—skills that may be also lacking (Kristoff, 1991). Although test administration procedures can be adjusted to a certain extent to accommodate the client's special needs, major changes might compromise the test norms.

Given the difficulties of using standardized tests with clients with autism, idiographic assessment procedures often prove more informative. Here the language specialist works one on one with the client in an effort to elicit the full range of verbal and nonverbal responses of which the client is capable. The content of the informal assessment overlaps to a great degree with the content of the standardized assessment. For example, receptive and expressive speech, auditory and semantic processing, articulation, and syntax are assessed.

The difference between formal and informal assessment is the degree of freedom and spontaneity afforded the language therapist. Thus, idiographic assessments allow the clinician to maximize the language demonstrated by the client because of the freedom to adjust phrasing, order of presentation, materials, or setting. For example, some individuals with autism respond to certain stereotypic phrases above all others (Kristoff, 1991). The client may respond to the direction "touch" (as in "touch the triangle") but not to the direction "show me." In addition, the language specialist may observe the client at home, since there is some evidence that language use is highest in the client's most familiar environment (Charlop, 1986). Observation might also take place in the classroom or in community settings, if appropriate.

Researchers have been creative in the methods employed to conduct language assessments. For example, Baltax and Simmons (1977) used audio recordings of an autistic child's bedtime soliloquies as a measure of linguistic competence. Others have studied recordings of language used by the child in the unstructured home setting to assess language use and language function (Cantwell, Howlin, & Rutter, 1978; Howlin, 1981), or used the child's symbolic and object play as a language assessment tool (Wulff, 1985).

This discussion of language assessment has focused on speech and language deficits. However, some persons with autism demonstrate a contrasting problem—speech excesses in the form of echolalia, self-stimulatory speech, and other disruptive verbal behaviors. As noted earlier, it may be important to conduct a functional assessment of such verbal behaviors to determine what communicative function, if any, they may have. For example, some research has shown that echolalia is more likely to occur when the client fails to comprehend a statement or question (Schreibman, 1988). In this case, the echolalia may be communicating the client's lack of understanding or lack of an appropriate response, such as "I don't know." Not all excesses of speech will have a communicative function, however; some idiosyncratic speech may be self-stimulatory. Yet, in all cases, a careful assessment of the client's language excesses and deficits will provide crucial information about his or her communication needs.

While the challenges of speech and language assessment with clients with autism are substantial, no client is untestable (Kristoff, 1991). Combining nomothetic and idiographic assessments with ongoing evaluation provides the clinician with comprehensive diagnostic information for assessing the language needs of the individual with autism.

Social Skills

As documented in DSM-III-R (American Psychiatric Association, 1987), deficits in social relatedness are salient aspects of autism. Such behaviors include a marked lack of awareness of the existence and feelings of others, impairments in imitative abilities, deficits in social play, and gross impairment in the ability to form friendships. Although these behaviors have not yet been studied in the same depth as other features of autism, there has been a recent increase in research examining social behaviors (e.g., Baron-Cohen, 1988; Mundy, Sigman, Ungerer, & Sherman, 1986; Walters, Barrett, & Feinstein, 1990) and affective experience and expression in individuals with autism (Braverman, Fein, Lucci, & Waterhouse, 1989; Hobson, 1986).

The clinician assessing the social and affective behavior of a person with autism is confronted by a number of questions. To what extent can the client discriminate among various emotional states (e.g., facial expression, voice tone, gesture, and other nonverbal cues, such as body language)? Can he or she recognize the emotional expressions of others within a particular social context? Is the behavior of the individual with autism responsive to the emotional expressions of others or to particular social contexts? To what extent does the individual express a full range of emotions and is he or she capable of communicating these emotional experiences by verbal or nonverbal means?

One way to assess social skills is to use a standardized scale. For example, social skills across the lifespan can be evaluated with the *Vineland Adaptive Behavior Scales* (Sparrow, Balla, & Cicchetti, 1984). This instrument is administered to a parent

or caretaker in an interview format and yields age-equivalent scores. The socialization domain is comprised of three subdomains: interpersonal relationships, play and leisure time, and coping skills. Because of the standardization of the scales and the comprehensive content, this device has been used extensively for diagnostic and program-planning purposes.

An alternative assessment instrument for very young children is the *Battelle Developmental Inventory* (Newborg, Stock, Wnek, Guidubaldi, & Svinicki, 1984), which has a personal-social domain that includes subdomains that assess interactions with adults, expression of feelings, self-concept, peer interactions, coping, and social role.

As with communication, nomothetic evaluation is typically not sufficient to develop a treatment plan for the person with social skills deficits. One must take an idiographic approach as well. For example, prior to teaching children with autism how to interact effectively with peers, one would assess such events as eye contact between the child with autism and the peer (duration, frequency, nature, and quality); physical proximity of one child to another; initiations of social interaction, as well as responses to initiation (e.g., latency or consistency of responding behavior); reciprocal interactions (e.g., conversational speech, discrete turn-taking, collaborative play); duration of interaction; level of interest in the interaction by the child with autism (attending behaviors); appropriateness of voice variables such as intensity and tone; level of affect during the interaction by the child with autism; and verbal communication between the children. It is also important to identify settings, persons, and antecedent conditions associated with high and low levels of social behaviors. Assessments of these kinds of variables have been an integral aspect of research in social relatedness (e.g., Egel & Gradel, 1988; Ragland, Kerr, & Strain 1978).

Assessing social skills is complex. Deficits in expressive language in many persons with autism prohibit the use of assessment formats such as self-monitoring, self-report, and role-playing that have been shown to be useful with more typical populations (Becker & Heimberg, 1988). Greenwood, Todd, Walker, and Hops (1978) developed a standardized observational system for assessing the social skills of withdrawn preschool-aged children, which may be useful for some children with autism. However, there is a particular need for assessment instruments to address the social skills of older individuals with autism who have similar deficits (Kratochwill & French, 1984).

Play skills. The play skills of children with autism are often particularly deficient (Romanczyk, Diament, Goren, Trunell, & Harris, 1975; Watters & Wood, 1983), especially symbolic play (Wing, Gould, Yeates, & Brierly, 1977; Wulff, 1985). The social and language impairments of even the highest-functioning children with autism render their play more isolated, more primitive, and more often typified by atypical behaviors (e.g., spinning, mouthing, repetitive or other stereotyped manipulation) than that of their nonhandicapped age-mates. These impairments pose serious obstacles to the development of cooperative play.

Assessment of independent play may address the following areas: the appropriateness of toy use; the nature of play (functional versus symbolic); the child's toy repertoire and toy choice; the duration of independent play; and the amount of adult prompting and reinforcement necessary to maintain the child's interest in the play activity. Attentional and affective factors may also be assessed during activity directed toward play materials, as well as maladaptive behaviors (e.g., stereotyped behavior) that emerge during unstructured activities.

Several assessment instruments are relevant for the play behaviors of children with autism. Quilitch, Christophersen, and Risley (1977) created an observational code for identifying a child's toy preferences, and the Play Assessment Scale (Fewell, 1984) is an experimental observational measure for examining play development. The Symbolic Play Test (Lowe & Costello, 1976), although more routinely used with typical populations of children, has been applied to socially impaired children with autistic features (Gould, 1986).

Because this test yields "play ages" that allow for comparisons to both children with mental retardation and normally developing children, it has potential value for assessment of children with autism.

In contrast to tests that focus on symbolic play behaviors, the Developmental Play Assessment Instrument (Lifter, Edwards, Avery, Anderson, and Sulzer-Azaroff, 1991) uses a developmental model to evaluate play. This observational instrument examines the topography of a child's play behavior across a set of hierarchical play categories in a free-play setting. One particularly beneficial aspect of this instrument for assessing children with autism is the coding of play behaviors independent of language responses.

Adaptive Behavior

Adaptive behavior can be defined as "behavior that is effective in meeting the natural and social demands of one's environment" (Sattler, 1988, p. 376). Assessment of adaptive behavior focuses on the ability to function independently and meet the culturally imposed demands of personal and social responsibility. This definition encompasses such skills as time management, telephone usage, meal preparation, use of public transportation, housekeeping, and street-crossing, in addition to such self-help skills as feeding, dressing, and toileting (Christian & Luce, 1985). These are behaviors in which many people with autism show deficits.

For purposes of simplicity, the following discussion focuses principally on that set of adaptive behaviors referred to as self-help or daily living skills. However, it should be noted that most of the comments regarding assessment of daily living skills apply equally to assessment of the full range of adaptive behaviors.

The importance to a client of learning daily living skills cannot be overemphasized. Facilitating the client's independence through teaching of skills of daily living embodies the value of helping clients to be as self-sufficient as possible (Powers & Handleman, 1984). Persons who lack self-help skills are restricted in the activities and environments in which they can take part. In contrast, clients with greater independence are eligible for less structured living settings and more normalized routines (Handleman & Harris, 1986). In addition, improving the client's self-help skills reduces the demands placed on staff and family caregivers; the individual is freed to participate more fully as a member of the family or group, and the other members have more time for more meaningful activities (Sisson, Kilwein, & Van Hasselt, 1988). Increasing the socially desirable behaviors in a client's repertoire (eating with a fork instead of fingers, for example) also allows the client to gain greater acceptance by nonhandicapped peers and other community members.

In order to assist a client in improving self-help skills, the clinician must undertake a thorough assessment of current skills, determining whether the client exhibits a skill or performance deficit. In addition, one must assess the degree of the client's motor impairment. Is a deficit in self-care skills due to poor muscle tone, strength, or motor coordination? Or is such an inability due to lack of knowledge, dependence on others, noncompliance, interfering behaviors, or other factors (Sisson et al., 1988)?

Browder (1991) articulated the goal of a thorough assessment of daily living skills—to "identify skills needed to function independently within domestic environments and to participate as a contributing member of the family, the household, and the immediate community" (p. 137). Browder also outlined several guidelines for conducting the assessment. First, one must address questions about long-range plans for community living options. Is the client expected to remain at home with the immediate family, live semi-independently in a supported apartment, or reside full-time in an outside facility? The expectations for current and future living arrangements significantly influence which skills are most crucial for the client to master.

A second guideline suggests that an assessment of self-help skills should reflect the culture and values of the individual's family and community. For example, different role expectations for men and women may influence a family's choice of which independence skills are most appropriate for their relative. A related guideline recommends that skills chosen for assessment and training should reflect the individual preferences of the learner and other family or residence members.

In addition, an assessment of daily living skills should address skills of general autonomy, such as making choices and scheduling one's time. For example, a client may have mastered dressing but still rely on others to select clothing for her. Improving her ability to choose appropriate clothing would further increase her self-sufficiency.

Assessment of any skill domain requires that the clinician first identify the potential range of skills and then subsequently select priorities. This can be accomplished in several ways. The clinician can review the client's prior records, have the caretakers complete an ecological inventory (surveys, interviews, or direct observations of the activities performed in, and skills required by, a given environment) (Browder, 1991), or perform a discrepancy analysis. In a discrepancy analysis, data are collected about the skills demonstrated by a nonhandicapped peer. The client's skills are then compared to this standard, and the discrepancies between the two become targets for intervention. Curriculum-based assessment is similar to discrepancy analysis in that published curricula are used as a checklist against which an individual's skills are compared (Browder, 1991).

After identifying the range of skills that the client potentially needs to master, the clinician works with the individual's caretakers and teachers to prioritize the skills that will be selected for full assessment. Taking into account the client's and family's preferences, the skills that are most crucial for success in current and future settings, the utility of various skills (i.e., usefulness across many activities or in only one isolated activity), and the practical issues involved in assessing and teaching the skills (i.e., time, money, and space constraints), the clinician assists in designating a set of skills to be assessed. Once the priorities have been determined, the remaining tasks of the clinician are conducting the actual assessments and subsequently developing an educational plan to address skill deficits.

Task analysis is one common method of assessing daily living skills. Assessment through task analysis involves breaking down complex skills or behaviors into component parts and assessing the client's skills against each component part (Powers & Handleman, 1984). Task analytic assessment is most useful for behaviors made up of finely grained skills, such as tying a shoelace. However, task analysis may also be used for broad behaviors, such as getting ready for school in the morning. Task analysis may also be useful when a client fails to complete a particular task, but it is believed that he or she possesses some of the component skills. For example, a client might be able to eat independently with the proper utensils but fail to do so because she cannot cut the food with a knife. A task analysis of each of the component behaviors of eating with utensils would reveal the area of skill deficit (Powers & Handleman, 1984). Task analysis can be carried out with either formally published versions or versions individually tailored for use in a particular setting with a particular client.

In addition to task analyses, published adaptive behavior scales and checklists have widespread use as a method for assessing daily living skills and other skills of independence. Sattler (1988) identified the applications and uses of adaptive behavior assessment instruments: well-normed scales and checklists identify the client's behavioral strengths and deficits, provide an objective basis for evaluating progress or results of intervention programs (e.g., using pre- and post-tests), and permit comparison of information across settings and informants. Behavioral scales are popular because they are economical, can be administered and scored easily, and survey a wide range of behaviors. To assess skills, most practitioners use information derived from adaptive behavior scales and checklists in combination with information gained from other sources (Browder, 1991; Sattler, 1988).

All scales and checklists of adaptive behavior are not equally sound and effective. A number of characteristics should be taken into account when determining which scales to select (Powers & Handleman, 1984; Sattler, 1988). Table 7.1 summarizes some characteristics of the better-known assessment instruments. For example, scales of adaptive behavior vary by informant. Informants may be parents, teachers, mental health workers, or caregiving staff at a residential facility. Because the information gained through these individuals is subject to their individual biases, lack of precise knowledge about the client, different expectations, and different degrees of familiarity with the client, the clinician must carefully consider whom to ask for the most reliable information. The choice of informant may narrow the available choices of instruments.

The psychometric properties of an instrument are another important consideration. Consequently, the clinician will want to be familiar with the reliability and validity of the instrument and the adequacy of the standardization procedures. Instruments also vary with respect to the comparison group used for the normative data. Some instruments permit the client's scores to be compared to several populations, such as handicapped and nonhandicapped; others allow comparisons to only a single group. Some instruments are not meant to provide normative data but are used as idiographic assessments. The *Balthazar Scales of Adaptive Behavior*, for example, is a checklist that permits the individual's skills and deficits to be catalogued in a detailed manner.

Additional factors to consider when selecting adaptive behavior assessment instruments include the scope of the items on the scale or checklist and the clinical utility. All the instruments shown in Table 7.1 assess several skill areas in addition to self-help skills. Some instruments contain more items and, therefore, assess some domains in greater detail than others. Clinicians need to select instruments based on their need for detail versus broad scope in the assessment procedure. A final consideration in the selection of assessment instruments is the clinical utility of the instrument. The ease of administration, time necessary to complete and score, and type of derived scores (e.g., standard

Table 7.1 Comparison of Adaptive Behavior Scales[1]

	AAMD Adaptive Behavior Scales[2]	Adaptive Behavior Inventory	Comprehensive Test of Adaptive Behavior	Functional Skills Screening Inventory	Scales of Independent Behavior
Reference	Lambert et al., 1981	Brown & Leigh, 1986	Adams, 1984	Becker et al., 1986	Bruininks et al., 1984
Age	3–adult	5–18	0–21	6–adult	0–adult
Informant and Format of Administration	Caregiver questionnaire or interview	Teacher questionnaire	Teacher or caretaker questionnaire or interview	Observation and caregiver interview	Caregiver interview
Areas Assessed and Number of Items per Area[3]	Self-care (17) Communication (9) Motor (6) Social (7) Vocational and academic (17)	Self-care (30) Communication (32) Social (30) Vocational (28) Academic (30)	Self-care, male (111), female (141) Home living (135) Communication and academic (68) Motor (51) Social (45) Vocational (87)	Self-care (> 100) Communication (20) Social (35) Community and vocational (85) Academic (20)	Self-care (195) Communication (33) Motor (34) Social (16) Vocational and academic (48)
Comparison Group[4]	Institutionalized MR persons	Persons with no disabilities; MR persons	Persons with no disabilities; MR persons	NA	Persons with no disabilities
Standard Score	No—percentile ranks	Yes	No	No—percentages	Yes
Standardization	Large sample, not nationally representative	Excellent	Small sample	Small sample	Good
Reliability and Validity	Questionable	Good	Questionable	Good	Good
Adaptations for Physical Disabilities	No	No	No	Yes	No
Maladaptive Behavior Items	Maladaptive, aggressive, and antisocial behavior (11)	No	No	Yes (35)	Yes (8)
Comments	Clinically useful, especially for daily living skills assessment. Maladaptive behaivor scale unreliable. School edition available.	Most useful in educational settings.	Standardization and validity of test make its use as a comparison instrument problematic. Most useful as a descriptive instrument—contains a large number of items in self-care domain.	Criterion-referenced checklist. Most appropriate as screening device to identify goals for severely disabled clients.	Can evaluate adaptive behavior scores in relation to score on Woodcock-Johnson Cognitive Ability Scale.

[1]The information in this table is an amalgamation of reviews by Browder (1989, 1991), Ehly (1989), Evans & Bradley-Johnson (1988), Perry & Factor (1989), Sattler (1988) and Svinicki (1989).
[2]AAMD = American Association on Mental Deficiency
[3]Some numbers in parentheses are approximate.
[4]MR = mentally retarded; ED = emotionally disturbed; VH = visually handicapped; HI = hearing impaired.

Table 7.1 Comparison of Adaptive Behavior Scales (continued)

	Vineland Adaptive Behavior Scales	Battelle Developmental Inventory	Balthazar Scales of Adaptive Behavior	Pyramid Scales
Reference	Sparrow et al., 1984	Newborg et al., 1984	Balthazar, 1976	Cone, 1984
Age	0–18	0–8	0–adult	0–adult
Informant and Format of Administration	Caregiver interview or questionnaire	Caregiver interview; structured test; observation	Observation and caregiver interview	Observation and caregiver interview
Areas Assessed and Number of Items per Area[3]	Self-care (92) Communication (67) Motor (34) Social (16) Vocational and academic (48)	Self-care (59) Communication (59) Motor (82) Social (85) Academic (56)	Self-care (> 100) Social (35)	Self-care (> 100) Communication (> 50) Social (35) Vocational and academic (> 100)
Comparison Group[4]	Persons with no disabilities; MR adults; ED children; VH; HI	Persons with no disabilities	NA	NA
Standard Score	Yes	Yes	No—percentile ranks	No—percentages
Standardization	Excellent	Good	Poor	Small
Reliability and Validity	Excellent	Questionable	NA—dependent on rater	Poor
Adaptations for Physical Disabilities	No	Yes—hearing, sight, motor impairments	NA	Yes
Maladaptive Behavior Items	Yes (36)	No	Yes (35)	No
Comments	Scores fluctuate across ages, so not good for longitudinal comparisons of the same individual. Complex to administer. Classroom edition available.	Provisions for evaluating physically handicapped children.	Used with severely impaired institutionalized persons. One of the most finely grained measures for assessing adaptive behaivor.	Criterion-referenced checklist. Most useful to describe individual's level of adaptive behavior.

scores versus percentiles) all influence the utility of a particular instrument in different settings.

Prevocational and Vocational Assessment

Determining the goodness of fit between a person with autism and a potential job placement is a crucial step toward creating a program that will enhance the person's self-sufficiency. It is important that the person with autism possess the requisite skills or be able to master them, and that the job be reinforcing and an ongoing source of motivation. Although a few instruments can assist in this assessment process, much of the assessment must be idiographic in nature.

The *Prevocational Assessment and Curriculum Guide* is one of the few standardized training measures available for assessing the vocational functioning of individuals with developmental disabilities (Mithaug, Mar, & Stewart, 1978). This instrument assesses three global areas: (a) worker behavior, (b) social/communication skills, and (c) self-help grooming skills. Examples from the worker behavior domain include the client's abilities to respond to external reinforcers, comply with facility rules, and respond to feedback. The social/communication domain includes the abilities to communicate basic needs, communicate work-related needs (e.g., needing additional materials), and respond appropriately to social overtures made by peers. The self-help/grooming domain covers the abilities to toilet independently, dress appropriately for work, and eat lunch independently.

In addition to assessment of abilities and skills, consideration of interests is also useful in selecting jobs and predicting job compatibility (Hansen, 1990). Formal instruments for assessing vocational interests of nonhandicapped populations, such as the *Strong Interest Inventory* (Hansen & Campbell, 1985) and the *Kuder General Interest Survey* (Kuder, 1988), have long been available. While these instruments may have some utility with higher-functioning individuals with autism, they are inappropriate for adolescents and adults whose expressive and receptive language abilities preclude the use of a self-report assessment.

An important focus for future work in this area is the development of vocational interest inventories that survey the types of prototypical employment experiences of adolescents and adults with autism. In the absence of such tools, the behavioral assessment should include exposure to a range of vocational activities and a careful evaluation of client response on an affective as well as a performance level.

Summary

Behavioral assessment is a powerful component of the planning and treatment process for the person with autism. Assessment techniques have been developed that are relevant to the broad range of behavioral excesses and skill deficits exhibited by persons with this diagnosis. It is important that assessments be sensitive to the family and social context in which the client lives, be developmentally appropriate, and be adjusted to the needs of each client. Although nomothetic techniques, including some norm-based data collection tools, have a role in the assessment process, the heart of behavioral assessment lies in the observation of the specific behaviors of each client. Assessment of behavioral excesses has been greatly enhanced by technological advances in the ability to examine the contextual and organismic variables that may contribute to or control these potentially dangerous or disruptive behaviors. Deficits in communication, social skills, adaptive behaviors, and vocational skills may be addressed by fine-grained analyses comparing the individual's present skills to those of others in a community, discriminating skill deficits from performance deficits, and setting priorities for intervention.

References

ADAMS, G. L. (1984). *Comprehensive test of adaptive behavior*. Columbus, OH: Charles E. Merrill.

AIKEN, J. M., & SALZBERG, C. L. (1984). The effects of a sensory extinction procedure on stereotypic sounds of two autistic children. *Journal of Autism and Developmental Disorders, 14*, 291–299.

AMERICAN PSYCHIATRIC ASSOCIATION. (1987). *Diagnostic and statistical manual of mental disorders* (3rd ed.). Washington, DC: Author.

ATKINSON, R. P., JENSON, W. R., ROVNER, L., CAMERON, S., VAN WAGENEN, L., & PETERSON, B. P. (1984). Brief report: Validation of the autism reinforcer checklist for children. *Journal of Autism and Developmental Disorders, 14*, 429–433.

BALTAX, C. A., & SIMMONS, J. Q. (1977). Bedtime soliloquies and linguistic competence in autism. *Journal of Speech and Hearing Disorders, 42*, 376–393.

BALTHAZAR, E. E. (1976). *Balthazar scales of adaptive behavior*. Palo Alto, CA: Consulting Psychologists Press.

BARON-COHEN, S. (1988). Social and pragmatic deficits in autism. *Journal of Autism and Developmental Disorders, 18*, 379–402.

BECKER, H., SCHUR, S., PAOLETTI-SCHELP, M., & HAMMER, E. (1986). *Functional skills screening inventory*. Austin, TX: Functional Resources Enterprises.

BECKER, R., & HEIMBERG, R. (1988). Assessment of social skills. In A. S. Bellack & M. Hersen (Eds.), *Behavioral assessment: A practical handbook* (3rd ed.) (pp. 365–395). Elmsford, NY: Pergamon.

BIRD, F., DORES, P. A., MONIZ, D., & ROBINSON, J. (1989). Reducing severe aggressive and self-injurious behaviors with functional communication training. *American Journal on Mental Retardation, 94,* 37–48.

BRAVERMAN, M., FEIN, D., LUCCI, D., & WATERHOUSE, L. (1989). Affect comprehension in children with pervasive developmental disorders. *Journal of Autism and Developmental Disorders, 19,* 301–316.

BROWDER, D. (1989). Functional skills screening inventory. In J. C. Conolly & J. J. Kramer (Eds.), *Tenth mental measurements yearbook* (pp. 315–317). Lincoln: University of Nebraska Press.

BROWDER, D. M. (1991). *Assessment of individuals with severe disabilities.* Baltimore: Paul H. Brooks.

BROWN, L., & LEIGH, J. E. (1986). *Adaptive behavior inventory.* Austin, TX: PRO-ED.

BRUINIKS, R. H., WOODCOCK, R. W., WEATHERMAN, R. F., & HILL, B. K. (1984). *Scales of independent behavior. Woodcock-Johnson psychoeducational battery: Part four.* Allen, TX: DLM Teaching Resources.

CANTWELL, D., HOWLIN, P., & RUTTER, M. (1978). The analysis of language level and language function: A methodological study. *British Journal of Disorders of Communication, 12,* 119–135.

CARR, E. G., & DURAND, V. M. (1985). Reducing behavior problems through functional communication training. *Journal of Applied Behavior Analysis, 18,* 111–126.

CHARLOP, M. H. (1986). Setting effects on the occurrence of autistic children's immediate echolalia. *Journal of Autism and Developmental Disorders, 16,* 472–487.

CHARLOP, M. H., BURGIO, L. D., IWATA, B. A., & IVANCIC, M. T. (1988). Stimulus variation as a means of enhancing punishment effects. *Journal of Applied Behavior Analysis, 21,* 89–95.

CHRISTIAN, W. P., & LUCE, S. C. (1985). Behavioral self-help training for developmentally disabled individuals. *School Psychology Review, 14,* 177–181.

CONE, J. D. (1984). *The pyramid scales: Criterion-referenced measures of adaptive behavior in severely handicapped persons.* Austin, TX: PRO-ED.

COWDERY, G. E., IWATA, B. A., & PACE, G. M. (1990). Effects and side effects of DRO as treatment for self-injurious behavior. *Journal of Applied Behavior Analysis, 23,* 497–506.

CREAK, M. (1964). Schizophrenic syndrome in childhood: Further progress of a working party. *Developmental Medicine and Child Neurology, 6,* 530–535.

DUKER, P. C., & RASING, E. (1989). Effects of redesigning the physical environment on self-stimulation and on-task behavior in three autistic-type developmentally disabled individuals. *Journal of Autism and Developmental Disorders, 19,* 449–460.

DUNLAP, G., KERN-DUNLAP, L., CLARKE, S., & ROBBINS, F. R. (1991). Functional assessment, curricular revision, and severe behavior problems. *Journal of Applied Behavior Analysis, 24,* 387–397.

DURAND, V. M., & CARR, E. G. (1987). Social influences on "self-stimulatory" behavior: Analysis and treatment application. *Journal of Applied Behavior Analysis, 20,* 119–132.

DURAND, V. M., & CARR, E. G. (1991). Functional communication training to reduce challenging behavior: Maintenance and application in new settings. *Journal of Applied Behavior Analysis, 24,* 251–264.

DURAND, V. M., & CRIMMINS, D. B. (1983, October). *The motivation assessment scale: A preliminary report on an instrument which assesses the functional significance of children's deviant behavior.* Paper presented at the conference of the Berkshire Association for Behavior Analysis and Therapy, Amherst, MA.

DURAND, V. M., & CRIMMINS, D. B. (1987). Assessment and treatment of psychotic speech in an autistic child. *Journal of Autism and Developmental Disorders, 17,* 17–28.

DURAND, V. M., & CRIMMINS, D. B. (1988). Identifying the variables maintaining self-injurious behavior. *Journal of Autism and Developmental Disorders, 18,* 99–117.

DYER, K., DUNLAP, G., & WINTERLING, V. (1990). Effects of choice making on the serious problem behaviors of students with severe handicaps. *Journal of Applied Behavior Analysis, 23,* 515–524.

EGEL, A. L., & GRADEL, K. (1988). Social integration of autistic children: Evaluation and recommendations. *The Behavior Therapist, 11,* 7–11.

EHLY, S. (1989). Review of the *Adaptive behavior inventory.* In J. C. Conolly & J. J. Kramer (Eds.), *Tenth mental measurements yearbook* (pp. 20–21). Lincoln: University of Nebraska Press.

EVANS, L. D., & BRADLEY, J. S. (1988). A review of recently developed measures of adaptive behavior. *Psychology in the Schools, 25,* 276–287.

FEWELL, R. R. (1984). *Play assessment scale.* Unpublished manuscript, University of Washington, Seattle, Experimental Education Unit.

FREEMAN, B. J., RITVO, E. R., GUTHRIE, D., SCHROTH, P., & BALL, J. (1978). The behavior observation scale for autism: Initial methodology, data analysis, and preliminary findings on 89 children. *Journal of the American Academy of Child Psychiatry, 17,* 576–588.

GOULD, J. (1986). The Lowe and Costello symbolic play testing of socially impaired children. *Journal of Autism and Developmental Disorders, 16,* 199–213.

GREENWOOD, C. R., TODD, N. M., WALKER, H. M., & HOPS, H. (1978). *Social assessment manual for preschool level* (SAMPLE). Eugene: University of Oregon, Center for Research in the Behavioral Education of the Handicapped.

HANDLEMAN, J. S., & HARRIS, S. L. (1986). *Educating the developmentally disabled: Meeting the needs of children and families*. San Diego, CA: College-Hill Press.

HANSEN, J. C. (1990). Interest inventories. In G. Goldstein & M. Hersen (Eds.), *Handbook of psychological assessment* (pp. 173–186). Elmsford, NY: Pergamon.

HANSEN, J. C., & CAMPBELL, D. P. (1985). *Manual for the SVIB-SCII*. Palo Alto, CA: Stanford University Press.

HARING, T. G., & KENNEDY, C. H. (1990). Contextual control of problem behavior in students with severe disabilities. *Journal of Applied Behavior Analysis, 23*, 235–243.

HARRIS, S. L. (in press). Treatment of family problems in autism. In E. Schopler & G. B. Mesibov (Eds.), *Assessment and management of behavior problems in autism*. New York: Plenum.

HARRIS, S. L., & FERRARI, M. (1983). Developmental factors in child behavior therapy. *Behavior Therapy, 14*, 54–72.

HENDRICKSON, J. M., STRAIN, P. S., TREMBLAY, A., & SHORES, R. E. (1982). Interaction of behaviorally handicapped children: Functional effects of peer social initiations. *Behavior Modification, 6*, 323–353.

HOBSON, R. P. (1986). The autistic child: Appraisal of expressions of emotion. *Journal of Child Psychology and Psychiatry, 27*, 321–342.

HOWLIN, P. (1981). The results of a home-based language training programme with autistic children. *British Journal of Disorders of Communication, 16*, 73–88.

IWATA, B. A., DORSEY, M. F., SLIFER, K. J., BAUMANN, K. E., & RICHMAN, G. S. (1982). Toward a functional analysis of self-injury. *Analysis and Intervention in Developmental Disabilities, 2*, 3-20.

IWATA, B. A., PACE, G. M., KALSHER, M. J., COWDERY, G. E., & CATALDO, M. F. (1990). Experimental analysis and extinction of self-injurious escape behavior. *Journal of Applied Behavior Analysis, 23*, 11–27.

KANNER, L. (1943). Autistic disturbances of affective contact. *Nervous Child, 2*, 217–250.

KERN, L., KOEGEL, R. L., & DUNLAP, G. (1984). The influence of vigorous versus mild exercise on autistic stereotyped behaviors. *Journal of Autism and Developmental Disorders, 14*, 57–67.

KRATOCHWILL, T. R., & FRENCH, D. C. (1984). Social skills training for withdrawn children. *School Psychology Review, 13*, 331–338.

KRISTOFF, B. (1991, September). *Evaluating communication skills*. Paper presented at the conference on Classification and Diagnosis of Autism, Rutgers University, New Brunswick, NJ.

KRUG, D. A., ARICK, J. R., & ALMOND, P. J. (1978). *Autism screening instrument for educational planning*. Portland, OR: ASIEP Educational.

KUDER, G. F. (1988). *Kuder general interest survey, Form E*. Chicago: Science Research Associates.

LAMBERT, N., WINDMILLER, M., THARINGER, D., & COLE, L. (1981). *American Association on Mental Deficiency adaptive behavior scales*. Monterey, CA: CTB/McGraw-Hill.

LIFTER, K., EDWARDS, G., AVERY, D., ANDERSON, S. R., & SULZER-AZAROFF, B. (1991). *The developmental play assessment instrument* (2nd ed.). Unpublished paper.

LOWE, M., & COSTELLO, A. (1976). *Symbolic play test*. Berkshire, England: NFER-Nelson.

MACE, F. C., BROWDER, D., & LIN, Y. (1987). Analysis of demand conditions associated with stereotypy. *Journal of Behavior Therapy and Experimental Psychiatry, 18*, 25–31.

MACE, F. C., & KNIGHT, D. (1986). Functional analysis and treatment of severe pica. *Journal of Applied Behavior Analysis, 19*, 411–416.

MACE, F. C., LALLI, J. S., & LALLI, E. P. (1991). Functional analysis and treatment of aberrant behavior. *Research in Developmental Disabilities, 12*, 155–180.

MACE, F. C., PAGE, T. J., IVANCIC, M. T., & O'BRIEN, S. (1986). Analysis of environmental determinants of aggression and disruption in mentally retarded children. *Applied Research in Mental Retardation, 7*, 203–221.

MASH, E. J., & TERDAL, L. G. (1988). Behavioral assessment of child and family disturbance. In E. J. Mash & L. G. Terdal (Eds.), *Behavioral assessment of childhood disorders* (2nd ed.) (pp. 3–65). New York: Guilford.

MITHAUG, D., MAR, D., & STEWART, D. (1978). *Prevocational assessment and curriculum guide*. Seattle: Exceptional Education Press.

MORGAN, S. (1988). Diagnostic assessment of autism. *Journal of Psychoeducational Assessment, 6*, 139–151.

MUNDY, P., SIGMAN, M., UNGERER, J., & SHERMAN, T. (1986). Defining the social deficit of autism: The contribution of non-verbal communication measures. *Journal of Child Psychology and Psychiatry, 27*, 657–669.

NATIONAL SOCIETY FOR AUTISTIC CHILDREN. (1978). National Society for Autistic Children definition of autism. *Journal of Autism and Childhood Schizophrenia, 8*, 162–167.

NEWBORG, J., STOCK, J. R., WNEK, L., GUIDUBALDI, J., & SVINICKI, J. (1984). *Battelle developmental inventory*. Allen, TX: DLM Teaching Resources.

O'NEILL, R. E., HORNER, R. H., ALBIN, R. W., STOREY, K., & SPRAGUE, J. R. (1990). *Functional analysis of problem behavior*. Sycamore, IL: Sycamore.

PAGGEOT, B., KAVALE, S., MACE, C. F., & SHARKEY, R. W. (1988). Some merits and limitations of hand-held computers for data collection. *Journal of Applied Behavior Analysis, 21*, 429.

PEINS, M. (Producer). (1983). *Speech and language assessment procedures with autistic children* [videotape]. New Brunswick, NJ: Rutgers University Office of Television and Radio.

PERRY, A., & FACTOR, D. C. (1989). Psychometric validity and clinical usefulness of the *Vineland adaptive behavior scales* and the AAMD *Adaptive behavior scale* for an autistic sample. *Journal of Autism and Developmental Disorders, 19*, 41–55.

POWERS, M. D., & HANDLEMAN, J. S. (1984). *Behavioral assessment of severe developmental disabilities*. Rockville, MD: Aspen.

QUILITCH, H. R., CHRISTOPHERSEN, E. R., & RISLEY, T. R. (1977). The evaluation of children's play materials. *Journal of Applied Behavior Analysis, 10*, 501–502.

RAGLAND, E. V., KERR, M. M., & STRAIN, P. S. (1978). Behavior of withdrawn autistic children: Effects of peer social initiations. *Behavior Modification, 2*, 565–578.

REPP, A. C., KARSH, K. G., FELCE, D., & LUDEWIG, D. (1989). Further comments on using hand-held computers for data collection. *Journal of Applied Behavior Analysis, 22*, 336–337.

RIMLAND, B. (1971). The differentiation of childhood psychoses: An analysis of checklists for 2,218 psychotic children. *Journal of Autism and Childhood Schizophrenia, 1*, 161–174.

ROMANCZYK, R. G., DIAMENT, C., GOREN, E., TRUNELL, G., & HARRIS, S. L. (1975). Increasing isolate and social play in severely disturbed children: Intervention and post intervention effectiveness. *Journal of Autism and Developmental Disorders, 5*, 57–70.

RUNCO, M. A., CHARLOP, M. H., & SCHREIBMAN, L. (1986). The occurrence of autistic children's self-stimulation as a function of familiar versus unfamiliar stimulus conditions. *Journal of Autism and Developmental Disorders, 16*, 31–44.

RUNCO, M. A., & SCHREIBMAN, L. (1987). Brief report: Socially validating behavioral objectives in the treatment of autistic children. *Journal of Autism and Developmental Disorders, 17*, 141–147.

RUTTENBERG, B. A., DRATMAN, M. L., FRANKNOI, J., & WENAR, C. (1966). An instrument for evaluating autistic children. *Journal of the American Academy of Child Psychiatry, 5*, 453–478.

RUTTENBERG, B. A., KALISH, B. I., WENAR, C., & WOLF, E. G. (1977). *Behavior rating instrument for autistic and other atypical children* (rev. ed.). Philadelphia: Developmental Center for Autistic Children.

RUTTER, M. (1978). Diagnosis and definition. In M. Rutter and E. Schopler (Eds.), *Autism: A reappraisal of concepts and treatment* (pp. 1–25). New York: Plenum.

SATTLER, J. M. (1988). *Assessment of children* (3rd ed.). San Diego, CA: Jerome M. Sattler.

SCHOPLER, E., REICHLER, R. L., DEVELLIS, R. F., & DALY, K. (1980). Toward objective classification of childhood autism: *Childhood autism rating scale* (CARS). *Journal of Autism and Developmental Disorders, 10*, 91–103.

SCHREIBMAN, L. E. (1988). *Autism*. Newbury Park, CA: Sage.

SCHWARTZ, I. S., & BAER, D. M. (1991). Social validity assessments: Is current practice state of the art? *Journal of Applied Behavior Analysis, 24*, 189–204.

SILVERMAN, K., WATANABE, K., MARSHALL, A. M., & BAER, D. M. (1984). Reducing self-injury and corresponding self-restraint through the strategic use of protective clothing. *Journal of Applied Behavior Analysis, 17*, 545–552.

SISSON, L. A., KILWEIN, M. L., & VAN HASSELT, V. B. (1988). A graduated guidance procedure for teaching self-dressing skills to multihandicapped children. *Research in Developmental Disabilities, 9*, 419–432.

SPARROW, S. S., BALLA, D. A., & CICCHETTI, D. V. (1984). *Vineland adaptive behavior scales*. Circle Pines, MN: American Guidance Service.

SVINICKI, J. G. (1989). Review of the *Pyramid scales*. In J. C. Conolly & J. J. Kramer (Eds.), *Tenth mental measurements yearbook* (pp. 671–673). Lincoln: University of Nebraska Press.

SWANSON, H. L., & WATSON, B. L. (1982). *Educational and psychological assessment of exceptional children*. St. Louis: Mosby.

VAN HOUTEN, R. V., AXELROD, S., BAILEY, J. S., FAVELL, J. E., FOXX, R. M., IWATA, B. A., & LOVAAS, O. I. (1988). The right to effective behavioral treatment. *Journal of Applied Behavior Analysis, 21*, 381–384.

WACKER, D. P., STEEGE, M. W., NORTHUP, J., SASSO, G., BERG, W., REIMERS, T., COOPER, L., CIGRAND, K., & DONN, L. (1990). A component analysis of functional communication training across three topographies of severe behavior problems. *Journal of Applied Behavior Analysis, 23*, 417–429.

WALTERS, A. S., BARRETT, R. P., & FEINSTEIN, C. (1990). Social relatedness and autism: Current research, issues and directions. *Research in Developmental Disabilities, 11*, 303–326.

WATTERS, R. G., & WOOD, D. E. (1983). Play and self-stimulatory behavior of autistic and other severely dysfunctional children with different classes of toys. *The Journal of Special Education, 17*, 27–35.

WING, L., GOULD, J., YEATES, S. R., & BRIERLY, L. M. (1977). Symbolic play in severely mentally retarded and in autistic children. *Journal of Child Psychology and Psychiatry, 18*, 167–178.

WOLF, M. M. (1978). Social validity: The case for subjective measurement or how behavior analysis is finding its heart. *Journal of Applied Behavior Analysis, 11*, 203–214.

WULFF, S. B. (1985). The symbolic and object play of children with autism: A review. *Journal of Autism and Developmental Disorders, 15*, 139–148.

CHAPTER 8

Self-Injury

Donald P. Oswald
Cynthia R. Ellis
Nirbhay N. Singh
MEDICAL COLLEGE OF VIRGINIA

Yadhu N. Singh
COLLEGE OF PHARMACOLOGY
SOUTH DAKOTA STATE UNIVERSITY

More has been written about self-injurious behavior in individuals with mental retardation than about any of their other behavior problems (Luiselli, Matson, & Singh, 1992; Repp & Singh, 1990). However, the literature dealing with self-injury in individuals with autism is rather limited. Although different diagnostic criteria are used to classify individuals as mentally retarded or autistic, the self-injurious behavior of the two groups appears to be functionally similar. It is our contention, therefore, that the principles that apply to the assessment and treatment of self-injury in the one population are also relevant to the other. Thus, in the absence of literature specifically on individuals with autism, we have included illustrative studies of self-injury in individuals with mental retardation to provide a more complete account of this topic.

Prevalence

Mental Retardation

The prevalence of self-injury in individuals with mental retardation ranges from 3 to 40 per 100 cases in institutions and is about 38 per 100 cases in the community (Johnson & Day, 1992). The wide variation in the prevalence rate reflects a number of factors, including the definition of "self-injury" used in the studies, the time frame within which the data were collected, the sampling strategy and data collection procedures used, and the characteristics of the subjects. Furthermore, the prevalence rate reported for self-injury in the community is based on only one study.

Autism

No large-scale studies have examined the prevalence of self-injury in individuals with autism, and the meager information available in the literature has been derived from studies with small, non-representative samples. For example, Bartak and Rutter (1976) provided data from two small samples of children with autism in England, one with mental retardation and the other with average intelligence. Among other differences, parental reports showed that more of the autistic children with mental retardation displayed self-injury (71%) than those with average intelligence (32%).

In a study of children in a special school program in Japan, Ando and Yoshimura (1979) reported that children with autism were significantly more likely to display self-injury (43% of the sample) than those with mental retardation (5%). In a more recent study of 19 individuals with autism from Connecticut, Volkmar, Hoder, and Cohen (1985) found that self-injury was negatively correlated with IQ but not significantly so. Further, in a statewide study from New York, Janicki and Jacobson (1983) identified 314 adults with autism; approximately 20% of this sample displayed self-injurious behavior. Finally, in a study conducted in Sweden, Gillberg, Persson, and Wahlstrom (1986) noted that five of their ten subjects with autism–Fragile-X syndrome (AFRAX) displayed self-injury "to a pronounced degree" (p. 36). As these studies indicate, self-injury occurs in individuals with autism, but the size of the problem remains to be determined.

Etiology

A number of theories of the etiology of self-injury have been advanced in the last 15 years (Luiselli et al., 1992). However, only the behavioral and neurochemical theories have provided testable hypotheses regarding causation; these are discussed in some detail below.

Behavioral Hypotheses

Behavioral hypotheses about self-injury in autism generally focus on maintenance and exacerbation of the problem rather than on its etiology. Behavioral principles traditionally employed to explain the mechanism by which behaviors enter an individual's repertoire (e.g., modeling and shaping) are neither helpful for explaining how self-injurious behaviors are initiated nor particularly useful for suggesting effective treatment strategies. For understanding how these problem behaviors are maintained, exacerbated, or ameliorated, behavioral hypotheses become more fruitful. Carr's (1977) exposition of these hypotheses remains the seminal

work on the topic and much of the research in the last 15 years on the behavioral treatment of self-injury in autism and mental retardation has consisted of testing and elaborating upon these hypotheses.

According to the positive reinforcement hypothesis, self-injury is a learned operant that is maintained by contingent positive reinforcement. Generally, it is presumed that attention provides social reinforcement and that the self-injurious individual has learned the contingency between self-injury and attention. According to the negative reinforcement hypothesis, self-injury is a learned operant that is maintained by the termination of an aversive event; that is, self-injury serves as an escape or avoidance response (Iwata, 1987). This hypothesis has been used to suggest that individuals with autism and mental retardation engage in self-injury to escape demand situations (e.g., academic tasks in the classroom or daily living skills tasks at home and in institutions). Indeed, an abundance of research supports the existence of such a phenomenon (e.g., Carr, Newsom, & Binkoff, 1980; Edelson, Taubman, & Lovaas, 1983). In addition, much of the recent applied work has been based on this hypothesis (e.g., Bird, Dores, Moniz, & Robinson, 1989; Iwata, Pace, Kalsher, Cowdery, & Cataldo, 1990).

There are two versions of the self-stimulation hypothesis, one dealing with hypoarousal and the other with hyperarousal. According to the hypoarousal hypothesis, a person needs an optimal level of stimulation (particularly in the tactile, vestibular, and kinesthetic modalities). If such stimulation is not available, he or she may engage in repetitive behaviors such as self-injury and stereotypy as a means of gaining sensory stimulation. Similarly, according to the hyperarousal hypothesis, when there is too much stimulation the person may engage in behaviors that will reduce sensory stimulation, thereby reducing arousal level.

In addition to these three behavioral hypotheses, Carr (1977) proposed psychodynamic and neurochemical hypotheses. The former is generally considered to be scientifically untestable (Carr, 1977; Favell et al., 1982) and need not be discussed here; the neurochemical hypothesis will be discussed next.

Neurochemical Hypotheses

Neurobiological changes associated with self-injury in autistic individuals have been postulated to involve either disturbances in neurotransmitter function, which may be associated with overt neuroanatomical abnormalities, or stress-induced analgesia modulated by both opioid and nonopioid systems. For example, cerebellar abnormalities and neuroanatomical changes in individuals exhibiting self-injury have been reported in the hippocampus, septal nuclei, and selected nuclei in the amygdala and neocerebellar cortex (Bauman & Kemper, 1985; Courchesne, Yeung-Courchesne, Press, Hesselink, & Jernigan, 1988). These changes may lead to disturbances in sensory modulation that result in a disruption of adaptive, integrative, and motivated behavior (Harris, 1992).

Various neurotransmitters, including dopamine and serotonin, and the endogenous opioid system have been found to be involved in autism. Based on neurotransmitter hypotheses, a variety of psychoactive drugs have been tested in individuals with autism. For example, in a placebo-controlled study of 33 children with autism, Campbell et al. (1982) found that Haloperidol, a drug that blocks the dopamine system, produces changes in behavior and learning. However, a positive correlation between clinical changes in behavior and central and peripheral dopamine turnover has not been clearly established (Minderaa, Anderson, Volkmar, Akkerhuis, & Cohen, 1989). This suggests the need for further studies, perhaps using more sophisticated neurochemical techniques.

The finding that D_1 or mixed D_1/D_2 dopamine agonists produce self-biting in monkeys who previously had nigrostriatal lesions has led to the suggestion that self-injury may involve an imbalance in dopamine/serotonin systems or that an interaction between dopamine and another neurotransmitter system leads to dopamine supersensitivity (Goldstein, Anderson, Reuben, & Dancis, 1985). Indeed, reduction in self-injury has been reported

in at least one patient treated with Fluphenazine, a mixed D_1/D_2 antagonist that predominantly blocks the D_1 system (Watts et al., 1982). It is hoped that the use of modern neurological techniques in future research will enable in vivo evaluation of the dopamine supersensitivity theory.

The discovery of endogenous opioid peptides and opioid receptors has led to extensive research on pain and pain-related behaviors, including self-injury. Three genetically distinct families of opioid peptides—beta-endorphins, dynorphins, and enkephalins—have been identified in the central nervous system (CNS). Increased opioid peptide secretion and reduction in pain responsiveness accompanying acutely stressful situations lead to stress-induced analgesia (SIA)—that is, an insensitivity to pain (Madden, Akil, Patrick, & Barchas, 1977; Willer, Dekers, & Cambier, 1981). The involvement of endogenous opioids—in particular, beta-endorphins—is indicated since SIA can be blocked or reduced by opioid antagonists such as Naloxone, whose administration is associated with increased pain perception (Buchsbaum, Davis, & Bunny, 1977).

Two theories have been advanced that implicate endophinergic mechanisms in the development and/or maintenance of self-injury: the congenital opioid excess hypothesis and the addiction hypothesis (DeMet & Sandman, 1991; Sandman, Barron, Chicz-DeMet, & DeMet, 1990). The congenital opioid excess hypothesis holds that the excessive activity of the endorphins results in opioid-mediated SIA. In some cases, this insensitivity to pain appears to be due to chronically elevated opioid levels. For example, increased levels of beta-endorphins in plasma and cerebrospinal fluid and reduction in pain threshold subsequent to Naloxone administration have been noted in individuals exhibiting self-injury compared to control subjects (Dehen, Willer, Boureau, & Cambier, 1977; Gillberg, Terenius, & Lonnerholm, 1985; Sandman et al., 1990).

According to the addiction hypothesis, self-injury itself stimulates the production and release of endorphins, with the resulting analgesic and euphoric effects of these opioids positively reinforcing self-injury (Harris, 1992; Singh, Ricketts, Ellis, & Singh, 1993). Assuming that production and release of endogenous opioids result from painful stimuli, it has been suggested that an individual can stimulate endorphin secretion by engaging in self-injury, thus experiencing analgesia and euphoria (Cataldo & Harris, 1982).

Interaction among neurotransmitter systems may also be involved in the genesis and maintenance of self-injury (Harris, 1992). Opioid peptides and dopamine are closely related to one another and are found in similar regions of the brain. Enkephalins might influence self-stimulation indirectly via dopamine neurons, which are thought to be presynaptically inhibited by enkephalins (Mulder, Wardeh, Hogenboom, & Frankhuyzen, 1984). Morphine alters dopamine turnover in the brain (Lal, 1975), and intrastriatal enkephalins have been shown to stimulate dopamine synthesis in the caudate nucleus. Furthermore, substantia nigra lesions have resulted in reductions in opiate receptor activity.

Centrally acting drugs may increase stereotypies and have been shown to lead to self-injury in animals. These substances include alcohol, caffeine, methylxanthine, Clonidine, Pemoline, and amphetamine (Harris, 1992). High-dose Pemoline is similar to amphetamine in its effects on self-injury and is blocked by Haloperidol, a dopamine antagonist, whereas low-dose Pemoline results in intermittent self-injury and stereotypy (Rylander, 1971). Underfed rats and rabbits developed self-injury after long-term treatment with high doses of caffeine or theophylline (methylpurine derivatives). The ability of these two methylpurines to cause self-injury in animals is of interest because it may provide important information about mechanisms related to the development of self-injury. Endogenous purine derivatives released from cells may influence neuronal activity as presynaptic modulators of neurotransmitter release and as regulators of receptor sensitivity (Kopin, 1981). Purine derivatives such as hypoxanthine interfere with the binding of diazepam to its receptors. Because caffeine also inhibits the binding of diazepam to its receptors,

Kopin suggested that a diazepam binding site may be involved in producing some of the behavioral manifestations of self-biting.

In summary, a number of neurochemical hypotheses may explain the genesis and maintenance of self-injury in individuals with autism who may or may not have concomitant mental retardation. However, current research data do not provide full support for any one hypothesis.

Assessment

Early behavioral research on the assessment of self-injury in individuals with autism was based on frequency counts of the behavior in a single setting. These data were used to compute the response rate of the behavior, whereupon a technique-driven treatment was instituted, with the base rate providing the comparison against which effectiveness of the intervention was judged. Because it did not lead to treatment based on the presumed cause of the behavior, this method of assessing self-injury proved inadequate. With increased understanding of the factors involved in the maintenance of self-injury, however, the current prerequisite for behavioral intervention is a functional analysis of the contingency or contingencies that maintain the behavior. The assumption is that behavioral techniques will prove to be more effective if chosen on the basis of the presumed causes of the behavior (Repp, Singh, Olinger, & Olson, 1990), and these can best be assessed through a functional analysis of the problem behavior.

Functional Analysis of Self-Injury

The most effective intervention for self-injury is likely to be one that is derived through a functional analysis of the presumed causes of the behavior. However, the majority of intervention studies of self-injury in individuals with autism or mental retardation have not been based on this premise. For example, in their analysis of intervention studies, Repp et al. (1990) report that few self-injury studies have addressed theoretical explanations of the contingencies maintaining self-injury. Repp et al. examined 75 intervention studies to determine whether a functional analysis was used to derive appropriate treatment strategies. They found that the treatments in a majority of the studies were based on "the *technology* of applied behavior analysis rather than on *functional analyses* of behavior" (p. 102; emphasis in original).

We believe that a scientific approach to the treatment of self-injury in individuals with autism must proceed from a functional analysis of the target behavior. The absence of such an approach to clinical assessment puts the treatment selection process at the mercy of such factors as clinician experience, program philosophy, and public policy. An adequate functional analysis, on the other hand, sheds light on the current functions of the target behavior and frequently provides a clear choice of treatment techniques.

Generally, functional analysis begins with structured observation in natural settings in an attempt to identify the motivation that appears to be associated with the target behavior (O'Neill, Horner, Albin, Storey, & Sprague, 1990). The motivations investigated are usually based on the fundamental behavioral hypotheses regarding the contingencies that maintain self-injury, such as positive reinforcement, negative reinforcement, and self-stimulation. The task of analyzing the function of a behavior involves manipulating the environment so that the behavior serves one, and only one, function in each of several otherwise similar conditions. By observing the rate of the behavior across conditions, the clinician can determine the function that is most strongly associated with the behavior. Of course, there is no guarantee that a target behavior will be maintained by a single motivation. However, a comprehensive functional analysis will uncover the strength of each motivation should the target behavior be maintained by more than one motivation.

Functional analysis technology has been developed to its present state largely by researchers in the area of self-injury. Though not specific to autism, this work has generally been carried out with individuals with developmental disabilities,

and for the most part, it is directly applicable to the treatment of self-injury in individuals with autism.

In the initial study using a functional analysis methodology, Iwata, Dorsey, Slifer, Bauman, and Richman (1982) described an analog approach to the functional analysis of self-injury. They designed four experimental conditions associated with four conceptually relevant maintaining variables: (a) unstructured play with social disapproval in response to self-injury; (b) structured, developmentally appropriate educational activities; (c) unstructured play with social approval for absence of self-injury; and (d) alone, without environmental stimulation of toys and materials. Nine subjects were exposed to each condition for 15 minutes twice each day, for a total of eight sessions per day, and self-injurious behavior was monitored by direct observation. Seven subjects displayed a pattern of behavior across conditions that yielded hypotheses about the motivation for their self-injury. For four of the subjects, self-injury was highest during the alone condition, suggesting that some form of self-stimulation was the maintaining variable. Two of the subjects displayed more self-injury during the academic task condition, where the behavior served to briefly terminate experimenter demands. One subject produced the highest rate of self-injury during the social disapproval condition, indicating that social attention was the key motivational variable. In a related study, Iwata et al. (1990) used similar functional analysis procedures to document the escape function of self-injurious behavior in seven developmentally delayed children and adolescents. In both studies, analog tasks were used to test for specific motivations for self-injury.

Based on the Iwata et al. (1982) analog tasks, Wacker, Northup, and Kelly (in press) present a much briefer assessment protocol for a functional analysis of self-injury. Further, they add a contingency-reversal phase to demonstrate that the function of the self-injury has been correctly identified. Wacker et al. (1990) used this approach in two cases of functional analysis of self-injury. Following an initial analog assessment, these researchers first repeated the conditions producing the highest and lowest rates of the target behavior. Then they implemented a contingency-reversal condition in which the conditions found to be maintaining the inappropriate behavior were differentially provided for appropriate behavior, thereby reversing the rates of the appropriate and inappropriate behaviors.

One common objection to an analog functional analysis procedure is that it requires a major commitment of time and effort by the clinician. As an alternative to the analog functional analysis procedure, Durand and Crimmins (1988) devised an informant rating scale, the *Motivation Assessment Scale* (MAS), designed "to assess the relative influence of social attention, tangibles, escape, and sensory consequences of self injury" (p. 100). In initial reliability and validity studies, teachers were asked to respond to the scale's 16 questions about the likelihood of a specific problem behavior occurring in different situations. While the psychometric data on the MAS reported by the authors were encouraging, more recent studies cast doubt on the scale's psychometric robustness (Singh et al., in press). Yet, as usually happens when an easy-to-use instrument with apparent face validity becomes available, this scale appears to be firmly entrenched in both research and clinical practice.

Bird et al. (1989) used the MAS to identify the motivation for self-injury in two adults with autism and profound mental retardation. Together with direct behavioral observations, the MAS data suggested that the two men used self-injury as a form of communication. Thus, the investigators devised a treatment program designed to achieve the same consequences through socially acceptable communication rather than self-injury. The reduction in self-injury achieved through functional communication training provided empirical support for the functional analysis of the two men's self-injury.

The technology of functional analysis has advanced considerably in recent years and has shown particular promise for the assessment of self-injurious and other challenging behaviors in individuals with autism and developmental disabilities. These procedures represent the state of the art in behavioral assessment and constitute valuable additions to the tools currently available for research and clinical practice.

Treatment Modalities

The neurochemical and behavioral hypotheses have provided the basis for most of the more effective treatments explored in this research area. However, as a prelude to discussing some of this intervention literature, it should be noted that, until very recently, neither the psychopharmacological nor the behavioral treatment studies were hypothesis-driven or had any substantial theoretical underpinnings.

Behavioral Interventions

As noted, studies employing a functional analysis to derive treatment options for self-injury in individuals with autism are a rarity. However, a number of investigations reported in the literature have used standard behavior reduction techniques to control self-injury in this population. We have chosen to discuss briefly those treatment procedures that have emerged as viable alternatives in the behavioral treatment literature. This discussion is based on the assumption that a sophisticated assessment process contributes immeasurably to the selection of the procedure most likely to control a specific behavior in a given individual. The aim here is not to provide a comprehensive evaluation of the treatment literature, because such evaluations are already available (e.g., Luiselli et al., 1992; Repp & Singh, 1990); the aim is to discuss the procedures that have shown promise as effective interventions.

Stimulus control. Little work has been carried out specifically on stimulus control interventions because stimulus control is a fundamental process occurring in conjunction with other processes, such as escape and avoidance. Nonetheless, if the cardinal principle of stimulus control (that self-injury occurs more frequently in some situations than in others) is accepted, it should be possible to alter the rate of self-injury by identifying the behavior and providing the self-injurious individual access to situations associated with infrequent occurrence. The alternative is to design an intervention that would change in some manner those situations associated with high rates of self-injury in an effort to decrease their salience as discriminative stimuli for self-injury (Favell et al., 1982).

A comprehensive functional analysis may suggest a stimulus control intervention for individuals whose self-injury is limited to a specific and idiosyncratic stimulus or stimulus complex. Clinical experience suggests that some individuals with autism become highly agitated by specific words, actions, or objects—responses that are not typically observed in their handicapped or nonhandicapped peers. The level of stimulus control over the self-injurious response can be demonstrated by a functional analysis in which the analog sessions involve systematic manipulations of antecedent environmental stimuli that are present during the occurrence of a self-injurious response. If the level of stimulus control is considerable, the most efficient short-term treatment may be to eliminate these antecedent stimuli from the individual's environment.

Although eliminating the antecedent stimulus may be a relatively easy and immediately effective solution, the potential difficulties of such an approach are considerable. For example, the removal of an antecedent stimulus or stimulus complex may restrict the individual's environment and unduly limit opportunities for growth and development. Further, control over the discriminative stimulus is rarely complete; in spite of the best efforts, the individual may be exposed to it after all, responding with self-injury. This would put the individual's self-injurious behavior on an intermittent schedule, making it even more difficult to extinguish in the future. Also, the self-injurious response may generalize to other stimuli, leading to a progressive restriction of the individual's environment and, in effect, providing the setting event for increased self-injury in more natural environments that contain such stimuli.

Thus, the removal of antecedent stimuli may be seen as a short-term solution for the control of only *severe* self-injury. However, for such control to be maintained, a gradual reintroduction of the stimuli in the individual's daily environment must occur without a clinically significant increase in self-injury.

Reinforcement-based procedures. The most frequently investigated reinforcement-based interventions in the treatment of self-injury are differential reinforcement of other behavior (DRO) and differential reinforcement of incompatible behavior (DRI) (Repp & Singh, 1990). DRO involves reinforcing the individual for refraining from self-injury; that is, the individual is reinforced following a period during which no self-injury has occurred. DRI interventions, in turn, consist of more specific differential reinforcement of appropriate or adaptive responses that are physically incompatible with self-injury. Response to DRO and DRI interventions in isolation has been mixed, and, in practice, these procedures are generally combined with some other interventions. Such a combination of techniques is generally supported in the self-injury literature (Favell et al., 1982).

In some circumstances, a functional analysis of self-injury may indicate the need to use a DRO procedure in isolation, such as when the behavior is found to be stereotypic or automatically reinforcing (Iwata, Vollmer, & Zarcone, 1990). Cowdery, Iwata, and Page (1990) reported on a case that illustrates this situation, although not involving an individual with autism. A child's severe self-excoriation was found to be largely limited to a condition in which he was left alone; conditions involving any other forms of stimulation—social, nonsocial, or academic tasks—reduced the incidence of the self-injurious response to near zero. Based on this analysis, the authors concluded that the behavior was "a form of self-stimulation, which usually implies some unidentified source of positive reinforcement associated with the behavior itself" (p. 499). A DRO treatment procedure was established, which involved earning pennies for refraining from self-scratching for gradually increasing amounts of time. This intervention quickly reduced the incidence of the self-injurious response to zero for up to 30 minutes at a time. The DRO procedure was eventually successfully incorporated in a token system that encompassed the waking hours of the child.

The Cowdery et al. (1990) study may be seen as a prototype for using reinforcement-based interventions derived through a functional analysis of an individual's self-injurious behavior. Those cases in which an individual's behaviors are found to be automatically reinforcing, to the exclusion of other functions, may call for a reinforcement-based approach, such as the exclusive use of DRO or DRI.

Extinction.   By definition, extinction is a process that reduces the frequency of a target behavior by eliminating its reinforcing consequences. Thus, extinction is not a procedure but an explanation of why certain clinical interventions are effective. The most commonly applied procedure that relies on extinction is time-out from positive reinforcement. Here, immediately following an occurrence of self-injury, the individual is removed from any opportunity to obtain reinforcement.

The reason for emphasizing the distinction between the procedure (time-out) and the process (extinction), in this context, is that the treatment literature on self-injury includes descriptions of interventions designated as time-out but indistinguishable from aversive conditioning procedures (cf. Favell et al., 1982). When such studies yield positive treatment outcomes, it is unclear which process—extinction or punishment—is actually responsible for the behavior reduction. In part because of this confusion, it is difficult to evaluate the efficacy of extinction in the treatment of self-injury.

To further complicate this picture, the assumption implicit in the use of procedures designed to bring about extinction is that the reinforcers that currently maintain the behavior have been accurately identified. However, it is rare to find a study in which the operant control of the reinforcer over the target behavior is unambiguously demonstrated prior to its systematic removal from the subject's environment. An exception is Iwata et al. (1990), who report on seven subjects whose self-injurious behavior was found to serve an escape function. A functional analysis showed that self-injury occurred most under conditions of demand when it resulted in brief attention time-out and termination of the demand. Implementing extinction involved eliminating the negative reinforcement inherent in escape from a demand situation by withdrawing the brief attention time-out and substituting physical guidance to complete the required task response. This procedure resulted in a marked reduction in the frequency of self-injury and an increase in task compliance.

The significance of this study lies in its use of experimental analysis to determine the function of self-injury and the subsequent tailoring of the treatment procedure—in this case, extinction—to that function. Iwata et al. (1990) emphasize the shift, inherent in this approach, from a focus on response topography to a focus on response function, maintaining that very different behaviors that serve the same function are more likely to respond to the same kind of intervention than are identical behaviors that serve very different functions across subjects.

Punishment procedures.   Punishment procedures, by definition, involve the presentation of a stimulus (usually aversive) immediately following the occurrence of a self-injurious response in an effort to decrease the frequency of that response. Given the current state of behavioral intervention, the use of punishment in the treatment of self-injury represents an implicit acknowledgment on the part of the clinician that the reinforcers maintaining the behavior are unknown or cannot be controlled. Considerable controversy has surrounded the use of punishment procedures with individuals who are developmentally disabled (see Repp & Singh, 1990). However, much of the controversy has emphasized ethical and philosophical issues rather than clinical efficacy.

Most informed readers would agree that punishment procedures are effective in suppressing specific target responses in specific contexts and that punishment must be used, as a last resort, when all alternatives have been exhausted. Although empirical investigations have yielded strong support for the efficacy of punishment, its use has decreased markedly because of cultural and political pressure.

Guess, Helmstetter, Turnbull, and Knowlton (1987) reviewed all reports on the use of punishment with disabled individuals in 16 professional journals between 1965 and 1984. Fourteen studies involving punishment procedures for self-injurious behavior were summarized. These procedures included restraint, electric shock, contingent tickling, hair tugs, ammonia capsule under nose, lemon juice into mouth, water squirted onto face, and water mist onto face. Since that time, a few reports on the use of punishment in the treatment of self-injury have appeared (e.g., Jenson, Rovner, Cameron, Petersen, & Kesler, 1985; Linschied, Iwata, Ricketts, Williams, & Griffin, 1990).

The punishment literature contains few examples of studies demonstrating adequate systematic control to clearly evaluate the effects of the procedure when compared to alternatives. In a notable exception, Jones, Singh, and Kendall (1991) compared the effects of visual screening (hand over subject's eyes) and gentle teaching procedures in reducing self-injury in an adult male with profound mental retardation. This study demonstrates the superiority, in this case, of the visual screening intervention and illustrates a methodology for evaluating punishment procedures for treating severe problem behaviors in single-case studies. Such findings notwithstanding, changing societal values regarding the field of developmental disabilities render it unlikely that a definitive scientific evaluation of the use of punishment in treating self-injury will be forthcoming in the near future.

The debate over the use of punishment procedures has frequently been cast in ethical, philosophical, or moral language, particularly by the opponents of punishment. In a recent review of Repp and Singh's (1990) book on the use of non-aversive and aversive interventions, Alberto and Andrews (1991) repeat the call for decisions to be based on empirical findings rather than rhetoric. Aside from the ethical and philosophical issues surrounding the use of aversive procedures in the treatment of self-injury, there is a clinical principle that takes precedence and, in many cases, avoids the struggle with those questions. Specifically, the principle involves employing the procedures that possess the best conceptual and empirical support—in this case, treatments driven by a functional analysis of the problem behavior. Clinical assessment that employs sophisticated functional analysis procedures rarely suggests a treatment procedure based on punishment effects, as punishment implies unknown or uncontrolled sources of reinforcement. The functional analysis of behavior is a technology for identifying salient reinforcers so that these can be controlled, and control over a reinforcer implies the capacity to shape the behavior that provides access to the reinforcer.

Overcorrection.   Overcorrection involves application of a mix of behavioral procedures immediately following the occurrence of a target response. Standard overcorrection procedures consist of two components—restitution and positive practice. Restitution is the correction of the consequence of the behavior, such as restoring the environment to its original or improved state; positive practice is the repeated performance of the appropriate behavior for interacting with the environment.

Aside from the issue of their efficacy, overcorrection procedures raise an interesting conceptual question: what is the relevant behavioral principle underlying the treatment effects? Few individuals with direct experience in implementing an overcorrection procedure would argue with the observation that the subject's experience of the procedure is generally unpleasant. The question that then arises is whether target responses decrease following overcorrection because of the effect of punishment (i.e., following a target response with an aversive event that decreases the frequency of that response) or because of the effect of instruction (i.e., establishing alternative, corrective responses). If the former is true, there seems to be little scientific reason to separate overcorrection procedures from punishment methods; in fact, there is considerable reason to avoid overcorrection in many cases because it may violate the principles of effective punishment. In such instances, semantic distinctions are being drawn that, while they may make overcorrection more palatable from a public relations point of view, are untenable from a scientific perspective. If the instruction effect is the true cause of the results, then most clinicians would argue that more effective and less aversive means exist for strengthening alternative responses.

Functional communication training. Functional communication training is perhaps the procedure most frequently and directly related to a functional analysis of self-injurious behavior. The procedure demands at least a tentative hypothesis about the function of the self-injury in order to be able to identify the specific communicative act to train. In brief, the central tenet of functional communication training as a treatment for self-injury is to identify the function served by the problem behavior and to provide training in alternative adaptive communication techniques so that these will provide the same outcome for the subject as the self-injurious behavior currently does. Take, for example, an autistic individual whose self-injury serves the function of escaping aversive, task-oriented events. Teaching this individual a sign or a signal that others interpret as "I need a break" and to which they respond accordingly substitutes a more adaptive (i.e., socially acceptable, less disturbing, and less painful) communication method for the self-injurious behavior.

This approach to the treatment of self-injury is particularly well suited to individuals with autism, for whom adaptive communication skills are almost always an area of relative, or absolute, weakness. Individuals with autism who lack even the most rudimentary communication skills may learn that self-injury quickly achieves desired results in the environment, thus reducing the incentive to develop more adaptive forms of communication.

Other procedures. An intervention that does not fit neatly into any of the above categories was recently described by Azrin, Besalel, Jamner, and Caputo (1988). Designated as "interruption," the intervention involved shadowing the subject's arm and hand movements and physically preventing the self-injurious response. Underwood, Figueroa, Thyer, and Nzeocha (1989) reported using interruption alone and interruption plus DRI procedures in the treatment of self-injury in two teenagers with autism and severe or profound mental retardation. Significant reduction was demonstrated in response to the combination treatment in one case, while the results were equivocal in the second case.

Reports of multicomponent treatments of self-injury in individuals with autism are not uncommon (e.g., Berkman & Meyer, 1988; Mohr & Sharpley, 1985; Smith, 1985). While such reports offer valuable ideas for clinical intervention, their scientific contribution is limited because it is impossible to determine which of the components of the intervention were effective in reducing the target behavior.

In summary, there appears to be an abundance of procedures for treating self-injury in individuals with autism. However, the efficacy of many of these procedures is not well established. Further, such procedures appear to be most effective when used on the basis of motivations isolated through a functional analysis of behavior. Certainly, further studies using analysis-driven treatments for self-injury in individuals with autism are indicated.

Psychopharmacological Interventions

Although behavioral intervention is typically viewed as the treatment modality of choice for severe self-injury, over the past two decades there has been a growing interest in the use of pharmacologic agents to treat self-injury (Singh, Singh, & Ellis, 1992). The neurochemical hypotheses related to the etiology of self-injury provide testable theoretical rationales for pharmacological trials with certain classes of drugs. In addition, psychopharmacological interventions have often been initiated as a "last resort" when all other forms of treatment have proven ineffective (Aman & Singh, 1991).

The majority of the scientific literature examining the psychopharmacology of self-injury is composed of studies of individuals with mental retardation, with relatively few studies specific to those with autism. Given the dearth of studies involving autistic subjects and the similarities in self-injury between the two groups, a brief overview of recent advances in the psychopharmacological treatment of self-injury both in individuals with autism and in those with mental retardation will be presented. The data specific to autism, however, will be highlighted and described in greater detail.

Antipsychotics. Antipsychotics are among the most frequently prescribed medications for individuals with developmental disabilities (Singh & Winton, 1989). Several studies have shown that certain antipsychotic medications, including Haloperidol (Aman, Teehan, White, Turbott, & Vaithianathan, 1989; Burk & Menolascino, 1968; Grossett & Williams, 1988; Le Vann, 1969) and Thioridazine (Abbott, Blake, & Vincze, 1965; Aman & White, 1988; Davis, Sprague, & Werry, 1969; Heistad, Zimmerman, & Doebler, 1982; Jakab, 1984; Singh & Aman, 1981), may be useful in the treatment of behavior problems and, more specifically, self-injury in individuals with mental retardation. However, there has been little research specific to using antipsychotic medications in the treatment of self-injury in individuals with autism.

In a double-blind, placebo-controlled study of the effects of Haloperidol on the behavior and learning of 40 children with autism, Anderson et al. (1984) found that doses in the range 0.019–0.217 mg/kg/day resulted in significant decreases in behavioral symptoms, general clinical improvement, and greater facilitation and retention of discrimination learning. The number of children who exhibited self-injury at baseline was not reported, but 6 of the 40 subjects had an increase in "aggressiveness against self" during the placebo condition, suggesting a decrease in their self-injury while on Haloperidol. Side effects, most commonly sedation, were noted only during dosage regulation or with above-optimum doses. Although other studies have been conducted on the effects of antipsychotics in individuals with autism, none have specifically targeted self-injury.

Opioid antagonists. Numerous studies and case reports have been published over the past 10 years on the effects of the opioid antagonists—Naloxone and Naltrexone—on self-injury in individuals with mental retardation (Ricketts, Ellis, Singh, & Singh, 1993). In addition, opioid antagonists have been the most frequently studied psychopharmacological agents in the treatment of self-injury among individuals with autism. Based on the hypothesized role of endogenous endorphins in the genesis and maintenance of self-injurious behavior (Singh et al., 1993), early studies used Naloxone, a short-acting, parenteral opioid antagonist. However, more recent trials have utilized Naltrexone, a substantially longer-acting, orally administered opioid antagonist.

In a placebo-controlled study, the effects of four doses of Naltrexone (0.5, 1.0, 1.5, and 2.0 mg/kg) on the frequency of self-injury in three male adolescents, two of whom had profound mental retardation and autism or autistic behavior, were investigated (Herman et al., 1987). Compared to placebo, there were significant decreases in the frequency of self-injury in all three subjects on the 0.5, 1.0, and 1.5 mg/kg doses of Naltrexone; the most dramatic and consistent decrease was with the 1.5 mg/kg dose. The highest dose (2.0 mg/kg), tested in two subjects, failed to show a beneficial response.

LeBoyer, Bouvard, and Dugas (1988) reported similar results in an open and acute dose trial of Naltrexone (1.0, 1.5, and 2.0 mg/kg) involving two girls with autism. A reduction in self-injury was reported at the 1.0 and 1.5 mg/kg doses but not at the 2.0 mg/kg dose.

Campbell, Adams, Small, Tesch, and Curren (1988) also reported an open and acute dose study of Naltrexone (0.5, 1.5, and 2.0 mg/kg) with eight boys with autism and moderate to profound mental retardation, four of whom engaged in self-injury. Although not directly measured in the study, treatment with Naltrexone appeared to reduce the self-injury in all four subjects. In a related study, Campbell et al. (1989) again noted that Naltrexone slightly reduced self-injury in 5 of 10 boys with autism and mental retardation who demonstrated self-injury at baseline.

In a more recent open trial of Naltrexone in four children with autism, Panksepp and Lensing (1991) found a reduction in several symptoms, including self-injury in the two subjects who had a history of self-injury. Intermittent administration of Naltrexone (e.g., once every 3 days) at low doses (0.4–0.5 mg/kg) was more beneficial in improving the target symptoms than more frequent daily administration of a higher dose (0.8 mg/kg).

In a double-blind, placebo-controlled trial, Barrett, Feinstein, and Hole (1989) reported that Naloxone and Naltrexone had a differential effect on the self-injury of a 12-year-old girl with autism and moderate mental retardation. Compared to placebo, no consistent reduction in self-injury was noted with either the 0.2 mg or 0.4 mg dose of Naloxone, but a dramatic reduction was observed with Naltrexone (1.2 mg/kg). In another study, Walters, Barrett, Feinstein, Mercurio, and Hole (1990) note that Naltrexone at a dose of 1.0 mg/kg was effective in decreasing the intractable self-injury of a 14-year-old boy with autism and mental retardation.

Several published uncontrolled case reports have described the effects of Naltrexone on the self-injury of individuals with autism. For example, Lienemann and Walker (1989) found a dramatic improvement in the severe self-injury of a woman with autism and mental retardation following the initiation of treatment with 50 mg/day of Naltrexone. At 1-year follow-up, she continued on the Naltrexone with no exacerbations in the frequency or severity of her self-injury. Knabe,

Schulz, and Richard (1990) also report two cases in which treatment with Naltrexone reduced self-injury in adult males with autism. However, the authors do note an initial increase in self-injury during the first few days of Naltrexone therapy.

In summary, the majority of studies involving the opioid antagonists were small, uncontrolled, and generally lacked methodological sophistication. Yet, the data indicate that opioid antagonists, particularly Naltrexone, may be useful in the treatment of self-injury in individuals with autism.

Fenfluramine.   The finding that a subgroup of individuals with autism have elevated blood levels of serotonin has led to increased interest in Fenfluramine, a serotonin-reducing agent, as a potential pharmacologic agent for improving the functioning of these individuals. Although numerous studies have examined the effects of Fenfluramine on IQ performance, adaptive behavior, and maladaptive behavior (see Aman & Kern, 1989, for review), few studies have specifically investigated the effects of Fenfluramine on self-injury in this population.

In an 8-week open trial of Fenfluramine employing a 2-week placebo baseline in 10 hospitalized children with autism, Campbell et al. (1986) found that the optimal dose ranged from 15 to 30 mg/day. Eight of the 10 children were aggressive, and 4 of those were also noted to engage in self-injury. Among the most consistent and dramatic therapeutic effects were decreases in self-injury and aggression. However, increased self-injury and aggression were reported in two children on Fenfluramine doses of 60 mg/day, who subsequently required a reduction in the dosage.

Stubbs, Budden, Jackson, Terdal, and Ritvo (1986) also evaluated the effects of Fenfluramine on the behavior of seven children with autism. The subjects received a placebo for 1 month, 1.5 mg/kg/day of Fenfluramine for four months, and then a placebo for an additional 2 months in a double-blind, placebo-controlled study. Target behaviors in two of the children included self-injury. During the active drug period, one of these subjects experienced an increase in self-injury, while the other initially showed a reduction in self-injury that reverted to baseline levels upon return to the placebo condition. These results are consistent with the other findings of the study, according to which two of the seven benefitted symptomatically from the Fenfluramine, while the remaining five subjects showed varying degrees of clinical response.

The effects of 2 mg/kg/day of Fenfluramine on several maladaptive behaviors were examined in 20 individuals with autism and mental retardation in a double-blind, placebo-controlled, crossover trial (Yarbrough, Santat, Perel, Webster, & Lombardi, 1987). The results indicated that Fenfluramine produced no significant clinical improvement in any of the problem behaviors, including self-injury.

Although the research contains a number of methodological flaws, the data suggest that Fenfluramine may play a role in the treatment of behavior problems in a subgroup of individuals with autism. Further research, however, is needed to delineate the effects of Fenfluramine on self-injury as well as to isolate the subtypes of individuals with autism likely to benefit from the drug.

Antihypertensives. Some evidence from case reports and uncontrolled studies suggests that beta-blockers may be useful in reducing self-injurious and aggressive behaviors in individuals with mental retardation (Luchins & Dojka, 1989; Ratey et al., 1986; Ruedrich, Grush, & Wilson, 1990; Yudofsky, Williams, & Gorman, 1981). In the only report in which self-injury was targeted in individuals with autism, eight subjects were included in an open clinical trial of Propranolol and Nadolol (Ratey et al., 1987). The dosages ranged from 100 mg/day to 420 mg/day for Propranolol (mean dose of 225 mg/day), and the dosage was 120 mg/day for Nadolol. In seven of the eight subjects who initially engaged in self-injury, self-injury was either eliminated or dramatically reduced following initiation of the beta-blocker. The time spent on the drug was an important factor in the clinical efficacy,

as the response was noted within 6 weeks to 3 months after initiation of the drug trial.

Anticonvulsants. In addition to controlling seizure disorders, anticonvulsants, typically Carbamazepine, have shown some promise in controlling behavioral problems among individuals with mental retardation (Sovner, 1991). However, there is no evidence from controlled studies that self-injury is reduced by Carbamazepine therapy, and, in the only study using self-injury as a specific target behavior, Carbamazepine had no effect in a subject with profound mental retardation (Singh & Winton, 1984).

Antidepressants. Little data are available on the effectiveness of antidepressants in the treatment of self-injury either in individuals with autism or in those with mental retardation. Huessy and Ruoff (1984) have reported anecdotal experience in using antidepressants to reduce self-injury, along with other behavioral symptoms, in individuals with mental retardation. In addition, Gedye (1991) reported a single-subject case study of a 17-year-old male with severe mental retardation and autism in which Trazodone was effective in reducing self-injurious movements, defined by the author as "involuntary self-injury."

Based on the same theoretical rationale as the Fenfluramine studies, a few reports have noted that Fluoxetine, an antidepressant that blocks the re-uptake of serotonin, may be useful in the treatment of symptoms characteristic of autism (e.g., Ghaziuddin, Tsai, & Ghaziuddin, 1991; Mehlinger, Scheftner, & Poznanski, 1990). Although several preliminary studies specifically identified self-injury as a target behavior for Fluoxetine treatment of individuals with mental retardation (see Ricketts et al., in press), only one Fluoxetine study included individuals with autism and self-injury (Markowitz, 1992). Markowitz reported a trial of Fluoxetine in 20 adults with self-injury and mental retardation. One of the subjects was diagnosed with autism, another 10 were noted to have symptoms suggestive of autism. Eighteen of the 20 subjects, including all 11 of the subjects with autistic features, showed a reduction in their self-injury following 12 weeks of treatment with 20–40 mg/day of Fluoxetine.

Antimanics.   Several case reports (e.g., Amin & Yeragani, 1987; Cooper & Fowlie, 1973) and two studies (Micev & Lynch, 1974; Tyrer, Walsh, Edwards, Berney, & Stephens, 1984) have suggested that lithium carbonate may be useful in the treatment of self-injury in individuals with mental retardation. However, no studies involving individuals with autism could be located.

Stimulants.   The effects of stimulants on self-injury have not been studied in individuals with autism. However, two well-controlled studies used stimulant medications to treat self-injury in individuals with severe or profound mental retardation (Aman & Singh, 1982; Davis et al., 1969). Both of these studies reported that stimulants were of little or no benefit in treating self-injury.

In summary, despite a paucity of psychopharmacological studies, extant data give us some cause to believe that certain pharmacological agents may provide a viable treatment option for self-injury in individuals with autism.

Summary

The empirical literature that specifically addresses self-injury in individuals with autism is not large. Controlled studies of the treatment of self-injury in such individuals are exceedingly rare. Further, investigation of self-injury in individuals with autism has suffered from a lack of coherent conceptual models to guide the research. The neurochemical literature has yielded some tentative research hypotheses, and the behavioral literature has generally remained within an operant framework, with occasional references to the functional analysis of behavior as a methodology for selecting an appropriate intervention. In a review of the extant literature, it was

striking, though not altogether surprising, that meaningful results that moved the field forward were found almost exclusively in those reports that adopted a clear theoretical framework with associated testable hypotheses. This chapter highlighted those studies in which investigators met this standard and clearly set forth conceptual models that were heuristic both in suggesting clinical intervention and in guiding future research.

References

ABBOTT, P., BLAKE, A., & VINCZE, L. (1965). Treatment of mentally retarded with Thioridazine. *Diseases of the Nervous System, 26,* 583–585.

ALBERTO, P., & ANDREWS, D. (1991). Are moral considerations sufficient for selecting nonaversive interventions? A review of Repp and Singh's *Perspectives on the use of nonaversive and aversive interventions for persons with developmental disabilities. The Behavior Analyst, 14,* 219–224.

AMAN, M. G., & KERN, R. A. (1989). Review of Fenfluramine in the treatment of developmental disabilities. *Journal of the American Academy of Child and Adolescent Psychiatry, 28,* 549–565.

AMAN, M. G., & SINGH, N. N. (1982). Methylphenidate in severely retarded residents and the clinical significance of stereotypic behavior. *Applied Research in Mental Retardation, 3,* 345–358.

AMAN, M. G., & SINGH, N. N. (1991). Pharmacological intervention: Update. In J. L. Matson & J. A. Mulick (Eds.), *Handbook of mental retardation* (pp. 347–373). New York: Pergamon.

AMAN, M. G., TEEHAN, C. J., WHITE, A. J., TURBOTT, S. H., & Vaithianathan, C. (1989). Haloperidol treatment with chronically medicated residents: Dose effects on clinical behavior and reinforcement contingencies. *American Journal of Mental Deficiency, 93,* 452–460.

AMAN, M. G., & WHITE, A. J. (1988). Thioridazine dose effects with reference to stereotypic behavior in mentally retarded residents. *Journal of Autism and Developmental Disabilities, 18,* 355–366.

AMIN, P., & YERAGANI, V. K. (1987). Control of aggressive and self-mutilative behavior in a mentally retarded patient with lithium. *Canadian Journal of Psychiatry, 32,* 162–163.

ANDERSON, L. T., CAMPBELL, M., GREGA, D. M., PERRY, R., SMALL, A. M., & GREEN, W. H. (1984). Haloperidol in the treatment of infantile autism: Effects on learning and behavioral symptoms. *American Journal of Psychiatry, 141,* 1195–1202.

ANDO, H., & YOSHIMURA, I. (1979). Effects of age on communication skill levels and prevalence of maladaptive behaviors in autistic and mentally retarded children. *Journal of Autism and Developmental Disorders, 9,* 83–93.

AZRIN, N. H., BESALEL, V. A., JAMNER, J. P., & CAPUTO, J. N. (1988). Comparative study of behavioral methods of treating self-injury. *Behavioral Residential Treatment, 3,* 119–152.

BARRETT, R. P., FEINSTEIN, C., & HOLE, W. T. (1989). Effects of Naloxone and Naltrexone on self-injury: A double-blind, placebo controlled analysis. *American Journal of Mental Retardation, 93,* 644–651.

BARTAK, L., & RUTTER, M. (1976). Differences between mentally retarded and normally intelligent autistic children. *Journal of Autism and Childhood Schizophrenia, 6,* 109–120.

BAUMAN, M., & KEMPER, T. L. (1985). Histoanatomical observations of the brain in early infantile autism. *Neurology, 35,* 866–874.

BERKMAN, K. A., & MEYER, L. H. (1988). Alternative strategies and multiple outcomes in the remediation of severe self-injury: Going "all out" nonaversively. *Journal of the Association for Persons with Severe Handicaps, 13,* 76–86.

BIRD, F., DORES, P. A., MONIZ, D., & ROBINSON, J. (1989). Reducing severe aggressive and self-injurious behaviors with functional communication training. *American Journal on Mental Retardation, 94,* 37–48.

BUCHSBAUM, M. S., DAVIS, G. C., & BUNNY, W. G. (1977). Naloxone alters pain perception and somatosensory evoked potentials in normal subjects. *Nature, 267,* 620–622.

BURK, H. W., & MENOLASCINO, F. J. (1968). Haloperidol in emotionally disturbed mentally retarded individuals. *American Journal of Psychiatry, 124,* 1589–1591.

CAMPBELL, M., ADAMS, P., SMALL, A. M., TESCH, L. M., & CURREN, E. L. (1988). Naltrexone in infantile autism. *Psychopharmacology Bulletin, 24,* 135–139.

CAMPBELL, M., ANDERSON, L. T., SMALL, A. M., PERRY, R., GREEN, W. H., & CAPLAN, R. (1982). The effects of Haloperidol on learning and behavior in autistic children. *Journal of Autism and Developmental Disorders, 12,* 167–175.

CAMPBELL, M., OVERALL, J. E., SMALL, A. M., SOKOL, M. S., SPENCER, E. K., ADAMS, P., FOLTZ, R. L., MONTI, K. M., PERRY, R., NOBLER, M., & ROBERTS, E. (1989). Naltrexone in autistic children: An acute open dose range tolerance trial. *Journal of the American Academy of Child and Adolescent Psychiatry, 28,* 200–206.

CAMPBELL, M., PERRY, R., POLONSKY, B. B., DEUTSCH, S. I., PALIJ, M., & LUKASHOK, D. (1986). Brief report: An open study of Fenfluramine in hospitalized young autistic children. *Journal of Autism and Developmental Disorders, 16,* 495–506.

CARR, E. G. (1977). The motivation of self-injurious behavior: A review of some hypotheses. *Psychological Bulletin, 84,* 800–816.

CARR, E. G., NEWSOM, C. D., & BINKOFF, J. A. (1980). Stimulus control of self-destructive behavior in a psychotic child. *Journal of Abnormal Child Psychology, 4,* 139–153.

CATALDO, M. F., & HARRIS, J. C. (1982). The biological basis for self-injury in the mentally retarded. *Analysis and Intervention in Developmental Disabilities, 2,* 21–39.

COOPER, A. F., & FOWLIE, H. C. (1973). Control of gross self-mutilation with lithium carbonate. *British Journal of Psychiatry, 122,* 370–371.

COURCHESNE, E., YEUNG-COURCHESNE, R., PRESS, G. A., HESSELINK, J. R., & JERNIGAN, T. L. (1988). Hypoplasia of cerebellar vermal lobules VI and VII in infantile autism. *New England Journal of Medicine, 318,* 1349–1354.

COWDERY, G. E., IWATA, B. A., & PAGE, G. M. (1990). Effects and side effects of DRO as treatment for self-injurious behavior. *Journal of Applied Behavior Analysis, 23,* 497–506.

DAVIS, K. V., SPRAGUE, R. L., & WERRY, J. S. (1969). Stereotyped behavior and activity level in severe retardates: The effects of drugs. *American Journal of Mental Deficiency, 73,* 721–727.

DEHEN, H., WILLER, J. C., BOUREAU, F., & CAMBIER, J. (1977). Congenital insensitivity to pain, and endogenous morphine-like substances. *The Lancet, ii,* 293–294.

DEMET, E. M., & SANDMAN, C. A. (1991). Models of the opiate system in self-injurious behavior: A reply. *American Journal on Mental Retardation, 95,* 694–696.

DURAND, V. M., & CRIMMINS, D. B. (1988). Identifying the variables maintaining self-injurious behavior. *Journal of Autism and Developmental Disorders, 18,* 99–117.

EDELSON, S. M., TAUBMAN, M. T., & LOVAAS, O. I. (1983). Some social contexts of self-destructive behavior. *Journal of Abnormal Child Psychology, 11,* 299–312.

FAVELL, J. E., AZRIN, N. H., BAUMEISTER, A. A., CARR, E. G., DORSEY, M. F., FOREHAND, R., FOXX, R. M., LOVAAS, O. I., RINCOVER, A., RISLEY, T. R., ROMANCZYK, R. G., RUSSO, D.

C., SCHROEDER, S. R., & SOLNICK, J. V. (1982). The treatment of self-injurious behavior. *Behavior Therapy, 13,* 529–554.

GEDYE, A. (1991). Trazodone reduced aggressive and self-injurious movements in a mentally handicapped male patient with autism. *Journal of Clinical Psychopharmacology, 11,* 275–276.

GHAZIUDDIN, M., TSAI, L., & GHAZIUDDIN, N. (1991). Fluoxetine in autism with depression. *Journal of the Academy of Child and Adolescent Psychiatry, 30,* 508.

GILLBERG, C., PERSSON, E., & WAHLSTROM, J. (1986). The autism–Fragile-X syndrome (AFRAX): A population-based study of ten boys. *Journal of Mental Deficiency Research, 30,* 27–39.

GILLBERG, C., TERENIUS, L., & LONNERHOLM, G. (1985). Endorphin activity in childhood psychosis. *Archives of General Psychiatry, 42,* 780–783.

GOLDSTEIN, M., ANDERSON, L. T., REUBEN, R., & DANCIS, J. (1985). Self-mutilation in Lesch-Nyhan disease is caused by dopaminergic denervation. *Lancet, 1,* 338–339.

GROSSETT, D. L., & WILLIAMS, D. E. (1988, May). *Psychopharmacological intervention for the treatment of self-injurious behavior in a person with profound mental retardation and a psychiatric disorder.* Paper presented at the annual convention of the Association for Behavior Analysis, Philadelphia.

GUESS, D., HELMSTETTER, E., TURNBULL, H. R., & KNOWLTON, S. (1987). Use of aversive procedures with individuals who are disabled: An historical review and critical analysis. *Monographs of the Association for Individuals with Severe Handicaps, 2*(1).

HARRIS, J. C. (1992). Neurobiological factors in self-injurious behavior. In J. K. Luiselli, J. L. Matson, & N. N. Singh (Eds.), *Self-injurious behavior: Analysis, assessment and treatment* (pp. 59–92). New York: Springer-Verlag.

HEISTAD, G. T., ZIMMERMAN, T. L., & DOEBLER, M. I. (1982). Long-term usefulness of Thioridazine for institutionalized mentally retarded patients. *American Journal of Mental Deficiency, 87,* 243–251.

HERMAN, B. H., HAMMOCK, M. K., ARTHUR-SMITH, A., EGAN, J., CHATOOR, I., WERNER, A., & ZELNICK, N. (1987). Naltrexone decreases self-injurious behavior. *Annals of Neurology, 22,* 550–552.

HUESSY, H. R., & RUOFF, P. A. (1984). Towards a rational drug usage in a state institution for retarded individuals. *Psychiatric Journal of the University of Ottawa, 9,* 56–58.

IWATA, B. A. (1987). Negative reinforcement in applied behavior analysis: An emerging technology. *Journal of Applied Behavior Analysis, 20,* 361–387.

IWATA, B. A., DORSEY, M. F., SLIFER, K. J., BAUMAN, K. E., & RICHMAN, G. S. (1982). Toward a functional analysis of self-injury. *Analysis and Intervention in Developmental Disabilities, 2,* 3–20.

IWATA, B. A., PACE, G. M., KALSHER, M. J., COWDERY, G. E., & CATALDO, M. F. (1990). Experimental analysis and extinction of self-injurious escape behavior. *Journal of Applied Behavior Analysis, 23,* 11–27.

IWATA, B. A., VOLLMER, T. R., & ZARCONE, J. R. (1990). The experimental (functional) analysis of behavioral disorders: Methodology, applications, and limitations. In A. C. Repp & N. N. Singh (Eds.), *Perspectives on the use of nonaversive and aversive interventions for persons with developmental disabilities* (pp. 301–330). Sycamore, IL: Sycamore.

JAKAB, I. (1984). Short-term effect of Thioridazine tablet versus suspension on emotionally disturbed/retarded children. *Journal of Clinical Psychopharmacology, 4,* 210–215.

JANICKI, M. P., & JACOBSON, J. W. (1983). Selected clinical features and service characteristics of autistic adults. *Psychological Reports, 52,* 387–390.

JENSON, W. R., ROVNER, L., CAMERON, S., PETERSEN, B. P., & KESLER, J. (1985). Reduction of self-injurious behavior in an autistic girl using a multifaceted treatment program. *Journal of Behavior Therapy and Experimental Psychiatry, 16,* 77–80.

JOHNSON, W. L., & DAY, R. M. (1992). The incidence and prevalence of self-injurious behavior. In J. K. Luiselli, J. L. Matson, & N. N. Singh (Eds.), *Self-injurious behavior: Analysis, assessment and treatment* (pp. 21–56). New York: Springer-Verlag.

JONES, L. J., SINGH, N. N., & KENDALL, K. A. (1991). Comparative effects of gentle teaching and visual screening on self-injurious behavior. *Journal of Mental Deficiency Research, 35,* 37–47.

KNABE, R., SCHULZ, P., & RICHARD, J. (1990). Initial aggravation of self-injurious behavior in autistic patients receiving Naltrexone treatment. *Journal of Autism and Developmental Disorders, 20,* 591–593.

KOPIN, I. J. (1981). Neurotransmitters and the Lesch-Nyhan syndrome. *The New England Journal of Medicine, 305,* 1148–1150.

LAL, H. (1975). Narcotic dependence, narcotic action, and dopamine receptors. *Life Sciences, 17,* 483–496.

LEBOYER, M., BOUVARD, M. P., & DUGAS, M. (1988). Effects of naltrexone on infantile autism. *Lancet, 1,* 715.

LE VANN, L. J. (1969). Haloperidol in the treatment of behavioral disorders in children and adolescents. *Canadian Psychiatric Association Journal, 14,* 217–220.

LIENEMANN, J., & WALKER, F. (1989). Naltrexone for treatment of self-injury. *American Journal of Psychiatry, 146,* 1639–1640.

LINSCHIED, T. R., IWATA, B. A., RICKETTS, R. W., WILLIAMS, D. E., & GRIFFIN, J. C. (1990). Clinical evaluation of the self-injurious behavior inhibiting system (SIBIS). *Journal of Applied Behavior Analysis, 23,* 53–78.

LUCHINS, D. J., & DOJKA, D. (1989). Lithium and propranolol in aggression and self-injurious behavior in the mentally retarded. *Psychopharmacology Bulletin, 25,* 372–375.

LUISELLI, J. K., MATSON, J. L., & SINGH, N. N. (1992). *Self-injurious behavior: Analysis, assessment and treatment.* New York: Springer-Verlag.

MADDEN, J., AKIL, H., PATRICK, R. L., & BARCHAS, J. D. (1977). Stress-induced parallel changes in central opioid levels and pain responsiveness in the rat. *Nature, 265,* 358–360.

MARKOWITZ, P. I. (1992). Effect of Fluoxetine on self-injurious behavior in the developmentally disabled: A preliminary study. *Journal of Clinical Psychopharmacology, 12,* 27–31.

MEHLINGER, R., SCHEFTNER, W. A., & POZNANSKI, E. (1990). Fluoxetine and autism. *Journal of the American Academy of Child and Adolescent Psychiatry, 29,* 985.

MICEV, V., & LYNCH, D. M. (1974). Effects of lithium on disturbed severely mentally retarded patients. *British Journal of Psychiatry, 125,* 110.

MINDERAA, R. B., ANDERSON, G. M., VOLKMAR, F. R., AKKERHUIS, G. W., & COHEN, D. J. (1989). Neurochemical study of dopamine functioning in autistic and normal subjects. *Journal of the American Academy of Child and Adolescent Psychiatry, 28,* 190–194.

MOHR, C., & SHARPLEY, C. F. (1985). Elimination of self-injurious behavior in an autistic child by use of overcorrection. *Behavior Change, 2,* 143–147.

MULDER, A. H., WARDEH, G., HOGENBOOM, F., & FRANKHUYZEN, A. L. (1984). Kappa and delta opiate receptor agonists differentially inhibit striatal dopamine and acetylcholine release. *Nature, 308,* 278–280.

O'NEILL, R. E., HORNER, R. H., ALBIN, R. W., STOREY, K., & SPRAGUE, J. R. (1990). *Functional analysis of problem behavior: A practical assessment guide.* Sycamore, IL: Sycamore.

PANKSEPP, J., & LENSING, P. (1991). Brief report: A synopsis of an open-trial of Naltrexone treatment of autism with four children. *Journal of Autism and Developmental Disorders, 21,* 243–249.

RATEY, J. J., MIKKELSEN, E. J., SMITH, B., UPADHYAYA, A., ZUCKERMAN, S., MARTELL, D.,

SORGI, P., POLAKOFF, S., & BEMPORAD, J. (1986). Beta-blockers in the severely and profoundly mentally retarded. *Journal of Clinical Psychopharmacology, 6,* 103–107.

RATEY, J. J., MIKKELSEN, E. J., SORGI, P., ZUCKERMAN, S., POLAKOFF, S., BEMPORAD, J., BICK, P., & KADISH, W. (1987). Autism: The treatment of aggressive behaviors. *Journal of Clinical Psychopharmacology, 7,* 35–41.

REPP, A. C., & SINGH, N. N. (1990). *Perspectives on the use of nonaversive and aversive interventions for persons with developmental disabilities.* Sycamore, IL: Sycamore.

REPP, A. C., SINGH, N. N., OLINGER, E., & OLSON, D. R. (1990). The use of functional analyses to test causes of self-injurious behavior: Rationale, current status, and future directions. *Journal of Mental Deficiency Research, 34,* 95–105.

RICKETTS, R. W., ELLIS, C. R., SINGH, Y. N., & SINGH, N. N. (1993). Opiate antagonists. II. Clinical effects in the treatment of self-injury in individuals with developmental disabilities. *Journal of Developmental and Physical Disabilities, 5,* 17–28.

RICKETTS, R. W., GOZA, A. B., ELLIS, C. R., SINGH, Y. N., SINGH, N. N., & COOKE, J. C. (in press). Fluoxetine treatment of severe self-injury in young adults with mental retardation. *Journal of the American Academy of Child and Adolescent Psychiatry.*

RUEDRICH, S. L., GRUSH, L., & WILSON, J. (1990). Beta adrenergic blocking medications for aggressive or self-injurious mentally retarded persons. *American Journal of Mental Retardation, 95,* 110–119.

RYLANDER, G. (1971). Stereotypy in man following amphetamine abuse. In S. B. de Baker (Ed.), *The correlation of adverse effects in man with observations in animals* (pp. 28–31). Amsterdam: Excepta Medica.

SANDMAN, C. A., BARRON, J. L., CHICZ-DEMET, A., & DEMET, E. M. (1990). Plasma beta-endorphin levels in patients with self-injurious behavior and stereotype. *American Journal on Mental Retardation, 95,* 84–92.

SINGH, N. N., & AMAN, M. G. (1981). Effects of thioridazine dosage on the behavior of severely mentally retarded persons. *American Journal of Mental Deficiency, 85,* 580–587.

SINGH, N. N., DONATELLI, L. S., BEST, A., WILLIAMS, D. E., BARRERA, F. J., LENZ, M. W., LANDRUM, T. J., ELLIS, C. R., & MOE, T. L. (in press). Factor structure of the motivation assessment scale. *Journal of Intellectual Disability Research.*

SINGH, N. N., SINGH, Y. N., & ELLIS, C. R. (1992). Psychopharmacology of self-injury. In J. K. Luiselli,

J. L. Matson, & N. N. Singh (Eds.), *Self-injurious behavior: Analysis, assessment, and treatment* (pp. 307–351). New York: Springer-Verlag.

SINGH, N. N., & WINTON, A. S. W. (1984). Behavioral monitoring of pharmacological interventions for self-injury. *Applied Research in Mental Retardation, 5,* 161–170.

SINGH, N. N., & WINTON, A. S. W. (1989). Behavioral pharmacology. In J. K. Luiselli (Ed.), *Behavioral medicine and developmental disabilities* (pp. 152–179). New York: Springer-Verlag.

SINGH, Y. N., RICKETTS, R. W., ELLIS, C. R., & SINGH, N. N. (1993). Opioid antagonists. I. Pharmacology and rationale for its use in treating self-injury. *Journal of Developmental and Physical Disabilities, 5,* 5–15.

SMITH, M. D. (1985). Managing the aggressive and self-injurious behavior of adults disabled by autism. *Journal of the Association for Persons with Severe Handicaps, 10,* 228–232.

SOVNER, R. (1991) Use of anticonvulsant agents for treatment of neuropsychiatric disorders in the developmentally disabled. In J. J. Ratey (Ed.), *Mental retardation: Developing pharmacotherapies* (pp. 83–106). Washington, DC: American Psychiatric Press.

STUBBS, E. G., BUDDEN, S. S., JACKSON, R. H., TERDAL, L. G., & RITVO, E. R. (1986). Effects of Fenfluramine on eight outpatients with the syndrome of autism. *Developmental Medicine and Child Neurology, 28,* 229–235.

TYRER, S. P., WALSH, A., EDWARDS, D. E., BERNEY, T. P., & STEPHENS, D. A. (1984). Factors associated with a good response to lithium in affective mentally handicapped subjects. *Progress in Neuro-Psychopharmacology and Biological Psychiatry, 8,* 751–755.

UNDERWOOD, L. A., FIGUEROA, R. G., THYER, B. A., & NZEOCHA, A. (1989). Interruption and DRI in the treatment of self-injurious behavior among mentally retarded and autistic self-restrainers. *Behavior Modification, 13,* 471–481.

VOLKMAR, F. R., HODER, E. L., & COHEN, D. J. (1985). Compliance, negativism, and the effects of treatment structure in autism: A naturalistic, behavioral study. *Journal of Child Psychology and Psychiatry, 26,* 865–877.

WACKER, D., NORTHUP, J., & KELLY, L. (in press). Proactive treatment of self-injurious behavior based on functional analyses. In E. Cipani & N. N. Singh (Eds.), *Treatment of severe behavior disorders: Models, methods and applications.* Sycamore, IL: Sycamore.

WACKER, D., STEEGE, M., NORTHUP, J., REIMERS, T., BERG, W., & SASSO, G. (1990). Use of functional analysis and acceptability measures to assess and treat severe behavior problems: An outpatient clinic model. In A. C. Repp & N. N. Singh (Eds.), *Perspectives on the use of nonaversive and aversive interventions for persons with developmental disabilities* (pp. 349–359). Sycamore, IL: Sycamore.

WALTERS, A. S., BARRETT, R. P., FEINSTEIN, C., MERCURIO, A., & HOLE, W. T. (1990). A case report of Naltrexone treatment of self-injury and social withdrawal in autism. *Journal of Autism and Developmental Disorders, 20,* 169–176.

WATTS, R. W. E., SPELLACVY, E., GIBBS, D. A., ALLSOP, J., MCKERAN, R. O., & SLAVIN, G. E. (1982). Clinical, postmortem, biochemical, and therapeutic observations in Lesch-Nyhan syndrome. *Quarterly Journal of Medicine, 5,* 73–78.

WILLER, J. P., DEKERS, A., & CAMBIER, J. (1981). Stress induced analgesia in humans: Endogenous opioids and Naloxone reversible suppression of pain reflexes. *Science, 212,* 689–691.

YARBROUGH, E., SANTAT, U., PEREL, I., WEBSTER, C., & LOMBARDI, R. (1987). Effects of Fenfluramine on autistic individuals residing in a state developmental center. *Journal of Autism and Developmental Disorders, 17,* 303–314.

YUDOFSKY, S., WILLIAMS, D., & GORMAN, J. (1981). Propranolol in the treatment of rage and violent behavior in patients with chronic brain syndromes. *American Journal of Psychiatry, 138,* 218–220.

CHAPTER 9

Aggression and Noncompliance: Behavior Modification through Naturalistic Language Remediation

Robert L. Koegel
UNIVERSITY OF CALIFORNIA AT SANTA BARBARA

Stephen M. Camarata
VANDERBILT UNIVERSITY

Lynn Kern Koegel
UNIVERSITY OF CALIFORNIA AT SANTA BARBARA

Behavior modification has repeatedly proven effective in decreasing aggression and noncompliance in children, adolescents, and adults with autism and other developmental disabilities. Historically, developers of behavior modification treatments first defined individual target behaviors, then designed programs to decrease undesirable behaviors or increase or evoke desirable behaviors. Such programs typically relied heavily on the use of consequences to modify behavior. Unfortunately, the effectiveness of administering punishers led many well-meaning researchers and practitioners to excessive use of punishment.

Widespread concern over such interventions has resulted in an emerging new positive approach to ameliorating severe behavior problems. This positive approach to behavior management seldom employs a single intervention to address a specific undesirable behavior but typically involves interdisciplinary and multicomponent treatments designed to increase classes of positive behavior while simultaneously decreasing classes of undesirable behavior.

This chapter integrates many of the issues discussed in the other treatment chapters in this book.

For example, as we explain effective ways of dealing with aggression and noncompliance through behavior modification, we will necessarily stress the importance of language acquisition and social skills.

Disruptive Behavior as a Characteristic of Autism

As noted in other chapters, many children with autism exhibit severe behavioral excesses in the form of disruptive behavior, such as aggression toward others or self-injurious behavior. These children may hit, bite, kick, scratch, or otherwise attempt to injure themselves or others. Similarly, children with autism frequently disrupt their environments by being noncompliant to requests or social initiations from others.

Often these behaviors are discussed as isolated symptoms. However, the recent literature discusses the communicative function of classes of these behaviors. For example, infants meet their communicative needs through crying; however, as speech and language develop, they soon learn (usually by the second year of life) that verbal communication is more efficient by being more specific and desirable to a parent. When verbal skills fail to develop appropriately, however, extreme frustration may prompt the child to revert to earlier effective forms of communication, such as crying. As the child with verbal disabilities matures, more elaborate forms of disruptive behavior may emerge to accomplish those goals, such as tantrums, aggression, self-injury, and so on. It is the thesis of this chapter that any effective behavior modification program for treatment of aggression and noncompliance needs to consider the interrelationships between all communicative domains in the child's repertoire.

Although a number of alternative and augmentative systems provide communication to individuals who fail to develop oral language skills (see Reichle, Mirenda, Locke, Piche, & Johnston, 1992), the focus of this chapter will be on recent advances in teaching oral communication, with emphasis on the necessary phonological component that makes oral language intelligible. However, the procedures outlined below can be adapted to augmentative system users (see Dattillo & Camarata, 1991). Before we begin, it is important to review the general trends in the field believed to promote optimal teaching and learning conditions for language and other associated behaviors.

Trends in Treatment

Several major advances in the field of autism treatment will be considered. First, increased mainstreaming and integration into regular schools and community settings provides opportunities for social development that cannot occur when the children are in segregated settings with other socially isolated children (Koegel, Valdez-Menchaca, & Koegel, in press). In such settings, not only can more able peers assist the children, but the children are required to exhibit appropriate social behavior in order to participate in the regular education curriculum and other community settings.

Second, the treatment focus has shifted from considering individual target behaviors (such as aggression or noncompliance) as isolated events to a more global approach that treats "pivotal" target behaviors in order to affect more widespread changes in many areas of the child's functioning (Koegel et al., 1989). In this chapter, we will discuss the intelligibility of speech as a major pivotal behavior.

Third, researchers are increasingly noting the importance of considering the function of the disruptive behavior for the child. Thus, it is becoming increasingly common to conduct thorough functional analyses and/or assessments of the antecedents, consequences, and setting events for a given behavior. Treatments based on such assessments replace the disruptive behavior with appropriate behavior that is the functional equivalent of the disruptive behavior; that is, it achieves the same purpose (O'Neill, Albin, Horner, Storey, & Sprague, 1990). For example, in a now classic study, Carr and Durand (1985) identified aggressive behavior that served to help children escape difficult tasks. Teaching these children appropriate ways of seeking assistance or reducing the difficulty of the task eliminated the need for disruptive behaviors in order to escape or avoid the task.

Fourth, the importance of the child's motivation to engage in social and communicative interactions must be fully recognized. Much research has shown that children with autism are highly motivated to avoid such situations. However, through recent techniques, they can be taught to enjoy communicative interactions, thereby reducing or eliminating the need to be aggressive to avoid the interactions. For example, many of the components in naturalistic language behavior modification interventions not only teach language but also motivate the child to want to engage in appropriate communicative interactions (cf. Dunlap, 1984; Koegel & Johnson, 1989; Koegel & Mentis, 1985; Koegel, O'Dell, & Dunlap, 1988). For example, Koegel, Koegel and Surratt (1992) show that using variables that increase motivation to communicate through naturalistic language-teaching produces major decreases in disruptive behavior.

A number of studies have documented the importance of decreasing disruptive behaviors through improved communication skills. In particular, use of naturalistic behavior modification language-teaching procedures has resulted in positive effects not only on language, but also on associated disruptive behaviors and academic and social skills.

The Communication Problem

Language competence is one of the cornerstones of success in the educational arena. Unfortunately, children with autism, Down's syndrome, conduct disorders, developmental delays, and other learning disabilities have long been documented as exhibiting difficulties in the language skills that exacerbate many aspects of their educational and social development (see the discussion in Camarata, 1991). The pervasive nature of language disorders has sparked an increased interest in effective procedures for language remediation, resulting in a number of innovative generalized naturalistic intervention programs (Camarata & Nelson, 1992; Hart & Risley, 1975; Koegel, O'Dell, & Koegel, 1987; Valdez-Menchaca & Whitehurst, 1988; Warren & Kaiser, 1986; Warren & Reichle, 1992).

These techniques dramatically improve acquisition of an initial lexicon and language development. Recent attention, however, is focusing on an often neglected but critical area of language acquisition—intelligibility. The primary concern here is that many of the gains made by children with severe language disabilities are often greatly limited by difficulties they encounter with respect to the intelligibility of their speech. That is, their language progress is often limited because of (a) numerous phonological errors in their speech productions (the resulting lack of intelligibility to teachers and other community members frustrates productive developmental interactions and raises the prob-

ability of aggressive behavior as an outcome of the communicative attempt), and (b) the interrelationship between phonological development and other domains of language acquisition. A "bottleneck" occurs for much of the children's linguistic, social, and academic development, resulting in what others may erroneously see as isolated aggressive or noncompliant social interactions.

Therefore, the purpose of this chapter is to discuss the effect a lack of speech intelligibility can have on aggression and noncompliance as coping mechanisms during frustrated language interactions, and to discuss innovative ways to reduce such disruptive behavior while improving other large areas of the children's overall language, social, and academic development. We hypothesize that teaching improved speech-sound production using naturalistic language training can unlock rapid and generalized improvements in related language, academic, and social skills while specifically decreasing severe disruptive behaviors, such as aggression and noncompliance. For example, as the children's ability to communicate effectively increases, researchers (e.g., Dattilo & Camarata, 1991; Haley, Camarata, & Nelson, 1992) have reported improved affect (happiness, enthusiasm, and interest in conversational interactions), improved social integration in the school system with typically functioning children, and improved social acceptability within school and community environments.

These findings are corroborated by a number of recent studies that have revealed that delayed or atypically developing phonological skills (articulation) often limit acquisition and social use of newly acquired language and result in frustrating plateaus in language development. For example, programs designed to increase social language use may encounter major obstacles if the student's social language production attempts are largely unintelligible (see Camarata, in press). Yet this aspect of language remediation has not been systematically included in training protocols, nor has it been tested within recently developed naturalistic language intervention procedures that are beginning to make major headway in inducing rapid, generalized language production.

In this chapter, we will discuss intelligibility within the context of naturalistic language teaching procedures and explore the possibility of affecting major improvements in language development in general, as well as in the areas of social and academic development and community integration. In order to accomplish this goal, a review of the current practices in the area of phonological disorders will be presented. Phonology has incorrectly been viewed as an autonomous construct, leading to a lack of attention to its impact on communicative behavior and on disruptive, aggressive behavior. Following the review of traditional approaches, we will present a rationale and evidence for viewing phonological disorders within a larger linguistic context and for incorporating the management of phonological disorders into a comprehensive management plan to reduce aggression.

Traditional Approaches to Phonological Training

In spite of a number of recent advances in the methodologies used to analyze speech-sound errors (e.g., phonological processes and generative analyses), the actual nature of training has remained almost exclusively imitation-based and has been completed outside natural conversation and outside more general linguistic and social behavior. For example, Dinnsen, Elbert, Gierut, and their colleagues (Dinnsen, Chin, Elbert, & Powell, 1990; Elbert, Dinnsen, Swartzlander, & Chin, 1990; Elbert, Dinnsen, & Weismer, 1984; Gierut, 1989, 1990) have demonstrated the importance of applying generative analyses to the selection of remediation targets. However, the actual training is based upon imitation procedures, and generalization is often measured using a probe list elicited under conditions similar to the actual training without reference to the impact on the child's overall communicative competence (cf. Elbert et al., 1990; Gierut, 1990).

Earlier studies using different phonological analyses, for example, distinctive features (Costello & Onstine, 1976; McReynolds & Bennett, 1972),

phonological processes (Hodson & Paden, 1983; McReynolds & Elbert, 1981), or minimal pairs (Hoffman, Norris, & Monjure, 1990; Weiner, 1981), also have been conducted using imitation procedures *in isolation from* broader social competence issues. Moreover, such autonomous imitation-based training continues to dominate the phonological disorders literature, regardless of theoretical approach and despite the relative lack of data indicating that such procedures lead to generalized improvements in speech production, language skills or social competence (cf. Elbert et al., 1990; Siegel & Spradlin, 1985; Stoel-Gammon & Dunn, 1986). Worse, phonological skills have long been taught in isolation, as a skill that is independent from other kinds of language-learning tasks. As a result, the teaching of accurate speech-sound production to students with severe language disabilities has not been part of the dramatic progress in language teaching seen in the last few years, nor has the importance of including speech-sound production in these language training programs been evaluated directly.

New Developments in Language Training

In contrast to the work on speech-sound production, the procedures used to remediate language disabilities in general have undergone dramatic changes in the past decade. There has been a shift from imitation-based training that focuses on rote learning of semantic, syntactic, and morphologic targets removed from the natural context to training that involves naturalistic conversational presentation of the target structures (Camarata & Nelson, 1992; Cole & Dale, 1986; Connell, 1987; Friedman & Friedman, 1980; Koegel, O'Dell, & Koegel, 1987; Olswang, Bain, Rosendahl, Oblak, & Smith, 1986; Warren & Kaiser, 1986). Moreover, this shift in orientation has been applied to populations representing a wide range of disabilities (cf. Warren & Kaiser, 1986), including developmental delays (Hart & Risley, 1975, 1980; Warren, McQuarter, & Rogers-Warren, 1984), autism (Koegel, O'Dell, & Koegel, 1987), and hearing impairments (Prinz & Masin, 1985). These systematic, naturalistic language-teaching approaches not only have proven useful in remediating semantic, syntactic, and morphologic deficits in diverse populations, but also, more importantly, have generated rapid generalization of the target structures to spontaneous conversation outside of the specific teaching environment (Warren & Kaiser, 1986).

Despite these considerable advances in the field, speech-sound production and overall intelligibility have not been addressed to any significant extent, nor have the recent techniques been applied to the treatment of phonological (speech-sound) disorders in a large-scale systematic manner. Indeed, one could argue that teaching technology has lagged significantly in this aspect of communication. As seen below, it may be responsible for some of the critical plateaus reached by children with severe language disabilities.

Rationale for Teaching Phonological Skills Using Naturalistic Conversational Approaches

In populations of typical language learners, there is no evidence that children learning language in the ambient environment receive direct imitation training on phonological (speech-sound) skills from parents (cf. Brown & Hanlon, 1970; Cross, 1978; Ferguson, 1977; Stoel-Gammon, 1983). Similarly, studies of phonological input to children suggest only that parents speak more slowly and articulate more clearly when speaking to young children rather than extensively employing imitation-based strategies (Bernstein-Ratner, 1983; Malsheen, 1980; Stoel-Gammon, 1983). It was precisely this kind of observation that led researchers to embed targets in conversation within training programs for the other language domains (e.g., Warren, 1988). Clearly, the kinds of teaching that are applied to morphology, syntax, and semantics also may be employed for phonology (speech production). Thus, used with phonology, such naturalistic conversation training procedures are likely to lead to the kinds of rapid gains seen in other aspects of language (e.g., syntax and lexical development) and are likely to remove obstacles to improvements within other language domains as well, resulting in very broad gains.

Two implicit barriers have prevented such studies of improved speech production. First, many have assumed that naturalistic conversational training for specific phonological targets cannot be conducted in an experimentally rigorous manner. To be sure, some conversation procedures have been lacking in specificity with regard to both teacher and student behaviors. Yet, no a priori rationale suggests that naturalistic conversation training cannot be conducted in an experimentally rigorous manner. As noted, there is a long history of successfully applying such teaching to populations with severe language disabilities (cf. the review in Warren & Kaiser, 1986). Additionally, Camarata and Nelson (in press) demonstrate that it is possible to rigorously monitor teacher and student behavior for the kinds of targets that must be specified within phonological training.

The second implicit barrier to conducting naturalistic conversation training as treatment for phonological disorders has been the assumption that some type of perceptual and/or motor disability underlies phonological problems and that extensive imitation practice is, therefore, required for improvement (Bernthal & Bankson, 1988; Stoel-Gammon & Dunn, 1986). However, several types of evidence argue against such an a priori theoretical position. First, although typical or typically developing children commit extensive phonological errors, they make steady progress toward mastering the adult phonological system despite a lack of imitation practice. Second, many children with phonological disabilities, such as "functional misarticulation" or "phonological disorders of unknown origin," display no overt evidence of other motor disturbances (Elbert, Dinnsen, & Weismer, 1984; Shriberg, Kwiatkowski, Best, Hengst, & Terselic-Weber, 1986).

These and other authors note that phonology includes a linguistic aspect, in addition to the motor requirements, and emphasize the role of language abilities (rather than motor limitations) in their accounts of phonological disorders of this type (see Folkins & Bleile, 1990, for a recent discussion of motor and linguistic aspects of phonology). In light of such accounts, it is not surprising that many children with language disabilities suffer from phonological impairments as well (cf. Aram & Kamhi, 1982; Shriner, Holloway & Daniloff, 1969). Indeed, the population of individuals with severe language disabilities and the population of individuals with functional misarticulation greatly overlap. This is not unexpected when one considers that phonology is an integral part of language and is probably learned parallel with the other aspects of language. The children who exhibit the co-occurrence of phonological, morphological, semantic, and syntactic difficulties suffer mostly in their efforts to acquire verbal communication skills; thus, they are the most likely to meet barriers to their attempts to function in integrated settings. These same children are also most likely to be frustrated and exhibit associated disruptive and noncompliant behaviors.

Integration of Language Domains during Training

As noted, researchers have traditionally subdivided the study of language (and language handicaps) into autonomous parts. For example, Crystal (1987) divided language into morphology, phonology, phonetics, semantics, and syntax. Similarly, Camarata (in press) defines language along morphological, phonological, pragmatic, semantic, and syntactic dimensions. Historically, language researchers have attempted to isolate and study in detail these individual language components. Although the importance of conducting research in such a manner should not be minimized, advantages of studying these language dimensions simultaneously are abundantly clear, considering that disruptive behaviors such as aggression and noncompliance also serve a communicative function. For example, Jakobson (1980) argued that "it is important to approach language and its disruption in the framework of a given level [dimension], while remembering at the same time . . . that the totality and the interrelation between the different parts of the totality have to be taken into account" (pp. 94–95).

Not surprisingly, preliminary attempts to examine the interrelation among language dimensions have revealed important integration effects between phonology and the other dimensions of language. Indeed, such studies have indicated that each of the other language dimensions can be interrelated with phonology in typically functioning children and in children with phonological impairments. For example, Panagos and his colleagues (Panagos, 1974; Panagos & Prelock, 1982; Panagos, Quine, & Klich, 1979), Paul and Shriberg (1982), and Schwartz, Leonard, Folger, and Wilcox (1980) reported that changes in the accuracy of syntactic complexity result in changes in speech-sound production. That is, increased syntactic complexity is often associated with an increased number of phonological errors.

Bock (1982) provided a detailed model to account for this apparent trade-off between phonological and syntactic complexity, suggesting that processing constraints in the child's linguistic system result in a decay in phonological production. Thus, paradoxically, one is cautioned to expect certain types of phonological decay as an indicator of progress in other language skills. However, it is crucial to note that (a) these decays should occur only at certain prescribed points, (b) they should be temporary, and (c) they should co-vary with language *improvements in other domains* before phonological improvement again takes place.

Camarata and his colleagues (Camarata & Leonard, 1986; Camarata & Schwartz, 1985) conducted a series of studies that also revealed the interrelation between semantics and phonology. In these studies, greater semantic complexity (object words as compared to action words) was associated with a temporary decrease in phonological accuracy (lower percentage of consonants produced correctly). These studies included a high degree of control of confounding factors (e.g., diversity of morphological markers, frequency of presentation, and phonological structure of the lexemes within each class), suggesting once again that limitations may result in trade-offs among language domains.

Additionally, Campbell and Shriberg (1982) noted that phonology and pragmatics are interrelated during language acquisition. They reported that phonologically impaired children made fewer errors when producing words that were new topics in the conversational context than when producing words as comments in the discourse (i.e., words that reflected an already established "shared reference" were produced with more errors). In this case, phonological accuracy increased only when listener uncertainty was likely to be high, whereas lower levels of accuracy were considered sufficient when the conversational partner was already aware of the topic.

Finally, work by Camarata (1990), Camarata and Erwin (1988), and Camarata and Gandour (1985) also suggested a relationship between morphology and phonology. These authors reported that difficulty in producing grammatical markers (e.g., plurals) can lead to shifts in the phonological patterns used to signal the grammatical change (e.g., use of variations in duration, intensity, and/or frequency).

As noted, analysis and treatment of phonological disorders historically have been viewed as separate from analysis and treatment of language impairment. For example, the leading texts often examine phonological disorders to the exclusion of other kinds of language disorders (e.g., Bernthal & Bankson, 1988; Stoel-Gammon & Dunn, 1986). Similarly, a review of the literature reveals that studies examining the treatment of phonological disorders do not include attempts to monitor simultaneous acquisition of morphological, phonological, pragmatic, syntactic, and semantic milestones.

Yet, the above review suggests that phonological acquisition is integrated into these other domains and that simultaneous monitoring of these language domains can yield important information. Such a view has long been evident in the study of normal language acquisition. For example, Slobin (1973) noted that acquisition of new structures is often coordinated with existing (old) language structures. Indeed, he observed that any new form would first appear with an old (already established) function. Leonard (1976) reported precisely this kind of effect upon discovering that children first use grammatical morphemes within previously mastered

syntactic structures. In the phonological domain, Leonard et al. (1982) found that children are more likely to learn new words when the words contain previously mastered phonemes.

Conversely, Schwartz and Leonard (1982) reported that children avoid producing words containing phonemes that are not present in their phonological systems. Perhaps the most familiar example of phonological integration is the progressive idiom (Ingram, 1976; Leonard et al., 1982; Leopold, 1947). Here phonological competence regresses as the child's lexical inventory increases.

Clearly, there is the potential for such effects during language training as well. Crystal (1987) stated rather directly, "My view is that levels of interactions between levels are of considerable clinical import. Indeed, a good case can be made to say that the traditional preoccupation with levels has led us to ignore what may well be a central issue in the investigation of language disabilities" (p. 8). Consider the teaching implications of progressive idioms: a regression in phonological performance may signal advances in the lexical domain. However, traditional training paradigms that examine phonology as an autonomous construct fail to account for this regression, leading the practitioner or researcher to conclude that the training was not effective; in fact, it might lead the teacher to proceed by emphasizing an inappropriate target. Camarata and Nelson (1989) demonstrated precisely this effect when monitoring phonology during the treatment of specific language impairment. These researchers trained (and monitored) morphological and syntactic targets and reported that advances in these domains were often associated with regression or a lack of advance in phonological accuracy.

The Role of Phonology in Language Training

Based on the above literature review, it is clear that phonology can interact with other aspects of language to produce interesting and important co-variance. But there is evidence to suggest that phonological competence plays a more fundamental role in language acquisition and in the remediation of language disabilities. For example, Miller et al. (1990) report that speech intelligibility is the most predictive factor in the remediation of language disorders in children with Down's syndrome. Relatedly, in the Leonard et al. (1982) project cited above, children avoided producing forms that contained phonemes outside of their phoneme inventories. Schwartz and Leonard (1982) replicated this finding, reporting that children were much more likely to acquire words that contained phonemes that were in their sound systems prior to the exposure to the new words.

Conversely, Camarata (1990) has found that early acquisition of alveolar fricatives ([s], [z]) in word final position can lead to very rapid (and precocious) acquisition of the grammatical markers that use these phonemes (e.g., plurals). Thus, phonology can serve as a "choke point" or "flow restrictor" for the other aspects of language; children with language disabilities must be proficient in the phonological form of language in order to express the meanings required for successful language production.

Summary of the Problem

In recent years, the key role of language, and language disabilities, in the development of academic and social skills has been recognized. At a fundamental level, difficulty in expressing wants, needs, thoughts, and ideas can lead to communication breakdowns in the classroom and to frustration in the child with language disabilities. Building upon this foundation, it has become increasingly clear that preschool students with language disabilities often develop associated behavior problems (cf. Aram, Ekelman, & Nation, 1984; Carr & Durand, 1985).

In addition, there is increasing evidence that such students also develop a high number of learning disabilities (Cantwell & Baker, 1985; Strickland, 1988; Teale, 1986; vanKleek, 1990; and see the review in Koopenhaver, Coleman, Kalman, & Yoder, 1991). Finally, speech-sound production disorders have been shown to relate directly to the

incidence of reading disabilities (see the review in Catts & Kamhi, 1986).

Thus, it is clear that persistent language and phonological disabilities can have a negative impact on social and academic performance. Indeed, one could argue that basic levels of communicative competence are required for improvements in social and academic performance. As a result, improved programs need to include systematic evaluation of speech-sound production and language skills, in addition to measures pertaining to aggression and disruptive behavior. We hypothesize that improvements in speech-sound production will relate to advances in language and communicative skills and, thus, also to improvements in social and academic performance as well as in severe behavior problems, such as aggression and noncompliance.

Specifics of Naturalistic Behavior-Modification Treatment Procedures

The naturalistic language procedures (NLP) we have found to be most effective for motivating conversational interactions, and thus for reducing escape-motivated aggression and noncompliance, are described in detail below. In general, the essence of these procedures is the same as that of most behavior modification programs. The treatment provider delivers instructional stimuli, the child responds, and the treatment provider ensures that a reinforcer is delivered. However, three additional points are essential in the naturalistic paradigm described below. First, the entire intervention is conducted within a natural interchange, using natural training stimuli and natural reinforcers. Second, key variables shown to be important in maximizing motivation are utilized throughout the intervention. Third, the intervention focuses on pivotal behaviors that are likely to influence widespread areas of the child's functioning. The steps below are summarized from Koegel, Koegel, and Schreibman (1991).

Use of clear instructional stimuli. Stimuli must be clear, appropriate to the task, and uninterrupted. In addition, the child must be attending to the task (Koegel, Glahn, & Nieminen, 1978; Koegel, Russo, & Rincover, 1977). Elaborate or lengthy instructions may be confusing to a child with a severe disability. In addition to giving instructions and asking questions, the treatment provider should capitalize on situations where the child's spontaneous speech may be strengthened. Thus, if the treatment provider knows the child likes apples, an apple may be placed near the child to encourage the child to ask for the fruit.

Interspersal of maintenance tasks. Frequent interspersal of tasks the child has already acquired among new acquisition trials seems to greatly help motivate the child (Dunlap, 1984; Koegel & Koegel, 1986; Neef, Iwata, & Page, 1980).

Use of multiple cues. Because much of language involves using multiple cues (e.g., multiple phonemes, multiple words, and multiple objects), another important aspect of teaching pivotal behaviors lies in teaching the child to respond to multiple cues (cf. Koegel & Schreibman, 1977; Schreibman, Charlop, & Koegel, 1982). The issue of multiple cues is closely related to *overselectivity,* the tendency of children with autism to respond to only a limited number of cues within a complex stimulus. Thus, the treatment provider must emphasize or otherwise ensure that the child responds to critical phonemes in a word, as well as to all the phonemes in the word, before delivering reinforcement.

Reinforcing of both correct responses and attempts at correct responses. This step deals with the question of whether a reward is given only after correct responses or also after any obvious try or attempt to perform the task. Recent research suggests that reinforcing attempts is dramatically more effective in motivating children with autism to try difficult tasks (Koegel, O'Dell, & Dunlap, 1988). We speculate that children with severe disabilities become increasingly unmotivated to respond if most of their attempts to respond are met with punishing interactions. Camarata and Nelson's

work (Camarata, 1992; Camarata & Nelson, 1992) suggests that, along with reinforcing a misarticulated attempt at pronouncing a word, it is important for the treatment provider to recast the word back to the child with the correct pronunciation as the reinforcer is delivered. For example, if the child said "Do car," meaning "Go car," the treatment provider would both make the car go and say "That's right, go car." According to the literature and our pilot data described below, under such conditions, motivation to respond and intelligibility improve, and aggression and other disruptive behaviors decrease dramatically.

Child's choice of stimulus materials. Choice is another variable that has been identified in recent years as important for promoting children's motivation to interact with others (Koegel, Dyer, & Bell, 1987; Koegel et al., 1987; Koegel et al., 1988). Previously, entire communicative interaction topics were planned by the treatment provider, and the children had to engage in the activities whether they wanted to or not. Present research, however, has indicated that if children are permitted to participate in choosing the task or topic, they are much more motivated to engage in the interaction, and escape-motivated disruptive behavior is greatly reduced. This approach can be carried out in a controlled fashion, such as asking the children which book they would like to read during reading time or which toy, topics, or games they would like to interact with during language activities (Paslawski, 1991).

Use of functional reinforcers. This and the next step relate to the consequences of the child's targeted treatment behaviors. First, in order to be functional, it is important that rewards are clearly delivered, immediate, contingent, uninterrupted, and effective. The reinforcer must be chosen based on evidence that the child will work to obtain it.

Natural reinforcers. Given the above requirements, it appears to be important that the reinforcer be a direct, natural part of the activity. For example, if a child wishes to play with a toy airplane and says "pane," the treatment provider should let her play with the airplane (while recasting the word correctly, saying "plane"), rather than giving her an indirect reinforcer, such as a piece of candy (Koegel & Williams, 1980; Skinner, 1979; Williams, Koegel, & Egel, 1981).

Natural reinforcers that are a direct part of the activity have several potential advantages. For example, their delivery is immediate, with no intervening, unrelated behavior between the targeted speech and the reinforcer (such as reaching out to receive a candy reinforcer). Perhaps relatedly, such natural reinforcers have the potential to emphasize the connection between the target behavior and the consequence. Making it clear to the child that the communicative behavior is related to the consequences appears to be important in enhancing motivation to communicate.

Measures of Improvement

The central message of this chapter is that if one wishes to reduce disruptive behavior, such as aggression and noncompliance, one must be concerned with modifying and measuring a core cluster of behaviors related to communication and social interactions with others. We have argued that, in order to do this, it is necessary to modify the child's speech intelligibility so that communicative social interactions may proceed smoothly with maximum reinforcement for the communicative partners. In order to measure improvement, we recommend that several areas be assessed. First, in addition to measuring the presenting target behaviors of aggression and noncompliance, we suggest measuring (a) phonology (speech sounds, including generalization measures), (b) language development (including morphology, pragmatics, semantics, and syntax), (c) social skills (including friendship patterns and school functioning), and (d) academic performance (including classroom teacher ratings and standardized academic assessments).

Pilot Studies

To provide preliminary evaluation of the effects of naturalistic conversation training on speech-sound production and the reduction of disruptive behavior, the authors have completed a series of pilot studies. The first of these pilot studies includes validation of the naturalistic conversation training procedures that form the core of the proposed program. These studies (Camarata & Nelson, 1992; Koegel, Koegel, & Surratt, 1992) indicate that sharp procedural contrasts can be implemented within training (procedural fidelity), and that real improvements in both disruptive behavior and language can be achieved by students with severe language disabilities under naturalistic training. Also, these gains have been associated with gains in social and academic skills as well (see Figure 9.1).

A second pilot study indicating that naturalistic conversation procedures are likely to result in gains in speech-sound production skills was conducted by Koegel, O'Dell, and Dunlap (1988). This study demonstrated that gains in speech-sound production could be achieved by reinforcing the communicative attempts of children with severe language handicaps arising from autism. The results also showed marked improvements in the children's affect and general degree of cooperation and compliance during the interactions.

Summary

The crux of this chapter is to emphasize the relationship between language disability and noncompliance, aggression, self-injury, and other harmful behaviors. Because of this documented co-variation, we have focused on the behavioral treatment of language and phonology and described research demonstrating the concomitant changes that occur in disruptive behavior as language skills improve. We have described preliminary phonology treatments patterned after the procedures described

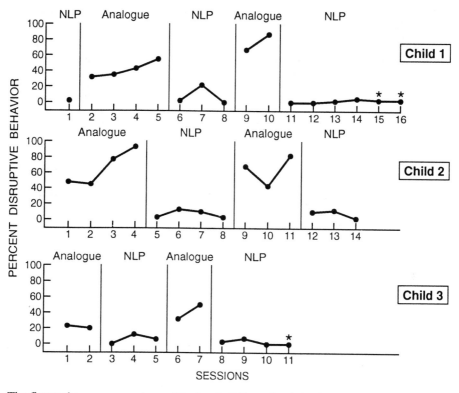

Figure 9.1. The figure shows a comparison of the level of disruptive behavior for naturalistic (NLP) versus analog language treatment conditions. Percentage of disruptive behavior is plotted on the ordinate, and session numbers are plotted on the abscissa for each child. The asterisks indicate final sessions that were conducted by the child's parents (who had been trained in implementation of the NLP treatment procedures).

SOURCE: *"Language intervention and disruptive behavior in preschool children with autism" by R. L. Koegel, L. K. Koegel, and A. V. Surratt, 1992.* Journal of Autism & Developmental Disorders, 22, *pp. 141–154.*

in Koegel, O'Dell, and Koegel (1987) and applied to children with language impairments by Camarata and Nelson (1992). We have suggested the use of activities designed to prompt student productions that contain target attempts. In terms of phonology, this includes toys and objects that contain the target speech sounds. After the student attempts the target, the teacher responds in a conversationally appropriate way that includes the core attributes of the student production while adding a correct production of the targeted speech sound. If the

student produces the target correctly, the teacher simply responds in a conversationally appropriate way (e.g., a conversationally natural reinforcer is provided). For example, assume that the target /s/ has been assigned to conversational training and the student says "Ti it go" for "See it go." The teacher would respond "Oh, see it go," and then set the toy into motion. These procedures have been shown to be effective in training a wide range of linguistic targets (cf. Camarata & Nelson, 1992; Koegel, O'Dell, & Koegel, 1987; Warren & Kaiser,

Table 9.1 Difference between Imitation Training and Naturalistic Conversation Training

	Imitation Training	Naturalistic Conversation Training
Stimulus items	a. Chosen by trainer b. Pictures/photographs of words containing target sounds	a. Chosen by student b. Objects and toys whose names contain target sounds c. Selection of items of high interest to the student
Steps	a. Begin with sounds in isolation; drill until mastery b. Sounds in syllables; drill until mastery c. Sounds in words and phrases; drill until mastery d. Elaborate transfer and generalization procedures	a. Begin with word production of item b. Productions are immediately imbedded in conversation c. Elaborate generalization procedures not required
Interaction	a. Trainer models sound production b. Direct metalinguistic feedback (e.g., motor placement cues) c. Stimulus items not functional within interaction	a. Teacher models word following student attempts b. Teacher and student play with stimulus items c. Stimulus items are functional within interaction

1986). Table 9.1 summarizes the major components of the treatment procedures.

Although reduction of aggression and noncompliance through improved intelligibility is only recently being studied, we believe it holds much promise for the success of those with severe language disabilities who are learning oral communication. We anticipate that such techniques will result in greatly reduced levels of noncompliance, aggression, and related disruptive behaviors.

Note

Preparation of this manuscript was supported in part by the National Institute on Disability and Rehabilitation Research Cooperative Agreement No. G0087C0234; the U. S. Public Health Service Research Grant MH28210 from the National Institutes of Mental Health; the National Institute on Deafness and Other Communicative Disorders, Award NS26437; and an endowment from the Scottish Rite Foundation of Nashville.

References

ARAM, D., EKELMAN, B., & NATION, J. (1984). Preschoolers with language disorders: 10 years later. *Journal of Speech and Hearing Research, 27,* 232–244.

ARAM, D., & KAMHI, A. (1982). Perspectives on the relationship between phonological and language disorders. *Seminars in Speech, Language, and Hearing, 3,* 101–114.

BERNSTEIN-RATNER, N. (1983, November). *Increased vowel precision in the absence of increased vowel duration.* Paper presented at the annual convention of the American Speech-Language-Hearing Association, Cincinnati.

BERNTHAL, J., & BANKSON, N. (1988). *Articulation disorders.* Englewood Cliffs, NJ: Prentice-Hall.

BOCK, K. (1982). Toward a cognitive psychology of syntax: Information processing contributions to sentence processing. *Psychological Review,* 1–47.

BROWN, R., & HANLON, C. (1970). Derivational complexity and the order of acquisition in child speech. In R. Brown (Ed.), *Psycholinguistics* (pp. 155–207). New York: Free Press.

CAMARATA, S. (1990). Semantic iconicity in plural acquisition: Extending the argument to include normal children. *Clinical Linguistics and Phonetics, 4*, 319–325.

CAMARATA, S. (1991). Assessment of oral language. In J. Salvia & J. Ysseldyke (Eds.), *Assessment in special and remedial education* (pp. 263–301). Boston: Houghton-Mifflin.

CAMARATA, S. (1992). *The application of naturalistic teaching procedures to speech production in children with speech disabilities.* Manuscript submitted for publication.

CAMARATA, S. (in press). *Phonological disorders in children.* Chicago: Mosby-Yearbook.

CAMARATA, S., & ERWIN, L. (1988). Rule invention in the acquisition of morphology revisited: A case of transparent semantic mapping. *Journal of Speech and Hearing Research, 31*, 425–431.

CAMARATA, S., & GANDOUR, J. (1984). On describing idiosyncratic phonologic systems. *Journal of Speech and Hearing Disorders, 49*, 262–266.

CAMARATA, S., & GANDOUR, J. (1985). Rule invention in the acquisition of morphology by a language impaired child. *Journal of Speech and Hearing Disorders, 50*, 40–45.

CAMARATA, S., & LEONARD, L. (1986). Young children produce object words more accurately than action words. *Journal of Child Language, 13*, 51–65.

CAMARATA, S., & NELSON, K. (1989). Interactions among language domains within the treatment of specific language impairment. Paper presented at the American Speech-Language-Hearing Association conference, St. Louis.

CAMARATA, S., & NELSON, K. (1990, November). *Patterns of acquisition in language impaired children.* Paper presented at the annual convention of the American Speech-Language-Hearing Association, Seattle.

CAMARATA, S., & NELSON, K. (1992). Treatment efficiency as a function of target selection in the remediation of child language disorders. *Clinical Linguistics and Phonetics, 6*, 167–178.

CAMARATA, S., & SCHWARTZ, R. (1985). Production of action words and object words: Evidence for a relationship between semantics and phonology. *Journal of Speech and Hearing Research, 28*, 323–330.

CAMPBELL, T., & SHRIBERG, L. (1982). Associations among pragmatic functions, linguistic stress, and natural phonological processes in speech delayed children. *Journal of Speech and Hearing Research, 25*, 547–553.

CANTWELL, D. P., & BAKER, L. (1985). Psychiatric and learning disorders in children with speech and language disorders: A descriptive analysis. *Advances in Learning and Behavior Disorders, 4*, 29–47.

CARR, E., & DURAND, V. (1985). Reducing behavior problems through functional communication problems. *Journal of Applied Behavior Analysis, 18*, 111–126.

CATTS, H., & KAMHI, A. (1986). The linguistic basis of reading disorders: Implications for the speech-language pathologist. *Language, Speech, and Hearing Services in Schools, 17*, 329–341.

COLE, K., & DALE, P. (1986). Direct language instruction and interactive language instruction with language delayed preschool children: A comparison study. *Journal of Speech and Hearing Research, 22*, 389–402.

CONNELL, P. (1987). Teaching language rules as solutions to language problems: A baseball analogy. *Language, Speech, and Hearing Services in Schools, 18*, 194–215.

COSTELLO, J., & ONSTINE, J. (1976). The modification of multiple articulation errors based upon distinctive feature theory. *Journal of Speech and Hearing Disorders, 41*, 199–215.

CROSS, T. (1978). Mother's speech and its association with rate of linguistic development in young children. In N. Waterson & C. Snow (Eds.), *The development of communication*. New York: Wiley.

CRYSTAL, D. (1987). Towards a bucket theory of language disability: Taking account of interaction between linguistic levels. *Clinical Linguistics and Phonetics, 1*, 7–21.

DATTILO, J., & CAMARATA, S. (1991). Facilitating conversation through self-initiated augmentative communication treatment. *Journal of Applied Behavior Analysis, 24*, 369–378.

DINNSEN, D., CHIN, S., ELBERT, M., & POWELL, T. (1990). Some constraints on functionally disordered phonologies: Phonetic inventories and phonotactics. *Journal of Speech and Hearing Research, 33*, 28–37.

DUNLAP, G. (1984). The influence of task variation and maintenance tasks on the learning and affect of autistic children. *Journal of Experimental Child Psychology, 37*, 41–64.

ELBERT, M., DINNSEN, D., & POWELL, T. (1984). On the prediction of phonological generalization learning patterns. *Journal of Speech and Hearing Disorders, 49*, 309–317.

ELBERT, M., DINNSEN, D., SWARTZLANDER, P., & CHIN, S. (1990). Generalization to conversational speech. *Journal of Speech and Hearing Disorders, 55*, 694–699.

ELBERT, M., DINNSEN, D., & WEISMER, G. (1984). Phonological theory and the misarticulating child. *ASHA Monograph, 22*. Rockville, MD: American Speech-Language-Hearing Association.

FERGUSON, C. (1977). Baby talk as a simplified register. In C. Snow & C. Ferguson (Eds.), *Language input and acquisition*. Cambridge, MA: Cambridge University Press.

FOLKINS, J., & BLEILE, K. (1990). Taxonomies in biology, phonetics, phonology, and speech motor control. *Journal of Speech and Hearing Disorders, 55*, 596–611.

FRIEDMAN, P., & FRIEDMAN, K. (1980). Accounting for individual differences when comparing the effectiveness of remedial language teaching differences. *Applied Psycholinguistics, 1*, 151–170.

GIERUT, J. (1989). Maximal opposition approach to phonological treatment. *Journal of Speech and Hearing Disorders, 54*, 9–19.

GIERUT, J. (1990). Differential learning of phonological oppositions. *Journal of Speech and Hearing Research, 33*, 540–549.

HALEY, K., CAMARATA, S., & NELSON, K. E. (1992). *Social valence during language intervention*. Manuscript submitted for publication.

HART, B., & RISLEY, T. (1975). Incidental teaching of language in the preschool. *Journal of Applied Behavior Analysis, 8*, 411–420.

HART, B., & RISLEY, T. (1980). In vivo language intervention: Unanticipated general effects. *Journal of Applied Behavior Analysis, 11*, 407–432.

HODSON, B., & PADEN, E. (1983). *Targeting intelligible speech*. San Diego, CA: College-Hill.

HOFFMAN, P., NORRIS, J., & MONJURE, J. (1990). Comparison of process targeting and whole language treatments for phonologically delayed preschool children. *Language, Speech, and Hearing Services in Schools, 21*, 102–109.

INGRAM, D. (1976). *Phonological disability in children*. New York: Elsevier.

JAKOBSON, R. (1980). On aphasic disorders from a linguistic angle. In R. Jakobson (Ed.), *The framework of language*. Ann Arbor: University of Michigan Press.

KOEGEL, R. L., DYER, K., & BELL, L. K. (1987). The influence of child-preferred activities on autistic children's social behavior. *Journal of Applied Behavior Analysis, 20*, 243–252.

KOEGEL, R. L., GLAHN, T. J., & NIEMINEN, G. S. (1978). Generalization of parent-training results. *Journal of Applied Behavior Analysis, 11*, 95–109.

KOEGEL, R. L., & JOHNSON, J. (1989). Motivating language use in autistic children. In G. Dawson (Ed.), *Autism: New perspectives on diagnosis, nature and treatment* (pp. 310–325). New York: Guilford.

KOEGEL, R. L., & KOEGEL, L. K. (1986). Promoting generalized treatment gains through direct instruction of self-monitoring procedures. *Direct Instruction News, 5*, 13–15.

KOEGEL, R. L., KOEGEL, L. K., & SCHREIBMAN, L. (1991). Assessing and training parents in teaching pivotal behaviors. In R. Prinz (Ed.), *Advances in behavioral assessment of children and families* (pp. 65–82). London: Jessica Kingsley.

KOEGEL, R. L., KOEGEL, L. K., & SURRATT, A. V. (1992). Language intervention and disruptive behavior in preschool children with autism. *Journal of Autism and Developmental Disorders, 22*, 141–154.

KOEGEL, R. L., & MENTIS, M. (1985). Annotation motivation in childhood autism: Can they or won't they? *Journal of Child Psychology and Psychiatry, 26*, 185–191.

KOEGEL, R. L., O'DELL, M. C., & DUNLAP, G. (1988). Producing speech use in nonverbal autistic children by reinforcing attempts. *Journal of Autism and Developmental Disorders, 18*(4), 525–538.

KOEGEL, R. L., O'DELL, M. C., & KOEGEL, L. K. (1987). A natural language paradigm for teaching nonverbal autistic children. *Journal of Autism and Developmental Disorders, 17*, 187–199.

KOEGEL, R. L., RUSSO, D. C., & RINCOVER, A. (1977). Assessing and training teachers in the generalized use of behavior modification with autistic children. *Journal of Applied Behavior Analysis, 10*, 197–205.

KOEGEL, R. L., & SCHREIBMAN, L. (1977). Teaching autistic children to respond to simultaneous multiple cues. *Journal of Experimental Child Psychology, 24*, 299–311.

KOEGEL, R. L., SCHREIBMAN, L., GOOD, A., CERNIGLIA, L., MURPHY, C., & KOEGEL, L. K. (1989). *How to teach pivotal behavior to children with autism: A training manual*. Santa Barbara: University of California.

KOEGEL, L. K., VALDEZ-MENCHACA, M. C., & KOEGEL, R. L. (in press). Autism: A discussion from a social communication perspective. In V. B. Van Hasselt & M. Hersen (Eds.), *Advanced abnormal psychology*. New York: Plenum.

KOEGEL, R. L., & WILLIAMS, J. A. (1980). Direct vs. indirect response-reinforcer relationships in teaching autistic children. *Journal of Abnormal Child Psychology, 4*, 537–547.

KOOPENHAVER, D., COLEMAN, P., KALMAN, S., & YODER, D. (1991). The implications of emergent literacy research for children with developmental disabilities. *American Journal of Speech-Language Pathology, 1*, 38–44.

LEONARD, L. (1976). *Meaning in child language.* New York: Grune & Stratton.

LEONARD, L., SCHWARTZ, R., CHAPMAN, K., ROWAN, L., PRELOCK, P., TERRELL, B., WEISS, A., & MESSICK, C. (1982). Early lexical acquisition in children with specific language impairment. *Journal of Speech and Hearing Research, 25,* 554–559.

LEOPOLD, W. F. (1947). *Speech development of a bilingual child: A linguist's record. Volume II: Sound learning in the first two years.* Evanston, IL: Northwestern University Press.

MALSHEEN, B. (1980). Two hypotheses for phonetic clarification in the speech of mothers to children. In G. Yeni-Komshian & C. Ferguson (Eds.), *Child phonology* (Vol. 2) (pp. 173–184). New York: Academic.

McREYNOLDS, L., & BENNETT, S. (1972). Distinctive feature generalization in articulation training. *Journal of Speech and Hearing Disorders, 37,* 462–470.

McREYNOLDS, L. & ELBERT, M. (1981). Criteria for phonological process analysis. *Journal of Speech and Hearing Disorders, 46,* 197–204.

MILLER, J., MIOLO, G., MURRAY-BRANCH, J., PIERCE, K., ROSIN, M., SEDEY, A., & SWIFT, E. (1990, November). *Facilitating speech and language development in children with Down's syndrome.* Paper presented at the annual convention of the American Speech-Language-Hearing Association, Seattle.

NEEF, N. A., IWATA, B. A., & PAGE, T. J. (1980). The effects of interspersal training versus high density reinforcement on spelling acquisition and retention. *Journal of Applied Behavior Analysis, 13,* 153–158.

OLSWANG, L., & BAIN, B. (1985). The natural occurrence of generalization during articulation treatment. *Journal of Communication Disorders, 18,* 109–129.

OLSWANG, L., BAIN, B., ROSENDAHL, P., OBLAK, S., & SMITH, A. (1986). Language learning: Moving performance from context dependent to independent state. *Child Language Teaching and Therapy, 2,* 180–210.

O'NEILL, R. E., ALBIN, R., HORNER, R. H., STOREY, K., & SPRAGUE, J. (1990). *Functional analysis of problem behavior: A practical assessment guide.* Sycamore, IL: Sycamore.

PANAGOS, J. (1974). String complexity increases phonemic interference. *Perceptual and Motor Skills, 38,* 1219–1222.

PANAGOS, J., & PRELOCK, P. (1982). Phonological constraints on the sentence productions of language disordered children. *Journal of Speech and Hearing Research, 25,* 171–176.

PANAGOS, J., QUINE, M., & KLICH, R. (1979). Syntactic and phonological influences on children's articulation. *Journal of Speech and Hearing Research, 22,* 841–848.

PASLAWSKI, T. (1991). *The effects of number of stimuli on the verbal responding, affect and disruptive behavior of autistic children.* Unpublished master's thesis, University of California, Santa Barbara.

PAUL, R., & SHRIBERG, L. (1982). Associations between phonology and syntax in speech delayed children. *Journal of Speech and Hearing Research, 25,* 536–546.

PRINZ, P., & MASIN, L. (1985). Lending a helping hand: Linguistic input and sign language acquisition in deaf children. *Applied Psycholinguistics, 6,* 357–370.

REICHLE, J., MIRENDA, P., LOCKE, P., PICHE, L., & JOHNSTON, S. (1992). Beginning augmentative communication systems. In S. F. Warren & J. Reichle (Eds.), *Causes and effects in communication and language intervention* (pp. 131–158). Baltimore: Brookes.

SCHREIBMAN, L., CHARLOP, M. H., & KOEGEL, R. L. (1982). Teaching autistic children to use extra stimulus prompts. *Journal of Experimental Child Psychology, 33,* 475–491.

SCHWARTZ, R., & LEONARD, L. (1982). Do children pick and choose? Phonological selection and avoidance in early lexical acquisition. *Journal of Child Language, 9,* 319–336.

SCHWARTZ, R., LEONARD, L., FOLGER, K., & WILCOX, M. J. (1980). Evidence for a synergistic view of language disorders. *Journal of Speech and Hearing Disorders, 45,* 357–377.

SHRIBERG, L., KWIATKOWSKI, J., BEST, S., HENGST, J., & TERSELIC-WEBER, B. (1986). Characteristics of children with phonological disorders of unknown origin. *Journal of Speech and Hearing Disorders, 51,* 140–160.

SHRINER, T., HOLLOWAY, M., & DANILOFF, R. (1969). The relationship between articulatory deficits and syntax in speech deficient children. *Journal of Speech and Hearing Research, 12,* 319–325.

SIEGEL, G., & SPRADLIN, J. E. (1985). Therapy and research. *Journal of Speech and Hearing Disorders, 50,* 226–230.

SKINNER, B. F. (1979, May). *The role of the contrived reinforcer.* Paper presented at the tenth annual Southern California Behavior Modification Conference, Los Angeles.

SLOBIN, D. (1973). Cognitive prerequisites for the acquisition of grammar. In C. Ferguson & D. Slobin (Eds.), *Studies of child language development* (pp. 175–208). New York: Holt, Rinehart, & Winston.

STOEL-GAMMON, C. (1983, November). *Variations of style in mother's speech to young children.* Paper presented at the annual convention of the American Speech-Language-Hearing Association, Cincinnati.

STOEL-GAMMON, C., & DUNN, C. (1986). *Normal and disordered phonology in children.* Austin, TX: PRO-ED.

STRICKLAND, D. (1988). Reading, writing and oral language. *Reading Teacher, 42,* 240–241.

TEALE, W. (1986). Home background and young children's literacy development. In W. Teale & E. Sulzby (Eds.), *Emergent literacy: Writing and reading* (pp. 173–206). Norwood, NJ: Ablex.

VALDEZ-MENCHACA, M. C., & WHITEHURST, G. J. (1988). What is the role of reinforcement in early language acquisition? *Child Development, 59,* 1451–1459.

VANKLEEK, A. (1990). Emergent literacy: Learning about print before learning to read. *Topics in Language Disorders, 10,* 25–45.

WARREN, S. F. (1988). A behavioral approach to language generalization. *Language, Speech, and Hearing Services in Schools, 19,* 292–303.

WARREN, S. F., & KAISER, A. (1986). Incidental language teaching. A critical review. *Journal of Speech and Hearing Disorders, 51,* 291–299.

WARREN, S. F., McQUARTER, R., & ROGERS-WARREN, A. (1984). The effects of mands and models on the speech of unresponsive language-delayed preschool children. *Journal of Speech and Hearing Disorders, 49,* 43–52.

WARREN, S. F., & REICHLE, J. (1992). The emerging field of communication and language intervention. In S. F. Warren & J. Reichle (Eds.), *Causes and effects in communication and language intervention* (pp. 1–8). Baltimore: Brookes.

WEINER, F. (1981). Treatment of phonological disability using the method of minimal contrast: Two case studies. *Journal of Speech and Hearing Disorders, 46,* 97–103.

WILLIAMS, J. A., KOEGEL, R. L., & EGEL, A L. (1981). Response-reinforcer relationships and improved learning in autistic children. *Journal of Applied Behavior Analysis, 14,* 53–60.

CHAPTER 10

Aggression and Noncompliance: Behavior Modification

Debra Farrar-Schneider

LOUISIANA STATE UNIVERSITY

Disruptive behaviors, including aggression and noncompliance, are common characteristics of autistic and developmentally disabled individuals and usually preface long-term negative outcomes (Durand & Carr, 1989; Lovaas, 1987; Schreibman, 1988). Aggression and noncompliance have been variously defined, but they usually have several behaviors in common, which (a) interfere with the development/expression of adaptive behaviors, (b) may represent a danger to others, and (c) often result in restrictions from educational, residential, and vocational programs (Gardner & Cole, 1990). Autistic and mentally retarded individuals with conduct difficulties are also more likely to be institutionalized than persons who do not demonstrate these traits (Gardner & Cole, 1990). For these reasons, it is important to use effective treatments with autistic individuals to ensure that they may reach their full potential in relevant areas.

Initially, treatment for autism was based on psychoanalytic theory, which suggested that autism was a result of parental psychopathology. Traditional psychotherapy has not proven useful, however (Durand & Carr, 1989; Lovaas, 1987; Schreibman, 1988). In addition, few methodologically sound studies have found pharmacological therapy—another treatment approach—to be effectual (Schreibman, 1988).

Over the past 30 years, empirically validated behavioral interventions have become the treatment of choice (Durand & Carr, 1989; Harris, 1988). Behavioral treatments are based on the premise that the disorder is made up of specific behaviors and that these behaviors should be treated rather than the "disease" itself (Schreibman, 1988). Thus, individual aberrant behaviors are the targets of treatment.

Behavior modification serves to reduce inappropriate behaviors, while increasing low-incidence appropriate behaviors, and usually involves three steps (Schreibman, 1988). First, target behaviors are defined. Second, these behaviors are reliably measured. Third, treatment interventions are devised and executed.

Several methods of behavior modification have been studied with autistic and developmentally disabled individuals (see Table 10.1). The purpose of this chapter is to describe and exemplify empirical-

Table 10.1 Breakdown of Studies by Treatment and Target Behaviors

Type of Intervention and Authors	Target Behaviors
Differential Reinforcement	
Frankel, Moss, Schofield, & Simmons (1976)	Biting, pinching, hair-pulling
Luiselli & Slocumb (1983)	Hitting, kicking, hair-pulling, spitting, screaming
Smith (1985)	Hitting, kicking
Smith & Coleman (1986)	Hitting, destroying property
Exercise	
Allison, Basile, & MacDonald (1991)	Hitting, kicking, biting, scratching, grabbing
Luce, Delquadri, & Hall (1980)	Hitting, kicking, choking, pushing
Extinction	
Carr, Newsom, & Binkoff (1980)	Hitting, kicking, biting, scratching
Relaxation Therapy	
Hughes & Davis (1980)	Hitting, cursing, destroying property
Response Cost	
Woods (1982)	Hitting, kicking, biting, destroying property
Restraint	
Luiselli, Suskin, & Slocumb (1984)	Hitting, kicking, grabbing
Friman, Barnard, Altman, & Wolf (1986)	Pinching
Matson & Keyes (1988)	Hitting, kicking, biting, destroying property, scratching, hair-pulling, pushing
Van Houten & Rolider (1988)	Biting, stomping
Sensory Aversions	
Doke, Wolery, & Sumberg (1983)	Hitting, kicking, pushing, pinching, destroying property, scratching, hair-pulling, spitting, screaming, noncompliance
Fleece, O'Brien, & Drabman (1982)	Biting
St. Lawrence & Drabman (1984)	Spitting
Overcorrection	
Foxx & Azrin (1972)	Biting, destroying property, scratching
Hung, Cosentino, & Henderson (1979)	Noncompliance
Luiselli (1984)	Hitting, grabbing, hair-pulling
Stimulus-Control Procedures	
Carr, Newsom, & Binkoff (1980)	Hitting, kicking, biting, scratching, pinching, hair-pulling
Charlop, Burgio, Iwata, & Ivancic (1988)	Hitting, biting, pinching, hair-pulling, destroying property
Dyer, Dunlap, & Winterling (1990)	Hitting, kicking, biting, pinching, scratching, destroying property
Touchette, MacDonald, & Langer (1985)	Hitting, kicking, destroying property
Winterling, Dunlap, & O'Neill (1987)	Hitting, kicking, biting, scratching, hair-pulling, grabbing, destroying property
Teaching Alternative Behaviors	
Carr, Newsom, & Binkoff (1980)	Hitting, kicking, biting, scratching
Wacker et al. (1990)	Hitting, biting
Time-out	
Luiselli, Myles, & Littman-Quinn (1983)	Hitting, scratching, destroying property
Nordquist & Wahler (1973)	Screaming, noncompliance

ly validated techniques designed to eliminate or reduce aggression and noncompliance in autistic children and adults. Such procedures include extinction, differential reinforcement of other behavior, exercise, overcorrection, response cost, restraint, sensory aversions, time-out, relaxation therapy, stimulus-control procedures, and teaching alternative behaviors. While this review is not exhaustive, it should give the reader a basic understanding of the use of behavior modification with autistic individuals for treatment of noncompliance and aggression.

Extinction

Extinction is a commonly employed intervention for eliminating aggression or noncompliance (Schreibman, 1988). This approach entails contingent removal or minimization of a response that has been shown to reinforce the disruptive behavior. Frequently, social attention is the reinforcing consequence of belligerent behavior; consequently, its removal can eliminate aggressive or noncompliant behavior (Gardner & Cole, 1990; Schreibman, 1988).

Carr, Newsom, and Binkoff (1980) studied the effects of extinction on aggression in a mentally retarded boy with autistic characteristics. The child was placed in demand situations from which he could not escape by exhibiting aggressive behaviors. As expected with extinction procedures, aggression first escalated before declining to a near-zero level. The procedure was so effective that demands on the child were increased without a concomitant rise in aggression.

Although extinction has proven effective, it is not always possible or desirable to ignore inappropriate behavior. Since this procedure often results in an increase in targeted behaviors (i.e., extinction burst) before a decrease occurs, severe or dangerous behaviors often require a more active treatment procedure. Several other interventions have been shown to produce dramatic, rapid effects.

Differential Reinforcement

Differential reinforcement typically involves providing reinforcement if an individual does not display aberrant target behaviors for a specified time interval (Gardner & Cole, 1990). The occurrence of the target behavior or the delivery of reinforcement results in restarting the time period. The behaviors that must be demonstrated to obtain reinforcement may be (a) any behaviors not addressed by the intervention (i.e., differential reinforcement of other behavior), (b) a specific behavior that competes with the target behavior (i.e., differential reinforcement of incompatible behavior), or (c) target behavior levels lower than those seen in baseline (i.e., differential reinforcement of low rates of behavior).

Differential reinforcement of other behavior (DRO) was used to control multiple forms of aggression in a 9-year-old autistic female (Luiselli & Slocumb, 1983). Although baseline conditions included using restraint, the child continued to exhibit high levels of aggressive behavior until a DRO procedure was added. The procedure consisted of furnishing praise and a favorite edible at the end of intervals in which the child did not display aggression. This procedure resulted in a significant decline in aggression, which had been maintained at a 34-week follow-up.

Another study found two forms of time-out to be ineffective in decreasing the aggression of a mentally retarded female with autistic behaviors (Frankel, Moss, Schofield, & Simmons, 1976). In fact, aggression continued to occur an average of 5 to 12 times during baseline and time-out conditions. However, when a DRO procedure (i.e., reinforcing appropriate behavior with praise and candy every 5 seconds) was executed, daily rates of aggression were rapidly reduced to an average of 1.17.

Smith (1985) used differential reinforcement to treat aggression in two autistic adults living in group homes. One client was rewarded with favorite foods, drinks, activities, or staff attention when he was not engaged in aggressive or stealing behavior; the other client was rewarded with physical proximity to staff and food when not displaying aggressive and self-injurious behaviors. This procedure successfully decreased the number of aggressive incidents to almost zero for both participants. This decline was subsequently associated with improvements in home and work tasks, as well as trips outside the home.

Differential reinforcement was also used to treat aggressive and off-task behaviors in a 26-year-old autistic male (Smith & Coleman, 1986). The subject was able to earn points for appropriate work behaviors, which, in turn, could be used to obtain attention from favorite staff members. The mean number of points the individual acquired increased by 20 upon implementation of treatment. Tantrums interfering with work productivity were treated in two other autistic males using comparable procedures, with similar results.

Available research suggests that differential reinforcement is an effective treatment for aggression and noncompliance. Thus, common reinforcers, such as preferred edibles, praise, and staff attention, have reliably reduced disruptive behaviors. However, reinforcement alone is not always effective and, therefore, is often used in conjunction with punishment. Exercise, overcorrection, response cost, restraint, sensory aversions and time-out are forms of punishments that have been used to treat problematic behaviors.

Exercise

To decrease aberrant behaviors, vigorous physical exercise may be used contingently or noncontingently (Harris, 1988). Contingent exercise entails having the individual engage in physical activity for a time interval after each occurrence of an unwanted behavior, whereas noncontingent, or antecedent, exercise requires the individual to participate in intense exercise prior to entering situations in which difficulties are likely to occur. Both contingent and noncontingent exercise have proven effective in decreasing noncompliance and aggression.

For example, contingent exercise was used to suppress aggressive behavior in two developmen-

tally delayed children who exhibited autistic behaviors (Luce, Delquadri, & Hall, 1980). Each child was required to stand up and sit down 10 times for every episode of aggression. In both subjects, rapid reductions in extremely high aggression levels were noted during contingent exercise conditions. However, aggressive responding rose during returns to baseline conditions. Contingent exercise was also found to be more effective than DRO.

Allison, Basile, and MacDonald (1991) used antecedent exercise to decrease an autistic adult's aggressive behaviors. The antecedent exercise consisted of having the male subject jog 20 minutes each afternoon. This intervention produced significantly lower levels of aggression than no treatment or pharmacological therapy alone. Additionally, an exercise-plus-medication intervention decreased aggression, but to a lesser extent than exercise alone.

Overcorrection

Overcorrection generally consists of two components: restitution and positive practice (Schreibman, 1988). Restitution requires the individual to restore the environment to a state equal to or better than it was before the aberrant behavior (e.g., cleaning a work area that he or she messed up). In positive practice, the individual overtly practices correct forms of behavior in situations in which problems usually occur (e.g., cleaning up other work areas). Many studies utilize only one of these elements, while others employ routines that are not topographically similar. Often the procedures require graduated guidance (i.e., application of physical guidance only in the amount required by the individual's resistance).

Foxx and Azrin (1972) treated two profoundly mentally retarded females' aggression with overcorrection, using both restitution and positive practice. For example, when one client threw objects, she was required to return all of the thrown objects to their original state and straighten other objects in the residential facility. The other client was given oral hygiene training (i.e., teeth brushed with oral antiseptic) for biting. An apology to everyone in the area was also required for both clients. These overcorrection procedures resulted in reductions to zero for both target behaviors.

Luiselli (1984) achieved similar results using a form of overcorrection that was not topographically similar to the target behavior. Two developmentally delayed children who exhibited aggression had to participate in arm exercises for 30 seconds every time they hit or grabbed someone. The arm exercises consisted of moving the child's arms above the head, to the side, and to the front. In addition, social praise was delivered periodically when the children were not engaging in aggression. Significant reductions in aggression were obtained with this intervention.

Noncompliance in autistic children was addressed using mild overcorrection procedures in a study by Hung, Cosentino, and Henderson (1979). Four subjects were partially or completely physically guided to comply each time the teacher gave verbal instructions. Guidance was provided either slowly and gently or quickly and firmly. While most of the children demonstrated improvements when slow, gentle guidance was used, responding was not consistent. However, stable gains in compliance were achieved when quick and firm guidance was used. These findings reveal that one positive practice trial may be effective in gaining compliance with autistic children, provided that the physical guidance is firm and abrupt.

Response Cost

Response cost is another punishment procedure, which decreases aggression by removing positive reinforcement following its occurrence (Gardner & Cole, 1988; Woods, 1982). Typically, response cost involves the loss of something the individual has earned (e.g., privileges, points, or tokens). It has been suggested that repeated use of response cost may reduce an individual's motivation to

behave appropriately, but this has not been demonstrated in the available research with autistic individuals (Gardner & Cole, 1988; Woods, 1982).

Woods (1982) targeted aggressive and self-injurious behaviors in an autistic adolescent boy by training his mother and siblings how to use response cost. At the beginning of each day, the subject's family would attach a certain number of "treat" tickets to the refrigerator door. One ticket was removed each time the subject emitted a target behavior. If any tickets were left at the end of the day, he was allowed to trade them for a socially reinforcing event (e.g., baking cookies with his mother, listening to the radio an extra 15 minutes). Over time, the number of tickets on the refrigerator was reduced to three as target behaviors were successfully diminished. However, these gains were not maintained when the treatment was withdrawn. While not clearly illustrating the long-term value of response cost, these results do suggest that it may be an efficient way to decrease noncompliance and aggression.

Restraint

A more intrusive intervention frequently used to reduce troublesome behaviors is brief contingent physical restraint (Harris, 1988). Specifically, parts of the individual's body may be restricted from movement by a therapist or a mechanical device when the inappropriate behavior is exhibited. Several variations of physical restraint have been employed. The most common approach requires that the subject's hands be held by his or her sides for a period of time (i.e., immobilization time-out). Another common restraint method is movement suppression, which involves guiding the individual to a corner, placing his or her chin into the corner, crossing the hands behind his or her back, and placing the feet close together touching the wall (Van Houten & Rolider, 1988). In both procedures, the amount of force used is only that necessary to keep the individual in place (Luiselli, Suskin, & Slocumb, 1984; Van Houten & Rolider, 1988).

The use of immobilization time-out decreased aggressive behavior in an autistic girl and a mentally retarded boy (Luiselli, Suskin, & Slocumb, 1984). Time-out consisted of having the child sit in a chair while a teacher held his or her hands by the sides with the minimal amount of guidance required to keep them there. This procedure was applied contingently upon exhibition of tantrum and aggressive behaviors. When used in conjunction with DRO, immobilization time-out was more effective than DRO alone, and gains were maintained at 4-month follow-ups.

Friman, Barnard, Altman, and Wolf (1986) also used immobilization to treat a severely retarded girl who was nonverbal, resistant to social interactions, and aggressive. The child's mother and teacher were trained to intervene using DRO, DRO in combination with time-out, or DRO in combination with restraint. DRO combined with restraint, which consisted of reinforcing nonaggressive behavior every 12–15 seconds and holding the girl's hands motionless for 2 minutes each time she pinched, was the most effective treatment. The intervention that included restraint resulted in reduction of aggressive behaviors to near zero, which was maintained at 3- and 15-month follow-ups.

Matson and Keyes (1988) treated aggression in an autistic male using mechanical restraint. The baseline condition consisted of using pharmacotherapy, planned activities, and DRO, while the treatment condition combined those procedures with a 15-minute restraint period. It was only during employment of contingent restraint that aggression decreased to an acceptable level (baseline level of 30–80 episodes, treatment level of 6 episodes). Physical restraint also produced similar results in two mentally retarded females who exhibited aggressive behaviors.

An innovative approach to movement suppression time-out that allowed discipline to be delayed was used by Van Houten and Rolider (1988) to treat aggression in an autistic child. When a baseline condition of a reprimand and chair time-out was found not to be successful at erasing this behavior, a new treatment was implemented. This intervention involved re-creating the situation in which aggression occurred and placing the child in movement suppression time-out for 1 minute. Use of this procedure quickly eliminated aggressive behaviors. Thus, physical restraint has repeatedly been proven successful in reducing aggression.

Sensory Aversions

Several studies have demonstrated that contingent application of unpleasant stimuli involving the senses can be effective in treating aggression (Gardner & Cole, 1988). As with overcorrection, the aversive stimuli employed are often topographically similar to the aggressive target behavior. Treatments include aversive tastes (e.g., application of a distasteful substance, such as Tabasco sauce, to the individual's lips or tongue), noxious smells (e.g., exposure to ammonia under the nose), loud noises (e.g., presentation of intense sound, such as a clap), and visual/facial screening (e.g., covering of eyes or face with hands or a bib). Although little research is available on specific use of sensory aversions, the effectiveness of these procedures with autistic individuals is expected to correspond to effects seen in developmentally disabled persons.

Aggression was suppressed in a developmentally disabled preschool child using an aversive taste (Fleece, O'Brien, & Drabman, 1982). Upon each biting attempt or incident, a solution of mouthwash and water was squeezed into the subject's mouth. The frequency of attempted bites dropped significantly after treatment was initiated. Further, gains were maintained at a 10-month follow-up, suggesting that distasteful liquids may be successful in treating aggression.

Similarly, Doke, Wolery, and Sumberg (1983) used a noxious odor to treat aggression in a mentally retarded 7-year-old. Observations and treatment took place in a daily 30-minute session, during which the boy was expected to participate in learning tasks. Each time the child exhibited an aggressive response, a vial of ammonia was placed under his nose until he took a breath. While not directly intervened upon, inappropriate vocalizations and participation (compliance) were also monitored. Aggression was significantly reduced during treatment conditions, but high levels resumed during a return to baseline. Analogous changes in noncompliance and inappropriate vocalizations were observed, implying that the treatment generalized across behaviors. Behaviors remained improved at a 14-month follow-up, even though the ammonia treatment had been withdrawn. The aggressive behaviors observed in autistic individuals may be similar to those seen in mentally retarded individuals, so this intervention should be useful with autistic individuals as well.

Facial screening was effective in extinguishing aggressive spitting in a severely handicapped adolescent (St. Lawrence & Drabman, 1984). Upon each instance of spitting, the child's mouth and eyes were covered loosely with a towel, which remained in place until 4 seconds had elapsed without a spit. This method was found to be even more effective when it was combined with a DRO procedure that provided an edible reward approximately every 4 seconds if the target behavior was absent. Increased social attention from teachers followed the decrease in aggression, and teacher reports after 1 year revealed that positive results had been preserved.

Time-Out

In time-out, an individual is removed from access to the opportunity for reinforcement contingently after the occurrence of a targeted response (Schreibman, 1988). The duration of time-out varies from 2 minutes to 3 hours, but most research has used intervals of 5 to 20 minutes (Schreibman, 1988). With this intervention, it is important to ensure that the environment outside the time-out setting is more reinforcing than that of the time-out. For example, if an individual is placed in time-out for not complying with an instruction and time-out consists of an environment in which no demands are being placed on the individual, it is likely that he or she might find the time-out condition more reinforcing than the "time-in" situation.

Nordquist and Wahler (1973) used time-out to alter the behavior of an autistic child. Targeted responses included noncompliance, screaming, and ritualistic behaviors. Contingent upon the occurrence of these behaviors, the child was placed in his room for 10 minutes. While ritualistic behavior improved, noncompliance and screaming were only minimally affected. When a reinforcer more tangible than parental attention was offered for appropriate behaviors in addition to continued use of the time-out for inappropriate behaviors, stable reductions were seen in noncompliance and screaming. This demonstrates the importance of having a reinforcing environment outside of time-out situations.

Time-out and reinforcement eliminated aggression in a 15-year-old mentally retarded male, after reinforcement alone had failed to do so (Luiselli, Myles, & Littman-Quinn, 1983). Time-out consisted of placing the subject in a small room for 3 minutes upon each instance of aggression. Tokens, which could be accumulated and exchanged for preferred items and activities, were distributed as reinforcers for the absence of aggression during time intervals. This intervention package was first implemented at school, but treatment effects did not generalize across settings. It was not until the treatment was implemented at home that these results generalized.

Relaxation Therapy

Electromyographic (EMG) biofeedback has been used to encourage control of disruptive and aggressive behaviors (Hughes & Davis, 1980). The EMG system monitors muscle tension levels and relays that information to the subject. Typically, a baseline for aggressive and nonaggressive conditions is established without providing feedback to the subject (phase 1), after which the subject is trained to lower his muscle tension levels using the audio feedback (phase 2). The subject must then learn to lower the tone of the audio feedback when it is presented intermittently (phase 3) and after responses (phase 4).

Hughes and Davis (1980) used EMG biofeedback to decrease the frequency of verbally and physically aggressive responses in a high-functioning autistic adult. Under several conditions, the man was reinforced with praise and pennies for exhibiting relaxed responses based on feedback. A significant reduction in the number of aggressive responses was observed during the intervention. However, during a return to baseline, the subject resumed high levels of aggression. These modifications in aggressive responses corresponded with changes in muscle tension levels.

Stimulus-Control Procedures

Frequently, stimuli are identified as consistently associated with noncompliance or aggression. Stimulus-control procedures eliminate or rearrange those stimuli (Durand & Carr, 1989). Situations in which demands are high have been demonstrated to elicit problem behaviors in autistic children (Carr et al., 1980). However, Carr et al. demonstrated that aggressive acts by an autistic boy could be decreased during demand situations if positive reinforcers, such as toys and food, were available.

Touchette, MacDonald, and Langer (1985) used scatter plots to identify the frequency and time of aggressive incidents in autistic individuals. One adolescent exhibited aggression primarily in the afternoons, when demands were placed on her in group activities. To treat this behavior, her afternoon activity schedule was revised to resemble times in which aggression was unlikely. Assaultive behavior was reduced; in addition, components of the original program were gradually reintroduced into her afternoon schedule without a recurrence of problem behaviors.

Similar to the differences in behavior seen when demand situations change, manipulation of choice has also been shown to alter aggression levels (Dyer, Dunlap, & Winterling, 1990). For example, the aggressive behaviors of two children with autism and mental retardation were measured in two conditions: choice and no-choice. In the choice condition, the child was allowed to select tasks in which to participate as well as reinforcers he or she wished to obtain after earning a reward. The same tasks and reinforcers were available in the no-choice condition, but here the teacher determined their distribution. Both subjects, for whom aggression was considered to be a severe problem, evinced significant decreases in aggressive behavior in the choice condition.

Varying instructional tasks has resulted in fewer aberrant behaviors, including aggression, than has repeated presentation of one educational task (Winterling, Dunlap, & O'Neill, 1987). Two autistic children, who exhibited some form of aggression and out-of-seat behavior, showed declines in target behaviors when five individual tasks were taught, rather than continuous presentation of one task. Furthermore, an autistic adult's deviant behavior was lessened using varied assignments, providing evidence that these results may generalize to all ages.

Charlop, Burgio, Iwata, and Ivancic (1988) carried the variation idea a step further. These authors compared the effects of varied punishers (i.e., reprimand, overcorrection, loud noise, and time-out) to the presentation of a single punisher. Three children with developmental delays and aggressive behavior, two of whom were diagnosed as autistic, served as subjects. While both conditions significantly decreased inappropriate behavior, the use of various punishers resulted in greater modification.

The manipulation of stimuli that lead to inappropriate behaviors has been shown to have therapeutic value. However, it is not always possible to alter or eliminate such stimuli. For instance, demands cannot and should not always be withdrawn. Another treatment option involves identifying the function of the inappropriate behavior and replacing it with a more appropriate behavior.

Teaching Alternative Behaviors

As mentioned, one approach to dealing with problematic behaviors is to teach the individual an alternative behavior that serves the same purpose as the undesirable behavior (Durand & Carr, 1989). This method of dealing with aggressive or noncompliant behaviors relies heavily on conducting a functional analysis of behavior, which identifies the factors that maintain the inappropriate behavior. O'Neill, Horner, Albin, Storey, and Sprague (1990) describe this process in detail. When it is determined what function the behavior serves, the objective is to replace it with an equivalent behavior.

Frequently, it is determined that an individual who is noncommunicative exhibits aggressive behaviors to communicate needs and wants. In these cases, a subject may be taught some form of verbal communication or sign language to replace aggressive or noncompliant behavior (e.g., Wacker et al., 1990). This is the subject of Chapter 9 (Koegel, Camarata, & Koegel, in press) of this book.

Nonverbal behaviors may also be taught. Carr et al. (1980) placed an autistic child in demand situations in which he was known to exhibit frequent aggression. It was determined that this behavior was probably functional in communicating his desire to escape the demands being placed upon him. When escape was prevented during aggression but allowed if the boy tapped a finger on the back of his hand, aggressive responses were reduced. This example demonstrates how training a more appropriate behavior that is functionally equivalent to the aggressive response may decrease inappropriate responses (Durand & Carr, 1989).

New Developments and Future Trends

Behavior modification is not new in the treatment of aggression and noncompliance in aggressive individuals. However, in recent years, the focus of research to reduce aggressive and noncompliant behavior has shifted from decelerative procedures to interventions aimed at manipulating antecedent conditions and teaching alternative behaviors to replace the disruptive behaviors (Gardner & Cole, 1990). This move is due to a number of factors, including increased attention to conducting functional analyses, the controversy over the use of aversives, and attempts to develop less intrusive treatments. Nevertheless, the contribution of aversive techniques should not be ignored, especially when necessary for dealing with severe or life-threatening behaviors (Matson & Keyes, 1988).

Generalization is another issue to be addressed in behavioral research. While the literature in this area is replete with case studies, future research should expand the number of replications and subjects (Franks, 1984). Furthermore, generalization across behaviors and situations should be assessed. Several projects combine aggression toward others and self-injury. Separating these behaviors would clarify and extend the data. School and work settings are also important areas to evaluate, as the bulk of research has taken place in residential settings.

Social validation has also become another important topic related to behavior modification. All reported studies provide evidence that behavioral procedures significantly diminish problematic behavior. However, "clinical" significance is rarely, if ever, assessed (Allison et al., 1991; Franks, 1984). Staff views on the effectiveness of interventions are essential to determine their practical relevance and, therefore, should be incorporated into future research projects.

Finally, other areas that are likely to receive attention in future investigations with autistic individuals include social behaviors and occasions on which nonoccurrence of problematic behaviors is observed. Specifically, the effect of training social behaviors on aggression and noncompliance in autism has not been adequately assessed (Franks, 1984). Also, as Touchette et al. (1985) suggested, assessing the periods when problematic behaviors are not occurring can be useful in designing behavioral interventions. Both of these domains deserve considerable study.

Summary and Conclusions

Psychoanalytic therapy, in particular, and pharmaco-therapy to a lesser degree have not been established as valuable tools for treating aggression and non-compliance in autistic individuals (Durand & Carr, 1989; Matson & Keyes, 1988; Schreibman, 1988). Behavior modification, however, has shown considerable promise in this area. Extinction, differential reinforcement, exercise, overcorrec-tion, sensory aversions, response cost, restraint, time-out, relaxation therapy, stimulus-control procedures, and teaching alternative behaviors have been proven to be successful interventions and should continue to be examined.

Finding effective and practical treatments for aggression and noncompliance is critical because of the problems these behaviors cause for autistic individuals by interfering with adaptive functioning in several areas, including education and vocation (Gardner & Cole, 1990). Noncom-pliance is discussed jointly with aggression in this chapter because the literature on treatment of noncompliance alone is sparse. However, the treatment methods that are effective with aggres-sion can likely be generalized to noncompliance, although that assumption must be borne out in research.

Future research should address the generaliza-tion of treatments used to extinguish other inap-propriate behaviors, as well as interventions employed with other populations. Representative research conducted with mentally retarded indivi-duals has been included in this chapter because they share many characteristics with autistic individuals. However, replications demonstrating the effective-ness of these treatments with autistic populations are necessary before definite conclusions can be drawn. Thus, although there is an expansive literature on the behavioral treatment of aggres-sion and noncompliance in individuals with autism, much more research needs to be done in this area.

References

ALLISON, D. B., BASILE, V. C., & MacDONALD, R. B. (1991). Brief report: Comparative effects of antecedent exercise and Lorazepam on the aggressive behavior of an autistic man. *Journal of Autism and Developmental Disorders, 21,* 89–94.

CARR, E. G., NEWSOM, C. D., & BINKOFF, J. A. (1980). Escape as a factor in the aggressive behavior of two retarded children. *Journal of Applied Behavior Analysis, 13,* 101–117.

CHARLOP, M. H., BURGIO, L. D., IWATA, B. A., & IVANCIC, M. T. (1988). Stimulus variation as a means of enhancing punishment effects. *Journal of Applied Behavior Analysis, 21,* 89–95.

DOKE, L., WOLERY, M., & SUMBERG, C. (1983). Treating chronic aggression: Effects and side effects of response-contingent ammonia spirits. *Behavior Modification, 7,* 531–556.

DURAND, V. M., & CARR, E. G. (1989). Operant learning methods with chronic schizophrenia and autism: Aberrant behavior. In J. L. Matson (Ed.), *Chronic schizophrenia and adult autism: Issues in diagnosis, assessment, and psychological treatment* (pp. 231–273). New York: Springer.

DYER, K., DUNLAP, G., & WINTERLING, V. (1990). Effects of choice making on the serious problem behaviors of students with severe handicaps. *Journal of Applied Behavior Analysis, 23,* 515–524.

FLEECE, L., O'BRIEN, T., & DRABMAN, R. (1982). Suppression of biting behavior via contingent application of an aversive tasting liquid. *Journal of Clinical Child Psychology, 11,* 163–166.

FOXX, R. M., & AZRIN, N. H. (1972). Restitution: A method of eliminating aggressive-disruptive behavior of retarded and brain damaged patients. *Behavior Research and Therapy, 10,* 15–27.

FRANKEL, F., MOSS, D., SCHOFIELD, S., & SIMMONS, J. Q. (1976). Case study: Use of differential reinforcement to suppress self-injurious and aggressive behavior. *Psychological Reports, 39,* 843–849.

FRANKS, C. M. (1984). Behavior therapy with children and adolescents. In C. M. Franks, G. T. Wilson, P. C. Kendall, & K. D. Brownell, *Annual review of behavior therapy: Volume 10* (pp. 236–290). New York: Guilford.

FRIMAN, P. C., BARNARD, J. D., ALTMAN, K., & WOLF, M. M. (1986). Parent and teacher use of DRO and DRI to reduce aggressive behavior. *Analysis and Intervention in Developmental Disabilities, 6,* 319–330.

GARDNER, W. I., & COLE, C. L. (1988). Conduct disorders: Psychological therapies. In J. L. Matson (Ed.), *Handbook of treatment approaches in childhood psychopathology* (pp. 163–194). New York: Plenum.

GARDNER, W. I., & COLE, C. L. (1990). Aggression and related conduct difficulties. In J. L. Matson (Ed.), *Handbook of behavior modification with the mentally retarded* (pp. 225–251). New York: Plenum.

HARRIS, S. L. (1988). Infantile autism and childhood schizophrenia: Psychological therapies. In J. L. Matson (Ed.), *Handbook of treatment approaches in childhood psychopathology* (pp. 279–300). New York: Plenum.

HUGHES, H., & DAVIS, R. (1980). Treatment of aggressive behavior: The effect of EMG response discrimination biofeedback training. *Journal of Autism and Developmental Disorders, 10,* 193–202.

HUNG, D. W., COSENTINO, A., & HENDERSON, E. (1979). Teaching autistic children to follow instructions in a group by a firm physical prompting procedure. *Journal of Behavior Therapy and Experimental Psychiatry, 10,* 329–338.

KOEGEL, R. L., CAMARATA, S. M., & KOEGEL, L. K. (in press). Aggression and noncompliance: Behavior modification through naturalistic language remediation. In J. L. Matson (Ed.), *Autism in children and adults: Etiology, assessment, and intervention.* Sycamore, IL: Sycamore.

LOVAAS, O. I. (1987). Behavioral treatment and normal educational and intellectual functioning in young autistic children. *Journal of Consulting and Clinical Psychology, 55,* 3–9.

LUCE, S. C., DELQUADRI, J., & HALL, R. V. (1980). Contingent exercise: A mild but powerful procedure for suppressing inappropriate verbal and aggressive behavior. *Journal of Applied Behavior Analysis, 13,* 583–594.

LUISELLI, J. K. (1984). Therapeutic effects of brief contingent effort on severe behavior disorders in children with developmental disabilities. *Journal of Clinical Child Psychology, 13,* 257–262.

LUISELLI, J. K., MYLES, E., & LITTMAN-QUINN, J. (1983). Analysis of a reinforcement/time-out treatment package to control severe aggressive and destructive behaviors in a multihandicapped rubella child. *Applied Research in Mental Retardation, 4,* 65–78.

LUISELLI, J. K., & SLOCUMB, P. R. (1983). Management of multiple aggressive behaviors by differential reinforcement. *Journal of Behavior Therapy and Experimental Psychiatry, 14,* 343–347.

LUISELLI, J. K., SUSKIN, L., & SLOCUMB, P. R. (1984). Application of immobilization time-out in management programming with developmentally disabled children. *Child and Family Behavior Therapy, 6,* 1–15.

MATSON, J. L., & KEYES, J. (1988). Contingent reinforcement and contingent restraint to treat severe aggression and self-injury in mentally retarded and autistic adults. *Journal of the Multihandicapped Person, 1,* 141–153.

NORDQUIST, V. M., & WAHLER, R. G. (1973). Naturalistic treatment of an autistic child. *Journal of Applied Behavior Analysis, 6,* 79–87.

O'NEILL, R. E., HORNER, R. H., ALBIN, R. W., STOREY, K., & SPRAGUE, J. R. (1990). *Functional analysis of problem behavior: A practical assessment guide.* Sycamore, IL: Sycamore.

ST. LAWRENCE, J. S., & DRABMAN, R. S. (1984). Case study: Suppression of chronic high frequency spitting in a multiply handicapped and mentally retarded adolescent. *Child and Family Behavior Therapy, 6,* 45–55.

SCHREIBMAN, L. E. (1988). *Autism.* Newbury Park, CA: Sage.

SMITH, M. D. (1985). Brief report: Managing the aggressive and self-injurious behavior of adults disabled by autism. *Association for Persons with Severe Handicaps Journal, 10,* 228-232.

SMITH, M. D., & COLEMAN, D. (1986). Managing the behavior of adults with autism in the job setting. *Journal of Autism and Developmental Disorders, 16,* 145–154.

TOUCHETTE, P. E., MacDONALD, R. F., & LANGER, S. N. (1985). A scatter plot for identifying stimulus control of problem behavior. *Journal of Applied Behavior Analysis, 18,* 343–351.

VAN HOUTEN, R., & ROLIDER, A. (1988). Recreating the scene: An effective way to provide delayed punishment for inappropriate motor behavior. *Journal of Applied Behavior Analysis, 21,* 187–192.

WACKER, D. P., STEEGE, M. W., NORTHUP, J., SASSO, G., BERG, W., REIMERS, T., COOPER, L., CIGRAND, K., & DONN, L. (1990). A component analysis of functional communication training across three topographies of severe behavior problems. *Journal of Applied Behavior Analysis, 23,* 417–429.

WINTERLING, V., DUNLAP, G., & O'NEILL, R.E. (1987). The influence of task variation on the aberrant behaviors of autistic students. *Education and Treatment of Children, 10,* 105–119.

WOODS, T. S. (1982). Reducing severe aggressive and self-injurious behavior: A nonintrusive home based approach. *Behavioral Disorders, 7,* 180–188.

CHAPTER 11

Self-Help and Community Skills

CHAPTER 11

Self-Help and Community Skills

Phillip J. Belfiore
PURDUE UNIVERSITY
SCHOOL OF EDUCATION

F. Charles Mace
UNIVERSITY OF PENNSYLVANIA
SCHOOL OF MEDICINE

With assessment and instructional practices for persons with developmental disabilities moving away from clinics and classrooms and into the community, educators have begun to develop strategies to meet the needs identified in these settings. A life skills curriculum focuses on the education of learners with severe developmental disabilities that is specific to community and home environments. Curriculum areas in these settings are prioritized to include "core" learning, along with learning that promotes enrichment, expansion, extension, and flexibility.

Two principles are important for sound educational programs within a life skills curriculum. First, regardless of severity, persons with disabilities have the right to exert control in their lives, thereby affecting the community in which they live (Browder, 1991). To allow such an impact, the primary target of programming for persons with severe developmental disabilities should be more meaningful integration options, rather than simply an increase in the number of integration contacts.

Second, a functional curriculum of life skills should provide the underpinnings for assessment and assessment-driven instruction. Specifically, a life skills curriculum for community and home addresses educational programs in the areas of community-recreational, community-vocational, home economics, and personal maintenance. Within individual curriculum areas, routines may include clothing maintenance, library use, food preparation, bird-watching, using the company breakroom, and preparation of the work site. Routines within each curriculum area can be further defined into a sequence of subroutines or activities, such as washing machine use, circuit board manufacturing, bowling, bed-making, and 35mm photography. Finally, specific chains of skills (i.e., task analyses) are derived from the subroutines and activities. This type of curriculum gives instructors the flexibility to assess individual learners across common classes of functional skills designed from the content of the classroom curriculum.

One focus of this chapter is to encourage movement away from traditional assessment practice and toward addressing the assessment and instruction strategies for the learner with autism within the context of a life skills curriculum. Through the use of a life skills curriculum as the framework for educational practice, stress is placed not only on spatial inclusion of the individual with autism into society, but also on functional and adaptive participation in society as a contributing member. A second focus of this chapter is to show that by developing carefully planned assessment strategies that link assessment with curriculum and instruction, educators will be better able to implement, adapt, and expand self-help and community-based instruction. Finally, this chapter will examine future directions for community and self-help education for learners with autism based on increased self-sufficiency and flexibility.

Components of Educational Assessment

The development of specific components for conducting an educational assessment of life skills for learners with autism provides the educator with a framework on which to build an effective instructional plan. Three general components comprise an effective self-help and community assessment strategy: assessment prior to educational intervention, continued assessment during educational intervention, and data-based evaluation of continued assessment.

Assessment Prior to Educational Intervention

Developing a meaningful individual instructional plan begins with an educational assessment. Just as effective academic intervention uses a classroom academic curriculum (e.g., mathematics, language arts, and science) as the basis for assessment, assessment of life skills should incorporate the educational content from life skills curriculum areas. Steps of an initial assessment include (a) the identification of the person's current skills repertoire, (b) prioritization of mastered skills and skills to be learned, and (c) development of an individual education program (IEP).

Identification of skills repertoire prior to educational intervention. Through a determination based on direct observation, interviews, and surveys of skills mastered or not mastered and preferred or not preferred, the initial assessment becomes more focused on the individual learner. The outcome of the initial assessment allows prioritization of skills that can be incorporated into an IEP.

A first step in identifying potential target skills for instruction is to conduct preference assessments. Preference assessments provide the instructor with an array of skills and activities identified as important in various sources. Primary care-givers, friends, therapists, mainstreaming teachers, and the learner all provide valuable information that will assist the instructor in prioritizing skills to be targeted for instruction. Therapists and teachers responsible for student mainstreaming also can provide information on what skills are preferred in other educational settings. Because caregivers constitute an integral component of the educational program, their input is crucial from the onset of assessment (Haracopos, 1989).

Information on learner preferences may be obtained through written feedback to caregiver questionnaires (see Figure 11.1). Such a questionnaire provides valuable information in addition to that from learner preference instruments and assessments. It can be sent home with the learner to be completed, conducted in person with teacher and caregiver(s), or completed through interviews over the telephone. This instrument provides a mechanism for caregivers to voice their position regarding their son's or daughter's current and future educational plan.

Learner preferences may be the most important part of the information gathered during preference assessments. For learners who are nonverbal or limited in their expressive language, preference information may be obtained through direct observation of stimuli presentation (Mason, McGee, Farmer-Dougan, & Risley, 1989) and movement across various settings (Belfiore, 1990). Preference information can also be obtained through interviews with past teachers, siblings, and friends. However, "other person–identified" information regarding the learner's preferences is not as valid a

Learner's Name_____   Date_____

Instructor_____

Caregiver_____

This questionnaire will assist us in planning the individual education program for this learner. Please take five minutes to respond to each question. We thank you in advance for helping us plan the education program for this learner.

1. What progress has the learner made that you hope this program will maintain?

2. What skills and activities do you think are especially important for the learner's continuing education in each of the following areas?

   a. Personal maintenance
   b. Home economics
   c. Community-recreational
   d. Community-vocational

3. Please list any educational programs currently conducted at home that you think should be included in this program.

4. Please list activities and/or items that are enjoyable for the learner.

5. Do you have any specific concerns regarding our education program for the learner thus far?

6. Please list what you consider to be the top five (5) priorities for the learner's education program.

7. Please list what you consider to be the top three (3) priorities for the learner's future.

8. Please list three (3) opportunities you would like us to make available to the learner.

We thank you for taking the time to complete this questionnaire. Your input is greatly appreciated and will be valuable in developing the individual education program. Please feel free to bring any additional ideas or further issues with you to the education planning meeting.

Figure 11.1. Caregiver questionnaire in response to learner preference
SOURCE: *Lehigh Continuing Education for Adults with Severe Disabilities, Lehigh University, Bethlehem, PA.*

measure as direct observations in a preference situation.

A second means of skill identification prior to instruction is curriculum-based assessments. To incorporate curriculum assessment into the initial assessment, instructors must evaluate a learner's current level of performance across each educational content area. A curriculum-based assessment is a system for determining the instructional needs of the learner based on his or her performance in the current curriculum areas (Glickling, Thompson, & Hargis, 1991).

Curriculum-based assessments differ from traditional educational assessments, which are primarily designed for placement and diagnosis (Wolery, Jones-Ault, & Munson-Doyle, 1992). Components such as functional academics and communication training run across all curriculum areas; thus, within each identified curriculum area, academic and communication needs are identified in relation to curriculum routines. In a curriculum-based methodology, life skills assessment is linked directly to the development and implementation of instructional programs.

Instructors may use comprehensive curriculum guides, such as the *Syracuse Community-Referenced Curriculum Guide* (Ford et al., 1989), or develop a curriculum guide from the content areas used in their classroom or school district. Within each curriculum area (e.g., home economics, community-vocational, community-recreational, personal maintenance), routines and activities are identified. For example, in a home economics curriculum, clothing maintenance, garden maintenance, and dinner preparation may be identified as routines. Once routines are specified, a sequence of operationally defined activities that occur in the natural context of that routine is identified. For example, in the routine of clothing maintenance, sorting clothes, washing clothes, drying clothes, ironing clothes (when applicable), and hanging clothes are examples of activities. Activities can be used later as the operational objectives for the IEP. If difficulties are observed within activities, they can be assessed further by identifying chains of skills

that make up each activity. Such chains of skills (i.e., task analyses) can also be used for ongoing assessment during instruction. Once the "menu" of routines, activities, and skills has been identified, the learner is assessed across those routines, activities, and skills to obtain a current level of mastery within that curriculum area.

Figure 11.2 shows a task-analytic assessment for a work site preparation routine in a community-vocational curriculum. The assessment outcome of known and unknown activities and skills within each curriculum area is the source of information needed for prioritizing and developing IEPs. The dependent measures obtained from a routine, such as the one depicted in Figure 11.2, include level of prompts (e.g., gesture, verbal, model, or physical), level of independence, duration of individual activity completion, and duration of total routine completion. This routine is also used as an instructional task analysis for continued assessment after the initial assessment is completed.

The benefits of curriculum-based assessment for life skills are that instructors become actively involved in designing, implementing, revising, and expanding the assessment and instruction methodology. On the other hand, with more formal or standardized assessment instruments, where assessment information bears little direct application to the design and implementation of the instructional program, instructors only react to assessment results. In curriculum-based assessments, instructors can readily identify specific skills and activities within a curriculum area and target those skills and activities for intervention. Also, because the assessment is developed from the school-district or school-level curriculum, each learner is individually tracked across similar curriculum content. Once a curriculum-based assessment tool is designed, it can be implemented across all learners using any part of the curriculum.

After preferences have been obtained from a variety of sources and curriculum content areas have been assessed, the information is used to help identify community or domestic domains, from which an ecological inventory can be conducted.

NAME: _____

CURRICULUM: Community-vocational; custodial services

ROUTINE: Vocational site preparation

1. Exit vehicle upon arrival at work site
2. Pick up equipment and carry to site
3. Set down equipment/store belongings; use restroom/ have cigarette/have coffee (if applicable)

CAN EMPLOYEE SELF-SCHEDULE?

4a. (If yes) Continue routine
4b. (If no) Request task cues presentation
5. Procure necessary equipment
6. Move to cleaning site within work site
7. Perform task
8. Seek assistance if problems arise (if applicable)
9. Seek supervisory assessment of performance

DOES ASSESSMENT INDICATE NEED TO REDO?

10a. (If no) Continue routine
10b. (If yes) Return to step 8 and follow supervisor direction
11. Put equipment away; use restroom/have cigarette/have coffee (if applicable)

IS FURTHER WORK REQUIRED AT THE SITE?

12a. (If no) Continue routine
12b. (If yes) Repeat steps 4–10
13. Engage in mealtime routine
14. Repeat steps 4–10

DEPARTURE

15. Locate equipment and belongings
16. Take equipment and belongings to vehicle and store
17. Board vehicle and fasten seatbelt
18. Exit vehicle upon arrival at home

Figure 11.2. Task-analytic assessment of a routine in a community-vocational curriculum.

SOURCE: *Lehigh Continuing Education for Adults with Severe Disabilities, Lehigh University, Bethlehem, PA.*

Ecological inventories are conducted either in current environments in which skills are generalized and maintained (e.g., high school or movie theater) or future environments to which skills are to be generalized and extended (e.g., small business, diner, or community college).

Ecological inventories can be conducted through informal interviews with a significant person or persons at the environment in question (e.g.,

grocery store owner, restaurant manager, park ranger, landlord, or real estate agent) or through direct observation in the targeted environment. Figure 11.3 shows examples of questionnaire items that may be used to conduct an interview in either current or future environments.

When using direct observation in conducting the ecological inventory, instructors should plan to observe both the environment in which the learner

SITE PERSONNEL:_____   INSTRUCTOR:_____
SITE:_____   DATE:_____

TRANSPORTATION, ARRIVAL, DEPARTURE
1. What is the distance, and how long does it take to arrive at the site from (answer only those applicable)
   a. place of residence?
   b. educational center?
   c. place of employment?
2. What means of transportation do people use to arrive and depart from the site
   (public transportation, walking)?
3. Is the site wheelchair-accessible?
4. Is parking available?

ON-SITE
1. What are primary activities of the site?
2. What are some secondary activities available at the site (pay phone, vending machines)?
3. What are some locations within the site (snackbar, video room)?
4. What is the timetable for the site (opening, closing)?
5. Are there times when consumer traffic is light?
6. Are all locations in the site wheelchair-accessible?
7. What are some activities within the site that may require specific communication
   (ordering food/drink, purchasing a ticket)?
8. Is assistance available if needed?
9. Does the site alter locations, change displays, or rearrange the physical layout?
10. What is the range of acceptable behavior (e.g., movie house versus outdoor stadium)?

Figure 11.3. Ecological inventory interview form
SOURCE: *Lehigh Continuing Education for Adults with Severe Disabilities, Lehigh University, Bethlehem, PA.*

is to interact in the immediate future and several potential future environments in which the learner may interact in the coming years. Ecological inventories conducted through direct observation break the environment into (a) subenvironments or locations within the environment, (b) activities that are present in the subenvironments or locations, and (c) skills that make up the activities. Behaviors observed in the environment and subenvironments become the target for assessment and, depending on assessment outcomes, may become the target behaviors for instruction.

Prioritization of mastered skills and skills to be learned. Based on information obtained from direct observations in current and potential future environments, curriculum-based measures, and preference analyses, the instructor must prioritize for the IEP. A prioritization grid may be developed to get a clearer picture of the amassed information collected in the initial assessment. The grid contains identified skills and activities, as well as the titles of persons responding to the assessment (e.g., "caregiver," "teacher," and "recreational therapist"). Boxes are provided for the persons involved in the initial assessment to indicate if activities are a high priority, a moderate priority, or not a priority. A prioritization grid shows activities and skills identified within each curriculum area. When targeting prioritized skills, the instructor should consider various instructional issues before goal development: (a) amount of integration inherent in each activity, (b) accessibility to instructional components, (c) feasibility of programs, (d) social and school values, (e) ultimate function of skills to be learned, and (f) availability of resources. When prioritizing for the community-vocational curriculum, other issues to consider include wage adequacy, longitudinal expectancy, company benefits, promotion potential, and transportation needs.

Develop the individual education program (IEP). After skills and activities have been prioritized within curriculum areas and goals have been identified, the education program is developed. Individual education programs may include behavioral objectives for skills instruction (e.g., washing machine use), skills sequences for routine instruction (e.g., clothing maintenance), and incidental instruction for extensions and expansions of mastered skills, activities, and routines.

Behavioral objectives are developed for each skill, activity, and/or routine targeted for programming. Components of behavioral objectives include antecedent conditions for instruction, observable target behavior(s), criteria for performance mastery, and extension of mastery. Routines might include multiple behavioral objectives as they would appear in the natural context of the overall routine. Mastery extension is included as part of program development to cue the instructor to train for generalization and maintenance of mastered skills through the fading of instructional stimuli.

The multiple components incorporated in a preinstructional assessment are designed to provide the educational community with an individual curriculum. The resulting assessment and educational program is tailored for each person and designed to meet the curriculum needs identified.

Continued Assessment during Educational Programming

After the initial assessment, prioritization, and IEP development, the instructor must monitor the effects of instruction on the objectives identified. Continued assessment during instruction provides information about the effectiveness of the teaching strategy and the learner's progress in relation to each objective. Continued assessment also provides the instructor with a mechanism for identifying areas of mastery and nonmastery within each objective. The next section of this chapter will address systematic instruction and mechanisms for effective mastery extension.

Routine assessment of curriculum content. The information obtained from the initial curriculum-based assessment allows instructors to design ongoing assessment within each life skills area. Once mastered and nonmastered activities and skills are identified within each curriculum area, ongoing assessment can be planned. Routines have been defined as the behaviors (skills) within a naturally occurring activity that are initiated with a natural cue and terminated with a critical effect on the environment (Browder, 1991; Neel & Billingsley, 1989). Natural cues are stimuli that naturally set the occasion for activities of the instructional chain and the initiation of the entire routine. The critical effect is the defined end for which the routine was written (Browder, 1991). Through incorporation of natural cues, natural consequences, and an identified critical effect, skills can be taught in the context of routines. Teaching of skills within a routine context minimizes prompt dependency, skills taught out of context, and repeated trials taught in isolation.

Similar to academic direct instruction strategies, where known and unknown skills within a curriculum area are monitored to prevent student frustration as a result of increasing the unknown-to-known ratio (Glickling et al., 1991), mastered and nonmastered skills, activities, and routines are also monitored within a life skills curriculum area. Following the initial assessment, the instructor identifies what activities, routines, and/or skills the learner has mastered. Ongoing assessment includes continued monitoring of activities and skills within the routine. The instructor begins to provide systematic instruction to identified areas in which mastery has not yet been observed. Instruction takes place within the routine context. Mastered skills and activities within the routine are reinforced when completed. Length of time to complete the routine, prompt levels, and level of independence across skills and activities continue to be monitored. Such data are valuable for program evaluation. Instruction and continued assessment within the natural routine increase the use of natural cues and consequences paired in relation to instructional cues and feedback. The pairing of natural with instructional stimuli and of mastered with nonmastered skills and activities enhances maintenance and generalization.

Most of the skills and activities included in a personal maintenance curriculum are easily identified within natural daily routines. For example, learners undress for a shower, wash, and dress in a natural sequence. Meal preparation (from the home economics curriculum) is naturally followed by eating, drinking, and napkin use. This sequence is subsequently followed by kitchen clean-up, washing dishes, and cleaning the tabletop.

Reinforcement, pacing, and opportunities to respond are maintained at an increased level of instruction, as opposed to skills being taught in isolation, because mastered and nonmastered skills and activities make up the routine assessments. The duration of routine completion is reduced, the schedule of reinforcement is richer, and the instructional opportunities to respond are increased when ongoing assessment includes mastered as well as nonmastered materials. Further, natural cues and consequences are more easily identified and programmed in the instructional sequence when activities and skills are assessed within the context of the natural routine. Also, for social validity, instructors can monitor the skills and activities that age-equivalent, nondisabled learners engage in and the routine sequence those skills and activities follow.

Task-analytic assessment of chained instruction. The development of task-analytic measures for behaviorally defined objectives involves the breakdown and sequencing of the operational steps necessary to perform the overall activity. Data collected from individual activities can be assessed on (a) level of independence achieved, (b) current level of prompting necessary, (c) pattern of errors throughout the task analysis, and (d) duration of total activity completion.

Task-analytic assessment of chained skills gives information about the total activity as well as the individual components of the chain. A task analysis of a specific activity is a more fine-grained assessment than a routine assessment. A series of task-analytic assessments may be imbedded within one routine. For more efficient task analytic designs, Browder, Lin, Lim, and Belfiore (1991) developed assessments that monitor left- and right-hand movement. Through development of a task analysis that is concurrent across individual hand movements, time to complete vocational tasks decreased compared to "traditional" task analytic designs (Browder, Belfiore, & Lim; 1991).

Time-based assessment. Quality control, efficiency, and completion rate provide an additional dimension to ongoing assessment and instruction of educational objectives. For vocational routines (e.g., custodial maintenance), activities (e.g., floor waxing), and skills (e.g., electric buffer operation), quality control and completion rate are necessary assessment areas for job acquisition, job retention, and promotion purposes. Social validation checks are made by the on-site supervisor, customers, and professionals in the field.

Response effort assessment: More effective performance via more efficient task design. By assessing response effort, the instructor learns the most efficient method for instructional design. Effective task design for ongoing assessment and instruction hinges on two priorities: (a) elimination or reduction of inefficient responses, and (b) facilitation of efficient responses.

Methods for assessing these priorities focus on motion and time studies (Browder, Belfiore, & Lim, 1991; Browder, Lin, Lim, & Belfiore, 1991) and human factors analysis (Radwin, Vanderheiden, & Lin, 1990). Chained skills (e.g., bowling, recycling paper stock, and using a communication board) are systematically analyzed across the use of the human body, the structural analysis of the work or educational environment, and/or the design of tools and instructional equipment (Niebel, 1982). The design of activities across these variables economizes the movement within the sequence of skills.

Three areas can be readily addressed for a continued response effort assessment. First, the length of time required to complete a sequence of skills or activities can be reduced by initially redefining the sequence (Browder, Belfiore, & Lim, 1991). As the distance required to complete the activity is reduced, the total completion time is reduced. Reduction of the time to completion increases the number of opportunities to practice, instruct, and assess. The range of competitive employment completion times can be, in turn, socially validated through direct observation. Such ranges can be set as criteria for mastery and extension.

Second, distance to complete an activity can be measured in a non–time-based assessment. Reducing the distance within and between steps reduces movement. Movement may consist of the distance each hand has to travel during a seated operation (e.g., data entry or circuit board welding) or the distance the learner travels during a full-body activity (e.g., vacuuming). Also, arrangement of instructional materials, jig construction, and tool adaptation can all affect the physical distance a learner has to travel through a routine or activity (Lin & Browder, 1990).

Response modality is a third way whereby instructors can maximize instructional time and make assessment more efficient. For example, if communication skills and functional academics can be learned through self-verbalization or match-to-sample rather than writing the desired responses, more opportunities are provided to make instructional responses, rate of feedback is increased, and the temporal span between instructional cue and feedback is reduced.

Continued assessment of program objectives shows the daily progress of individual learners across routines, activities, and skills. The continued monitoring of program objectives allows the instructor more direct input into each educational plan through an assessment of the learner's progress in relation to instructional antecedent and consequence strategies.

Data-based Evaluation of Continued Assessment

To be able to monitor and evaluate ongoing educational programming, instructors must develop an effective system for analyzing instructional data. Evaluation of progress provides instructors with (a) verification of instruction efficacy, (b) validation of the assessment-instruction link (i.e., whether objectives are representative of assessment strengths and weaknesses), and (c) keys to maintenance and generalization of objectives.

Effective instruction can be validated by the instructor, on-site supervisor, or job specialist. Evaluation results lead to program continuation, program modification, or program extension and expansion. Instructional efficacy is evaluated at all levels of educational programming. Thus, annual IEP meetings monitor instructional efficacy across the calendar year. More specific analysis is conducted at quarterly review meetings, where quarterly reports should provide documentation of progress across all instructional objectives and anecdotal training. Biweekly training data are assessed for routines, activities, and skills outlined in the objectives. Similarly, data-based evaluations can be made on daily routines (Neel & Billingsley, 1989) and activities.

Instructional cues, instructional consequences, pacing, and sequencing are systematically adapted when following guidelines designed for instructional outcome data (Browder, 1991). By identifying effective and ineffective instructional programs or program components, instructors have direct, ongoing input into program changes and expansions. Data-based instructor decisions have been shown to be effective in skills evaluation and program modification (Belfiore & Browder, 1992).

By assessing instructional efficacy when analyzing training data, instructors can validate whether assessment priorities have been adequately met. Incorporating a curriculum-based assessment gives instructors greater confidence that the activities and skills identified in the initial assessment are functional. Further, the probability that assessment needs are met increases when instructional priorities are developed based on the curriculum that was monitored during assessment.

Evaluation of educational programs also provides instructors with information that will enhance maintenance and generalization of programs. Assessment and instruction of skills and activities in routines give teachers a framework from which maintenance and generalization can be planned. Maintenance of educational objectives over time is enhanced when the learner is taught material in relation to natural cues and consequences. Evaluating programs continually to ensure that consequences are identified and salient is a means of increasing the likelihood of learning maintenance.

Generalization can also be enhanced by evaluating program objectives. Again, by instruction couched in routines and subroutines, learners are exposed to activities already in natural context at the acquisition stage. Instruction and continued assessment in community environments also enhances the likelihood of generalization.

Educational Practices for Learners with Autism

Now that a model for initial assessment, continued assessment with instruction, and evaluation has been identified and methods for collecting assessment data have been outlined, the second section of this chapter will be devoted to the application of educational practices to learners with autism across a life skills curriculum. Two curriculum areas are identified: self-help and community. The curriculum area of self-help is divided into home economics and personal maintenance, whereas that of community is divided into community-recreational and community-vocational.

Educational Issues

Some researchers have suggested that a lack of responsivity to environmental stimuli (i.e., motivation) in learners with autism affects their acquisition of new skills in the primary educational environment and limits generalization and maintenance of already mastered skills beyond the primary educational environment (Koegel & Koegel, 1988; Koegel & Mentis, 1985). For learners with autism, a lack of motivation may result from repeated exposure to nonmastered skills so that the concurrent reinforcement is not forthcoming, resulting in failure to maintain responding (Koegel & Koegel, 1988), or from a lack of saliency in target cues to occasion response accuracy. Because of an increase in the ratio of nonmastered to mastered skills across a routine, learners with autism may demonstrate slower skill acquisition, limited maintenance, and sporadic generalization. In contrast, lowering the ratio between nonmastered skills and mastered skills across a given instructional routine may prevent learners with autism from encountering "educational frustration."

Two principles underlie educational practices for learners with autism in a life skills curriculum. First, assessment and instruction follow a functional approach as opposed to following a sequential hierarchy of prerequisite skill mastery. Assessment and instruction within one curriculum area (e.g., personal maintenance, drinking skills) does not preclude assessment and instruction in other curriculum areas (e.g., community-recreational, attending a dinner theater; community-vocational, photocopy training). In fact, routine instruction can span curriculum areas: personal maintenance activities, such as hair care, make-up use, and accessorizing, may be taught within the routine of having drinks and dinner at a tavern. Identifying the importance of life skill routines and activities during the preschool (e.g., personal maintenance, domestic-recreational) and elementary (e.g., home economics) years benefits the learner with autism later in life (Haracopos, 1989). Thus, frustration or lack of motivation may be diminished if functional skills are identified, and instruction initiated, in the elementary grades.

Second, whenever possible, assessment and instruction should include the settings of ultimate function (Lovaas & Smith, 1989; Rutter, 1985) with the tools and materials necessary in that setting. Although not all assessment and instruction during the school years can take place in the natural setting with the natural tools and materials, instructors should make every effort to offer some component of instruction in the setting of ultimate function. For example, work assessment and instruction should take place in the settings where the work is to be completed, using equipment on the job whenever possible. Fading of instructional stimuli after acquisition is less an issue when the natural cues are incorporated into learning at the acquisition stage. Purchasing should take place in the market, shopping center, or other community facility with actual purchases. Clothing maintenance should include a component in which natural routines are incorporated as opposed to, for example, the repeated practice of putting on and taking off shoes.

For learning eventually to come under the control of the naturally occurring stimuli and no longer be dependent on teacher-delivered cues, more salient instructional cues are paired continually with natural cues. Generalization and maintenance of skills are enhanced when natural cues and natural consequences are identified and imbedded into instructional routines. Issues of problem-solving, self-management, and "in-context" functional communication are identified and programmed for the time when instruction is developed from educational routines identified in curriculum-based assessments.

Self-Help

The curriculum area of self-help includes two general subcurricula. The first, personal maintenance, covers such areas as eating, personal hygiene, wellness, and dressing. The second subcurriculum in self-help, home economics, includes such areas as clothing maintenance (e.g., washing, drying, ironing, folding, and sewing), home maintenance (e.g., dusting, food stock maintenance, utilities management, and lawn care), domestic-leisure (e.g., computer games, astronomy, and home entertainment systems), finance management, and meal preparation.

Personal maintenance. The development of personal maintenance skills begins early in the lives of learners without disabilities, leading to independence in later life. For learners with autism, however, assessment and targeted instruction in personal maintenance may need to continue into secondary and postsecondary educational programs. Although findings are inconclusive for preschool children with autism (Loveland & Kelley, 1991), in adolescents and adults with autism, personal self-help skills, as identified on the *Vineland Adaptive Behavior Scales: Survey Form* (Sparrow, Balla, & Cicchetti, 1984), appear to be a relative strength (Loveland & Kelley, 1988).

These results may be open to a number of explanations, one of which concludes that personal maintenance skills (e.g., toileting and grooming) are required across most educational environments, from residential facilities to mainstreamed classrooms, and that repeated training over time and across settings increases learning. Ando (1977) found that an intervention package incorporating reinforcement and punishment components produced varied results when applied to toileting tasks for five elementary school–aged learners.

By teaching skills in isolation (Ando, 1977), instructors run the risk of "out-of-context" teaching. Besides, teaching out of a natural context relies more heavily on instructional cues to occasion and maintain responding, thus requiring more time to fade those cues. When teaching a toileting task, for example, other activities that occur in sequence with toileting should be incorporated to develop an instructional routine. Buttoning/unbuttoning pants, zipping/unzipping trousers, and pulling up/pulling down clothing all occur in the natural routine prior to the activity of toileting. Washing hands, using a trash can, and setting up the work materials (i.e., getting back on-task) all follow the activity of toileting and, therefore, should also be taught in the routine. By using a stopwatch and a system of instructional prompts, educators monitor level of independence, error rate and pattern, and duration to complete the restroom routine.

Other areas within the personal maintenance curriculum, such as dressing and eating, are also amenable to routine instruction. Activity sequences within a curriculum routine are identified from observations of nondisabled learners in similar situations. Each activity within the sequence is taught according to a system of least prompt (gesture, verbal, verbal-model, and verbal-physical). The routine is initiated with a cue from the instructor and paired with a natural cue (e.g., after the 4 o'clock news on Channel 11, we start dinner). If the first activity is not initiated within a given length of time following the instructor cue, the first prompt level is provided (a hand gesture to the kitchen). Once in the kitchen (a natural cue for the next activity), the learner proceeds to activity two.

To avoid disrupting the natural sequence of activities, instructors should identify specific steps to insert labeled praise. Error-correction procedures (e.g., "No, this is how you fold the napkins") are developed and imbedded within the instructional format. It is important to keep mastered activities or skills within the routine, so labeled praise for accurate responding is always delivered at some point in the routine. When acquisition is not observed across an activity, the instructor can target and further break down that activity into a smaller skill-task analysis. Task analyses for each activity are taught in the same manner as the overall routine. Task analyses are also taught within the framework of that routine.

Home economics. The second subcurriculum of self-help is home economics, which includes routines and activities similar to those found in a school home economics curriculum. Schoen and Sivil (1989) compared instructional techniques when teaching snack preparation and getting a drink of water to two clients. Increasing assistance, which included a prompt system ranging from verbal to full physical guidance, and a constant time

delay were compared across task analyses of the two activities. Schoen and Sivil found that (a) the constant time delay procedure was slightly more effective in teaching the chained responses of both activities, and (b) a second learner in the pair acquired similar levels of mastery solely from observing instruction.

Routine instruction for a home economics curriculum follows an outline similar to that described above. Each routine (e.g., apartment cleaning, cooking dinner, mowing the grass, or ironing and folding clothes) is broken into a sequence of activities. If elevated error rates are observed within one activity, a more discrete task analysis of skills that make up the activity may be planned.

The prompt system and constant time delay used by Schoen and Sivil (1989) to teach individual activities can also be used to teach routines. Each activity of the routine sequence is instructed identically to steps of a task analysis. Learner progress within routines can be demonstrated by (a) monitoring percentage of activities independently performed, (b) monitoring the level of prompt or time delay for each activity, (c) monitoring the time required to complete each activity of the routine, and/or (d) monitoring the time required to complete the entire routine. Individual progress can be monitored by assessing the skills of the task analysis across percentage of independent steps, error pattern, and/or time to completion.

Community

If school-aged learners with autism are going to be successful as adults in community-based environments, they will need to function in heterogeneous groupings with learners who are not disabled and be able to adapt to learning in the presence of highly diverse and complex stimulus arrangements (Donnellan, Mesaros, & Anderson, 1985). Educational strategies such as peer tutoring, cooperative learning, and group instruction are designed to foster life skills and social skills learning. Further, such strategies as self-management and routine instruction increase independence, self-sufficiency, and flexibility in community situations. These types of strategies are necessary to excel in postsecondary options (vocational or technical school, employment, and supported employment), which require adaptions to nondisabled situations and increases in problem-solving ability.

The curriculum area of community has two general subcurricula. First, community-recreational consists of such areas of instruction as joining a bowling league, attending a concert, visiting friends and neighbors, distance running, and playing golf. The second subcurriculum, community-vocational, includes such areas as commuter transportation, end-of-day clean-up, and machine assembly.

As with the self-help curriculum, components of communication training, functional academics, and social skills training are targeted across many of the instruction routines of the community curriculum. An added concern, when assessment and instruction occur in the community curriculum, is accurate data collection. To avoid drawing attention to community-based instruction, unobtrusive data collection techniques are preferred to clipboards. For example, task analysis data may be collected in a checkbook or magazine, frequency data may be collected using a golf stroke clicker or calculator, and time-based data can be collected using a runner's wristwatch, hand-held computer, or microcassette recorder with an earphone (Browder & Belfiore, 1991). Planning ahead for community instruction can minimize the potential reactive effects of data collection and instructor presence, and maximize the learner's normalized participation in the community.

Community-recreational. Community-recreational routines and activities are important for integration and social skills training. These areas become more immediate priorities for the student who attends class in segregated facilities or the adult who has not obtained employment. Without mainstreamed classes and employment options, the learner with autism may have limited access to the community environment outside the routines and activities designed in this curriculum.

As with the other life skill curriculum areas, community-recreational goals and objectives should be assessed, prioritized, and taught throughout the calendar year. As learners get older, priorities in the community-recreational area will change, but the quality of instruction should be maintained.

Blew, Schwartz, and Luce (1985) combined natural settings with peer tutoring to teach checking out a library book, buying an item at a convenience store, purchasing a snack, and crossing the street. The nondisabled peer tutors were instructed to (a) follow the task-analytic steps for each community activity, (b) model the activity in close proximity to the learner with autism with no instruction, and (c) model the task with instruction. The results showed that modeling alone was not effective in helping the learners with autism reach mastery, but modeling with instruction (i.e., peer tutoring) was effective across all subjects and all activities. Other reports have also suggested the incorporating of peer-instruction strategies for learners with autism as a means of promoting instruction of the target behavior and collateral social skills (Egel, Richman, & Koegel, 1981; Rotholz, 1987). Successful use of peer tutoring also demonstrates that learners with autism do benefit from mainstreamed classroom and community sites as environments targeted for instruction.

Whereas Blew et al. (1985) found modeling an ineffective method for teaching in the community, Haring, Kennedy, Adams, and Pitts-Conway (1987) found modeling an effective way to increase generalized community purchasing. A training package using a system of least-intrusive prompts and labeled praise in one setting was found not to increase generalized responding to the community sites. After Haring et al. had students view videotaped models of correct performance and answer questions to highlight key sequences on the tape, however, purchasing generalized to three other community settings.

In the area of physical education, Connor (1990) provides several practical suggestions for working with learners with autism. Specifically, the author suggests (a) minimizing unnecessary external stimuli that may prove distracting, (b) avoiding presenting multiple relevant stimuli simultaneously, (c) assessing and teaching to the preferred sensory modality, (d) instructing in natural settings, with as few added prompts as necessary for learning, and (e) incorporating natural cues and realistic materials wherever possible (Connor, 1990). Physical education and sports participation may also result in marked changes in the level of nonadaptive behavior that learners with autism exhibit (Haracopos, 1989). Physical education, like other areas in the community-recreational curriculum, can provide ideal routines for teaching communication and social skills as natural components in the activity sequence.

Community-vocational. Previously, learners with autism were exposed to methods and practices that increased adaption to institutional environments, with little attention or priority placed on work adjustment, job procurement, and long-term employment (Berkell, 1987; Smith & Coleman, 1986). In *America 2000: An Education Strategy*, Bush (1991) suggests a number of goals that have relevance to transition and vocational programs. High school drop-out rates and functional literacy are key issues related to transition services and vocational stability for learners with disabilities (Halpern, 1992), who include learners with autism. Without a sound school-based transition program that meets the learner's needs in the community-vocational curriculum, as well as in community-recreational (e.g., public transportation skills) and personal maintenance (e.g., dressing appropriately) curricula and in the content areas of social skills, communication skills, and functional academics, the community employment option is limited.

One key advantage to community-based assessment for employment is the potential for a more effective job match (Berkell, 1987; Browder & Belfiore, 1991). A first step in identifying an effective job match is to conduct a job market analysis. Such an analysis can be carried out by a classroom instructor or a job procurement specialist who identifies local job possibilities through newspaper classifieds, trade journals, business weeklies, and company job postings. After relevant job options in the community are identified, routine assessments are implemented and routine priorities are established. Work assessments should contain a component whereby performance is measured at an actual work site. Routine assessment should also include communication and social skills necessary to compete in the current job market. Also, ecological inventories must be conducted, and auxiliary employment components (i.e., job extensions, problem-solving, co-worker contacts, benefit options, and promotion potential) should be identified. Identification of auxiliary employment components will benefit job maintenance and increase job satisfaction. Finally, for school-aged learners, either an individual transition plan (ITP) or a transition goal for the IEP is developed based on previous assessment, preference, and prioritization data. For adults, employment goals are established for the individual habilitation plan (IHP).

Berkell (1987) described a program, Real Employment Alternatives for Developmentally Disabled Youth (READDY), which directs curriculum and training to link school and employment. In addition to the components described above, the READDY program targets family involvement in planning and interagency cooperation between special education facilities and the regional Office of Vocational Rehabilitation (OVR). Without interagency cooperation, training and assessment initiated within the school system may not be continued when school services end and funding streams change.

Training within the community-vocational curriculum may take place in a simulated work site designed around the criteria of the community site or in the identified employment site. Simulated sites provide more flexibility for the instructor but limit generalization and maintenance in the actual employment setting. Transition programs set up in school should include a practicum at several future employment sites. Adult programs should conduct the majority of assessment and training at the site of employment. Routines for work activity include social skills training and problem-solving scenarios to help learners function above minimal standards of employment. Without such social skills and communication training, the quality of employment, potential for advancement, and collateral work behavior are diminished.

The effectiveness of transition and community employment training for learners with autism is contingent on the adequacy of career development programs (Berkell, 1987). Two areas need to be enhanced in the field of community employment for learners with autism. First, to establish tested and practical teaching techniques, experimental analysis of instruction must be conducted. Noncontrolled demonstrations (i.e., case reports or narratives) of educational procedures will have questionable impact without experimental validation. Instruction in a community-vocational curriculum should be evaluated by (a) its functional relationship with behavior change and (b) the overall importance of change to the learner (Horner, 1981). This chapter has provided a mechanism for conducting assessment and instruction across other life skills curriculum areas. Curriculum-based assessment and empirical instructional strategies are readily applied to the community-vocational curriculum.

Second, if the ultimate vocational site for learners with autism is the community employment environment, assessment and training must be conducted in those settings. The goal is paid employment in real job venues. Sheltered workshops and institutional training sites are no longer the accepted norm of many advocates and professionals for employment options for learners with autism, regardless of severity.

Future Directions: Promotion and Maintenance of Integration

The direction of assessment and training in self-help and community areas of instruction has led to increases in integration for persons with developmental disabilities. To initiate, maintain, and/or enhance community-based programs, instructors and researchers must address areas that will maximize community involvement across all life skills curricula. One area to be addressed is the utilization of natural stimuli conditions. Incorporating natural stimuli, which include community training sites and "real" materials, across all phases of instruction as part of the education plan increases the probability of response generalization and maintenance in the site of ultimate function (i.e., home, workplace, postsecondary education, or community). A second area to be addressed involves the introduction of self-management techniques to community and home instruction (Koegel & Koegel, 1988; Litrownik, 1984). A third area that will maximize integration through home and community curricula is that of response flexibility. Response flexibility and problem-solving ability enhance all aspects of community and home life by providing the learner with effective methods for responding to subtle variations in daily events.

Integration into the community, workplace, and neighborhood involves more than just inclusion in those sites. Instead, integration should involve mutual participation of persons with and without disabilities. Integration into the community is not a hierarchical step in a readiness model, but a parallel educational domain dovetailing with school-based instruction, adult education, or employment.

Focus on Environmental Stimuli and Responses

The emphasis on environmental stimuli centers on the use of natural cues and consequences within assessment and instructional routines during acquisition, maintenance, and generalization, as well as the use of self-management for skill maintenance and generalization. Pairing instructional cues with natural cues during skill acquisition increases the likelihood of generalization (Kirby & Bickel, 1988), while decreasing the dependency on instructional cues. Thus, self-management for skill maintenance is enhanced if learners with autism are less dependent on teacher-initiated cues. Integration is further enhanced when problem solving skills are targeted and planned for within the community and the self-help curriculum.

Natural cues and consequences.   Instructional routines for skill acquisition focus teacher attention on natural stimuli present in the sequence of activities. By monitoring routines across the curriculum areas of home economics, personal maintenance, community-recreational, and community-vocational, teachers will readily identify the topography and function of natural stimuli specific to those environments. For example, in the area of self-help, a clothes maintenance routine developed for the home and the laundromat involve similar activities (e.g., clothes in washer, clothes in dryer, and fold clothes) but may have varied natural cues (e.g., auditory cue signaling cycle completion or number of steps to activate). While separate routines do not need to be developed for each environment, varied skills, activities, and cues must be identified and imbedded into each routine. The analysis of stimulus classes (i.e., natural cues and consequences) within each environment increases the likelihood of successful skill transfer from training to generalization sites (Kirby & Bickel, 1988).

The topography and temporal location of natural cues within a curriculum routine are important for structuring the routine. With natural cues in place, added instructional cues can be paired with those stimuli when they are present and omitted when they are not present in the routine. For example, in teaching a clothes maintenance routine, an added instructional cue ("Let's put the clothes in the dryer") can be paired with the natural cue of the buzzer indicating that the wash cycle is over, or an added instructional cue of a gesture to the washer drum can be paired with the natural cue of picking up soiled clothes from the laundry basket in the utility room. Using the natural stimulus conditions as part of the assessment and teaching program increases the probability of generalization (Kirby & Bickel, 1988).

Other specific methods for increasing maintenance and generalization include delayed contingencies and unscheduled supervision. Dunlap,

Koegel, Johnson, and O'Neill (1987) found that for learners with severe autism, appropriate on-task behavior could be maintained in community settings with infrequent and delayed instructor-delivered contingencies. Although not in an integrated setting, Dunlap and Johnson (1985) reported similar results when incorporating unpredictable supervision in a classroom site. Delayed contingencies, unpredicted supervision, and training routines incorporate the use of stimulus control and reinforcement schedules (i.e., fading from artificial to more naturally occurring stimuli while maintaining behavior on a "thinner," more natural, reinforcement schedule).

The incorporation of natural stimuli to occasion and maintain curriculum routines not only enhances learning of the target skills in the context of the routine, but also increases the opportunity to include in-context functional language (Browder, 1991).

Self-management.   The inclusion of self-management techniques in community-based educational plans assists learners with autism to function under reinforcement schedules similar to those for the general public. For example, in the community-vocational curriculum, self-management techniques can be employed to monitor units per hour on a specific assembly line job. Through self-management, the employee with autism will gradually no longer require constant employer-directed supervision or high rates of employer-directed feedback. Self-management also provides a mechanism for self-cueing and self-delivered reinforcement within the context of community or domestic routines.

Litrownik (1984) listed six steps in developing a self-management training program: (a) a general assessment of level of functioning, (b) identification and analysis of targeted outcome, (c) identification of a self-management system, (d) a second assessment of performance as it relates to targeted outcome and the self-management system, (e) designing of a training program, and (f) evaluation of program effectiveness.

Koegel and Koegel (1988) also suggested self-management as an effective system for learners with autism, referring to the acquisition of self-management behavior as a "pivotal target behavior" (p. 53). The authors recommended that general steps include such components as self-cueing, self-monitoring, self-evaluation, and self-reinforcement.

Average members of society come under the control of the weekly paycheck, hourly bonus, and 2-week vacation. With an effective self-management system imbedded within the work routine, the employee with autism can better adapt to the contingencies of everyday work. The maintenance of mastery under the gradual removal of instructional cues transfers skills from teacher-directed to learner-directed. Self-management and transfer of control may also lead to more effective performances across curriculum areas and training sites in the absence of immediate teacher prompting and feedback.

Response flexibility and problem-solving. A third area related to the promotion of integration and maintenance focuses on the learner's flexibility of behavior in response to subtle alterations in the educational environment. Burt, Fuller, and Lewis (1991) point to the inability to make decisions and solve problems and a lack of flexibility and work speed as two characteristics that lead to individual job failure in competitive employment sites. Whereas attention to natural cues and consequences and self-management directly influence maintenance and skill generalization across integrated sites, problem-solving is directed more towards enhancement, competency, and equality at integrated sites. Problem-solving skills give the learner with autism the ability to master curricula on a level with nondisabled learners.

Browder, Belfiore, and Lim (1991) and Browder, Lin, Lim, and Belfiore (1991) have assessed and compared the effectiveness of vocational task design in an attempt to construct more efficient job-related skills. Through task-design analysis, instructors can develop various means to job completion. Tasks designed around principles of motion economy have been shown to be more efficient (i.e, fewer trials to criteria, fewer errors, and decreased duration to task completion) than "traditional" task analyses developed by special education teachers. Instructional time was economized through subtle response modifications leading to maintenance and generalization (Browder, Belfiore, & Lim, 1991). The optimal task design and modified response output provided a mechanism for performing the target jobs in the community environment at levels comparable to those achieved by nondisabled custodians.

Problem solving requires responding to (a) a set of core stimuli that remain relatively constant across teaching opportunities or environments (e.g., toothbrush or mop) and (b) a second set of stimuli that vary in relation to specific situations across learning environments (e.g., cleaning supplies run out or washer unplugged). On-site training that integrates social interactions with educational routines not only increases the probability for target-response maintenance and generalization, it also provides opportunities to respond in subtly varied situations that arise daily. Harris, Handleman, and Alessandri (1990) found that learners with autism can discriminate subtle social cues from others. Once the cues were identified by the participants, they were taught how to offer assistance appropriately in integrated educational sites. On-site training for vocational or community activities exposes learners to situations that cannot be simulated in the classroom or sheltered workshop.

Conclusion

Integration is no longer an issue of inclusion alone, but an issue of equal partnership through functional participation. The curriculum areas addressed in this chapter have implications for community involvement. As education for learners with developmental disabilities shifts from segregated to integrated instructional environments, methods for ensuring quality assessment and teaching become necessary.

Assessment and instruction in self-help and community skills provide many opportunities for integration for individuals with autism. To adequately prepare learners with autism to participate meaningfully and impact the community in which they live, assessment must be developed from actual curricula, and teaching must be assessment-driven. The steps toward curriculum-based assessment and the assessment-instruction link presented in this chapter give instructors an outline from which community-based programs in curriculum areas of personal maintenance, home economics, community-vocational, and community-recreational can be initiated. Components of self-management, problem-solving, and natural stimuli identification will build on initial educational practices, so learners with autism are not only included in the community but participate and impact the community as contributing members.

References

ANDO, H. (1977). Training autistic children to urinate in a toilet using operant conditioning techniques. *Journal of Autism and Childhood Schizophrenia, 7*, 151–163.

BELFIORE, P. J. (1990, December). *Quantification and analysis of "quality of life" indicators for persons with the most severe disabilities.* Paper presented at the annual conference of the Association for Persons with Severe Handicaps, Chicago.

BELFIORE, P. J., & BROWDER, D. M. (1992). The effects of self-monitoring on teachers' data-based decisions and on the progress of adults with severe mental retardation. *Education and Training in Mental Retardation, 27,* 60–67.

BERKELL, D. E. (1987). Career development for youth with autism. *Journal of Career Development, 13,* 14–20.

BLEW, P. A., SCHWARTZ, I. S., & LUCE, S. C. (1985). Teaching functional community skills to autistic children using nonhandicapped peer tutors. *Journal of Applied Behavior Analysis, 18,* 337–342.

BROWDER, D. M. (1991). *Assessment of individuals with severe disabilities: An applied behavior approach to life skills.* Baltimore: Paul H. Brookes.

BROWDER, D. M., & BELFIORE, P. J. (1991). Assessment in and for the community. In D. Browder (Ed.), *Assessment of individuals with severe disabilities: An applied behavior approach to life skills* (pp. 177–212). Baltimore: Paul H. Brookes.

BROWDER, D. M., BELFIORE, P. J., & LIM, L. (1991). *The effects of applying the principles of motion economy in developing task designs.* Paper presented at the annual conference of the Association for Persons with Severe Handicaps, Washington, DC.

BROWDER, D. M., LIN, C. H., LIM, L., & BELFIORE, P. J. (1991, December). *A comparison of traditional task analytic instruction and therblig-based task analytic instruction in teaching vocational skills to adults with severe disabilities.* Paper presented at the annual conference of the Association for Persons with Severe Handicaps, Washington, DC.

BURT, D. B., FULLER, S. P., & LEWIS, K. R. (1991). Brief report: Competitive employment of adults with autism. *Journal of Autism and Developmental Disorders, 21,* 237–242.

BUSH, G. (1991). *America 2000: An education strategy.* Washington, DC: U. S. Department of Education.

CONNOR, F. (1990). Combating stimulus overselectivity: Physical education for children with autism. *Teaching Exceptional Children,* 30–33.

DONNELLAN, A. M., MESAROS, R. A., & ANDERSON, J. L. (1985). Teaching students with autism in natural environments: What educators need from researchers. *Journal of Special Education, 18,* 505–522.

DUNLAP, G. & JOHNSON, J. (1985). Increasing the independent responding of autistic children with unpredictable supervision. *Journal of Applied Behavior Analysis, 18,* 227–238.

DUNLAP, G., KOEGEL, R. L., JOHNSON, J., & O'NEILL, R. E. (1987). Maintaining performance of autistic clients in community settings with delayed contingencies. *Journal of Applied Behavior Analysis, 20,* 185–191.

EGEL, A. L., RICHMAN, G. S., & KOEGEL, R. L. (1981). Normal peer models and autistic children's learning. *Journal of Applied Behavior Analysis, 14,* 3–12.

FORD, A., SCHNORR, R., MEYER, L., DAVERN, L., BLACK, J., & DEMPSEY, P. (Eds.). (1989). *The Syracuse community-referenced curriculum guide for students with moderate and severe disabilities.* Baltimore: Paul H. Brookes.

GLICKLING, E. E., THOMPSON, V. P., & HARGIS, C. H. (1991). *Curriculum based assessment: A curriculum effectiveness approach to instruction.* Boston: Allyn and Bacon.

HALPERN, A. S. (1992). Transition: Old wine in new bottles. *Exceptional Children, 58,* 202–211.

HARACOPOS, D. (1989). Comprehensive treatment programs for autistic children and adults in Denmark. In Gillberg, C. (Ed.), *Diagnosis and treatment of autism* (pp. 251–261). New York: Plenum.

HARING, T. G., KENNEDY, C. H., ADAMS, M. J., & PITTS-CONWAY, V. (1987). Teaching generalization of purchasing skills across community settings to autistic youth using videotape modeling. *Journal of Applied Behavior Analysis, 20*, 89–96.

HARRIS, S. L., HANDLEMAN, J. S., & ALESSANDRI, M. (1990). Teaching youths with autism to offer assistance. *Journal of Applied Behavior Analysis, 23*, 297–305.

HORNER, R. H. (1981). Stimulus control, transfer, and maintenance of upright walking posture in a severely mentally retarded adult. *American Journal of Mental Deficiency, 86*, 86–96.

KIRBY, K. C., & BICKEL, W. K. (1988). Toward an explicit analysis of generalization: A stimulus control interpretation. *The Behavior Analyst, 11*, 115–130.

KOEGEL, R. L., & KOEGEL, L. K. (1988). Generalized responsivity and pivotal behaviors. In R. H. Horner, G. Dunlap, & R. L. Koegel (Eds.), *Generalization and maintenance: Life-style changes in applied settings* (pp. 41–66). Baltimore: Paul H. Brookes.

KOEGEL, R. L., & MENTIS, M. (1985). Motivation in childhood autism: Can they or won't they? *Journal of Child Psychology and Psychiatry, 26*, 185–191.

LIN, C. H., & BROWDER, D. M. (1990). An application of the engineering principles of motion study for the development of task analyses. *Education and Training in Mental Retardation, 25*, 367–375.

LITROWNIK, A. J. (1984). Cognitive behavior modification with psychotic children. In S. W. Meyers & W. E. Craighead (Eds.), *Cognitive behavior therapy with children* (pp. 229–260). New York: Plenum.

LOVAAS, I. O., & SMITH, T. (1989). A comprehensive behavioral theory of autistic children: Paradigm for research and treatment. *Journal of Behavior Therapy and Experimental Psychiatry, 20*, 17–29.

LOVELAND, K., & KELLEY, M. L. (1988). Development of adaptive behavior in adolescents and young adults with autism and Down syndrome. *American Journal on Mental Retardation, 93*, 84–92.

LOVELAND, K., & KELLEY, M. L. (1991). Development of adaptive behaviors in preschoolers with autism or Down syndrome. *American Journal on Mental Retardation, 96*, 13–20.

MASON, S. A., MCGEE, G. G., FARMER-DOUGAN, V., & RISLEY, T. R. (1989). A practical strategy for ongoing reinforcer assessment. *Journal of Applied Behavior Analysis, 22*, 171–179.

NEEL, R. S., & BILLINGSLEY, F. F. (1989). *IMPACT: A functional curriculum handbook for students with moderate to severe disabilities.* Baltimore: Paul H. Brookes.

NIEBEL, B. W. (1982). *Motion and time study.* Homewood, IL: Richard D. Irwin.

RADWIN, R. G., VANDERHEIDEN, G. C., & LIN, M. L. (1990). A method for evaluating head-controlled computer input devices using Fitts' Law. *Human Factors, 32*, 423–438.

ROTHOLZ, D. A. (1987). Current considerations on the use of one-to-one instruction with autistic students: Review and recommendations. *Education and Treatment of Children, 10*, 271–278.

RUTTER, M. (1985). The treatment of autism. *Journal of Child Psychology and Psychiatry, 24*, 193–214.

SCHOEN, S. F., & SIVIL, E. O. (1989). A comparison of procedures in teaching self-help skills: Increasing assistance, time delay, and observational learning. *Journal of Autism and Developmental Disorders, 19*, 57–71.

SMITH, M. D., & COLEMAN, D. (1986). Managing the behavior of adults with autism in the job setting. *Journal of Autism and Developmental Disorders, 16*, 145–153.

SPARROW, S. S., BALLA, P., & CICCHETTI, D. (1984). *The Vineland adaptive behavior scales: Interview edition, Survey Form.* Circle Pines, MN: American Guidance Service.

WOLERY, M., JONES-AULT, M., & MUNSON-DOYLE, P. (1992). *Teaching students with moderate to severe disabilities.* White Plains, NY: Longman.

CHAPTER 12

Speech and Language Acquisition and Intervention: Behavioral Approaches

Marjorie H. Charlop
CLAREMONT MCKENNA COLLEGE
Linda K. Haymes
CLAREMONT GRADUATE SCHOOL

One of the most striking characteristics of autistic children is their failure to acquire appropriate speech and language (Kanner, 1943; Lovaas, 1977; Schreibman & Charlop, 1989). Autistic children generally either are mute or are considered echolalic (Rutter, 1978). Autistic individuals are characterized as mute when they do not engage in speech. Thus, mute autistic persons generally do not form more than a few comprehensible words but commonly emit vocalizations, babble, and sounds. For example, one child in our program used all the consonant and vowel sounds (e.g.,"ga," "ba," and "ma") but never developed speech.

Echolalia, another characteristic of autism, has been defined as "parrot speech" in that words spoken by another person are repeated (Fay, 1969). This repetition may immediately follow another person's statement, as in immediate echolalia, or it may be repeated days, weeks, or months later, as in delayed echolalia. For example, when asked "How are you?" a child with immediate echolalia might respond with "How are you" rather than answering the question. A child engaging in delayed echolalia, on the other hand, frequently repeats statements out of context, such as "Coke adds life." The lack of normal speech development is so pervasive in autistic children that it usually prompts parents to get their child diagnosed.

Description of Speech

Muteness

Fifty percent of the autistic population are mute and remain that way all of their lives (Ricks & Wing, 1975; Rutter, 1966). It is unclear, however, whether this statistic includes those who have been exposed to treatment. Some children with autism engage in very limited early speech of a few words, primarily using labels, but typically lose this speech between 18 and 30 months (Schreibman, 1988). It has never been confirmed why this occurs. Data on the incidence of muteness range from 28% (Wolff & Chess, 1965) to 61% (Fish, Shapiro, & Campbell, 1966). A long period of muteness inhibits subsequent language development.

When, or if, language does emerge depends partially on the child's level of intellectual functioning.

Bartak and Rutter (1976) studied children who exhibited delayed onset of speech. The children with IQs above 70 had a mean age of onset for first single words of 2 years, 6 months, while for autistic children with IQs below 70, the mean age of onset was 4 years, 7 months. In another study, Rutter and Lockyer (1967) followed children with infantile autism for 5 to 15 years and determined that the majority of those who learned to speak did so before the age of 5. Indeed, it is generally considered a better prognostic sign to acquire speech before the age of 5 years (Lovaas, 1977). This finding supports the necessity for early speech intervention with mute children.

Echolalia

Those autistic children who are not mute are generally considered echolalic. When Kanner (1943) first identified children with autism, one predominant feature that separated these children from those with other disorders was echolalia. Echolalia is considered to be both a bizarre behavior and an inappropriate speech form. Children who engage in echolalic speech appear strikingly different from peers. Their failure to engage in conversations due to their echolalia interferes with social interactions. In addition, echolalia affects acquisition of academic skills. When a child repeats the teacher's instructions in lieu of responding correctly, the child does not learn. It has been estimated that 75% of verbal autistic children display echolalia (Baltaxe & Simmons, 1981).

Immediate and delayed echolalia are the most common forms of autistic children's echolalia. As mentioned, immediate echolalia is the meaningless repetition of a verbal stimulus immediately after its presentation. Researchers have questioned the view that immediate echolalia is a completely meaningless verbalization (Charlop, 1983; Prizant & Rydell, 1984), citing evidence that echolalia may serve a linguistic function. According to Charlop (1983), the foundation of such questioning goes back to Skinner (1957), who noted that normal children and adults engaged in a similar type of behavior, referred to as "echoic behavior." Indeed,

Nakanishi and Owada (1973) found echoic behavior in their sample of normal children up to age 2½ years. Eventually, the echoes disappeared and were replaced with an expanding vocabulary. The use of echoic behavior in normal speech development peaks at around the age of 30 months, after which it is replaced with appropriate speech (Van Riper, 1963). It is important to note the distinction that while echoic behavior has been identified as a normal step in language development (e.g., Fay, 1969; Van Riper, 1963), echolalia is considered pathological in that the meaning of words is not acquired. It has been hypothesized that autistic echolalia may be at the far end of the continuum of normal speech acquisition (Fay, 1969; Philips & Dyer, 1977). While normal infants echo, replacing random sounds or babble upon learning appropriate speech, autistic children may plateau at this stage and continue their high frequency of echoing well into adolescence (Simmons & Baltaxe, 1975).

As mentioned earlier, not all view echolalia as having no function. For example, Philips and Dyer (1977) suggested that echolalia is a necessary step in the acquisition of language for autistic children. Rutter and Lockyer (1967) confirmed that immediate echolalia is an early form of speech for autistic children. Indeed, the presence of echolalia before age 5 is associated with a better prognosis for language acquisition. Howlin (1981) compared the speech of autistic children in treatment with those not receiving treatment. She determined that among the children who were echolalic, 80% used appropriate speech at follow-up, whether or not they received treatment. Prior to treatment, approximately 20% of the children's utterances were classified as echolalic. After treatment, the incidence of echolalic speech decreased to 10%. At follow-up, the children who did not receive treatment increased their frequency of echolalic speech. Even though the autistic children increased appropriate phrases, they continued to display echolalia.

Fay (1969) compared the echoic speech of three children. One child, age 30 months with normal IQ, engaged in echoic behavior that abated after one follow-up session. The second child, age 36 months with an IQ of 75, engaged in delayed echoes that decreased upon follow-up. A third child, diagnosed as autistic with an IQ of 53, demonstrated no decline in echoes upon follow-up. The researcher hypothesized that this finding supported the existence of echoic behavior in normal children, but that the autistic child's echolalia was abnormal in its longer duration. However, it is difficult to draw any conclusions from a sample of three children. In addition, the difference in the children's IQs, not their diagnoses, may have accounted for their speech differences.

In addition to the amount and duration of echolalia, there is a qualitative difference between autistic children's echolalia and normal children's echoic behavior. The first distinction is that autistic children have a later onset of verbalizations, including echolalic responses (Ricks & Wing, 1975). Second, the content of autistic children's echoes may include profanity and phrases out of context (Fay, 1969; Ricks & Wing, 1976). Finally, autistic echolalia includes verbatim repetition of others' phrases (Ricks & Wing, 1975).

As mentioned earlier, echolalic children repeat the content of statements without acquiring the meaning of words. Shipley, Smith, and Gleitman (1969) investigated the relationship between immediate echoic behavior and comprehension. They demonstrated that children echoed foreign words and nonsense syllables more often than English (comprehended) words.

Carr, Schreibman, and Lovaas (1975) confirmed that verbal incomprehensibility is the antecedent to some echolalia. In this study, the children echoed neutral verbal stimuli for which they had no response more frequently than discriminative stimuli for known responses (statements understood by the child). The discriminative stimuli were verbal statements presented in the children's everyday environment (e.g.,"What is this?" and "Drink the water"), while the neutral stimuli consisted of nonsense syllables (e.g., "Min dar snick" and "Fop vit gerpy"). The neutral stimuli were matched with the discriminative stimuli on the

number of phrases and syllables. Thus, echolalia may be used to pinpoint when a child is not comprehending the question or command. For example, one 6-year-old autistic child in our program repeated questions when he did not know the answer. When asked "What is this?" he responded with "Is this" instead of providing the correct answer.

Charlop (1986) investigated the effects of the familiarity of the person presenting the task, the room, and the task stimuli upon the occurrence of autistic children's immediate echolalia. The greatest amount of echolalia occurred in settings where an unfamiliar person presented an unfamiliar task, whereas the second highest frequency occurred when a familiar person presented unfamiliar stimuli. This is consistent with the finding of Carr et al. (1975) that the novelty or unfamiliarity of the stimuli affects echolalic responses.

Immediate echolalia, which involves the repetition of what was just said, can be distinguished from delayed echolalia by the amount of time that passes between the original statement and the subsequent repetition. Delayed echolalia involves the repetition of contextually inappropriate phrases heard in the past (Fay & Schuler, 1980; Kanner, 1943). The delayed echo may be uttered hours, days, or even years later (Kanner, 1946; Ricks & Wing, 1975, 1976). Often, the children echo a verbalization that was presented in an arousing format (Gonzales, 1987; Kurtz & Charlop, 1992). For example, one child's delayed echoes consisted of repeating his mother's reprimands ("Go wash your hands now" and "Bill, get out"). Also, television commercials and songs are frequently echoed. Statements more likely to be echoed include reprimands, expletives, and verbalizations that are stated in a loud tone of voice (Bucher & Lovaas, 1968; Hermelin & O'Connor, 1970; Kurtz & Charlop, 1992).

Lovaas, Newsom, and Hickman (1987) suggested that some delayed echolalia is merely a higher form of self-stimulation. Like any type of self-stimulation, echolalic phrases may be repeated for the sensory input they provide to the child—in this case, auditory input. As additional evidence that some delayed echolalia may be self-stimulatory in nature, Lovaas, Varni, Koegel, and Lorsch (1977) demonstrated that children's use of delayed echoes is not affected by social consequences. Also, Charlop, Kurtz, and Casey (1990) effectively used delayed echoes as reinforcers.

Some research has suggested that delayed echolalia, in some instances, may have communicative functions (Fay & Schuler, 1980; Prizant & Rydell, 1984; Schreibman & Charlop, 1989). Such communicative function is seen in the classic example described by Kanner (1946) of a child who echoed a previously heard reprimand, "Don't throw the dog off the balcony" (initially stated when the child tried to throw a toy dog off a balcony), whenever he was tempted to throw an object. This echo seemed to serve as a self-instruction to inhibit the inappropriate behavior (Kanner, 1946). That is, the child engaged in the echo and then refrained from throwing. Delayed echoes may also serve communicative functions such as requesting items and answering questions (Kurtz & Charlop, 1992). For example, one child echoed "Do you want a cookie, honey?" while standing by the cookie jar. Another child, when asked what he did at school that day, responded with "Greg, you didn't finish your worksheet." Both of these statements demonstrate some attempt at communication within an appropriate context.

Despite a few early reports, a descriptive analysis of the functions of echolalia was not conducted until more recently. Prizant and Rydell (1984) observed three children with their teachers in regular classroom activities for a period of 30–45 minutes. The observed echoes were classified as interactive or noninteractive, comprehended or noncomprehended, and relevant or irrelevant. Echoes were scored as interactive if the child was engaged in turn-taking, labeling objects or actions, requesting objects by pointing or showing, and/or providing information. Noninteractive echoes were self-stimulatory or self-directive. Comprehension was indicated by the accompaniment of gestures, reaching, or pointing or if the verbal response was appropriate to a prior discourse. The echo was scored as relevant to the situation or context if it referred to an object, person, action, activity, or topic. Roughly half of the delayed echoes were determined to be interactive, relevant, and comprehended. These results, however, are considered only preliminary because of the limited number of participants and observations (only two observations for each child).

Kurtz and Charlop (1992) conducted a more extensive analysis of the functions of delayed echolalia. Six autistic children were each observed four times in eight conditions, totaling 32 observations per child. They were observed during free-play alone, free-play with an unfamiliar person at their after-school behavior therapy program, therapy sessions, breaktime from therapy, free-play at home, in their school classroom, and in an unfamiliar setting with a parent. All speech and vocalizations were transcribed by the experimenter and assistants.

The results suggest definite functions of the echoes. As in the Prizant and Rydell study (1984), 50% of the echoes were classified as communicatively functional (see Figure 12.1), including labeling, self-instructions, communicative requests, communicative information, and communicative answers. Figure 12.2 depicts the various categories of delayed echolalia delineated in Kurtz and Charlop (1992). As shown, 15% of the delayed echoes were self-instructions. This finding is important since this function may be used to facilitate other appropriate behaviors. For example, one autistic child who frequently engaged in self-stimulatory hand-flapping repeated "Better settle down," which appeared to serve as a reminder to abstain from the behavior.

Other Characteristics of Autistic Children's Speech

Another prevalent feature of autistic children's speech and language is lack of generalization. Generalization involves transferring treatment gains from training to nontraining settings.

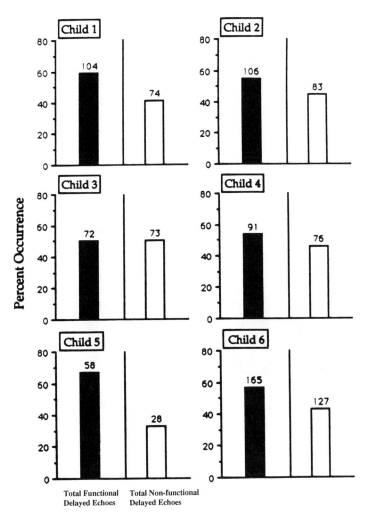

Figure 12.1. Use of functional and nonfunctional delayed echoes

Generalization occurs when children use trained words and/or phrases in various appropriate contexts. Behavior change is meaningless if the children engage in newly acquired behaviors only in the presence of trainers and training stimuli. Stokes and Baer (1977) specified that generalization of behavior change does not occur naturally and that it usually requires training with multiple exemplars (many persons, teaching stimuli, and settings).

Generalization of language skills has been especially difficult to achieve with autistic children (Lovaas, Koegel, Simmons, & Stevens-Long, 1973).

Monotone speech is another characteristic of autistic children's speech identified by Kanner (1946). Monotone speech is the utterance of successive words without change in pitch or key. Ricks and Wing (1975) and Bartak, Rutter, and Cox (1975) reported that, even as infants, autistic

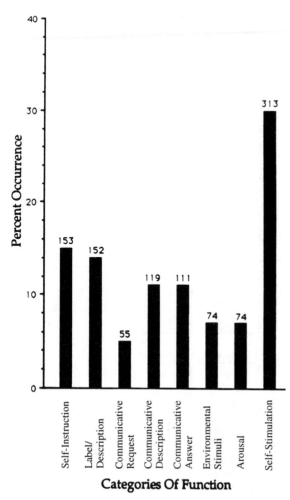

Figure 12.2. Cumulative distribution of delayed echoes across categories

Needleman, Ritvo, and Freeman (1980) compared the speech of children diagnosed as autistic, mentally retarded, or language-delayed. The autistic children displayed significantly more atypical intonation and stress of speech sounds than the other populations. Typically, autistic speech is characterized by dysprosody, which includes inaccurate inflection, pitch, rhythm, intonation, and pace (Baltaxe, 1981; Baltaxe & Simmons, 1975; Schreibman, Kohlenberg, & Britten, 1986). Schreibman et al. determined that dysprosody in speech may be due to the children's overselectivity of certain aspects of auditory stimuli. In this study, the children were trained to bar press at the sound of a complex auditory stimulus (S+) and to withhold responding when presented with a different auditory stimulus (S–). The complex auditory stimulus consisted of two features—content and intonation. The content sounds were "min min" and "nur nur," and the intonation was either monotone or varied. The children were presented with various combinations of intonation and content totaling four different stimulus pairs. The children with echolalia tended to selectively respond to the intonation of the stimulus, while the nonverbal children selectively responded to the content component. This finding is consistent with previous observations of autistic children's speech; that is, echolalic children display varied intonation but demonstrate little comprehension of the verbal stimuli, whereas nonverbal children who acquire speech (content) demonstrate dysprosody.

Another characteristic of autistic children's speech is a lack of spontaneity. Kanner (1946) described his sample as lacking spontaneous sentence formation. Typically, autistic children's speech is a response to a prompt or question. Seldom do they speak without being requested to do so (Charlop, Schreibman, & Thibodeau, 1985). Charlop et al. proposed that spontaneous speech can be viewed as a continuum. At one end is speech elicited by the presence of an obvious physical referent or nonverbal cue (e.g., saying "I want cookie" when presented with a cookie). At the other end of the continuum is speech under the

children's babble lacks inflection. Ricks and Wing (1976) noted that autistic infants' noises were qualitatively different from those of normal children in that the autistic infants had "idiosyncratic articulated methods of expression" (p. 104). The infants' expressions of requests, frustration, greetings, and surprise were recorded. After listening to audiotapes of these expressions, the parents were able to identify their own child's emotions but were unable to tell the emotions expressed by other autistic infants.

stimulus control of an internal, historical, or future event (e.g., saying "Potty, please" when feeling bladder pressure). Charlop et al. defined spontaneity as "a verbal response to a nonverbal discriminative stimulus in the absence of a verbal discriminative stimulus" (p. 156). This definition applies to spontaneous speech at all points along the continuum. Echolalia can be mistaken as spontaneous speech since it is frequently not a response to a verbal prompt. However, echolalia has been distinguished from spontaneous speech in that it is generally spoken out of context.

Lovaas (1977) and Lovaas et al. (1973) determined that most children who received speech training still failed to use speech spontaneously. To remediate this problem, Lovaas (1977) suggested that structure during the language training session needs to be loosened so that control can be shifted to features in the environment, not the adult's requests for speech. However, spontaneous speech continues to be a difficult component of speech to teach. Spontaneity in speech is important in that it is extremely limiting for an individual to respond only following verbalizations from others. Additionally, spontaneous speech is necessary because it enables one to establish control over the environment by requesting toys, food, and the bathroom, for example.

Another characteristic of autistic children's speech is literal or concrete interpretation of speech. This involves interpreting spoken words in a strict sense. For example, when one 9-year-old autistic boy was told to put his hand down during a therapy session, he responded by using one hand to pull the other hand down. In another example, when a parent preparing to leave the house said to her autistic child "Let's hit the road," the child ran to the street and hit the road with his hand. Similarly, Wing (1976) confirmed that speech can be comprehended and produced with complete literalness; hence, idiomatic expressions can be confusing to children with autism. For example, one child described by Ricks and Wing (1976) was terrified when her mother said that she "cried her eyes out."

Autistic children also demonstrate a pronounced lack of nonverbal accompaniment to language (Fay & Schuler, 1980). That is, they do not exhibit occasional nods of agreement, hand movements, changing facial expressions, and appropriate body postures that coincide with conversation. These subtle accompaniments do not develop naturally. Autistic children have been taught the extremes of facial expressions (Ricks & Wing, 1975), but the rote use of such expressions in social interaction gives the impression of awkwardness.

Pronoun reversal is another common characteristic of autistic children's speech (Kanner, 1943). The children generally make statements with "you" replacing "I." For example, an autistic child may say "You want a cookie" instead of "I want a cookie." Originally, Bettelheim (1967) postulated that the pronoun reversal reflected a rejection by these children of their own existence. However, Bartak and Rutter (1974) demonstrated that pronoun reversal is a consequence of echolalia. In this study, the children were presented with sentences with the pronouns in the first, middle, and end positions (e.g., "I am big," "Can I come," and "How can I?"). Children with autism tend to echo statements with pronouns at the end of sentences. When Bartak and Rutter controlled sentence position of the various pronouns (as in the previous example), the children repeated "I" with the same frequency as for other pronouns. Nevertheless, autistic children generally have problems using all pronouns correctly and often need extensive training to do so. For those children who do develop good verbal repertoires, invariably one of the last skills acquired is the correct use of pronouns. It is also common for autistic children to avoid using pronouns altogether, referring to themselves and others directly by names (Schreibman & Charlop, 1989). For example, when one autistic child wanted to use the bathroom, he stated "You want, I want, Mark wants the bathroom."

One final characteristic of speech of children with autism is their pronounced lack of conversational speech (Charlop & Milstein, 1989). Autistic children's speech is generally limited to simple responses, lacking the give-and-take interactions and question-asking of conversational speech. Ricks and Wing (1975) described speaking to an autistic child as "holding a discussion with a well-programmed computer." The children tend to rely on stereotyped phrases and repetition, limited to a range of topics that interest them.

Charlop (1989) compared autistic children's conversations about toys with their conversations about obsessive topics. The children emitted more novel responses, elaborated more, and had a longer MLU (mean length of utterances) when the conversations focused on obsessions. Ricks and Wing (1975) noted that once the conversation departs from the exchange of concrete information that interests them, autistic children may withdraw from further contact. As seen in the Charlop study, using toys of little interest to the children as topics of conversation resulted in a limited variation of responses and a limited number of elaborations. Question-asking is a component of conversational speech that has been taught to autistic individuals (Hung, 1977) and mentally retarded clients (Twardosz & Baer, 1973; Warren, Baxter, Anderson, Marshall, & Baer, 1981). Although question-asking has helped naturalize autistic children's speech, the children still lack the natural give-and-take interaction and continued participation found in conversational speech.

In summary, speech abnormalities and deficits are by far one of the most prominent features of autism, ranging from complete mutism to lack of spontaneity and conversational skills. Autistic children engage in many different speech patterns. First, delayed and immediate echolalia are common, with verbal autistic children having a combined frequency of approximately 75%. Second, many of the verbal children display abnormal intonation, rhythm, and pitch. Third, there is a profound lack of generalization of speech and language skills. In addition, these children demonstrate almost completely literal interpretations of speech. Finally, verbal children generally lack the nonverbal accompaniments to language.

These major deficits in speech and language interfere with social interactions. The children appear bizarre and different from their peers, which may hinder peer initiations. Autistic children generally lack social responsiveness to others (Kanner, 1943). They seldom initiate social interactions and frequently do not respond to others' attempts to interact. Their speech and language deficits compound this profound social deficit. For example, echolalia interferes with communication of desires and also hinders learning. Frequently, the children repeat instructions instead of providing the correct answer. Since much of the academic curriculum is language-based, these children are at a severe disadvantage in educational areas. Speech and language not only facilitate social interactions, they are necessary for communicating desires, maintaining control over one's environment, and learning new skills.

The remainder of this chapter will focus on speech and language intervention for autistic children. We will cover basic intervention procedures that have been devised to teach appropriate speech and language to both mute and echolalic children. In addition, we will outline the latest advances in naturalizing speech and in teaching complex and conversational speech. Some autistic children fail to develop speech despite these intervention procedures. Therefore, we will also provide an overview of alternative methods of communication.

Behavioral Intervention for Speech and Language

The behavioral approach to language training for autistic children has been demonstrated to be the most successful method of intervention. A substantial database demonstrates the effectiveness of operant techniques in the development of speech and language (Guess, Sailor, Rutherford, & Baer, 1968; Hewett, 1965; Stevens-Long & Rasmussen, 1974). Skinner (1957) first examined the role of operant techniques in the development of language in organisms. He suggested that all verbal behavior is shaped and maintained by contingencies of reinforcement. It is this basic operant technique that has been used by researchers in the development of language-acquisition procedures for children with autism. The basic behavioral methods involve shaping speech to criterion by using imitation, verbal prompts, and reinforcement of approximations.

Imitation, Prompting, and Reinforcement: Teaching Basic Speech and Language

Teaching speech to mute children is extremely difficult and time-consuming (Lovaas, 1977). Children who have not learned to talk on their own need intense interventions to develop what generally "comes naturally" to normal children. The first study to present language-acquisition procedures for an autistic child was by Hewett (1965). An autistic boy was initially taught to imitate hand movements. Then, a preferred song was introduced to develop imitation of vocalizations. Eventually, words were differentially reinforced. This procedure involved the shaping of vocal imitation by reinforcing successive approximations and prompt-fading techniques. The child eventually developed a 32-word vocabulary that was used for spontaneous requesting. Similarly, Baer, Peterson, and Sherman (1967) chained together motor and vocal responses following motor-imitative training. They hypothesized that the children developed generalized imitation, which facilitated vocal imitation.

In an outline of the traditional behavioral approach to language acquisition, Lovaas (1977) and Lovaas, Schreibman, and Koegel (1974) suggested that once researchers have established attending behaviors, nonverbal imitative behaviors should be targeted. The motor-imitative skills are brought under verbal control so that they become receptive responses to commands. For example, the therapist states "Raise arms," and the child responds by raising his or her arms. It is important to distinguish between expressive and receptive language. Receptive language involves a nonverbal response to a verbal command, whereas expressive language involves a verbal response to either a verbal or a nonverbal stimulus. Thus, in the example above, receptive language consists of following the instruction "Raise arms" with the motor response. An example of expressive language is saying "cow" when a picture of a cow is presented. Skinner refers to the latter example as a "tact" (Skinner, 1957).

Lovaas's verbal imitation paradigm has been successful in teaching expressive language skills to nonverbal autistic children. Initially, for children who are mute, all vocalizations need to be reinforced. This includes babbling and other seemingly inappropriate sounds. The goal is to increase the overall rate of the child's vocalizations. Once the rate of vocalizations is high, any vocalization that follows the therapist's verbal prompt (e.g., "Say ah") within 5–10 seconds is reinforced. Gradually, the responses are shaped by reinforcing closer and closer approximations to the therapist's discriminative stimulus ("ah"). Initial vocal imitations include sounds such as "mm," "ah," and "bah," plus other sounds that include visual components that can be exaggerated, such as widening of the mouth or curling under the lips (Lovaas, 1977).

During the training session, the child and the therapist sit facing each other so that distractions are limited and the adult can maintain behavioral control of the child. Sometimes light physical prompts are necessary to shape appropriate mouth movements. For example, in training the "mm" sound, the therapist says "mm" and simultaneously lightly holds the child's lips closed until the child vocalizes. The physical prompt is gradually faded from the child's mouth until the child emits "mm" following the adult's verbal stimulus with no physical prompt. Once the child has mastered imitation of an initial sound, a new sound is introduced. When criterion is reached with the new sound, the presentations of new and old sounds are then systematically intermixed so that the child maintains responses to variations of verbal stimuli. More sounds are added, sounds are increased to words, words are made into phrases, and, finally, phrases are increased to sentences (as described below).

After the child has been taught to imitate the therapist's vocalizations, the child needs to learn the meaning of the words. The child is taught the labels of common objects. The therapist can present the stimulus item to be labeled either alone or with the question "What is it?" The therapist presents an item (e.g., a cookie) and prompts the word "cookie." The prompt is faded until the child responds "cookie" upon presentation of the item. Then, a second stimulus item is introduced in the same manner. Once the child reaches criterion on the second item, the presentations of the two stimuli are systematically intermixed and new objects are introduced. Thus, the child learns to discriminate between the sample items. Over time, more complex grammatical phrases are required to receive reinforcement. Instead of one-word labels ("cookie"), the child is required to respond with phrases ("It is cookie"). It has been suggested that verbal imitation, as outlined above, is a prerequisite to development of functional speech in nonverbal autistic children (Goetz, Schuler, & Sailor, 1979; Hartung, 1970).

Children who engage in echolalia do not have to develop imitative behaviors as mute children do. Instead, they simply need to be taught when it is, and when it is not, appropriate to imitate others' speech. Thus, children who engage in echolalia, especially prior to age 5, respond more positively to language intervention and ultimately have a better prognosis for appropriate speech and language (Howlin, 1981). Speech and language training for echolalic children is consequently less time-consuming (Lovaas, 1977). For example, Risley and Wolf (1967) established functional speech in echolalic children through shaping and transferring stimulus control from the experimenter's verbal prompt (e.g., "cow") to the stimulus items (picture of a cow). Initially, the children's verbal responses were reinforced if they followed within 5 seconds of the experimenter's statements. Eventually, the children's responses were reinforced when they labeled the presented items. The children's speech developed into functional phrases ("That is a cow"). Although teaching speech and language to echolalic children is much easier than teaching mute children,

speech and language training, in general, is still an arduous task for all autistic children.

Lovaas (1977) also outlined a method of speech acquisition for echolalic children. Like nonverbal children, echolalic children are taught labeling through imitation and differential reinforcement of approximations. However, full words and sentences can initially be taught. As mentioned, the goal is to shape the children's responses by reinforcing closer and closer approximations to the therapist's model. To limit echoing of instructions and prompts, Lovaas suggested using volume cueing and instructing the children with "don't echo." The goal of volume cueing is to have the child echo only the desired response, not the question or prompt. Using this procedure, the question or instruction is presented quietly, and the desired response is presented in a louder tone to emphasize for imitation. For example, the therapist quietly says "What is this?" and then immediately says in a louder tone "It is car." Gradually, the discriminative stimulus is raised to a normal level, and the imitative prompt level is decreased. The prompt is eventually eliminated.

Stevens-Long and Rasmussen (1974) expanded the literature on operant language procedures for developing complex language skills in echolalic children when they demonstrated that imitative prompts and differential reinforcement were effective for acquiring compound sentences. In this study, an echolalic autistic child was taught to chain two simple sentences using the conjunction "and." The children were presented with a card and asked "What do you see?" They were taught to respond with compound sentences, such as "The girls are swinging, *and* the boy is walking."

Lovaas (1977) provided a detailed account of behavior modification techniques for teaching speech to autistic children. Not only did Lovaas and his colleagues successfully develop basic imitative skills, but the children were taught functional speech and sentence formation. Despite the development of appropriate speech with echolalic children, elimination of echolalia is generally not expected (Howlin, 1981; Kurtz & Charlop, 1992; Lovaas et al., 1973).

Another important feature of language development is receptive language skills. As mentioned, receptive language involves a nonverbal response to a verbal instruction or request. For example, the therapist requests "Give me bowl," and the child responds by handing the therapist the bowl. Lovaas (1977) recommended that receptive responding be targeted prior to expressive speech, just as receptive language precedes expressive language in normal language development (Gesell & Thompson, 1934). Mann and Baer (1971) suggested that training receptive vocabulary facilitates expressive usage of those words. However, Guess and Baer (1973) concluded that automatic generalization from receptive to expressive language does not inevitably result from language training of retarded children. Therefore, it is recommended that children be taught both receptive and expressive tasks. Verbal and nonverbal imitation can often be taught at the same time in the course of the child's treatment. Therefore, we recommend that receptive and expressive language be taught simultaneously for some children, based on our observations of successful simultaneous acquisition of expressive and receptive repertoires by many children.

The techniques described are the foundation for establishing control over autistic children's verbal responses and development of basic language. These methods have been successful in teaching children to speak who previously could not speak (mute children), as well as teaching children with some speech (echolalic) to speak appropriately. However, autistic children's speech still presents significant problems. First, the children fail to generalize speech from training situations to the natural environment (Lovaas et al., 1973). Second, their verbal skills are often limited to rote responses and answers, not conversational speech (Charlop & Milstein, 1989). Finally, they speak only when they are spoken to and generally lack spontaneity in their speech (Charlop et al., 1985).

More elaborate speech and language training programs have targeted the areas where autistic children display deficits. These include developing spontaneity, conversational speech, question-asking, and generalization and decreasing rote responses while increasing variation in responses. The procedures discussed below have been designed to address some or all of these concerns. The procedures take advantage of natural interactions and include environmental cues to enhance conversational speech and generalization while still maintaining a rigorous empirical base.

Expanding Speech and Language Repertoires

Modeling

Numerous investigators have examined the effectiveness of observational learning with non-handicapped children. For example, observational learning has been used to modify self-reinforcement (Bandura & Kupers, 1964), sharing (Hartup & Coates, 1967), and emotional reactions (Bandura & Menlove, 1968). In these studies, a peer, situated near the target child, modeled the appropriate behavior. This paradigm has been extended to include the use of nonhandicapped peer models to facilitate learning for handicapped children (Apolloni, Cooke, & Cooke, 1976; Peterson, Peterson, & Scriven, 1977).

Varni, Lovaas, Koegel, and Everett (1979) conducted the first analysis of observational learning of instruction-following, using adult models with autistic children. Once the target child was oriented toward the model, the teacher instructed the model to engage in a particular behavioral sequence. For example, the teacher handed the model a ball and said "truck." The model then placed the ball in the dumping section of the truck. The model received social approval and food for performing the task. The autistic children in this study were "low-functioning" and failed to acquire most of the adult responses. The investigators suggested that stimulus overselectivity accounted for the lack of success, hypothesizing that the children failed to attend to the total complex stimulus since some of them responded to only certain components of the model's response. The data from Varni et al. demonstrated that modeling is not successful with low-functioning autistic children and that their failure to learn through observation in their natural environment may contribute to further behavioral deficits.

More positive results using modeling with autistic children have been demonstrated more recently. Charlop, Schreibman, and Tryon (1983) addressed the effect of modeling on receptive labeling tasks. Using low-functioning autistic children, the researchers assessed the effects of peer modeling (using other low-functioning autistic children) and compared them with typical trial-and-error learning. Autistic peer models were chosen as they were more likely to be encountered by the target children on a daily basis (e.g., in their classroom). The target child was cued to pay attention while observing the autistic peer perform the receptive labeling task and receive reinforcement and praise for correct responses. Following 20 observational trials, the target child was tested to determine whether he or she had acquired the receptive labels through observation. Both trial-and-error and modeling procedures were effective for acquisition; however, peer modeling was superior in facilitating generalization.

Charlop et al. (1983) hypothesized that the loose structure of the peer modeling facilitated generalization. Since the intervention was not directly presented to the target child, there was less stimulus control in the learning environment. In addition, the use of autistic peer models may have facilitated generalization since they were part of both the training and the natural environment. Thus, discriminability between training setting and generalization setting was decreased, leading to improved generalization (Stokes & Baer, 1977).

Coleman and Stedman (1974) also had success using modeling when shaping an autistic child's verbalizations with a nonhandicapped peer model. The model demonstrated appropriate voice volume and received social praise and food for correct responses. Upon viewing the model, the autistic child increased her volume of vocalizations and

maintained this level without the presence of her peer. Vocabulary (labeling) was also increased using the same peer modeling technique. Within 8 weeks, the autistic child had acquired 40 labels. Coleman and Stedman pointed out that it took less time to train therapists to implement the modeling procedure than to teach them to provide direct intervention.

Egel, Richman, and Koegel (1981) also reported positive results from using nonhandicapped peer models. The participants in their study were higher functioning than those in the studies by Varni et al. (1979) and Charlop et al. (1983), and all but one child had a functional vocabulary prior to the modeling program. The modeling procedure was successful at teaching receptive labeling and expressive discrimination tasks that the children had failed to learn using more traditional teaching procedures. Importantly, all the children maintained the treatment gains in the absence of the peer models.

Modeling has been shown to be a promising method for teaching autistic children both expressive and receptive language skills. Modeling is also a cost-effective and convenient teaching tool. Charlop and Milstein (1989) investigated an even more cost-efficient method of modeling—video modeling. The use of videos enhances cost and personnel efficiency, since less staff need to be trained with the modeling procedures and staff do not need to provide in vivo modeling once the videos are made. In this study, three autistic children were taught conversational skills after viewing two familiar adult models engage in conversations about specific toys and abstract concepts on a video. All the autistic children had some expressive and receptive language skills prior to modeling training. However, they had very limited conversational speech, with their existing speech generally characterized as perseverative or echolalic.

Several conversation scripts were created, using back-and-forth exchange of questions and answers in which an adult and child both answered and asked questions. (Table 12.1 provides examples of

Table 12.1 Examples of Conversations Used in Video Modeling

Conversation A	Therapist:	What do you have?
	Child:	A box. Are you holding something?
	Therapist:	Yes, a box. What's in your box?
	Child:	A ball. Is there something in your box?
	Therapist:	Yes, a puppet. Do you want to play with the toys?
	Child:	Yes. Can I play with the puppet?
	Therapist:	Yes.
Conversation A´	Therapist:	What do you have?
	Child:	A barrel. Are you holding something?
	Therapist:	Yes, a barrel. What's in your barrel?
	Child:	A duck. Is there something in your barrel?
	Therapist:	Yes, bubbles. Do you want to play with the toys?
	Child:	Yes. Can I play with the bubbles?
	Therapist:	Yes.
Abstract 1	Therapist:	How are you?
	Child:	Fine. How are you?
	Therapist:	Fine. Did you have fun at school today?
	Child:	Yes. What did you do at school today?
	Therapist:	Read. What did you do at school today?
	Child:	A puzzle, colored. What's the name of your school?
	Therapist:	Claremont.
Abstract 2	Therapist:	Do you like to swim?
	Child:	Yes. Do you swim?
	Therapist:	Yes. What do you wear when you swim?
	Child:	A bathing suit. Where do you swim?
	Therapist:	Claremont. Do you play with beach balls?
	Child:	Yes. Do you like rafts?
	Therapist:	Yes.

Note: From "Teaching Autistic Children Conversational Speech Using Video Modeling" by M. H. Charlop and J. P. Milstein, 1989, *Journal of Applied Behavior Analysis, 22.*

the conversations.) Videos were made of two adults engaging in the specific conversations and subsequently shown to the children (video modeling). Acquisition of the conversations via observation of the videos was assessed. That is, the experimenter and the child engaged in the conversation that was presented on the video. Novel responses were encouraged by continuing along any topic proposed by the child during testing of observational learning. Video modeling was implemented sequentially, if needed, for each of several conversations. In addition, probes were conducted in extra-therapy conditions such as outside, at home, and with unfamiliar persons, siblings, and various toys.

The children acquired the conversation skills in as few as three presentations of a 45-second video (one session), the highest number of presentations being 20 viewings, or only 16 minutes of actual treatment with the videos. At a 15-month follow-up, the children maintained all previously trained conversations. Also, generalization to other settings, persons, and conversations occurred. An increase in spontaneous response variation was an important positive side effect of this intervention. During baseline, the children exhibited less than

1% of varied responses; following treatment, this increased to 13% for one child and as high as 100% for another child. This suggests that the children did not merely memorize the videos but perhaps acquired a learning set of how to have conversations. An increase in question-asking during free operant settings was another positive side effect from the video modeling.

Question-asking and conversational speech are complex language skills that have been successfully taught through modeling procedures. Modeling has also proven beneficial for basic language acquisition. It has been hypothesized that one reason why modeling is effective for speech training is that it takes advantage of the autistic children's tendency to echo. For example, in the study by Charlop and Milstein (1989), echoing of the appropriate lines in the conversation was considered a correct response. These initially echolalic responses later served as functional communicative speech and were either contextually appropriate, substituted with other novel appropriate responses, or in some way modified by the child. Thus, the tendency to echo may have enhanced the effects of modeling since these children would more readily imitate (or echo) the model's speech. Modeling is a cost-efficient intervention technique that can be useful in both mainstreamed and special education classrooms, especially when there is a high teacher-child ratio.

The video-modeling procedure includes many features that have been recommended for enhancing generalization of trained responses (Stokes & Baer, 1977). These include multiple exemplars (of conversations and models), natural contingencies (answering of questions and access to toys), and sequential administration of treatment as needed (sequential modification). Garcia and DeHaven (1974) suggested that generalization should be the criterion in determining the success of a language program.

Time Delay

Time delay is another successful speech intervention for autistic children, especially for teaching spontaneous speech (Charlop et al., 1985; Charlop & Trasowech, 1991; Charlop & Walsh, 1986; Ingenmey & Van Houten, 1991; Matson, Sevin, Fridley, & Love, 1990). This procedure entails inserting a delay between the presentation of the target stimulus, such as an object, and the presentation of the prompted response.

As mentioned, Charlop et al. (1985) defined spontaneity as "a verbal response to a nonverbal discriminative stimulus in the absence of a verbal discriminative stimulus" (p. 156). These researchers proposed that spontaneity can be viewed on a continuum. At one end of the continuum is speech occurring in response to a visible nonverbal stimulus (e.g., "I want cookie" when shown a cookie). In the middle of the continuum may be speech that is under the control of a less clearly defined physical referent, such as an activity (e.g., hugging). Further along this continuum may be speech controlled by general environmental cues (e.g., a particular room). Finally, at the "most spontaneous" end of the continuum may be speech under the control of internal, historical, or future events (e.g., "I want bathroom" when bladder pressure is felt). Time-delay procedures have been studied along this hypothesized continuum.

Several studies have demonstrated the efficacy of time-delay procedures for increasing spontaneous speech in response to a physical referent. For example, Risley and Wolf (1967) established the functional speech of echolalic children by implementing a delayed prompt. They taught autistic children to label spontaneously when shown an object or a photograph. The experimenter presented the object and the response simultaneously and then gradually lengthened the time between the object presentation and the presentation of the prompt (graduated time-delay procedure).

Halle, Marshall, and Spradlin (1979) increased the spontaneous requesting of six retarded institutionalized children. They implemented a constant (15-second) time-delay procedure, instead of the graduated method used by Risley and Wolf (1967). The attendants held the child's food tray and at the end of the 15-second interval provided the verbal prompt "Tray, please." Two children acquired spontaneous requesting after the delay and model; one child required intensive training using a gradually incremented time delay. The requesting behavior generalized across trainers and meals when given the delay in these conditions.

Like Halle et al. (1979), Charlop et al. (1985) introduced a time-delay procedure to increase autistic children's spontaneous requesting for desired items. The experimenter presented an item (e.g., cookie) and immediately modeled the request (e.g., "I want cookie"). Gradually, as the child imitated the experimenter's prompt (modeled phrase), the time between presentation of the object and the modeled phrase was lengthened by 2-second increments. The time-delay procedure was designed to transfer stimulus control of the child's verbalizations from the experimenter's model ("I want cookie") to the presence of the object (cookie). All the children acquired spontaneous requesting of desired items and generalized such spontaneous speech to unfamiliar settings, unfamiliar people, and untrained stimuli.

Moving further along the continuum, Charlop and Walsh (1986) taught spontaneous speech in the presence of an activity. Specifically, they used a time delay to teach autistic children to spontaneously verbalize "I like (love) you" in response to a hug by a familiar person or parent. In this study, the activity of hugging served as the nonverbal discriminative stimulus for spontaneous verbalizations of affection. All the children increased spontaneous use of such statements with concomitant increases in eye contact. They also appeared to discriminate as to when certain phrases were more appropriate than others. For example, the children responded with "I love you" when hugged by family members and "I like you" when hugged by the experimenter and more "favored" persons and did not respond with either statement when hugged by less familiar persons (e.g., new staff members). Autistic children are characteristically unresponsive and lack appropriate affect (Rutter, 1978). Thus, the display of affection via such a verbal statement can have positive effects on

those interacting with these children. One positive effect of the program was that parents reported that their children were more sociable and lovable following treatment. This change in parents' attitude may account for their increased time interacting with their children following treatment.

Schreibman, Charlop, and Tryon (1981) taught autistic children to request playground equipment spontaneously when the items were not in the children's view. Thus, the speech was controlled by environmental cues. Using a graduated time delay, stimulus control was shifted from the verbal prompt ("I want slide") to the environment (playground).

Finally, Charlop and Trasowech (1991) increased the daily spontaneous speech of three autistic children with a graduated time-delay procedure. This study demonstrates that the children can learn to greet people appropriately in multiple situations and with various people and engage in appropriate conversational "small talk." For each child, settings that were a part of the child's daily routine, such as morning, after school, clinic arrival, school bus, and bedtime, were used. In addition, the parents and family members were trained and served as therapists to implement the program. The responses taught were contextually appropriate phrases typically used by nonhandicapped peers—for example, saying "Good morning" when woken up in the morning; "See ya later" when leaving the clinic; and "What's for dinner, Mom?" while she prepares dinner in the kitchen.

The children increased their spontaneous speech across settings and familiar people. In many circumstances, the same room and person were part of the setting for two different targeted responses. For example, the children stated "Good morning, Mom" and "Goodnight, Mom" in their bedroom with their mother present. In this example, the setting and the person were the same, the difference being the time of the day. Thus, the statements were not under the control of one object, person, or location. Instead, the control appeared to be temporal, or time-bound, environmental cues. The generalization data were also encouraging, and the behaviors were maintained at the 30-month follow-up. Charlop and Trasowech (1991) utilized multiple exemplars of training settings and phrases. The training in several settings may have contributed to the acquisition of the spontaneous phrases in various generalization situations (Stokes & Baer, 1977). Using parents as therapists in the natural environment increases the likelihood of generalization and maintenance of spontaneous speech. This study significantly extended the utility of time-delay procedures by increasing spontaneous speech further along the continuum specified in Charlop et al. (1985). That is, the children engaged in discriminative spontaneous speech based on contextual cues (e.g., the time of the day).

Initially, a time-delay procedure was introduced as an experimental method for analyzing the moment of transfer of stimulus control (Touchette, 1971). In addition to its original purpose, the procedure has been beneficial in modifying and establishing communication skills. Three important aspects are inherent in using time-delay procedures. First, the method can be virtually errorless if the prompt is presented simultaneously with the associative stimulus, gradually lengthening the time between presentation of the stimulus and the prompt. Learning can progress faster when there are no or few errors (Etzel, McCartney, & LeBlanc, 1986; Sidman & Stoddard, 1966; Terrace, 1963). Second, the children's language is transferred from control by the teacher's verbal prompt to control by environmental cues (e.g., presence of a glass of milk, proximity to parent, or returning from school). Finally, control by nonspecific environmental stimuli can lead to more generalizable spontaneous speech (Charlop & Trasowech, 1991).

The use of time delay has eliminated the problem of transferring stimulus control of trained responses from the training location to the natural environment (Charlop & Trasowech, 1991; Halle et al., 1979; Ingenmey & Van Houten, 1991). In the long run, inclusion of natural maintaining contingencies, parental implementation, and control by environmental cues or events will facilitate maintenance of spontaneous speech and generalization to the natural contingencies of multiple environments (Stokes & Baer, 1977). Training parents to use the procedures outside of therapy may add to the successful generalization and maintenance (e.g., Charlop & Trasowech, 1991; Laski, Charlop, & Schreibman, 1988). Another facilitator of generalization is training with multiple exemplars. Griffiths and Craighead (1972) suggested that all target responses should be reinforced in at least one extra-therapy setting and more if necessary. Charlop and Trasowech (1991) implemented training in various settings (6 or 7 both in the home and at the after-school program) and trained a variety of responses (at least 6). In conclusion, the benefits of time-delay procedures in increasing spontaneous speech and facilitating generalization have been encouraging.

Incidental Teaching

Similar to the time-delay procedures that use the natural environment, the basis of incidental teaching involves teaching functional language within a natural context. Incidental teaching requires an interaction between an adult and a child in the natural environment, such as during free-play, self-care, or meal preparation. That is, instruction does not occur during formal language-training sessions; instead, the teachers take advantage of events occurring in the everyday environment, such as a child requesting assistance or information. The child's request may be either verbal (asking for toy or food) or nonverbal (pointing, crying). When the child initiates the incidental teaching situation with such a request, the teacher can respond and set up a learning situation. The goal of incidental teaching is for the child to learn in naturally occurring opportunities.

Hart and Risley (1982) suggested that spontaneous speech may be elicited from children when the natural environment is arranged so that desirable items are stored out of reach. The teacher then must be available to provide instruction when the children initiate. Incidental teaching has been extremely successful with disadvantaged children who already have basic speech skills (Hart & Risley, 1974, 1975). However, it may not be as successful with autistic children who are much more language-deficient. Halle (1984) questioned whether incidental teaching provides enough occasions for language instruction. It has been suggested that massed trials may be necessary for initial acquisition, paired with simultaneous training in the natural environment (Halle, 1984; Hart & Risley, 1980; McGee, Krantz, Mason, & McClannahan, 1983). Nevertheless, incidental teaching has been demonstrated as effective with autistic children in several studies.

Incidental teaching has been effective in establishing receptive object-labeling in autistic children. McGee et al. (1983) implemented an incidental teaching program with gestural prompts, descriptive praise, and contingent access to materials. The program was conducted during lunch preparation in the kitchen, which was a daily activity within the group home environment. The materials necessary for lunch preparation and distractor items were placed on the kitchen table. The teaching parent instructed "Give me (lunch material)." If the autistic person failed to make the correct discrimination, the instruction was repeated with a gestural prompt. Correct discriminations resulted in access to the lunch preparation materials. All the clients increased correct responding, and responses generalized to the dining room. This program focused on teaching receptive language while simultaneously training an adaptive skill in the group home environment.

Incidental teaching programs are designed to address some of the concerns resulting from use of basic operant techniques. Use of speech learned through incidental training is facilitated when the environment is arranged to include desirable items that are not readily available. The children can then initiate requests to receive the desired items. In addition, there is opportunity to generalize speech learned in separate teaching settings (Halle, 1984). The spontaneous speech is maintained through naturally occurring contingencies, such as access to desired items in environments that contain the desirable reinforcers. Programming common stimuli is also a feature of incidental teaching that has been recommended to facilitate generalization and maintenance. For example, McGee et al. (1983) used household materials as the training stimuli. Similarly, Hart and Risley (1974) used classroom play materials to modify the language of preschool children.

Natural Language Paradigm (NLP)

Incidental teaching was developed to aid transfer of stimulus control to environmental cues and provide more naturalistic instruction to facilitate generalization and maintenance. Koegel, O'Dell, and Koegel (1987) investigated another language-training program for autistic children that included adult-child interaction, naturalistic instruction, direct reinforcement, and task variation. The natural language paradigm (NLP) systematically incorporates variables found in typical language interactions with nonhandicapped persons (e.g., turn-taking, natural consequences, and sharing). The natural language paradigm begins when the child selects an item (e.g., a toy) from an array; the adult uses the item and models the target verbal response. If the child responds with the correct verbal response or an approximation, the child receives the item and praise.

O'Dell and Koegel (1981) presented the following example of use of multiple stimuli and phrases during NLP interaction. A child is presented with a ball, and the therapist prompts the word "roll" as he or she rolls the ball. Then, the child is presented with a car. Again, the therapist says "roll" while rolling the car. Importantly, if a correct verbalization or approximation is made, the therapist says "your turn," and the child is given the toy to roll while the therapist continues to repeat the verbalization (i.e., says "roll" several times). In another example of multiple phrases for the same toy, the teacher says "blow bubbles" while blowing bubbles and then prompts "pop bubbles" while breaking them.

Laski et al. (1988) demonstrated that parents may be trained to implement NLP and increase their children's speech. The parents were trained in the clinic and instructed to conduct daily 15-minute NLP sessions at home. Generalization probes were conducted in structured free-play sessions at home and in the clinic and during breaktime at the school. Teaching parents to use language acquisition procedures offers an additional way to enhance generalization and long-term maintenance of speech gains. The parents of the echolalic children reported that they were inconsistent in implementing NLP at home. Yet, the children increased their speech in both trained and nontrained situations. This indicates that NLP was extremely successful in eliciting speech from these children. In addition to generalizable effects, NLP allows for response variation by including multiple verbalizations.

Echolalia as a Speech Facilitator

As previously discussed, echolalia has been beneficial for speech training. Many of the programs used to teach appropriate speech to autistic children have been successful because of the children's tendency to echo and subsequently imitate appropriate speech. Indeed, treatment has focused on emphasizing the discrimination between words and phrases that are appropriate to imitate and those that are not (e.g., Charlop, Schreibman, & Kurtz, 1991; Lovaas, 1977). However, it is often difficult to replace echolalia with appropriate speech, and elimination of echolalia is seldom reported. Thus, reductive procedures have frequently been used to suppress echolalia. Reductive procedures have ranged from instructions to refrain from echoing to verbal reprimands contingent upon echoing to time-out procedures (Lovaas, 1977; Lovaas et al., 1973). Unfortunately, such reductive procedures have been unsuccessful at eliminating echolalia, and the generalized suppression of echolalia may be an unattainable goal.

In light of the literature demonstrating the faciliatory effect of echolalia upon speech and language acquisition as well as the failure of existing programs to eliminate echolalia, it seems more feasible to explore the ways in which echolalia can be used to advantage to teach speech, rather than to

continue efforts to punish echolalia. Recently, researchers have been focusing upon a more pragmatic approach—that of exploring the functional uses of echolalia (e.g., Charlop, 1983; Kurtz & Charlop, 1992).

Freeman, Ritvo, and Miller (1975) devised a procedure to teach an autistic child with rapid immediate echolalia to answer questions appropriately. The questions were structured to guarantee correct responding, taking advantage of the child's tendency to echo. The child was presented with a picture and the experimenter said "Sitting. What is the girl doing?" As soon as the child echoed "sitting," he received a food reinforcer and, thus, was prevented from echoing the remainder of the statement. Later, the child discontinued echoing the question and responded with the appropriate answer to the question.

Charlop (1983) developed a procedure that used autistic children's echoes to advantage for the acquisition and generalization of receptive labels. A two-choice discrimination task for receptive labeling was presented. The therapist said the label of one of the objects, waited a few seconds to allow the child an opportunity to echo the label, placed the objects in front of the child, and requested the child to hand her the object by repeating the label once more while holding out her hand to receive the object. For example, a trial consisted of the therapist saying "boat," the child echoing "boat," the therapist putting the two objects (boat and horse) before the child and then extending her hand and asking for the boat, and the child ending the trial by handing the therapist the boat. Echoing the label prior to the manual response facilitated the receptive labeling. In a second experiment, Charlop demonstrated that for echolalic children, but not for functionally mute children, this procedure increased generalization to different settings. As a result, Charlop proposed that the echolalia may have served as the children's self-imposed discriminative stimulus that they took with them to the generalization settings. This is an example of what Stokes and Baer (1977) described as "mediated generalization." It suggests that immediate echolalia can be used to teach generalizable language skills to echolalic children.

Freeman et al. (1975) and Charlop (1983) directly used immediate echolalia to increase autistic children's appropriate language skills. Charlop has replicated the use of her "echo procedure" across several language tasks (e.g., Ball, 1989; Charlop, 1992). The natural language paradigm (NLP) does not purposefully incorporate echolalia but is successful partly because the children echo the experimenter's verbalizations. Similarly, the use of time delay also takes advantage of the children's tendency to echo verbalizations. Gradually, the therapist's prompt is delayed and the children anticipate the model, thereby transferring from echolalic responding to spontaneous speech. It has also been suggested that video modeling is facilitated by the children's initial tendency to echo the video (Charlop & Milstein, 1989; Charlop, Milstein, Moore, Trasowech, & Spitzer, 1990). Programs that take advantage of children's tendency to echo can be implemented at home or at school.

Alternative Methods of Communication

The programs designed to teach autistic children speech and language have been promising. Researchers have taught autistic children a wide range of speech and language skills, ranging from labeling (Hewett, 1965), use of plurals (Guess et al.,1968), and compound sentences (Stevens-Long & Rasmussen, 1974) through spontaneous speech (Charlop & Trasowech, 1991) and conversational skills (Charlop & Milstein, 1989). However, some children require thousands of trials before they master simple language tasks (Lovaas, 1977), while others fail to acquire speech altogether. For those who do not benefit from verbal programs, it is imperative that alternative methods of communication be investigated. More and more efforts have been directed toward teaching nonverbal systems of communication to autistic children. Below is a brief description of the most frequently used nonverbal communication systems.

Sign Language

Sign language, an effective mode of communication for autistic children, is the most commonly used alternative system (Creedon, 1973; Konstantareas, Oxman, & Webster, 1977; Miller & Miller, 1973). It has been recommended that sign language be considered as an alternative only after it has been determined that the child cannot learn speech (Lovaas, 1977). Some autistic children who do not respond to verbal programs benefit from sign language apparently because they perform better with visual modes of sensory input (Hermelin & O'Connor, 1970). Carr (1982) suggested that signs are effective because they are generally concrete and function as iconic stimuli. For example, Carr presented the sign for "banana," which consists of "peeling" the index finger of one hand with the fingers of the other hand. This action resembles the peeling of a banana and is, therefore, more easily understood than an abstract concept such as the word "banana." Unfortunately, many signs are not related to the object at all. For example, "shoe" is signed by joining together the right and left fists.

Most of the literature on sign language consists of repeated demonstrations of sign acquisition by individuals, concentrating on the results but not the process of learning signs. However, Carr, Binkoff, Kologinsky, and Eddy (1978) specified how they used a three-step procedure to teach sign labels. This process was similar to operant methods for speech acquisition. The child was presented with an object and then prompted manually or through imitation to construct the sign. Eventually, the prompts were faded out.

Carr (1982) provided a detailed description of the process used to teach two-word signing. First, the child was taught to sign labels of objects. Second, an adult pantomimed an action, such as moving a car across the table (minus the car). The child was prompted to sign "move" (or the targeted verb). The adult's prompts were faded, and the adult verbally asked "What am I doing?" Once one verb was mastered, other verbs were introduced. Finally, the noun (object) was reintroduced so that the actions and nouns were combined.

Through prompting and prompt fading, differential reinforcement, and incidental teaching, Carr and Kologinsky (1983) taught children with handicaps to create new sign combinations and to use signs spontaneously. Sign language appears to have generative qualities such as those found in speech. For example, an institutionalized, low-functioning autistic child was served pepperoni pizza for the first time and signed "I want meat pie" since he did not know the specific sign for pizza. In addition, incidental teaching of signs facilitated generalization across settings and experimenters. Similarly, incidental teaching has successfully facilitated spontaneous speech and generalization (Hart & Risley, 1980; McGee, Krantz, & Mc-Clannahan, 1985).

Simultaneous Communication

Simultaneous communication, or total communication, is a method for teaching sign language that consists of the simultaneous presentation of spoken words and signs. Barrera, Lobato-Barrera, and Sulzer-Azaroff (1980) and Miller and Miller (1973) suggested that receptive or expressive communication may be enhanced when sign and speech are presented simultaneously.

Carr and Dores (1981) analyzed the effects of simultaneous communication on the language acquisition of autistic children. They studied the individual components of the simultaneous presentation separately to determine whether it was the auditory (verbal) or the visual (signed) element that maintained control over the children's responding. Two of the children acquired receptive signing, but there was no demonstration of control by auditory stimuli. Four other participants showed control by both visual and auditory components and acquired receptive signs and receptive speech. Prior to training, all the children were administered a verbal imitative test. The children who scored high on verbal imitation acquired receptive speech and signs, but the poor verbal imitators only acquired signs.

Similarly, Carr, Pridal, and Dores (1984) analyzed the role of verbal imitative skills on the acquisition of receptive labels. All the "good" verbal imitators acquired receptive language skills with both speech and sign language. It has been hypothesized that the high score on the verbal imitation test indicated that the children were proficient at responding to auditory stimuli (Carr, 1982). Therefore, children who are capable of verbal imitation respond to auditory stimuli. This means that those who learn language with simultaneous communication may learn language without the accompanying signs. Thus, children who are good verbal imitators may be responsive to learning speech and may not need alternative communication methods.

The facilitative effects of simultaneous communication on speech has not been widely replicated. Some researchers report little or no change in mute autistic children's speech following simultaneous communication training (Bonvillian & Nelson, 1976; Salvin, Routh, Foster, & Lovejoy, 1977). The literature on stimulus overselectivity demonstrates that simultaneous presentation of two modalities would lead to response to only one of the modalities. When presented with visual and auditory (or multiple) stimuli, an autistic child generally responds to only one of the stimuli (Lovaas & Schreibman, 1971; Rincover & Koegel, 1975). Thus, the advantage of simultaneous communication over sign language alone for nonspeakers remains unclear.

Symbols and Written Words

A number of systems involving symbols and signs as methods of communication are available for autistic children. While sign language is the most widely used and best researched alternative communication method (Kiernan, 1983), written words and pictures have clear advantages over sign language. One benefit of written words and pictures is that the symbols are durable, in contrast to the transitory nature of speech and signs. Thus, the children are given a longer presentation time as well as a permanent concrete cue. A second benefit of most picture and word communication programs is that, unlike signs, the symbols can be comprehended by the general public, thus providing the children with more opportunities to use them in generalization settings. Finally, the symbol and word programs can be trained with errorless procedures, such as time delay. A reduction in errors may lead to a faster acquisition rate and reduce behavior problems caused by a lack of reinforcers during training (Berkowitz, 1990).

A representational system of communication that has generalized utility is pictograms (Hollis & Carrier, 1978). This system consists of photographs, detailed drawings of objects, line drawings, or pictures from magazines. Such pictures are more easily interpreted by the general public than abstract symbol systems. Murphy, Steele, Gilligan, Yeow, and Spare (1977) outlined the method they used to teach a boy with developmental delays and autistic features to use a picture communication system. First, they trained him to match objects and pictures. Second, they tested his comprehension of the pictures. The boy was given an array of objects and had to choose one when presented with the accompanying picture. Third, expressive use of pictures was trained, followed by spontaneous requesting. When the child pointed to a picture of a readily available reinforcer, this was defined as spontaneity. The authors noted anecdotally that the child's expressive use of pictures generalized to similar objects.

Studies on picture communication with autistic children are limited, and relatively few address how to teach the children to use the pictures (Berkowitz, 1990). Berkowitz compared the effectiveness of time delay and decreasing assistance (fading of prompts) in the acquisition of communication pictures with autistic adolescents. Results indicate that time delay results in fewer errors during training and requires fewer trials to criterion. Picture communication seems to be a promising alternative communication method; however, further research is needed on generalization and spontaneous use of pictures.

Hollis and Carrier (1978) outlined non-SLIP (non-speech language initiation program), which consists of a set of symbols. Each symbol is abstract or designed in an arbitrary configuration.

The word represented by each symbol is written on a movable plastic piece. The system is based on earlier research by Premack (1970), who used a similar system with chimpanzees. This system has had limited success with autistic children (Schuler & Baldwin, 1981).

A similar system is Bliss, which consists of line drawings that are semi-pictographical (Bliss, 1965). Since the symbols represent ideas, they are conceptual. For example, symbols involving emotions include a heart. According to surveys, these systems are rarely used in schools in the United States (Kiernan, 1983). Since the symbols are non-recognizable to untrained people, the system has little utility for communication in public.

Printed words offer a promising alternative communication method for autistic children. For example, Wolff and Chess (1965) noted that some autistic children exhibited precocious reading skills. Nine of the 14 children in their sample acquired reading skills without a particular effort to teach reading. Also, some autistic children show poor speech comprehension but perform better on visual discrimination tasks (Hermelin & O'Connor, 1970). Both superior reading and visual skills make written words a practical alternative method of communication. Using an errorless discrimination procedure, La Vigna (1977) taught autistic adolescents to select the appropriate referent on a receptive task when presented with labeled cards (mint, corn, drop). Similarly, De Villiers and Naughton (1974) used a board with magnetic word cards to teach two autistic children expressive requests for food. Eventually, single-word cards were lengthened to chains of words (e.g., "Joe give cracker" and "Who has cracker?"). One child acquired four-word statements and questions in addition to some accompanying speech, while the second child acquired two-word card use.

Careful consideration is necessary when selecting the appropriate communication system for an individual with autism. For example, various personal characteristics should be considered when choosing a method of communication. The first is age—the older the child, the slimmer the chances that speech will evolve. (This is not to suggest that all older children should be taught alternative communication methods.) The second is the individual's vocal or motor imitative skills. Carr and Dores (1981) and Carr et al. (1984) examined the role of verbal imitation in language acquisition and determined that good verbal imitators were more likely to acquire speech concomitantly when taught simultaneous communication. Those with good motor imitative skills may benefit from sign language training. Baer et al. (1967) demonstrated that a child who had acquired motor imitative skills developed a generalized response class of imitative skills, which was used to facilitate language. The third personal characteristic to be considered is the individual's visual discrimination skills, which determine whether he or she can use symbols such as written words or pictures. Modality preference is another factor to be taken into account when selecting communication methods. For example, Kolko, Anderson, and Campbell (1980) performed a modality preference test with autistic children and later tested these children on a discrimination task. During the discrimination task, the autistic children only attended to one aspect of the stimulus (either the visual or the auditory). This aspect was the same sensory modality they selected on the preference test. The investigators recommended that instructional procedures be developed based on the preferred modality, or the "overselected" modality.

Summary

The speech of autistic children is characterized by major deficits and abnormalities, and speech is absent in 50% of cases. The severity of language deficits warrants intervention as early as possible. We have outlined some of the operant techniques that have been successful in the development of basic speech and language skills in both mute and echolalic children. These procedures include imitation training of verbal responses and shaping by differential reinforcement of approximations to adult verbalizations. Additionally, recent techniques have addressed more complex language skills, beyond basic labeling and requesting. Conversational skills, spontaneity, and generalization of speech and language have been the focus of some of the more recent interventions (i.e., modeling, time delay, incidental teaching, NLP, and using echolalia as a facilitator). In addition, alternative communication methods should be considered if a child fails to acquire speech. Such alternative systems include sign language, symbols, written words, and pictures.

Based on our review of the literature and our own research and clinical experience with autistic children, we would like to close with a few recommendations for speech and language intervention. First, we recommend that initial speech training for mute children begin with the verbal imitation paradigm suggested by Lovaas (1977). This increases the child's generalized verbal imitation skills and production of sounds and improves clarity of vocalizations. Once the child has acquired some verbal imitation skills, NLP procedures may be introduced to increase the production of sounds while also potentially increasing the enjoyment of speech training. Both of these programs are easy to teach parents and teachers to use with the children. We do not find it necessary to teach nonverbal imitation skills before verbal imitation skills. Rather, we have been successful in teaching nonverbal and verbal imitation concurrently in the child's treatment (Charlop, Trasowech, Calkin, Kurtz, & Bott, 1990). We believe that early intervention is especially important with speech training; therefore, we do not delay the onset of speech training, if at all possible.

The verbal imitation paradigm is helpful for teaching acquisition of single words and, subsequently, full sentences to mute children. This paradigm may also be used for teaching words and sentences to echolalic children, although generally they can quickly proceed to learning answers to questions as opposed to rote imitation. NLP is strongly recommended for echolalic children who can more readily imitate phrases and full sentences, and we have seen powerful results with such children (e.g., Laski et al., 1988). While both mute and echolalic children are learning expressive speech, we recommend that they also be taught receptive language. We do not find it necessary to teach receptive language first. Although some mute children acquire receptive skills much faster than they do even minimal expressive imitative responses, we recommend that both be taught concurrently in the child's course of treatment, since receptive skills do not necessarily generalize to expressive skills (Guess & Baer, 1973).

One of the most important questions is whether to teach verbal speech or an alternative communication method. Clearly, if the child is echolalic or if echolalia is beginning to emerge, verbal speech is recommended. For mute children, the question is more difficult to answer. It has been suggested that if verbal speech is not acquired by the age of 5, the prognosis for learning it sharply decreases. Additionally, it has been suggested that if no verbal speech is present, sign language should be taught either as a precursor to verbal speech or simultaneously with verbal speech.

The literature has not provided consistent and compelling evidence suggesting that teaching sign language has any faciliatory effect on later verbal speech acquisition. Additionally, the literature on the simultaneous teaching of sign language and verbal speech has not provided clear evidence of its efficacy. Based on these findings, as well as our experience, we do not recommend automatically teaching sign language or simultaneous communication to children because they are mute— even if they are over 5 years old. Rather, it is important to test for responsiveness to verbal imitation training. If the child demonstrates such responsiveness, we recommend verbal speech training, even though such training may have to proceed slowly. We believe that each child is entitled to receive training in the communication method that is least restrictive and less handicapping. Since few people use and understand sign language in the natural environment, it is unlikely that sign language will function as an effective means of communication. Thus, we strongly recommend teaching verbal speech.

If speech training proves unsuccessful, we then recommend an alternative communication method. As mentioned, the number of people who speak and understand sign language is limited. Thus, if an alternative method of communication is necessary, we recommend one that will be widely understood, such as picture communication or written word communication. These communication methods can be widely used in the natural environment and are generally no more difficult to acquire than signing. At present, we are studying written word communication methods for children who have interest and skills in use of alphabet letters, word discrimination, and word recognition (Knize & Charlop, 1992).

For those children who learn verbal speech, speech and language intervention is far from complete. Rather, teaching of more naturalized speech becomes the next challenge for researchers and practitioners. The procedures discussed in this chapter (e.g., modeling, time delay, NLP, incidental teaching, and using echolalia as a speech facilitator) appear promising for teaching more complex speech, such as spontaneous speech, conversational speech, generalized speech, and other more natural verbal interactions. We encourage researchers to replicate and expand upon such encouraging procedures.

This chapter has not covered all speech and language programs that are available for children with speech delays. We have focused predominantly on programs heavily researched with autistic children. Clearly, other programs designed for developmentally delayed populations may be appropriate for autistic children. Further research is needed as speech and language deficits remain major obstacles to autistic children's overall improvement.

However, we are optimistic about the research being conducted on speech and language training for autistic children. Empirical research has demonstrated the success of the programs discussed in this chapter. The targeted verbal skills have been seriously lacking from autistic children's repertoires prior to this research. It is encouraging that behavior analysts continue to develop new methods for improving autistic children's speech and language skills. Remediation of speech and language deficits can lead to changes in social skills, academic achievement, and increased integration into society. We believe that the speech and language programs discussed in this chapter may lead to a much more promising future for autistic persons.

References

APOLLONI, T., COOKE, S. A., & COOKE, T. P. (1976). Establishing a normal peer as a behavioral model for developmentally delayed toddlers. *Perceptual and Motor Skills, 43,* 1155–1165.

BAER, D. M., PETERSON, R. F., & SHERMAN, J.A. (1967). The development of imitation by reinforcing behavioral similarity to a model. *Journal of the Experimental Analysis of Behavior, 10,* 405–416.

BALL, K. L. (1989). *Using immediate echolalia to teach autistic children a memory task.* Unpublished senior thesis, Claremont McKenna College.

BALTAXE, C. A. (1981). Acoustic characteristics of prosody in autism. In P. Mittler (Ed.), *Frontiers of knowledge in mental retardation* (pp. 223–233). Baltimore: University Park Press.

BALTAXE, C. A., & SIMMONS, J. Q. (1975). Language in childhood psychosis: A review. *Journal of Speech and Hearing Disorders, 30,* 439–458.

BALTAXE, C. A., & SIMMONS, J. Q. (1981). Disorders of language in childhood psychosis: Current concepts and approaches. In J. Darby (Ed.), *Speech evaluation in psychiatry* (pp. 285–328). New York: Grune and Stratton.

BANDURA, A., & KUPERS, C. J. (1964). Transmission of patterns of self-reinforcement through modeling. *Journal of Abnormal and Social Psychology, 69,* 1–9.

BANDURA, A., & MENLOVE, F. L. (1968). Factors determining vicarious extinction of avoidance behavior through symbolic modeling. *Journal of Personality and Social Psychology, 8,* 99–108.

BARRERA, R. D., LOBATO-BARRERA, D., & SULZER-AZAROFF, B. (1980). A simultaneous treatment comparison of three expressive language training programs with a mute autistic child. *Journal of Autism and Developmental Disorders, 10,* 21–37.

BARTAK, L., & RUTTER, M. (1974). The use of personal pronouns by autistic children. *Journal of Autism and Childhood Schizophrenia, 4,* 217–222.

BARTAK, L., & RUTTER, M. (1976). Differences between mentally retarded and normally intelligent autistic children. *Journal of Autism and Childhood Schizophrenia, 6,* 109–120.

BARTAK, L., RUTTER, M., & COX, A. (1975). A comparative study of infantile autism and specific developmental receptive language disorder. I. The children. *British Journal of Psychiatry, 126,* 127–145.

BERKOWITZ, S. (1990). A comparison of two methods of prompting in training discrimination of communication book pictures by autistic students. *Journal of Autism and Developmental Disorders, 20,* 255–262.

BETTELHEIM, B. (1967). *The empty fortress.* New York: Free Press.

BLISS, C. K. (1965). *Semantography-Blissymbolics.* Sydney, Australia: Semantography Publications.

BONVILLIAN, J. D., & NELSON, K. E. (1976). Sign language acquisition in a mute autistic boy. *Journal of Speech and Hearing Disorders, 41,* 339–347.

BUCHER, B., & LOVAAS, O. I. (1968). Use of aversive stimulation in behavior modification. In M. R. Jones (Ed.), *Miami symposium on the predication of behavior: Aversive stimulation* (pp. 77–140). Coral Gables, FL: University of Miami Press.

CARR, E. G. (1981). Sign language. In O. I. Lovaas, A. Ackerman, D. Alexander, D. Firestone, M. Perkins, & D. Young (Eds.), *The me book: Teaching manual for parents and teachers of developmentally disabled children.* Baltimore: University Park Press.

CARR, E. G. (1982). Sign language. In R. Koegel, A. Rincover & A. L. Egel (Eds.), *Educating and understanding autistic children* (pp. 142–157). San Diego, CA: College-Hill.

CARR, E. G., BINKOFF, J. A., KOLOGINSKY, E., & EDDY, E. (1978). Acquisition of sign language by autistic children. I. Expressive labeling. *Journal of Applied Behavior Analysis, 11,* 489–501.

CARR, E. G., & DORES, P. A. (1981). Patterns of language acquisition following simultaneous communication with autistic children. *Analysis and Intervention in Developmental Disabilities, 1,* 347–361.

CARR, E. G., & KOLOGINSKY, E. (1983). Acquisition of sign language by autistic children. II. Spontaneity and generalization effects. *Journal of Applied Behavior Analysis, 16,* 297–314.

CARR, E. G., PRIDAL, C., & DORES, P. (1984). Speech versus sign comprehension in autistic children: Analysis and prediction. *Journal of Experimental Child Psychology, 37,* 587–597.

CARR, E. G., SCHREIBMAN, L., & LOVAAS, O. I. (1975). Control of echolalic speech in psychotic children. *Journal of Abnormal Child Psychology, 3,* 331–351.

CHARLOP, M. H. (1983). The effects of echolalia on acquisition and generalization of receptive labeling in autistic children. *Journal of Applied Behavior Analysis, 16,* 111–126.

CHARLOP, M. H. (1986). Setting effects on the occurrence of autistic children's immediate echolalia. *Journal of Autism and Developmental Disorders, 16,* 473–483.

CHARLOP, M. H. (1989). *Using autistic children's echolalia to teach speech.* NIH grant proposal.

CHARLOP, M. H. (1992). *Using immediate echolalia to increase verbal reporting of prior actions.* Working manuscript.

CHARLOP, M. H., KURTZ, P. F., & CASEY, F. G. (1990). Use of aberrant behaviors as reinforcers for autistic children. *Journal of Applied Behavior Analysis, 23,* 163–181.

CHARLOP, M. H., & MILSTEIN, J. P. (1989). Teaching autistic children conversational speech using video modeling. *Journal of Applied Behavior Analysis, 22,* 275–285.

CHARLOP, M. H., MILSTEIN, J. P., MOORE, M., TRASOWECH, J. E., & SPITZER, S. L. (1990, May). *Direct and indirect effects of video modeling on autistic children's play, social behaviors, and speech.* Paper presented at the annual meeting of the Association for Behavior Analysis, Nashville, TN.

CHARLOP, M. H., SCHREIBMAN, L., & KURTZ, P. F. (1991). Childhood autism. In T. R. Kratochwill & R. J. Morris (Eds.), *The practice of child therapy* (2nd ed.) (pp. 257–297). New York: Pergamon.

CHARLOP, M. H., SCHREIBMAN, L., & THIBODEAU, M. G. (1985). Increasing spontaneous verbal responding in autistic children using a time delay procedure. *Journal of Applied Behavior Analysis, 18,* 155–166.

CHARLOP, M. H., SCHREIBMAN, L., & TRYON, A. S. (1983). Learning through observation: The effects of peer modeling on acquisition and generalization in autistic children. *Journal of Abnormal Child Psychology, 11,* 355–366.

CHARLOP, M. H., & TRASOWECH, J. E. (1991). Increasing autistic children's daily spontaneous speech. *Journal of Applied Behavior Analysis, 24,* 747–761.

CHARLOP, M. H., TRASOWECH, J. E., CALKIN, J., KURTZ, P. F., & BOTT, M. (1990, November). *Program evaluation of autistic children.* Paper presented at the annual convention of the Association for the Advancement of Behavior Therapy, San Francisco.

CHARLOP, M. H., & WALSH, M. E. (1986). Increasing autistic children's spontaneous verbalizations of affection: An assessment of time delay and peer modeling procedures. *Journal of Applied Behavior Analysis, 19,* 307–314.

COLEMAN, S. L., & STEDMAN, J. M. (1974). Use of a peer model in language training in an echolalic child. *Journal of Behavior Therapy and Experimental Psychiatry, 5,* 275–279.

CREEDON, M. P. (1973). *Language development in nonverbal autistic children using a simultaneous communication system.* Paper presented at the biennial meeting of the Society for Research in Child Development, Philadelphia.

DE VILLIERS, J. G., & NAUGHTON, J. M. (1974). Teaching a symbol language to autistic children. *Journal of Consulting and Clinical Psychology, 42,* 111–117.

EGEL, A. L., RICHMAN, G. S., & KOEGEL, R. L. (1981). Normal peer models and autistic children's learning. *Journal of Applied Behavior Analysis, 14,* 3–12.

ETZEL, B. C., McCARTNEY, L. L., & LEBLANC, J. M. (1986, May). *An update on errorless stimulus control technology.* Paper presented at the annual convention of the Association for Behavior Analysis, Milwaukee.

FAY, W. H. (1969). On the basis of autistic echolalia. *Journal of Communication Disorders, 2,* 38–47.

FAY, W. H., & SCHULER, A. L. (1980). *Emerging language in autistic children.* Baltimore: University Park Press.

FISH, B., SHAPIRO, T., & CAMPBELL, M. (1966). Long-term prognosis and the response of schizophrenic children to drug therapy: A controlled study of Trifluoperazine. *American Journal of Psychiatry, 123,* 32–39.

FREEMAN, B. J., RITVO, E., & MILLER, R. (1975). An operant procedure to teach an echolalic autistic child to answer questions appropriately. *Journal of Autism and Childhood Schizophrenia, 5,* 169–176.

GARCIA, E., & DEHAVEN, E. D. (1974). Use of operant techniques in the establishment and generalization of language: A review and analysis. *American Journal on Mental Deficiency, 79,* 169–178.

GESELL, A., & THOMPSON, H. (1934). *Infant behavior: Its genesis and growth.* New York: McGraw-Hill.

GOETZ, L., SCHULER, A., & SAILOR, W. (1979). Teaching functional speech to the severely handicapped: Current issues. *Journal of Autism and Developmental Disorders, 9,* 325–343.

GONZALES, J. (1987). *Delayed echolalia in autistic children: Contributing factors and beneficial effects.* Unpublished senior thesis, Claremont McKenna College.

GRIFFITHS, H., & CRAIGHEAD, W. E. (1972). Generalization in operant speech therapy for misarticulation. *Journal of Speech and Hearing Disorders, 37,* 485–494.

GUESS, D., & BAER, D. M. (1973). An analysis of individual differences in generalization between receptive and productive language in retarded children. *Journal of Applied Behavior Analysis, 6,* 311–329.

GUESS, D., SAILOR, W., RUTHERFORD, G., & BAER, D. M. (1968). An experimental analysis of linguistic development: The productive use of the plural morpheme. *Journal of Applied Behavior Analysis, 1,* 297–306.

HALLE, J. (1982). Teaching functional language to the handicapped: An integrative model of natural environment teaching techniques. *Journal of the Association for the Severely Handicapped, 7,* 29–36.

HALLE, J. (1984). Natural environment language assessment and intervention with severely impaired preschoolers. *Topics in Early Childhood Special Education, 4,* 36–56.

HALLE, J.W., MARSHALL, A. M., & SPRADLIN, J. E. (1979). Time delay: A technique to increase language use and facilitate generalization in retarded children. *Journal of Applied Behavior Analysis, 12,* 431–439.

HART, B., & RISLEY, T. R. (1974). Using preschool materials to modify the language of disadvantaged children. *Journal of Applied Behavior Analysis, 7,* 243–256.

HART, B., & RISLEY, T. R. (1975). Incidental teaching of language in the preschool. *Journal of Applied Behavior Analysis, 8,* 411–420.

HART, B., & RISLEY, T. R. (1980). In vivo language intervention: Unanticipated general effects. *Journal of Applied Behavior Analysis, 13,* 407–432.

HART, B., & RISLEY, T. R. (1982). *How to use incidental teaching for elaborating language.* Lawrence, KS: H & H Enterprises.

HARTUNG, J. R. (1970). A review of procedures to increase verbal imitation skills and functional speech in autistic children. *Journal of Speech and Hearing Disorders, 35,* 203–217.

HARTUP, W. W., & COATES, B. (1967). Imitation of a peer as a function of reinforcement from the peer and rewardingness of the model. *Child Development, 38,* 1003–1016.

HERMELIN, J. B., & O'CONNOR, N. (1970). *Psychological experiments with autistic children.* Oxford, England: Pergamon.

HEWETT, F. (1965). Teaching speech to an autistic child through operant conditioning. *American Journal of Orthopsychiatry, 35,* 927–936.

HOLLIS, J. H., & CARRIER, J. K. (1978). Intervention strategies for nonspeech children. In R. L. Schiefelbusch (Ed.), *Language intervention strategies* (pp. 57–100). Baltimore: University Park Press.

HOWLIN, P. (1981). The effectiveness of operant language training with autistic children. *Journal of Autism and Developmental Disorders, 11,* 89–105.

HUNG, D. (1977). Generalization of curiosity questioning behavior in autistic children. *Journal of Behavior Therapy and Experimental Psychiatry, 8,* 237–245.

INGENMEY, R., & VAN HOUTEN, R. (1991). Using time delay to promote spontaneous speech in an autistic child. *Journal of Applied Behavior Analysis, 24,* 591–596.

KANNER, L. (1943). Autistic disturbances of affective contact. *Nervous Child, 2,* 217–250.

KANNER, L. (1946). Irrelevant and metaphonical language in early infantile autism. *American Journal of Psychiatry, 103,* 242–245.

KIERNAN, C. (1983). The use of nonvocal communication techniques with autistic individuals. *Journal of Child Psychology and Psychiatry, 24,* 339–375.

KNIZE, L., & CHARLOP, M. H. (1992, May). *Using printed labels to facilitate receptive labeling by a nonverbal autistic child.* Paper presented at the annual meeting of the Association for Behavior Analysis, San Francisco.

KOEGEL, R. L., O'DELL, M. C., & KOEGEL, L. K. (1987). A natural language teaching paradigm for nonverbal autistic children. *Journal of Autism and Developmental Disorders, 17,* 187–200.

KOLKO, D. J., ANDERSON, L., & CAMPBELL, M. (1980). Sensory preference and overselective responding in autistic children. *Journal of Autism and Developmental Disorders, 10,* 259–271.

KONSTANTAREAS, M. M., OXMAN, J., & WEBSTER, C. D. (1977). Simultaneous communication with autistic and other severely dysfunctional children. *Journal of Communication Disorders, 10,* 267–282.

KURTZ, P. F., & CHARLOP, M. H. (1992). *Analysis and application of autistic children's delayed echolalia.* Unpublished dissertation, Claremont McKenna College.

LASKI, K. E., CHARLOP, M. H., & SCHREIBMAN, L. (1988). Training parents to use the natural language paradigm to increase their autistic children's speech. *Journal of Applied Behavior Analysis, 21,* 391–400.

LAVIGNA, G. W. (1977). Communication training in mute autistic adolescents using the written word.

Journal of Autism and Childhood Schizophrenia, 7, 135–149.

LOVAAS, O. I. (1977). *The autistic child.* New York: Irvington.

LOVAAS, O. I., KOEGEL, R. L., SIMMONS, J. Q., & STEVENS-LONG, J. (1973). Some generalization and follow-up measures on autistic children in behavior therapy. *Journal of Applied Behavior Analysis, 6,* 131–166.

LOVAAS, O. I., NEWSOM, C., & HICKMAN, C. (1987). Self-stimulatory behavior and perceptual reinforcement. *Journal of Applied Behavior Analysis, 20,* 45–68.

LOVAAS, O. I., & SCHREIBMAN, L. (1971). Stimulus overselectivity of autistic children in a two-stimulus situation. *Behavior Research and Therapy, 9,* 305–310.

LOVAAS, O. I., SCHREIBMAN, L., & KOEGEL, R. L. (1974). A behavior modification approach to the treatment of autistic children. *Journal of Autism and Childhood Schizophrenia, 4,* 11–129.

LOVAAS, O. I., VARNI, J., KOEGEL, R. L., & LORSCH, N. (1977). Some observations on the non-extinguishability of children's speech. *Child Development, 48,* 1121–1127.

MANN, R., & BAER, D. M. (1971). The effects of receptive language training on articulation. *Journal of Applied Behavior Analysis, 4,* 291–299.

MATSON, J. L., SEVIN, J. A., FRIDLEY, P., & LOVE, S. R. (1990). Increasing spontaneous language in three autistic children. *Journal of Applied Behavior Analysis, 23,* 227–233.

McGEE, G., KRANTZ, P. J., MASON, D., & McCLANNAHAN, L. E. (1983). A modified incidental teaching procedure for autistic youth: Acquisition and generalization of receptive object labels. *Journal of Applied Behavior Analysis, 16,* 329–338.

McGEE, G., KRANTZ, P. J., & McCLANNAHAN, L. E. (1985). The facilitative effects of incidental teaching on preposition use by autistic children. *Journal of Applied Behavior Analysis, 18,* 17–31.

MILLER, A., & MILLER, E. E. (1973). Cognitive-development training with elevated boards and sign language. *Journal of Autism and Childhood Schizophrenia, 3,* 65–85.

MURPHY, G. H., STEELE, K., GILLIGAN, T., YEOW, J., & SPARE, D. (1977). Teaching a picture language to a non-speaking retarded boy. *Behavior Research and Therapy, 15,* 198–201.

NAKANISHI, Y., & OWADA, K. (1973). Echoic utterances of children between the ages of one to three years. *Journal of Verbal Learning and Verbal Behavior, 12,* 658–665.

NEEDLEMAN, R., RITVO, E. R., & FREEMAN, B. J. (1980). Objectively defined linguistic parameters in children with autism and other developmental disabilities. *Journal of Autism and Developmental Disorders, 10,* 389–398.

O'DELL, M. C., & KOEGEL, R. L. (1981, November). *The differential effects of two methods of promoting speech in non-verbal autistic children.* Paper presented at the annual convention of the American Speech-Language-Hearing Association, Los Angeles.

PETERSON, C., PETERSON, J., & SCRIVEN, G. (1977). Peer imitation by nonhandicapped and handicapped preschoolers. *Exceptional Children, 43,* 223–224.

PHILIPS, G. M., & DYER, C. (1977). Late onset echolalia in autism and allied disorders. *British Journal of Disorders of Communication, 12,* 47–59.

PREMACK, D. (1970). A functional analysis of language. *Journal of the Experimental Analysis of Behavior, 14,* 107–125.

PRIZANT, B. M., & RYDELL, P. J. (1984). Analysis of functions of delayed echolalia in autistic children. *Journal of Speech and Hearing Research, 27,* 183–192.

RICKS, D. M., & WING, L. (1975). Language, communication, and the use of symbols in normal and autistic children. *Journal of Autism and Childhood Schizophrenia, 5,* 191–220.

RICKS, D. M., & WING, L. (1976). Language, communication and the use of symbols. In L. Wing (Ed.), *Early childhood autism* (2nd ed.) (pp. 93–134). New York: Pergamon.

RINCOVER, A., & KOEGEL, R. L. (1975). Setting generality and stimulus control in autistic children. *Journal of Applied Behavior Analysis, 8,* 235–246.

RISLEY, T. R., & WOLF, M. (1967). Establishing functional speech in echolalic children. *Behavior Research and Therapy, 5,* 73–88.

RUTTER, M. (1966). Behavioral and cognitive characteristics of a series of psychotic children. In J. Wing (Ed.), *Early childhood autism* (pp. 51–81). Oxford, England: Pergamon.

RUTTER, M. (1978). Diagnosis and definition of childhood autism. *Journal of Autism and Childhood Schizophrenia, 8,* 139–161.

RUTTER, M., & LOCKYER, L. A. (1967). A five to fifteen year follow-up study of infantile psychosis: I. Description of the sample. *British Journal of Psychiatry, 113,* 1169–1182.

SALVIN, A., ROUTH, D. K., FOSTER, R. E., & LOVEJOY, K. M. (1977). Acquisition of modified American sign language by a mute autistic child. *Journal of Autism and Childhood Schizophrenia, 7,* 359–371.

SCHREIBMAN, L. (1988). *Autism.* Newbury Park, CA: Sage.

SCHREIBMAN, L., & CHARLOP, M. H. (1989). Infantile autism. In T. H. Ollendick & M. Hersen (Eds.), *Handbook of child psychopathology* (pp. 105–129). New York: Plenum.

SCHREIBMAN, L., CHARLOP, M. H., & TRYON, A. S. (1981, August). *The acquisition and generalization of appropriate spontaneous speech in autistic children.* Paper presented at the annual convention of the American Psychological Association, Los Angeles.

SCHREIBMAN, L., KOHLENBERG, B., & BRITTEN, K. R. (1986). Differential responding to content and intonation components of a complex auditory stimulus by nonverbal and echolalic autistic children. *Analysis and Intervention in Developmental Disabilities, 6,* 109–125.

SCHULER, A. L., & BALDWIN, M. (1981). Nonspeech communication and childhood autism. *Language, Speech and Hearing Services in the School, 12,* 246–256.

SHIPLEY, E. F., SMITH, C., & GLEITMAN, L. (1969). A study of the acquisition of language: Free response to commands. *Language, 45,* 322–342.

SIDMAN, M., & STODDARD, L. (1966). *International review of research in mental retardation* (pp. 151–208). New York: Academic.

SIMMONS, J. Q., & BALTAXE, C. A. (1975). Language patterns of adolescent autistics. *Journal of Autism and Childhood Schizophrenia, 5,* 333–351.

SKINNER, B. F. (1957). *Verbal behavior.* New York: Appleton-Century-Crofts.

STEVENS-LONG, J., & RASMUSSEN, M. (1974). The acquisition of simple and compound sentence structure in an autistic child. *Journal of Applied Behavior Analysis, 7,* 473–479.

STOKES, T. F., & BAER, D. M. (1977). An implicit technology of generalization. *Journal of Applied Behavior Analysis, 10,* 349–367.

TERRACE, H. S. (1963). Discrimination learning with and without "errors." *Journal of the Experimental Analysis of Behavior, 6,* 1–27.

TOUCHETTE, P. (1971). Transfer of stimulus control: Measuring the moment of transfer. *Journal of the Experimental Analysis of Behavior, 15,* 347–354.

TWARDOSZ, S., & BAER, D. M. (1973). Training two severely retarded adolescents to ask questions. *Journal of Applied Behavior Analysis, 6,* 655–661.

VAN RIPER, C. (1963). *Speech correction.* Englewood Cliffs, NJ: Prentice-Hall.

VARNI, J. W., LOVAAS, O. I., KOEGEL, R. L., & EVERETT, N. L. (1979). An analysis of observational learning in autistic and normal children. *Journal of Abnormal Child Psychology, 7,* 31–43.

WARREN, S. F., BAXTER, D. K., ANDERSON, S. R., MARSHALL, A., & BAER, D. M. (1981). Generalization of question-asking by severely retarded individuals. *Journal of the Association for the Severely Handicapped, 6,* 15–22.

WING, L. (1976). Diagnosis, clinical description, and prognosis. In L. Wing (Ed.), *Early childhood autism: Clinical, educational and social aspects* (2nd ed.) (pp. 15–48). Oxford, England: Pergamon.

WOLFF, S., & CHESS, S. (1965). An analysis of the language of fourteen schizophrenic children. *Journal of Child Psychology and Psychiatry, 6,* 29–41.

CHAPTER 13

Social Skills Training with Autistic Children

Johnny L. Matson
LOUISIANA STATE UNIVERSITY

Naomi Swiezy
THE KENNEDY KRIEGER INSTITUTE,
JOHNS HOPKINS UNIVERSITY

Definition of Social Skills

A clear and generally accepted definition of social skills does not yet exist (Davies & Rogers, 1985). According to Bernstein (1981), this lack of a consistent definition of social skills may result in several difficulties. These include slowed development of useful assessment instruments, confusion about what is being measured, use of vague or simplistic terminology, and neglect of crucial areas of investigation.

Some confusion in the definition and conceptualization of social skills may have resulted from the populations investigated. That is, in the general child population, interpersonal skills have typically been the primary target of social skills intervention (e.g., Rathjen, 1984). However, in the mentally retarded population, social skills often encompass a wider range of skills, including dressing and hygiene (e.g., Lee, 1977). In addition, as a result of the definitional and conceptual confusion, professionals from various disciplines and of diverse orientations have become motivated and interested in investigating social skills. The contributions from these sources have led to even further confusion (Matson & Ollendick, 1988).

Some researchers favor a more molar focus to defining and conceptualizing social skills, whereas others prefer a more molecular approach (Eisler, 1976; McFall, 1982). Some have suggested that the concept of social skills encompasses perceptual, cognitive, and performance components (Trower, 1979), while others prefer a more limited view (Curran, 1979). The latter is more appropriate with individuals of lower intellectual functioning who would have difficulty relating to the more complex, cognitive aspects of social skills (e.g., empathy and interpersonal problem-solving) (Davies & Rogers, 1985).

According to the narrower definition, individuals with adequate social skills are able to adapt to their environment and can avoid interpersonal conflicts by exhibiting appropriate motoric behaviors (e.g., hand-waving and appropriate mealtime behavior). Conversely, individuals deficient in social skills tend to exhibit conduct problems (e.g., physical fights), to be unpopular with others, to fail to get along with authority, and to appear uncaring about others' rights and privileges (Davies & Rogers, 1985; Matson & Ollendick, 1988). A more general definition of social skills involves appropriate application of motoric, cognitive, and affective skills and behaviors according to the situation, setting, and individual (Eisler, 1976; Hersen & Bellack, 1976; Trower, Bryant, & Argyle, 1978).

In addition, the terms "social skills" and "social competence" have often been used simultaneously (Cartledge & Milburn, 1986). However, Hops (1983) clarified the distinction between the two concepts. Social competence may be considered a summary term that reflects an overall judgment of the quality of an individual's behavior in a specific situation. Conversely, social skills may be conceptualized as specific identifiable skills that form the basis for or lead to socially competent behavior.

Importance of Social Skills

General Population

Despite the lack of a clear conceptualization of social skills, concern and interest in this area have continued. Appropriate social skills are of considerable importance in the population at large. For example, recent research has highlighted the importance of children's social relationships for emotional functioning and later psychological adjustment. Thus, social skills deficiencies have been associated with major adjustment problems in the school and home settings (Matson & Ollendick, 1988). In fact, social skills deficiencies have been noted to correlate highly with rates of juvenile delinquency (Roff, Sell, & Golden, 1972), dropping out of school (Ullman, 1975), bad conduct military discharges (Roff, 1961), and mental illness (Cowen et al., 1973). Further, social skills deficits often result in the development of negative stereotypes among peers (Koslin et al., 1986) and other lifelong problems (Guinouard & Rychlak, 1982).

Autistic Population

The development of appropriate social skills is particularly important for developmentally dis-abled individuals. Social interest and skills are considered two of the most important factors in treatment outcome with this population. Unfortunately, research with developmentally disabled individuals does not reflect the importance of social skills training (Schopler & Mesibov, 1983).

It is generally accepted that children with autism are deficient in social skills and peer interactions (e.g., Stone & Lemanek, 1990; Ungerer, 1989). Despite considerable disagreement on the nature and behavioral characteristics of autism, one characteristic has been consistently recognized as salient—impaired social and interpersonal functioning (American Psychiatric Association, 1987; Kanner, 1943; Ritvo & Freeman, 1977; Rutter, 1978; Schopler, 1983). Because of this salience and the negative repercussions of the social and interpersonal skills deficits of autistic individuals, many have cited the need to remediate problems in this area (Bemporad, 1979; Stokes, 1977).

Support for this view has been provided by research suggesting that social interest and skills are among the most crucial variables determining autistic individuals' long-term adjustment (Schopler & Mesibov, 1983). The social skills deficits are further compounded by the fact that most autistic individuals are mentally retarded, and social behavior is also central to the latter diagnosis (Marchetti & Campbell, 1990). That is, to be classified as mentally retarded, an individual must display impaired adaptive behavior and be of significantly subaverage intelligence (Grossman, 1983).

Furthermore, adaptive behavior assessment typically involves some measure of social functioning (Meyers, Nihira, & Zetlin, 1979), a lack of which is an integral part of developmental disabilities. Also, given the recent trend toward deinstitutionalization, assessment and treatment of social skills are important considerations in the prognosis for the developmentally disabled individuals' adjustment within the community (Davies & Rogers, 1985). Development of acceptable social behavior may facilitate placement in a less restrictive environment (Hill, Wehman, & Horst, 1982).

History of Social Skills Training

The conceptual basis for and the specific techniques utilized in social skills training were largely derived from social learning theory. The assumption was that many responses that help people adapt to their physical and social environments are learned. Consequently, types of responses displayed and behaviors found successful in enhancing social adjustment are thought to be determined by observations of and reinforcement from others (Matson & Ollendick, 1988).

Empirically derived treatments of social skills are a recent phenomenon. The first studies in this area focused on assertiveness training with an adult diagnosis (e.g., McFall & Marston, 1970). Soon, other interpersonal problems were investigated within the realm of social skills deficits (Matson & Ollendick, 1988). In addition, the focus of research efforts changed from generally "normal" populations with minor problems to populations with more severe diagnoses such as schizophrenia and depression (e.g., Hersen & Bellack, 1976; Liberman & Davis, 1975).

Given the success of social skills training with adults, social skills programs were eventually pursued with children (Combs & Slaby, 1977; Rathjen & Foreyt, 1980). Assessment and treatment techniques are generally derived from operant conditioning or social learning theory (Matson & Ollendick, 1988).

Research pertaining to social skills in children has primarily focused on improving school adjustment or enhancing normalization in individuals with mental retardation, learning disabilities, or emotional disturbances (LaGreca & Mesibov, 1981; Matson & Ollendick, 1988; Morris & Dalker, 1974). Other socially important results of social skills training noted in the literature include acceptance by peers and others, good mental health, and avoidance of legal difficulties (Cartledge & Milburn, 1986; Gresham, 1984).

Considerable research with children was initially conducted by psychologists using operant training. More recently, professionals from a variety of disciplines and using a variety of approaches have become involved in social skills. This change has led to the development of diverse assessment and treatment strategies of varied theoretical orientations, which may be utilized for intervention within different settings (Matson & Ollendick, 1988).

Selecting Social Skills for Training

General Population

Before social skills training may begin, it is important to identify what skills are important for the child to learn. To identify which social skills are to be taught requires consideration of several issues. First, the child's developmental level should be taken into account. Some behaviors may be more easily taught and maintained at one developmental stage than at another. In addition, some behaviors require instruction, while others develop naturally. It is debatable whether behavior always develops according to the stages proposed in different theories. Nevertheless, these theories suggest the general sequence in which social behaviors develop and, therefore, should be taught.

There has been a tendency to conceptualize social skills within a developmental context, although the field of social skills has historically been dominated by a behavioral orientation (Cartledge & Milburn, 1986). Reinforcement contingencies may be used to alter behavior; however, children's beliefs about the causes of behavior are often inaccurate and vary with developmental level rather than with reinforcement contingencies (Gelfand & Hartmann, 1979). Harris and Ferrari (1983) stressed the need for normative information that suggests which social skills are relevant for training at each developmental level and helps evaluate treatment outcomes.

Certain social criteria should also be considered when selecting social skills to be trained. Various societies, professionals, and families differ in their opinions of how a child should act. Therefore, it is important to determine the norms of the child's social environment before deciding how to assist him or her (Cartledge & Milburn, 1986). Behaviors considered desirable by the child and his or her peers should also be considered in order to determine motivation for treatment. Finally, behavior classified as appropriate or demonstrative of good social skills may vary with the particular situation.

Ultimately, selecting social skills to be trained depends on which skills will be of reinforcing and adaptive value to the child. That is, skills that are likely to be appreciated and reinforced by others and have an effect on the individual's social and community adjustment should be selected (Cartledge & Milburn, 1986; Davies & Rogers, 1985). A good rule of thumb in selecting social skills is the relevance of behavior rule, which states that only behaviors that will continue to be reinforced after training should be taught (Allyon & Azrin, 1968). This approach also helps in the generalization and maintenance of social behaviors. Generally, skills selected for remediation programs must have some social validity and address specific outcomes (e.g., improve family relationships or classroom behavior) (Cartledge & Milburn, 1986).

Autistic Population

The social behaviors of autistic individuals considered to be in need of remediation are typically integral to the diagnosis of autism. For example, autistic individuals often fail to engage in reciprocal social interactions. In an investigation of the social responsiveness of autistic, Down's syndrome, and normal youngsters, both groups of handicapped individuals engaged in less social interaction with their parents than did the normal children (Sigman, Ungerer, Mundy, & Sherman, 1984). When these researchers compared other social behaviors of the same groups, other striking differences occurred. That is, although both the mentally retarded and autistic groups were capable of initiating or responding to simple social games, the autistic children were much less likely to share toys, seek adult attention, or respond to adults' attempts to gain their attention. Likewise, in another comparison of normal, autistic, and mentally retarded children, the autistic children failed to display the

high levels of positive affect exhibited by the other two groups during joint attention situations (Kasari, Sigman, Mundy, & Yirmiya, 1990). The findings from both of these studies seem to support the tendency of autistic individuals to relate to others only as objects, not in a more socially oriented and reinforcing way.

Autistic children also often fail to appreciate or respond to the emotions of others (Howlin, 1986). It has been suggested that this deficit may be more related to mental age than to pathology (Ferrari & Matthews, 1983). Regardless, this lack of empathy tends to be problematic as it hampers the development of friendships (Rutter, 1984). Although lack of sensitivity to emotional cues has not been investigated directly, analog studies have been conducted to examine some limited aspects of social behavior (Howlin, 1986). For instance, Hobson (1983, 1984) conducted a series of studies to investigate autistic individuals' ability to identify emotions from facial expressions as well as their ability to differentiate between sexes and ages. Autistic individuals were found to be less responsive than controls to emotional and other bodily cues. In another study, autistic individuals were able to discriminate male from female faces in photographs but were unable to interpret the emotions represented by different facial expressions (Sherman, Sigman, Ungerer, & Mundy, 1984).

Autistic individuals are often described as avoiding eye contact (Rutter, 1978; Wing, 1976). However, definitions of what constitutes normal levels of eye contact are often imprecise, the level of eye contact can change considerably throughout development, and the behavior is more complex than some researchers suggest (Howlin, 1986; Scheman & Lockard, 1979; Stern, 1976). Failure to attend to these factors has led to conflicting results in the literature.

For example, some researchers (e.g., Richer & Coss, 1976) have reported less eye contact from autistic children, while others (e.g., Gardner, cited in Howlin, 1986) have failed to find differences in frequency or duration of eye contact by these children. Still other researchers (e.g., Mirenda,

Donnelan, & Yoder, 1983; Tiegerman & Primavera, 1984) have suggested that among autistic individuals, eye contact varies depending on the conditions (i.e., type of interaction and familiarity with social partner).

Possibly the deviance noted in individuals with autism lies more in failure to reciprocate eye contact or to exhibit eye contact appropriately (e.g., when interacting with another person) than in complete avoidance of it (Rutter, 1978). Moreover, other factors may influence eye contact. For instance, children with Down's syndrome also tend to show abnormalities in eye contact, indicating that maturational factors may influence the appropriate use of this behavior (Howlin, 1986; Sinson & Wetherick, 1981). The extent of eye contact and imitative behaviors by the person interacting with the autistic child may also influence eye contact from the child (Tiegerman & Primavera, 1984). Finally, avoidance of eye contact may be a function of low mental age rather than extreme psychopathology (Howlin, 1986).

Another behavior often targeted in addressing social skills in autistic individuals is their tendency to remain aloof and avoid physical contact. However, it appears that this aloofness and withdrawal have been overemphasized in the literature and that some behavior (e.g., stereotypies) has been interpreted as, without truly being, avoidant (Howlin, 1986).

Common interpretations of autistic behavior have been challenged. For instance, Churchill and Bryson (1972) found that degree of physical avoidance did not differ significantly between normal and autistic children. Furthermore, Hutt and Ounsted (1966) noted that although autistic children rarely initiated social interactions, they often exhibited a greater tolerance than other children for proximity and close physical contact once contact was established. Perhaps the stereotypic behavior common in autistic individuals gives the appearance of aloofness and withdrawal (Strain & Fox, 1981). In addition, stereotypic behaviors may interfere with autistic individuals' ability to respond adequately to the environment. This contention has been supported by a finding of increased responsiveness to the environment as a result of attempts to minimize such behaviors (Koegel & Covert, 1972).

As autistic children grow older, they tend to develop relationships with adults and peers, although much of their social behavior may be considered abnormal (Howlin, 1986). For instance, autistic individuals display a wide range of play behaviors; however, such play behaviors are qualitatively different from the social play engaged in by other children. For example, autistic individuals tend to engage more in stereotypical behaviors involving simple manipulation of objects rather than the functional, symbolic, and cooperative play of other children. Also, autistic children tend to exhibit fewer complex and imitative behaviors, probably limiting the frequency and duration of interactions with peers (Stone, Lemanek, Fishel, Fernandez, & Altemeier, 1990; Ungerer & Sigman, 1981).

These problematic social behaviors, along with a lack of reciprocity and empathy, can result in isolation for autistic individuals (Howlin, 1986). However, social behavior and communication partly depend on the individual's cognitive and social skills level and may improve over time (Howlin, 1986; McHale, Simeonsson, Marcus, & Olley, 1980). Autistic students gradually show increases in social interaction and decreases in solitary activity when nonhandicapped individuals are introduced to the classroom (McHale, 1983; McHale, Olley, Marcus, & Simeonsson, 1981). However, generalization of these improvements to less structured settings tends to be limited.

Finally, as mentioned, many autistic individuals are mentally retarded. Social skills deficits are considered common with mental retardation. Many researchers have recognized that mentally retarded individuals require assistance in developing appropriate social skills (Andrasik & Matson, 1985; Grossman, 1983). However, the specific skills in need of remediation vary with the level of cognitive ability (Matson & Ollendick, 1988).

In sum, various social behaviors have been targeted for evaluating and treating in autistic individuals. However, the data may be misinterpreted if certain factors are not taken into account. For instance, when solely quantitative analyses are utilized, behaviors assumed to be specific to autism may actually occur as often in normals (Van Engeland, Bodnar, & Bolhuis, 1984). In addition, normative data on age-appropriate skills are necessary, as social behaviors appropriate for one age may be inappropriate for another. When social skills are considered within such a developmental framework, it becomes evident that many behaviors exhibited by autistic individuals may be more indicative of low mental age than of distinct pathology (Howlin, 1986).

Therefore, autistic individuals should not be treated as a homogeneous group. Findings must be interpreted based on particular samples of developmental and cognitive levels (Sigman et al., 1984). In addition, social skills of autistic individuals should be interpreted based on the context in which the behaviors are exhibited. What are considered appropriate behaviors in one situation may not be considered appropriate in another. Although autistic individuals exhibit similar rates of certain behaviors relative to other children (especially within highly structured situations), they may lack the ability to be flexible and adapt such behaviors to the demands of changing situations (Howlin, 1986).

Assessment of Social Skills

Once behavior in need of remediation is selected, the next consideration is how to accurately measure and evaluate specific skills. Measures typically used in this assessment process are based in social learning theory. Multiple assessment measures are used whenever possible to obtain comprehensive data. Other considerations include ensuring standardized and controlled testing conditions (Bernstein & Nietzel, 1977; Kazdin, Esveldt-Dawson, & Matson, 1982). Furthermore, the examiner should attempt to enhance the child's motivation (e.g., through social and/or tangible rewards) so as to increase the likelihood that the child will perform

the desired skills to the fullest extent possible. Often, skills that are not performed are believed to be nonexistent because of a performance deficit (i.e., lack of motivation) rather than a true skills deficit (i.e., lack of ability) (Matson & Ollendick, 1988).

The most commonly employed procedures for assessing social skills are checklists, direct observation of social situations, contrived or analog settings, and sociometric ratings (Matson & Ollendick, 1988). Each form of assessment has its own advantages and disadvantages. Therefore, a multimethod approach to assessment is warranted (Frame & Matson, 1987).

Checklists and Rating Scales

Checklists and rating scales have been used to assess a wide range of childhood problems. These measures are often used to screen for potential problem behaviors or social skills deficits (Cartledge & Milburn, 1986; Matson & Ollendick, 1988). Rating scales provide choices along a continuum for designating the extent of a behavior, whereas checklists tend to involve binary decisions regarding the presence or absence of a behavior. Ratings and checklists are typically administered to individuals closely associated with the child (e.g., parents or teachers) (Cartledge & Milburn, 1986).

The advantages of these techniques include ease of administration and analysis. Copies of the same measure may be used to obtain information from different informants regarding the same individual. Comparison of responses from different informants can provide critical information about the most salient problem behaviors and the way the individual functions in different settings (Cartledge & Milburn, 1986). However, the accuracy of the responses on behavioral checklists and ratings depends on the amount of opportunity the informant has had to observe relevant behavior. Other factors influencing accuracy of responses include interfering perceptions and attitudes and difficulties in remembering accurately. Lastly, the extent to which items are clearly defined and consistently interpreted by informants may also influence the accuracy of responses (Cartledge & Milburn, 1986; Humphreys & Ciminero, 1979; Reardon, Hersen, Bellack, & Foley, 1979; Rie & Friedman, 1978).

The two most empirically sound general measures of child behavior are the *Child Behavior Checklist* (CBCL) and *Behavior Problem Checklist* (Matson & Ollendick, 1988). These checklists have been used to conduct initial screenings for social dysfunction and to compare the responses of different informants. However, they may only be used as general measures, as few items are specific to social skills (Matson & Ollendick, 1988). In addition, the items tend to refer more to classes of behavior than to distinct behavioral skills or deficits (Cartledge & Milburn, 1986). Subsequently, a more specialized assessment of social dysfunction could be conducted to identify specific areas and severity of social skills deficits and excesses (Cartledge & Milburn, 1986; Matson & Ollendick, 1988).

The self, teacher, and parent versions of the CBCL (Achenbach & Edelbrock, 1983) are popular methods of assessing overall child psychopathology. The checklist contains 118 items designed for children between 4 and 18 years of age. Categories are based on factor analyses and include the following: social withdrawal, aggression, cruelty, and uncommunicativeness.

Another popular general measure of aberrant childhood behavior is the *Behavior Problem Checklist* (Quay & Peterson, 1975). The categories of this scale (like those of the other measure previously mentioned) were defined via a factor-analytic approach. Categories include socialized aggression and anxiety/withdrawal. This measure has not been as well accepted as the CBCL, as the categories diverge from the widely accepted DSM-III-R categories.

In addition to more general measures of child behavior problems, instruments specifically designed to assess social skills have been used when it has been established, through the above screening measures or otherwise, that social skills problems exist (Matson & Ollendick, 1988). The *Matson Evaluation of Social Skills with Youngsters*

(MESSY) (Matson, Rotatori, & Helsel, 1983) is the most extensively researched instrument. The scale consists of 62 items for the self-report version and 64 items for the teacher/parent report. Using factors established through factor analyses, items were selected from general scales of psychopathology, behaviors targeted in research on social skills in children, clinical observations, and discussions with professionals working with children.

The MESSY has been found useful because of its applicability to a broad array of subgroups within the general childhood population (Matson & Ollendick, 1988). In addition to being used with children of superior intelligence (Matson, Esveldt-Dawson, & Kazdin, 1981), the measure has been used with mildly mentally retarded (Matson, Macklin, & Helsel, 1985), deaf and hearing-impaired (Macklin & Matson, 1985; Matson et al., 1985), visually impaired (Matson et al., 1986), and emotionally disturbed (Helsel & Matson, 1984; Kazdin, Rodgers, & Colbus, 1986) children. The MESSY has also been applied to individuals of more average intellectual, physical, and emotional functioning. Finally, because the items of the MESSY pertain more to specific behaviors than to particular settings, it may be completed by a variety of informants (Matson & Ollendick, 1988).

Another measure, the *Social Skills Rating System* (SSRS) (Clark, Gresham, & Elliott, 1985), was also developed to measure social skills. Like the MESSY, the SSRS can be used to evaluate a wide range of social and interpersonal behaviors, particularly within the classroom setting. The scale consists of 52 items completed by the teacher and derived from other rating scales, target behaviors employed in empirical studies of social skills, and social behaviors found to predict peer acceptance and/or popularity. The subscales, derived through factor analyses, consist of academic performance, social initiation, cooperation, and peer reinforcement. The SSRS is especially useful to screen social skills in children (Matson & Ollendick, 1988). In addition, it may be utilized to assess a variety of children, including those of normal intelligence (Clark et al., 1985) and those with behavior disorders, learning disabilities, and mild mental retardation (Gresham, Elliott, & Black, 1986).

Both the MESSY and the SSRS represent recent and very critical developments in the area of social skills assessment. Beyond identifying social skills excesses and deficits in a variety of subgroups within the child population, these measures are important as a means of evaluating treatment programs designed to remediate the problems in these groups (Matson & Ollendick, 1988).

Behavioral Observation

Another important way to assess social skills is behavioral observation. This technique involves identifying discrete behaviors (e.g., eye contact, speech latency, number of words spoken, and frequency of aggression), which are operationally defined (Matson & Ollendick, 1988). Data collection may involve simple counts of behavior or use of elaborate coding systems, and the data may be expressed as the rate, frequency, or percent of behavior (Howlin, 1986). Direct observation may be conducted in both naturalistic (e.g., classroom or home) and analog settings.

Despite the accuracy that can be attained through observation in naturalistic settings, the potential expense and threat of reactivity often prohibit widespread use. Other threats to accurate interpretation of findings include variability in sampling procedures, observer and subject expectancies, and observer drift. Furthermore, a substantial amount of data must be gathered to ensure representativeness of the individual's performance. However, unless such data are collected in a variety of settings, the generalizability of the data to other settings must be questioned (Gottman, 1977; Howlin, 1986; Matson & Ollendick, 1988; Van-Hasselt et al., 1979).

Determining which facets of social behavior to observe also presents problems. Defining and observing a particular behavior does not guarantee that it is important to adaptive social functioning and relevant for study. Given this confusion, it is debatable whether behaviors rated across different studies are comparable (Howlin, 1986). Finally,

observational methods seem to be based on the assumption that behavioral variables are solely responsible for social acceptance. However, nonbehavioral variables such as sex, race, physical attractiveness, and observable handicaps also influence peer acceptance (LaGreca, 1981). Therefore, behavioral and nonbehavioral variables probably interact in influencing peer acceptance as well as the development of socially competent behavior (Howlin, 1986).

Another difficulty in collecting observational data in naturalistic settings is the inefficiency of having to wait for low-frequency behaviors to occur naturally. Therefore, behavioral observation has often occurred in contrived or analog settings.

Contrived and Analog Settings

In contrived settings, the natural environment may be arranged in a way that requires or facilitates occurrence of the target behavior rather than waiting for it to happen naturally (Stephens, 1978). For example, one might put an individual in a task-oriented group situation to observe his or her ability to stay on task or to work cooperatively (Cartledge & Milburn, 1986).

In analog settings, several target behaviors may be evaluated by one or two observers based on responses to role-play scenes that represent natural interpersonal encounters. Responses are rated by observers on accuracy of performance (Cartledge & Milburn, 1986; Matson & Ollendick, 1988). However, behavior exhibited in role-play situations has not been correlated with behavior in more natural social situations (Bellack, Hersen, & Lamparski, 1979; Bellack, Hersen, & Turner, 1978; Kazdin, Matson, & Esveldt-Dawson, 1984). Therefore, conclusions based on role-play assessments have limited generalizability to the natural environment. In addition, responses on these tests may be susceptible to motivational factors.

These facts do not preclude role-play assessments altogether, but indicate that it should not be used as the sole means of evaluation. Role-play assessments are a simple and convenient means of assessment, which are also more sensitive than checklists to changes in actual behavior. Furthermore, analog settings allow control of extraneous variables, avoid the possibility of harmful consequences that might occur in the natural situation, and offer efficiency and economy. This type of assessment might be particularly useful as an initial indicator of behavior change in response to treatment and may, therefore, help determine the utility of specific interventions (Matson & Ollendick, 1988).

Several role-play tests have been developed, including some standardized assessments such as the *Behavioral Assertiveness Test for Children* (BAT-C) (Bornstein, Bellack, & Hersen, 1977) and the *Social Skills Test for Children* (SST-C) (Williamson et al., 1983).

Sociometric Ratings

Social skills may also be evaluated by means of sociometric ratings, or ratings by peers. Such ratings often prove highly accurate (Matson & Ollendick, 1988). In addition, given the established relationship between childhood social rejection and later social maladjustment (Roff et al., 1972), sociometric ratings may serve as effective means of predicting behavior. The predictive validity of these measures has yet to be established, however (Cartledge & Milburn, 1986).

Also, several problems are inherent in this methodology. For example, LaGreca (1981) pointed out that sociometric ratings may be time-consuming to administer and score. Also, attaining such ratings may be difficult if the individual is seen at an out-patient facility, an in-patient facility in which client turnover is rapid, or some other facility outside of the school setting. Furthermore, some professionals have questioned the ethics of having individuals rated and discussed by their peer groups (LaGreca, 1981). With increasing emphasis on confidentiality and the necessary consent of all involved, the procedure is becoming less feasible (Matson & Ollendick, 1988).

Yet, of the sociometric techniques currently in use, peer nomination is a commonly used form of evaluation (e.g., McCandless & Marshall, 1957;

Moreno, 1953). Individuals are asked to identify peers who are their best friends or with whom they would most like to play or work. The score is then calculated as the number of nominations received (Cartledge & Milburn, 1986; Matson & Ollendick, 1988). A similar procedure has also been used to identify individuals who are least liked and most in need of assistance (Moore & Updegraff, 1964).

Another form of sociometric evaluation is the peer rating procedure. This method is more time-consuming since all individuals in the peer group are evaluated by all others in the group and sometimes by the teacher. However, more stable scores may be obtained since all individuals are evaluated, and ratings may provide such information as rankings of likability (Matson & Ollendick, 1988).

A major limitation of sociometric procedures is that determining whether an individual is generally accepted or rejected by peers does little to specify the particular behavioral characteristics or deficits that contribute to that given social status (Connolly, 1983; Foster & Ritchey, 1979; Hymel, 1983). Therefore, more structured peer assessment procedures have been developed in which several characteristics are listed, allowing the individual to rate particular children on their similarity to particular characteristics. Examples of this type of assessment include the *Guess Who Technique* (Hortshore, May, & Maller, 1929) and the *Bower Class Play Method* (Bower, 1960). Typically, accepted children exhibit behaviors reflecting cooperativeness, support, and physical attractiveness, whereas rejected children typically exhibit disruptiveness and aggression (Coie, Dodge, & Coppotelli, 1982; Di Lorenzo & Foster, 1984; Quay & Jarrett, 1984).

Autistic Population

The techniques just described for assessing social skills have generally been used with developmentally disabled individuals as well. Social skills assessment techniques used with the general population can be adapted for use with special populations (Matson & Ollendick, 1988). Three basic approaches have typically been utilized in evaluating the social behavior of autistic individuals. While quantitative measures such as frequency or duration of peer contact have been used (Romanczyk, Diamant, Goren, Trunell, & Harris, 1975; Strain, Kerr, & Ragland, 1979), more qualitative and informative measures are often required to measure the complex behaviors generally encountered in social interactions. Lastly, measures designed to examine the relationship among different behaviors exhibited during social interaction and to determine effective means of interaction have also been utilized.

When autistic individuals are also mentally retarded, some assessment techniques commonly used to evaluate social skills may prove difficult to use. For example, the cognitive limitations of mentally retarded individuals may prohibit the use of role-playing and other techniques dependent on client sources of information (Marchetti & Campbell, 1990). Instead, the *American Association on Mental Deficiency Adaptive Behavior Scale* (AAMD-ABS) (Nihira, Foster, Shellhaas, & Leland, 1974) and the *Vineland Adaptive Behavior Scales* (Sparrow, Balla, & Cicchetti, 1984) have proven effective means of evaluating social skills in the mentally retarded population. Detailed norms have been specifically devised for interpreting these social skills assessment results (McCarver & Campbell, 1987). The AAMD-ABS includes the following items for assessing global social skills: cooperation, consideration for others, awareness of others, interaction with others, participation in group activities, selfishness, and social maturity. The *Vineland Scales* have 37 items contained within three socialization domains (i.e., interpersonal relationships, play and leisure time, and coping skills).

Treatment Approaches

Once the skills to be remediated and the extent of the excesses or deficits have been identified, intervention may begin. Social skills training programs have generally been successful and have primarily derived from a behavioral orientation. That is, early

intervention studies typically focused on reinforcing isolated behaviors with tangible or social reinforcers for limited periods. More recently, treatment has begun to consider internal control and self-control of behavior, emphasized involvement of peers and family members, and involved training that occurs for substantial periods of the day (Matson & Ollendick, 1988). Treatment approaches that reflect these trends will be discussed below.

Operant Approach

Operant conditioning was the basis for the methods that were first effectively implemented to treat social skills. The basic characteristics of this approach involve identifying the antecedents and consequences of the selected observable and operationally defined target behaviors to which reinforcement and punishment are contingently applied as treatment.

Despite the general effectiveness of this technique, the lack of generalization and the recognized importance of considering the entire social environment for effective treatment have led to a shift from more traditional and focused methods to newer and more general methods (Marchetti & Campbell, 1990). Consequently, several different behaviors may be considered at once (e.g., Bryant & Budd, 1984; Filipczak et al., 1979), and individuals besides parents and teachers (e.g., siblings, classmates) may be involved in treatment (Kohler & Fowler, 1985; Sainato, Maheady, & Shook, 1986).

Cognitive-Behavioral Approach

The cognitive-behavioral approach refers to a wide range of treatments (Marchetti & Campbell, 1990). This approach is based on the belief that internal events (e.g., perceptions, thoughts, or beliefs) are intimately related to problem behavior and that the modification of these factors is important for promoting behavior change (Thase, 1986).

Cognitive-behavior therapy places great emphasis on internal control and active participation through self-reinforcement and other self-regulation strategies. Therefore, the extent of time required from the therapist can be greatly minimized. In addition, development of internal control can lead to increased generalization and maintenance. However, this approach requires significant cognitive ability, verbal responses, and motivation (Matson & Ollendick, 1988; Thase, 1986).

Several cognitively based methods have been employed. For example, in a social problem-solving strategy (Shure, Spivack, & Jaeger, 1971), general problem-solving skills believed to bear directly on social adjustment are taught in a systematic, step-by-step manner. Individuals are taught to identify problems, determine alternatives to problematic behaviors, predict consequences, and evaluate new behaviors (Castles & Glass, 1986; Matson & Ollendick, 1988). A recent extension of this strategy was developed by Christoff and colleagues (Christoff et al., 1985). Their procedure involves written work as well as discussions and encourages individuals to apply problem-solving to interpersonal problems of their choice. Role-playing and homework are also integral parts of the program. However, this procedure is likely to work best with individuals who are verbal and well-motivated (Matson & Ollendick, 1988).

Another popular cognitive strategy is the self-control strategy. Rehm's (1977) self-control strategy emphasized increasing rates of self-rewarding behaviors and/or decreasing rates of self-punitive behaviors. In this approach, covert events are viewed as observable behaviors, capable of being modified with reinforcement and punishment. Treatment may involve behavioral rehearsal and role-playing within a therapist-client setting and training in self-monitoring and functional analyses to be utilized outside of the treatment setting. In addition, homework and problem-solving discussions are part of the program. Again, intelligence and motivational levels may affect the success of this program (Matson & Ollendick, 1988).

Social Learning Approach

Social learning theory, also used in social skills training, focuses primarily on modeling and role-playing. The basic premise is that social skills can be markedly improved by observing and practicing various socially acceptable behaviors. This framework presumes a skills deficit. Therefore, if the problem is a performance deficit (i.e., poor motivation), other methods might be more appropriate. Verbal communication is necessary, making the approach less effective with younger children and the severely mentally handicapped (Matson & Ollendick, 1988).

Nevertheless, this technique has been subject to fewer modifications than the others, and it has proven effective with a wide range of individuals, including those who are mentally retarded (e.g., Matson, Kazdin, & Esveldt-Dawson, 1980). The general procedures involve instructions, modeling, role-playing, practice, feedback, and social reinforcement (Cartledge & Milburn, 1986; Marchetti & Campbell, 1990; Matson & Ollendick, 1988). These techniques have been applied singly and in combination (Marchetti & Campbell, 1990). Utilization of all of the techniques at once is usually referred to as a social skills training package (Matson & Stephens, 1978). Social reinforcement is typically promoted more strongly than self-reinforcement and/or tangible reinforcement (Matson & Ollendick, 1988). The treatment may be conducted on a one-to-one basis (e.g., Matson & Adkins, 1980; Matson et al., 1980) or in a group format (e.g., Matson et al., 1980; Matson & Senatore, 1981); it may involve training the patient (e.g., Matson et al., 1980; Turner, Hersen, & Bellack, 1978) or the family unit (e.g., Arnold, Sturgis, & Forehand, 1977; Serna et al., 1986); and it may be conducted in a contrived (e.g., Meredith, Saxon, Doleys, & Kyzer, 1980) or a naturalistic setting (e.g., Matson & Andrasik, 1982; Matson & Zeiss, 1979; Pravder & Israel, 1983).

Autistic Population

The above models are not mutually exclusive. In fact, most effective programs incorporate aspects of all three treatment approaches (Cartledge & Milburn, 1986). The differential effectiveness of the approaches is more apparent when they are applied to children or developmentally disabled populations. More specifically, the operant approach to social skills training has been particularly useful with the developmentally disabled population because (a) verbal communication and behavior is typically not employed, (b) treatment is generally carried out on a one-to-one basis, (c) behavior is controlled by external reinforcement, and (d) reinforcement is often frequent, direct, and tangible (Marchetti & Campbell, 1990; Matson & Ollendick, 1988).

As mentioned, the cognitive-behavioral approach places great emphasis on internal control and active participation through self-management strategies and often requires significant cognitive ability, verbal responses, and motivation. These characteristics greatly limit the use of this approach with child or handicapped populations. The social learning approach is also viewed as more effective with verbally expressive, intelligent, and motivated individuals (Matson & Ollendick, 1988).

The social skills training literature is replete with treatment outcome studies targeting social behavior of developmentally disabled (e.g., autistic) individuals. However, this research (e.g., Ragland, Kerr, & Strain, 1978; Strain et al., 1979; Tremblay, Strain, Hendrickson, & Shores, 1981) has primarily involved simple frequency counts of behaviors prior to and following training, because of the problems inherent in assessing the social skills of individuals in this population (Howlin, 1986). Although the analyses are usually sufficiently reliable, limiting them in such a way tends to lead to an overestimation of treatment effects.

When evaluating treatment outcomes it is important to recognize that, although autistic or other developmentally disabled individuals' behavior may improve through treatment, it is unlikely that intervention will result in "normalcy." Rather, some difficulty in the coordination of social skills, use of language and play, and initiation of social contact will probably remain (Howlin, 1986). More meaningful information could be derived from treatment outcome research that investigated behavior change within the context of the individual's social environment and drew conclusions about the functional nature of this behavior change (Marchetti & Campbell, 1990). For instance, autistic children are handicapped by both their uneven patterns of development and their failure to provide sufficient reinforcement to maintain reciprocal interactions with normal children (Howlin, 1986). However, as suggested by Berler, Gross, and Drabman (1982), merely improving social behavior does not necessarily result in altered peer acceptance ratings. The ultimate goal of treatment is improved social interaction, not merely the improvement of isolated behaviors.

Treatment Maintenance and Generalization

Once the target behaviors have been trained, the next task is to program generalization and maintenance of those behaviors. That is, for training to be considered effective, the child should be able to exhibit the behaviors in various contexts and across time (Cartledge & Milburn, 1986).

As Stokes and Baer (1977) indicated, generalization does not occur naturally but must be programmed into the treatment process. Methods for programming generalization include varying aspects of training (e.g., training in different settings and with different people), using training mediators, and changing the contingencies of reinforcement. Ideally, social skills training should occur in the setting in which the behavior is likely to be exhibited (Cartledge & Milburn, 1986). However, for the behavior to generalize, the instruction should occur in multiple settings (e.g., Van Den Pol et al., 1981). Formal instruction need not occur in every setting. Rather, practicing the target behavior in role-play situations, reinforcing the target behavior in other settings, and self-monitoring and subsequent rewarding of the behavior in different settings may also facilitate generalization (Cartledge & Milburn, 1986).

An important consideration in programming for generalization is highlighted by Rincover and Koegel (1975). In this study with autistic children, the behaviors learned in instructional settings did not generalize to another setting since the children were responding to incidental stimuli (i.e., hand movements) rather than the intended stimuli (i.e., verbal commands). Therefore, the authors determined that is it important not only to train in different situations, but also to ensure that the behavior is being triggered by the appropriate social stimuli across situations. Similarly, individuals must learn not only how to generalize, but also how to discriminate and adapt behavior to the particular setting and people involved (e.g., use different greetings with authorities and peers) (Cartledge & Milburn, 1986). This may be accomplished by providing a variety of practice examples in training and by assigning homework exercises that allow experience with different settings and people (e.g., Gelfand & Hartmann, 1984; Kaufman & Wagner, 1972).

To ensure generalization across people as well as across settings, training should ideally be conducted with more than one trainer (e.g., Stokes, Baer, & Jackson, 1974). Individuals in different settings (e.g., parents, teachers, and peers) might be taught how to instruct, prompt, and reinforce appropriate social behaviors (Stokes & Baer, 1977; Wiig & Bray, 1983). Group contingency programs in which individuals are taught the behaviors of and interact with more competent peers to achieve a specified goal have been found to be particularly effective in encouraging peer support of the maintenance and transfer of desirable social behavior (Strain, Kerr, & Ragland, 1981).

Another approach utilized to achieve generalization and maintenance of trained social skills is the development of cognitive mediators. Behavior learned through observation may be acquired and retained more effectively through use of mental and verbal as well as behavioral rehearsal (Cartledge & Milburn, 1986). Specifically, language-mediated techniques (e.g., self-instruction and problem-solving) (Meichenbum, 1977; Richards & Perri, 1978), imagery (e.g., Harris & Johnson, 1983), and expectations of self-efficacy (e.g., Nicki, Remington, & MacDonald, 1984) have been utilized to facilitate generalization and maintenance of learned behaviors. However, since these techniques require more verbal, cogni-

tive, and motivational skills than are expected to exist in developmentally disabled (i.e., autistic) individuals, we will not go into greater detail here.

Maintenance of behavior (i.e., generalization across time) may also be influenced by reinforcement contingencies. Timing of reinforcement may change from a continuous and immediate schedule during behavior acquisition to one that is more intermittent and unpredictable or delayed during behavior maintenance. The rationale for this change is to establish conditions in which the individual has difficulty determining which social or other behaviors will be reinforced. Therefore, in the case of social skills training, social skills are targeted on a more continuous basis in hopes that the chances of obtaining the desired reward will be increased (Stokes & Baer, 1977).

Contingency contracts (e.g., Dardig & Heward, 1980; Kanfer, 1975) in which social behavior, performance criteria, and rewards are defined have also proven effective for generalization and maintenance of social skills. Besides serving as a reminder to exhibit the appropriate behavior, these contracts are useful in that rewards can be delayed, the source of reinforcement can change, and the conditions of reinforcement may be revised as necessary (Cartledge & Milburn, 1986).

The most effective means of maintaining appropriate behavior are self-management strategies (e.g., Bandura, 1977). Using these strategies, individuals learn to regulate their own behavior by learning the appropriate standards for performance, as well as by subsequently monitoring, evaluating, and self-reinforcing their own behavior (Cartledge & Milburn, 1986). The self-management techniques may be taught using such procedures as modeling and behavioral rehearsal (i.e., Stevenson & Fantuzzo, 1984). An eventual goal is for individuals to progress from providing extrinsic rewards (i.e., tangible reinforcers) to themselves to self-administering intrinsic rewards (i.e., positive self-statements and thoughts) for the performance of appropriate social skills. Shaping and fading procedures may be utilized to accomplish this task (Cartledge & Milburn, 1986). Again, these techniques may prove less successful with less cognitively, verbally, and motivationally oriented individuals (e.g., developmentally disabled).

Occasionally, incorporating generalization and maintenance strategies into treatment programs is not sufficient, making further training necessary. Booster sessions have been suggested as a way to ensure maintenance of acquired behaviors, particularly if conducted before behavior deteriorates completely (Franks & Wilson, 1978; Hersen, 1979; Stevenson & Fantuzzo, 1984). As Baer (cited in Cartledge & Milburn, 1986) indicated, even though a behavior may require occasional reteaching to facilitate generalization and maintenance, sufficient time taken for initial instruction may help minimize the time and effort required for subsequent teachings.

Summary

Social skills training has generally been established as an important area of research both for the general population and for autistic individuals. In fact, impaired social and interpersonal functioning has consistently been recognized as a salient characteristic of autistic individuals. Therefore, social skills training has become an important aspect of treatment programs with these and other developmentally disabled individuals in attempts to promote deinstitutionalization, facilitate placement in less restrictive environments, and encourage adaptive functioning within the community.

A clear conceptualization of what is meant by "social skills" is lacking. However, the specific social behaviors believed to be in need of remediation in the autistic population have been fairly consistently agreed upon. These behaviors are typically those integral to the diagnosis of autism (e.g., lack of social responsiveness, empathy, eye contact, physical contact, and appropriate social play).

Several basic techniques are commonly used to assess social skills. Some of these techniques have also been effective, or effectively adapted for use,

with developmentally disabled individuals as well. When mental retardation is a factor, however, adaptive behavior scales are the most suitable means of assessment.

The assessment approaches utilized with the autistic population primarily reflect effective adaptations of techniques utilized with the general population. However, when autistic individuals are also mentally retarded, measures that depend on client sources of information and higher cognitive functioning may prove difficult to use. In these cases, adaptive behavior scales have proven more effective.

Treatment approaches have derived from a behavioral orientation. However, more recent intervention has followed the cognitive-behavioral and social learning approaches. That is, intervention has expanded to consider cognitive aspects of behavior and involvement of peers and family in the adaptation of social skills. Suggestions for generalization and maintenance of behaviors acquired through treatment interventions have been offered.

Despite widespread recognition of the importance of training social skills, research on this topic has been minimal. A good starting point for advancing this line of research would be to reach a consensus on the definition and conceptualization of social skills. In addition, in order to reach more meaningful conclusions regarding treatment outcomes, research should investigate behavior change within the context of an individual's environment and as it relates to adaptive functioning within that environment. Finally, an emphasis on generalization and maintenance of social skills will enhance the success of many social skills training programs.

References

ACHENBACH, T. M., & EDELBROCK, C. (1983). *Manual for the child behavior checklist and revised child behavior profile.* Burlington, VT: Queen City Printers.

ALLYON, T., & AZRIN, N. (1968). *The token economy.* New York: Appleton-Century-Crofts.

AMERICAN PSYCHIATRIC ASSOCIATION. (1987). *Diagnostic and statistical manual* (3rd ed.). Washington, DC: Author.

ANDRASIK, F. S., & MATSON, J. (1985). Social skills training for the mentally retarded. In L. L'-Abate & M. Milan (Eds.), *Handbook of social skills training and research* (pp. 418–454). New York: Wiley.

ARNOLD, S., STURGIS, E., & FOREHAND, R. (1977). Training a parent to teach communication skills: A case study. *Behaviour Modification, 1,* 259–276.

BANDURA, A. (1977). *Social learning theory.* Englewood Cliffs, NJ: Prentice-Hall.

BELLACK, A. S., HERSEN, M., & LAMPARSKI, D. (1979). Role-play tests for assessing social skills: Are they valid? Are they useful? *Journal of Consulting and Clinical Psychology, 47,* 335–342.

BELLACK, A. S., HERSEN, M., & TURNER, S. M. (1978). Role-play tests for assessing social skills: Are they valid? *Behavior Therapy, 9,* 448–461.

BEMPORAD, J. R. (1979). Adult recollections of a formerly autistic child. *Journal of Autism and Developmental Disorders, 9,* 179–197.

BERLER, E., GROSS, A., & DRABMAN, R. (1982). Social skills training with children: Proceed with caution. *Journal of Applied Behavior Analysis, 15,* 41–53.

BERNSTEIN, D. A., & NIETZEL, M. T. (1977). Demand characteristics in behavior modification: The natural history of a "nuisance." In M. Hersen, R. M. Eisler, & P. M. Miller (Eds.), *Progress in behavior modification* (Vol. 4) (pp. 119–162). New York: Academic.

BERNSTEIN, G. (1981). Research issues in training interpersonal skills for the mentally retarded. *Education and Training of the Mentally Retarded, 16,* 70–74.

BORNSTEIN, M. R., BELLACK, A. S., & HERSEN, M. (1977). Social-skills training for unassertive children: A multiple-baseline analysis. *Journal of Applied Behavior Analysis, 10,* 183–195.

BOWER, E. M. (1960). *Early identification of emotionally handicapped children in school.* Springfield, IL: Charles C. Thomas.

BRYANT, L. E., & BUDD, K. S. (1984). Teaching behaviorally handicapped preschool children to share. *Journal of Applied Behavior Analysis, 17,* 45–46.

CARTLEDGE, G., & MILBURN, J. F. (Eds.). (1986). Assessment and evaluation. *Teaching social skills to children: Innovative approaches* (2nd ed.). New York: Pergamon.

CASTLES, E., & GLASS, C. (1986). Training in social and interpersonal problem-solving skills for mildly retarded and moderately retarded adults. *American Journal of Mental Deficiency, 91,* 35–42.

CHRISTOFF, K. A., SCOTT, W. O. N., KELLEY, M. L. SCHLUNDT, D., BAER, G., & KELLY, J. A. (1985). Social skills and social problem training shy young adolescents. *Behavior Therapy, 16,* 468–477.

CHURCHILL, D. W., & BYSON, C. (1972). Looking and approach behaviour of psychiatric and normal children as a function of adult attention or preoccupation. *Comprehensive Psychiatry, 13,* 171–177.

CLARK, L., GRESHAM, F. M., & ELLIOTT, S. N. (1985). Development and validation of a social skills assessment measure: The TROSS-C. *Journal of Psychoeducational Assessment, 4,* 347–358.

COIE, J. D., DODGE, K. A., & COPPOTELLI, H. (1982). Dimensions and types of social status: A cross-age perspective. *Developmental Psychology, 18,* 557–570.

COMBS, M. L., & SLABY, D. A. (1977). Social skills training with children. In B. Lahey & A. Kazdin (Eds.), *Advances in clinical child psychology* (Vol. 1) (pp. 161–201). New York: Plenum.

CONNOLLY, J. A. (1983). A review of sociometric procedures in the assessment of social competencies in children. *Applied Research in Mental Retardation, 4,* 315–327.

COWEN, E. L., PEDERSON, A., BABJIAN, H., IZZO, L. D., & TROST, M. A. (1973). Long term follow-up of early detected vulnerable children. *Journal of Consulting and Clinical Psychology, 43,* 438–446.

CURRAN, J. P. (1979). Social skills: Methodological issues and future directions. In A. S. Bellack & M. Hersen (Eds.), *Research and practice in social skills training* (pp. 319–354). New York: Plenum.

DARDIG, J. C., & HEWARD, W. L. (1980). *Sign here: A contracting book for children and their parents.* Columbus, OH: Charles E. Merrill.

DAVIES, R. R., & ROGERS, E. S. (1985). Social skills training with persons who are mentally retarded. *Mental Retardation, 23,* 186–196.

DI LORENZO, T. M., & FOSTER, S. L. (1984). A functional assessment of children's ratings of interaction patterns. *Behavioral Assessment, 6,* 291–302.

EISLER, R. M. (1976). Behavioral assessment of social skills. In M. Hersen & A. A. Bellack (Eds.), *Behavioral assessment: A practical handbook* (pp. 369–395). Elmsford, NY: Pergamon.

FERRARI, M., & MATTHEWS, S. (1983). Self-recognition deficits in autism: Syndrome-specific or general developmental delay. *Journal of Autism and Developmental Disorders, 13,* 317–325.

FILIPCZAK, J., ARCHER, M. B., NEALE, M. S., & WINETT, R. A. (1979). Issues in multivariate assessment of a large-scale behavioral program. *Journal of Applied Behavior Analysis, 12,* 593–613.

FOSTER, S. L., & RITCHEY, W. L. (1979). Issues in assessment of social competence in children. *Journal of Applied Behavior Analysis, 12,* 625–638.

FRAME, C. L., & MATSON, J. L. (1987). *Handbook of assessment in childhood psychopathology: Applied issues in differential diagnosis and treatment evaluation.* New York: Plenum.

FRANKS, C. M., & WILSON, T. (1978). *Annual review of behavior therapy: Theory and practice* (Vol. 6). New York: Brunner/Mazel.

GELFAND, D. M., & HARTMANN, D. P. (1979, August). *Behavior analysis and developmental psychology. What we can learn from one another.* Paper presented at the convention of the American Psychological Association, New York.

GELFAND, D. M., & HARTMANN, D. P. (1984). *Child behavior analysis and therapy* (2nd ed.). New York: Pergamon.

GOTTMAN, J. (1977). The effects of a modeling film on social isolation in preschool children: A methodological investigation. *Journal of Abnormal Child Psychology, 5,* 69–78.

GRESHAM, F. M. (1984, August). *Social skills: Social validation of assessment and treatment methods.* Paper presented at the annual meeting of the American Psychological Association, Toronto.

GRESHAM, F. M., ELLIOTT, S. N., & BLACK, F. L. (1986). *Factor structure replication and bias investigation of the teacher rating of social skills.* Baton Rouge: Louisiana State University.

GROSSMAN, H. J. (Ed.). (1983). *Manual on terminology and classification in mental retardation.* Washington, DC: American Association on Mental Deficiency.

GUINOUARD, D. E., & RYCHLAK, J. F. (1982). Personality correlates of sociometric popularity in elementary school children. *Personnel and Guidance Journal, 40,* 438–442.

HARRIS, G. M., & JOHNSON, S. B. (1983). Coping imagery and relaxation instructions in a covert modeling treatment for test anxiety. *Behavior Therapy, 14,* 144–157.

HARRIS, S. L., & FERRARI, M. (1983). Developmental factors in child behavior therapy. *Behavior Therapy, 14,* 54–72.

HELSEL, W. J., & MATSON, J. L. (1984). The assessment of depression in children: The internal structure of the *Child depression inventory* (CDI). *Behaviour Research and Therapy, 22,* 289–298.

HERSEN, M. (1979). Limitations and problems in the clinical application of behavioral techniques in psychiatric settings. *Behavior Therapy, 10,* 65–80.

HERSEN, M., & BELLACK, A. S. (1976). Social skills training for chronic psychiatric patients: Rationale, research findings and future directions. *Comprehensive Psychiatry, 17,* 559–580.

HILL, J., WEHMAN, P., & HORST, G. (1982). Toward generalization of appropriate leisure and social behavior in severely handicapped youth: Pinball machine use. *Journal of the Association for the Severely Handicapped, 6,* 38–44.

HOBSON, R. P. (1983). The autistic child's recognition of age-related features of people, animals and things. *British Journal of Developmental Psychology, 1,* 343–352.

HOBSON, R. P. (1984). Early childhood autism and the question of egocentrism. *Journal of Autism and Developmental Disorders, 14,* 85–104.

HOPS, H. (1983). Children's social competence and skill: Current research practices and future directions. *Behavior Therapy, 14,* 3–18.

HORTSHORE, H., MAY, M. A., & MALLER, J. B. (1929). *Studies in the nature of character. II. Studies in service and self-control.* New York: Macmillan.

HOWLIN, P. (1986). An overview of social behavior in autism. In E. Schopler & G. B. Mesibov (Eds.), *Social behavior in autism* (pp. 103–131). New York: Plenum.

HUMPHREYS, L. E., & CIMINERO, A. R. (1979). Parent report measures of child behavior: A review. *Journal of Clinical Child Psychology, 8,* 56–63.

HUTT, C., & OUNSTED, C. (1966). The biological significance of gaze aversion with particular reference to the syndrome of infantile autism. *Behavioral Science, 11,* 346–356.

HYMEL, S. (1983). Preschool children's peer relations: Issues in sociometric assessment. *Merrill-Palmer Quarterly, 29,* 237–260.

KANFER, F. H. (1975). Self-management methods. In F. H. Kanfer & A. P. Goldstein (Eds.), *Helping people change* (pp. 309–355). Elmsford, NY: Pergamon.

KANNER, L. (1943). Autistic disturbance of affective contact. *Nervous Child, 2,* 217–250.

KASARI, C., SIGMAN, M., MUNDY, P., & YIRMIYA, N. (1990). Affective sharing in the context of joint attention interactions of normal, autistic, and mentally retarded children. *Journal of Autism and Developmental Disorders, 20,* 87–100.

KAUFMAN, L. M., & WAGNER, B. R. (1972). Barb: A systematic treatment technology for temper control disorders. *Behavior Therapy, 3,* 84–90.

KAZDIN, A. E., ESVELDT-DAWSON, K., & MATSON, J. L. (1982). Changes in children's social performance as a function of preassessment experiences. *Journal of Clinical Child Psychology, 11,* 243–248.

KAZDIN, A. E., MATSON, J. L., & ESVELDT-DAWSON, K. (1984). Social skill performance among normal and psychiatric inpatient children as a function of assessment conditions. *Behaviour Research and Therapy, 22,* 129–139.

KAZDIN, A. E., RODGERS, A., & COLBUS, D. (1986). The hopelessness scale for children:

Psychometric characteristics and concurrent validity. *Journal of Consulting and Clinical Psychology, 54,* 241–245.

KOEGEL, R. L., & COVERT, A. (1972). The relationship of self-stimulation to learning in autistic children. *Journal of Applied Behavioral Analysis, 5,* 381–387.

KOHLER, F. W., & FOWLER, S. A. (1985). Training prosocial behaviors to young children: An analysis of reciprocity with untrained peers. *Journal of Applied Behavior Analysis, 18,* 187–200.

KOSLIN, B. L., HAARLOW, R. N., KARLINS, M., et al. (1986). Predicting group status from member's cognitions. *Sociometry, 31,* 64–75.

LAGRECA, A. M. (1981). Peer acceptance: The correspondence between children's sociometric scores and teacher's ratings of peer interaction. *Journal of Abnormal Child Psychology, 9,* 167–178.

LAGRECA, A. M., & MESIBOV, G. B. (1981). Facilitating interpersonal functioning with peers in learning-disabled children. *Journal of Learning Disabilities, 14,* 197–199; 238.

LEE, D. Y. (1977). Evaluation of a group counseling program designed to enhance social adjustment of mentally retarded adults. *Journal of Counseling Psychology, 24,* 318–323.

LIBERMAN, R. P., & DAVIS, J. (1975). Drugs and behavior analysis. In M. Hersen, R. M. Eisler, & P. M. Miller (Eds.), *Progress in behavior modification* (pp. 307–330). New York: Academic Press.

MACKLIN, G. F., & MATSON, J. L. (1985). A comparison of social behaviors among non-handicapped and hearing impaired children. *Behavior Disorders, 1,* 60–65.

MARCHETTI, A. G., & CAMPBELL, V. A. (1990). Social skills. In J. L. Matson (Ed.), *Handbook of behavior modification with the mentally retarded* (2nd ed.) (pp. 333–355). New York: Plenum.

MATSON, J. L., & ADKINS, J. (1980). A self-instructional social skills training program for mentally retarded persons. *Mental Retardation, 18,* 245–248.

MATSON, J. L., & ANDRASIK, F. (1982). Training leisure time social interaction skills to mentally retarded adults. *American Journal of Mental Deficiency, 86,* 533–542.

MATSON, J. L., ESVELDT-DAWSON, K., & KAZDIN, A. E. (1981). Validation of methods for assessing social skills in children. *Journal of Clinical Child Psychology, 12,* 174–180.

MATSON, J. L., HEINZE, A., HELSEL, W. J., KAPPERMAN, G., & ROTATORI, A. F. (1986). Assessing social behaviors in the visually handicapped. The *Matson evaluation of social skills with youngsters* (MESSY). *Journal of Clinical Child Psychology, 15,* 78–87.

MATSON, J. L., KAZDIN, A. E., & ESVELDT-DAWSON, K. (1980). Training interpersonal skills among mentally retarded and socially dysfunctional children. *Behaviour Research and Therapy, 18,* 419–427.

MATSON, J. L., MACKLIN, C. F., & HELSEL, W. J. (1985). Psychometric properties of the *Matson evaluation of social skills with youngsters* (MESSY) with emotional problems and self concept in deaf children. *Journal of Behavior Therapy and Experimental Psychiatry, 16,* 117–123.

MATSON, J. L., & OLLENDICK, T. H. (1988). *Enhancing children's social skills: Assessment and training.* New York: Pergamon.

MATSON, J. L., ROTATORI, A. F., & HELSEL, W. J. (1983). Development of a rating scale to measure social skills in children: The *Matson evaluation of social skills with youngsters* (MESSY). *Behaviour Research and Therapy, 21,* 335–340.

MATSON, J. L., & SENATORE, V. (1981). A comparison of traditional psychotherapy and social skills training for improving interpersonal functioning of mentally retarded adults. *Behavior Therapy, 12,* 369–382.

MATSON, J. L., & STEPHENS, R. M. (1978). Increasing appropriate behaviour of explosive chronic psychiatric patients with a social-skills training package. *Behaviour Modification, 2,* 61–76.

MATSON, J. L., & ZEISS, R. A. (1979). The buddy system: A method of generalized reduction of inappropriate interpersonal behaviour of retarded psychotic patients. *British Journal of Social and Clinical Psychology, 18,* 401–405.

McCANDLESS, B. R., & MARSHALL, H. R. (1957). A picture sociometric technique for preschool children and its relation to teacher judgements of friendships. *Child Development, 28,* 139–147.

McCARVER, R. B., & CAMPBELL, V. A. (1987). Future developments in the concept and application of adaptive behavior. *Journal of Special Education, 21,* 197–207.

McFALL, R. M. (1982). A review and reformulation of the concept of social skills. *Behavioral Assessment, 4,* 1–33.

McFALL, R. M., & MARSTON, A. R. (1970). An experimental investigation of behavior rehearsal in assertive training. *Journal of Abnormal Psychology, 76,* 295–303.

McHALE, S. (1983). Social interactions of autistic and non-handicapped children during free play. *American Journal of Orthopsychiatry, 53,* 81–91.

McHALE, S., OLLEY, J., MARCUS, L., & SIMEONSSON, R. (1981). Non-handicapped peers as tutors for autistic children. *Exceptional Children, 48,* 263–265.

McHALE, S., SIMEONSSON, R., MARCUS, L., & OLLEY, J. (1980). The social and syntactic quality of autistic children's communications. *Journal of Autism and Developmental Disorders, 10,* 299–314.

MEICHENBAUM, D. (1977). *Cognitive-behavior modification: An integrative approach.* New York: Plenum.

MEREDITH, R. L., SAXON, S., DOLEYS, D., & KYZER, B. (1980). Social skills training with mildly retarded young adults. *Journal of Clinical Psychology, 36,* 1000–1009.

MEYERS, C. E., NIHIRA, K., & ZETLIN, A. (1979). The measurement of adaptive behavior. In N. R. Ellis (Ed.), *Handbook of mental deficiency, psychological theory and research* (2nd ed.) (pp. 431–481). Hillsdale, NJ: Lawrence Erlbaum.

MIRENDA, P., DONNELAN, A., & YODER, D. (1983). Gaze behavior: A new look at an old problem. *Journal of Autism and Developmental Disorders, 13,* 397–409.

MOORE, S. G., & UPDEGRAFF, R. (1964). Sociometric status of preschool children related to age, sex, nurturance giving and dependency. *Child Development, 35,* 519–524.

MORENO, J. L. (1953). *Who shall survive?* New York: Beacon House.

MORRIS, R. J., & DALKER, M. (1974). Developing cooperative play in socially withdrawn retarded children. *Mental Retardation, 12,* 24–27.

NICKI, R. M., REMINGTON, R. E., & MACDONALD, G. A. (1984). Self-efficacy, nicotine-fading/self-monitoring and cigarette-smoking behavior. *Behavior Research and Therapy, 22,* 477–485.

NIHIRA, K., FOSTER, R., SHELLHAAS, M., & LELAND, H. (1974). *AAMD adaptive behavior scale.* Washington, DC: American Association on Mental Deficiency.

PRAVDER, M. D., & ISRAEL, A. C. (1983). The effect of peer influence systems on children's coercive behavior. *Journal of Clinical Child Psychology, 12,* 145–152.

QUAY, H. C., & JARRETT, O. S. (1984). Predictors of social acceptance in preschool children. *Developmental Psychology, 20,* 793–796.

QUAY, H. C., & PETERSON, D. R. (1975). *Manual for the behavior problem checklist.* Champaign: University of Illinois, Children's Research Center.

RAGLAND, E., KERR, M., & STRAIN, P. (1978). Effects of social imitations on the behavior of withdrawn autistic children. *Behavior Modification, 2,* 565–578.

RATHJEN, D. P. (1984). Social skills training for children: Innovations and consumer guidelines. *School Psychology Review, 13,* 302–310.

RATHJEN, D. P., & FOREYT, J. P. (1980). *Social competence: Interventions for children and adults.* New York: Pergamon.

REARDON, R. C., HERSEN, M., BELLACK, A. S., & FOLEY, J. M. (1979). Measuring social skill in grade school boys. *Journal of Behavioral Assessment, 1,* 87–105.

REHM, L. P. (1977). A self-control model of depression. *Behavior Therapy, 8,* 787–804.

RICHARDS, C. S., & PERRI, M. D. (1978). Do self-control treatments last? An evaluation of behavioral problem-solving and faded counselor contact as treatment maintenance strategies. *Journal of Counseling Psychology, 25,* 376–383.

RICHER, J., & COSS, R. (1976). Gaze aversion in autistic and normal children. *Acta Psychiatrica Scandinavica, 53,* 193–210.

RIE, E. D., & FRIEDMAN, D. P. (1978). *A survey of behavior rating scales for children.* Columbus, OH: Office of Program Evaluation and Research, Ohio Department of Mental Health and Mental Retardation.

RINCOVER, A., & KOEGEL, R. L. (1975). Setting generality and stimulus control in autistic children. *Journal of Applied Behavior Analysis, 8,* 235–246.

RITVO, E. R., & FREEMAN, B. J. (1977). National Society for Autistic Children definition of the syndrome of autism. *Journal of Pediatric Psychology, 2,* 146–148.

ROFF, M. (1961). Childhood social interactions and young adult bad conduct. *Journal of Abnormal and Social Psychology, 63,* 333–337.

ROFF, M., SELL, B., & GOLDEN, M. M. (1972). *Social adjustment and personality development in children.* Minneapolis: University of Minnesota Press.

ROMANCZYK, R., DIAMANT, C., GOREN, E., TRUNELL, G., & HARRIS, S. (1975). Increasing isolate and social play in severely disabled children: Intervention and postintervention effectiveness. *Journal of Autism and Childhood Schizophrenia, 5,* 57–70.

RUTTER, M. (1978). Diagnosis and definition. In M. Rutter & E. Schopler (Eds.), *Autism: A reappraisal of concepts and treatment* (pp. 1–25). New York: Plenum.

RUTTER, M. (1984). Infantile autism and other pervasive developmental disorders. In M. Rutter & L. Hersov (Eds.), *Child and adolescent psychiatry: Modern approaches* (Vol. 2) (pp. 717–749). Oxford, England: Blackwell Scientific.

SAINATO, D. M., MAHEADY, L., & SHOOK, G. L. (1986). The effects of a classroom management role on the social interaction patterns and social status of withdrawn kindergarten students. *Journal of Applied Behavior Analysis, 19,* 187–195.

SCHEMAN, J., & LOCKARD, J. (1979). Development of gaze aversion in children. *Child Development, 50,* 594–596.

SCHOPLER, E. (1983). New developments in the definition and diagnosis of autism. In B. B. Lahey & A. E. Kazdin (Eds.), *Advances in clinical child psychology* (Vol. 6) (pp. 93–127). New York: Plenum.

SCHOPLER, E., & MESIBOV, G. B. (Eds.). (1983). *Autism in adolescents and adults.* New York: Plenum.

SERNA, L. A., SCHUMAKER, J. B., HAZEL, J. S., & SHELDON, J. B. (1986). Teaching reciprocal social skills training to parents and their delinquent adolescents. *Journal of Clinical Psychology, 15,* 64–77.

SHERMAN, T., SIGMAN, M., UNGERER, J., & MUNDY, P. (1984). *Knowledge of categories in autistic children.* Manuscript in preparation.

SHURE, M. B., SPIVACK, G., & JAEGER, M. (1971). Problem-solving thinking and adjustment among disadvantaged preschool children. *Child Development, 42,* 1791–1803.

SIGMAN, M., UNGERER, J., MUNDY, P., & SHERMAN, T. (1984). Cognitive functioning in autistic children. In D. Cohen, A. Donnelan, & R. Paul (Eds.), *Handbook of autism and atypical development.* New York: Wiley.

SINSON, J., & WETHERICK, N. (1981). The behaviour of children with Down's syndrome in normal play groups. *Journal of Mental Deficiency Research, 25,* 113–120.

SPARROW, S. S., BALLA, D. A., & CICCHETTI, D. V. (1984). *Vineland adaptive behavior scales.* Circle Pines, MN: American Guidance Service.

STEPHENS, T. M. (1978). *Social skills in the classroom.* Columbus, OH: Cedars Press.

STERN, D. (1976). Mothers and infants at play: The dyadic interaction involving facial, vocal and gaze behaviors. In M. Lewis & L. Rosenblum (Eds.), *The effects of the infant on its caretaker* (pp. 187–213). New York: Wiley.

STEVENSON, H. C., & FANTUZZO, J. W. (1984). Application of the "generalization map" to a self-control intervention with school-aged children. *Journal of Applied Behavior Analysis, 17,* 203–212.

STOKES, K. S. (1977). Planning for the future of a severely handicapped autistic child. *Journal of Autism and Childhood Schizophrenia, 7,* 288–297.

STOKES, T. F., & BAER, D. M. (1977). An implicit technology of generalization. *Journal of Applied Behavior Analysis, 10,* 349–367.

STOKES, T. F., BAER, D. M., & JACKSON, R. L. (1974). Programming the generalization of a greeting response in four retarded children. *Journal of Applied Behavior Analysis, 7,* 599–610.

STONE, W. L., & LEMANEK, K. L. (1990). Parental report of social behaviors in autistic preschoolers. *Journal of Autism and Developmental Disorders, 20,* 513–522.

STONE, W. L., LEMANEK, K. L., FISHEL, P. T., FERNANDEZ, M. C., & ALTEMEIER, W. A. (1990). Play and imitation skills in the diagnosis of young autistic children. *Pediatrics, 86,* 267–272.

STRAIN, P., & FOX, J. (1981). Peer social initiations and the modification of social withdrawal: A review and future perspective. *Journal of Pediatric Psychology, 6,* 417–433.

STRAIN, P., KERR, M., & RAGLAND, K. E. (1979). Effects of peer-mediated social initiations and prompting/reinforcement procedures in the social behavior of autistic children. *Journal of Autism and Developmental Disorders, 9,* 41–54.

STRAIN, P. S., KERR, M. M., & RAGLAND, E. U. (1981). The use of peer social initiations in the treatment of social withdrawal. In P. S. Strain (Ed.), *The utilization of classroom peers as behavior change agents* (pp. 101–128). New York: Plenum.

THASE, M. E. (1986). Cognitive therapy. In A. Bellack & M. Hersen (Eds.), *Dictionary of behavior therapy techniques* (pp. 60–63). New York: Pergamon.

TIEGERMAN, E., & PRIMAVERA, L. (1984). Imitating the autistic child: Facilitating communicative gaze behavior. *Journal of Autism and Developmental Disorders, 14,* 27–38.

TREMBLAY, A., STRAIN, P., HENDRICKSON, J., & SHORES, S. (1981). Social interactions in normal preschool children. *Behavior Modification, 5,* 237–253.

TROWER, P. (1979). Fundamentals of interpersonal behavior: A social-psychological perspective. In A. Bellack & M. Hersen (Eds.), *Research and practice in social skills training* (pp. 3–40). New York: Plenum.

TROWER, P., BRYANT, B., & ARGYLE, M. (1978). *Social skills and mental health.* Pittsburgh: University of Pittsburgh Press.

TURNER, S. M., HERSEN, M., & BELLACK, A. S. (1978). Social skills training to teach prosocial behaviors in an organically impaired and retarded patient. *Journal of Behaviour Therapy and Experimental Psychiatry, 9,* 253–258.

ULLMAN, C. A. (1975). Teachers, peers, and tests as predictors of adjustment. *Journal of Educational Psychology, 48,* 257–267.

UNGERER, J. A. (1989). The early development of autistic children: Implications for defining primary deficits. In G. Dawson (Ed.), *Autism: Nature, diagnosis, and treatment* (pp. 75–91). New York: Guilford.

UNGERER, J., & SIGMAN, M. (1981). Symbolic play and language comprehension in autistic children.

Journal of the American Academy of Child Psychiatry, 20, 318–337.

VAN DEN POL, R. A., IWATA, B. A., IRANCIC, M. T., PAGE, T. J., NEEF, N. A., & WHITLEY, F. P. (1981). Teaching the handicapped to eat in public places: Acquisition, generalization, and maintenance of restaurant skills. *Journal of Applied Behavior Analysis, 14,* 61–69.

VAN ENGELAND, H., BODNAR, F., & BOLHUIS, G. (1984). Some qualitative aspects of the social behavior of autistic children: An ethological approach. *Journal of Child Psychology and Psychiatry, 26,* 879–893.

VANHASSELT, V. B., HERSEN, M., WHITEHALL, M. B., & BELLACK, A. S. (1979). Social skill assessment and training for children: An evaluative review. *Behaviour Research and Therapy, 23,* 395–405.

WIIG, E. H., & BRAY, C. M. (1983). *Let's talk for children.* Columbus, OH: Charles E. Merrill.

WILLIAMSON, D. A., MOODY, S. C., GRANBERRY, S. W., LETHERMON, V. R., & BLOVIN, D. C. (1983). Criterion-related validity of a role-play social skills test for children. *Behavior Therapy, 14,* 466–481.

WING, L. (1976). *Early childhood autism* (2nd ed.). London: Pergamon.

AUTHOR INDEX

SUBJECT INDEX